Dawn of the Arcana

9

Story & Art by

Rei Toma

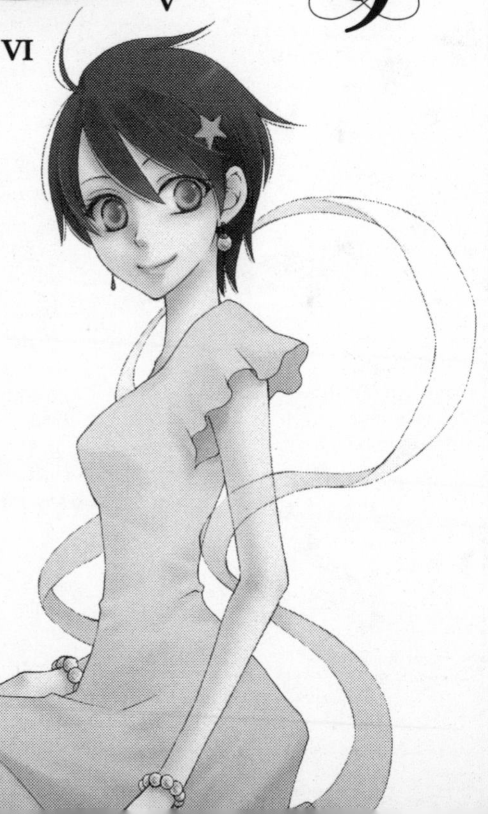

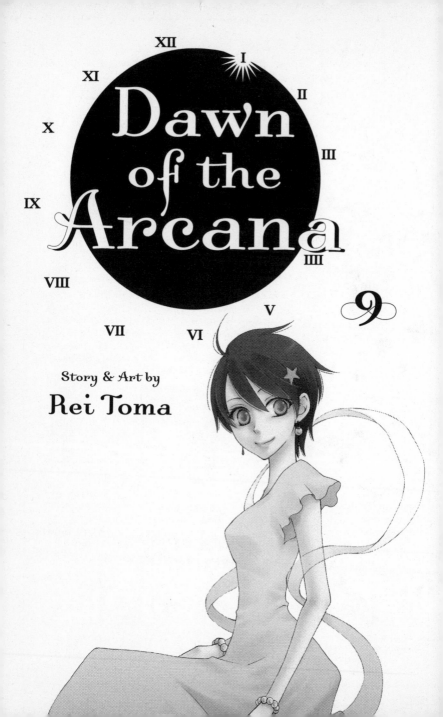

characters

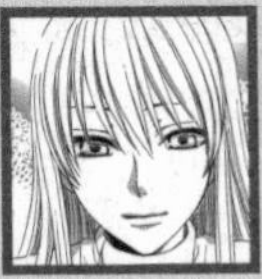

Sara
King Guran's concubine. Deceased.

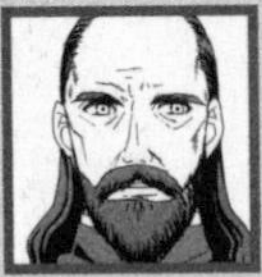

Guran
King of Belquat.

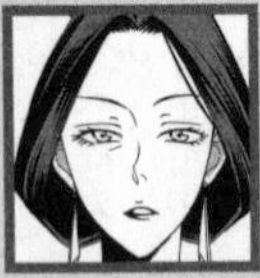

Rosenta
Queen of Belquat.

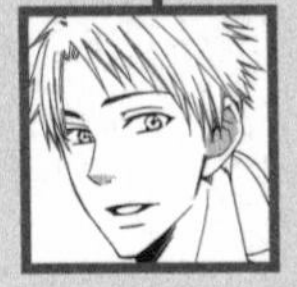

Cain
First-born prince of Belquat. Caesar's brother. He was killed by Loki.

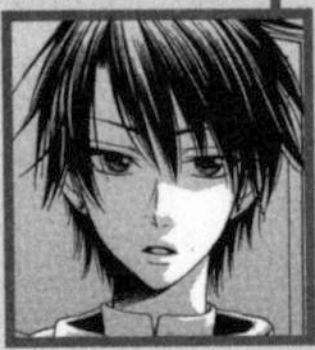

Caesar
The second-born prince of Belquat. Nakaba's husband through a marriage of political convenience. Headstrong and selfish.

Married

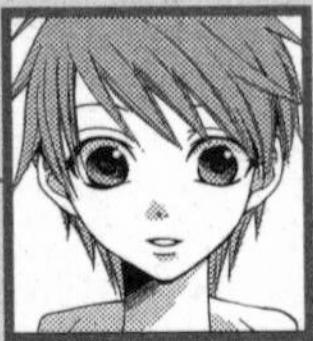

Nakaba
The princess royal of Senan. Strong of will and noble of spirit, she possesses a strange power.

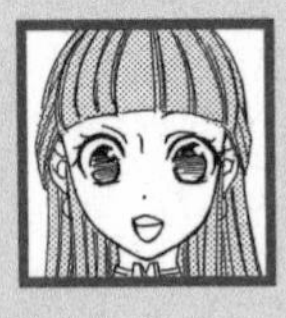

Lemiria
Bellinus's younger sister. Fond of her big brother.

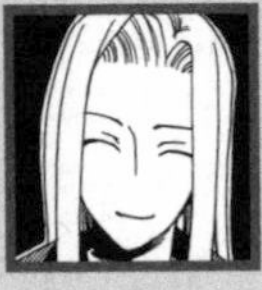

Bellinus
Caesar's attendant. Always cool and collected.

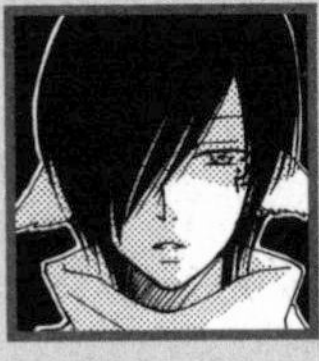

Loki
Nakaba's attendant. His senses of perception are unmatched.

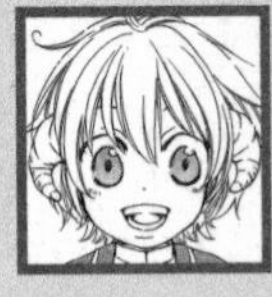

Rito
Nakaba's attendant. Recently arrived from Senan.

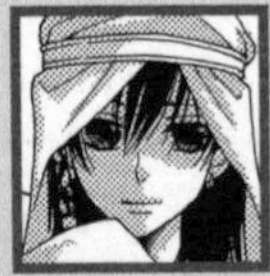

Akhil
Fifth-born prince of Lithuanel.

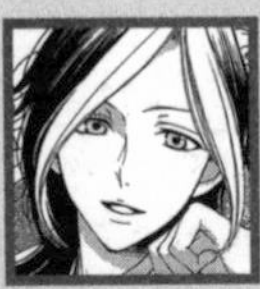

Azhal
Second-born prince of Lithuanel.

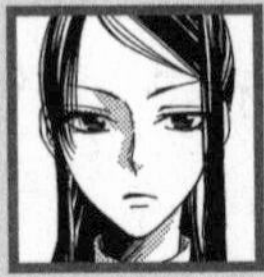

Batal
First-born prince of Lithuanel.

story

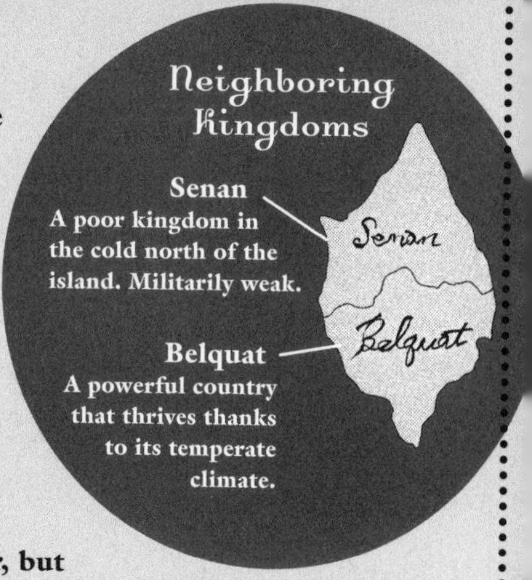
Neighboring Kingdoms
Senan
A poor kingdom in the cold north of the island. Militarily weak.
Belquat
A powerful country that thrives thanks to its temperate climate.
Senan
Belquat

• Nakaba, a survivor of a race which has been nearly wiped out, possesses the ability to see into the past and the future—a power known as the Arcana of Time. Wed to Prince Caesar as a symbol of peace between their two countries, Nakaba is actually little more than a hostage. At first, Nakaba and Caesar are distant and cold to each other, but their relationship has been slowly warming.

• King Guran sends soldiers to a demi-human village to test a powerful new weapon. In order to protect Nakaba, Loki kills Cain, who was leading the mission. Realizing that pursuit from Belquat is inevitable after Cain's death, Nakaba and the others travel to Senan and visit the castle. The king of Senan is as eager as the king of Belquat to form ties with Lithuanel, and on his orders, the group makes the journey to Lithuanel.

• Being acquainted with Akhil, the fifth prince of Lithuanel, they reach out to him for help upon arrival. He agrees, on the condition that they help capture a group of bandits plaguing the country, thus bolstering support for the second prince, Azhal, in his bid to be crowned king. Nakaba uses the Arcana of Time to identify the bandits' next target, but despite her knowledge, Akhil and his people are unable to vanquish them. Meanwhile, Caesar decides to return to Belquat to fulfill his duties as prince.

• With everything seeming to fall apart around her, Nakaba grows increasingly anxious. Then, to make matters worse, she's taken prisoner by Batal, the first-born prince of Lithuanel. She loses consciousness and learns, through the Arcana of Time, just how much Loki has sacrificed for her—and the painful depths of the feelings that have driven him to do so!

Dawn of the Arcana

Volume 9

XII

XI

X

CONTENTS

Chapter 32

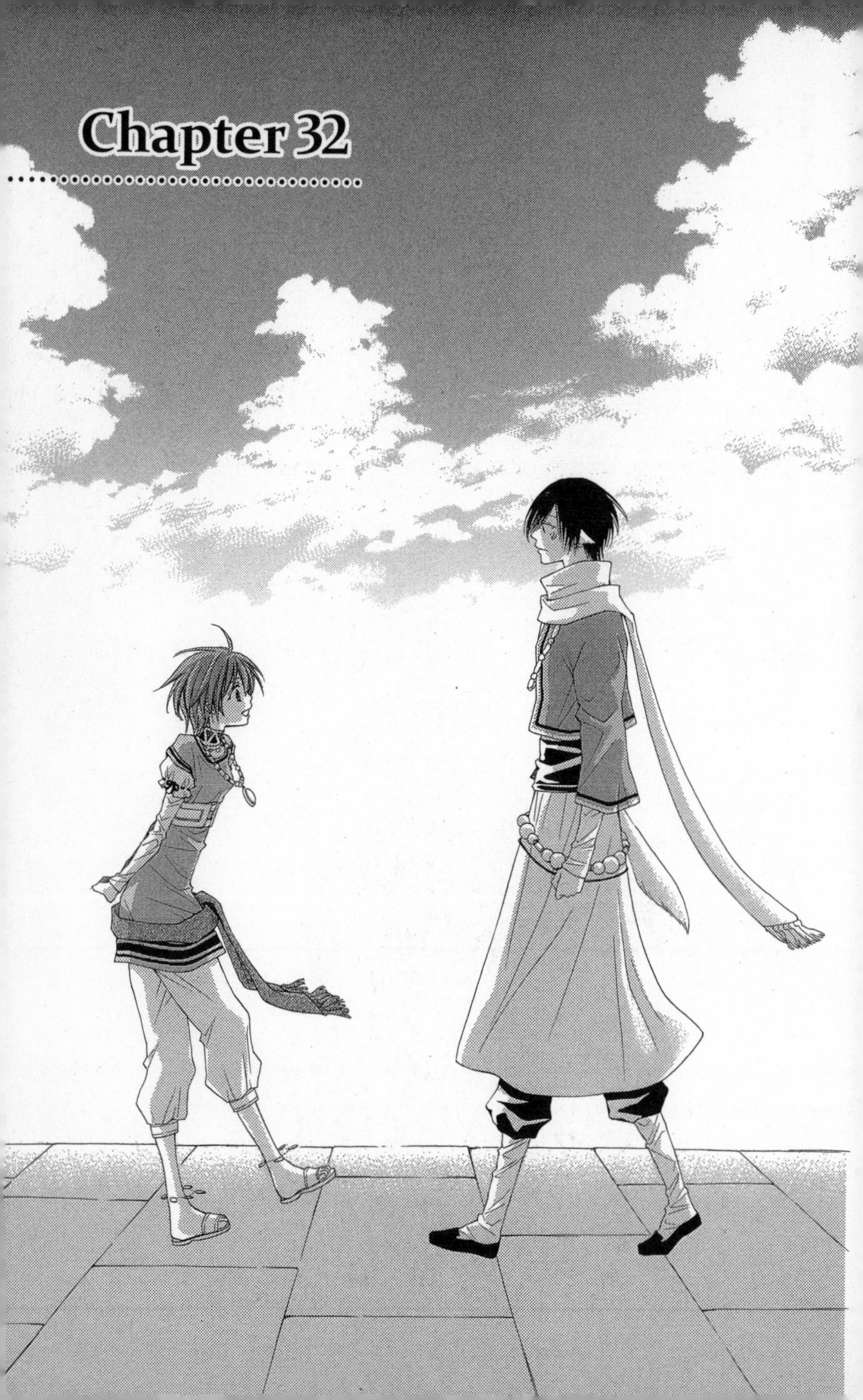

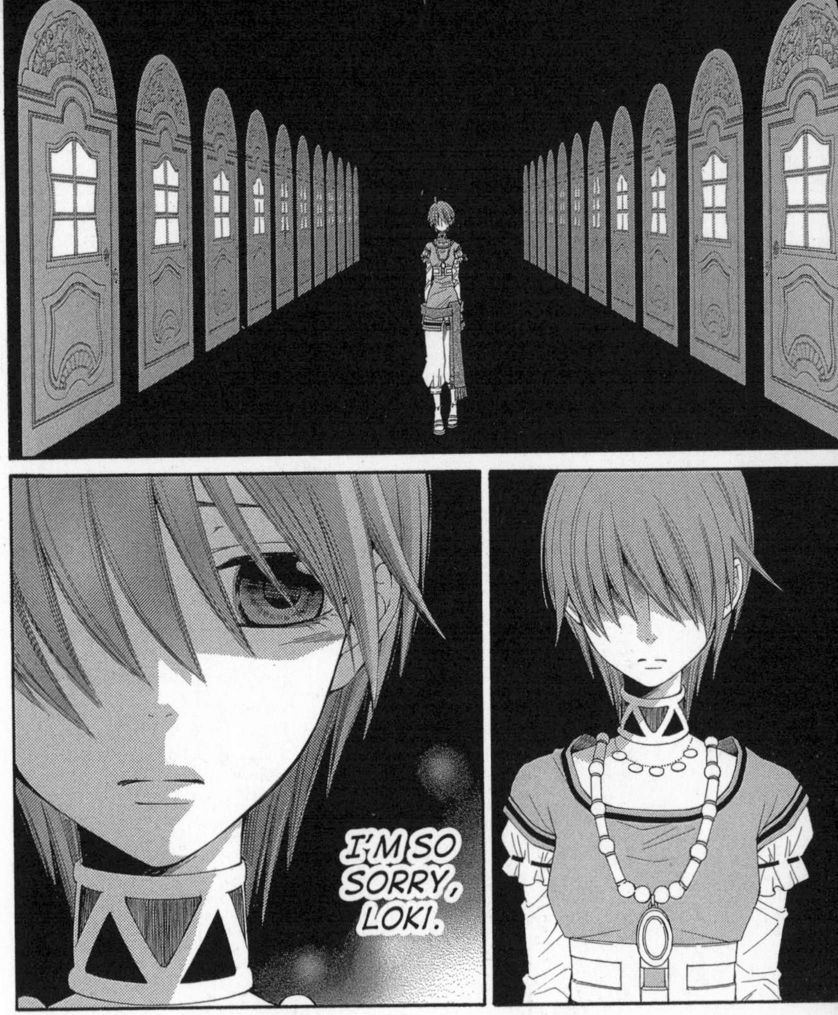
I'M SO SORRY, LOKI.

Dawn of the Arcana

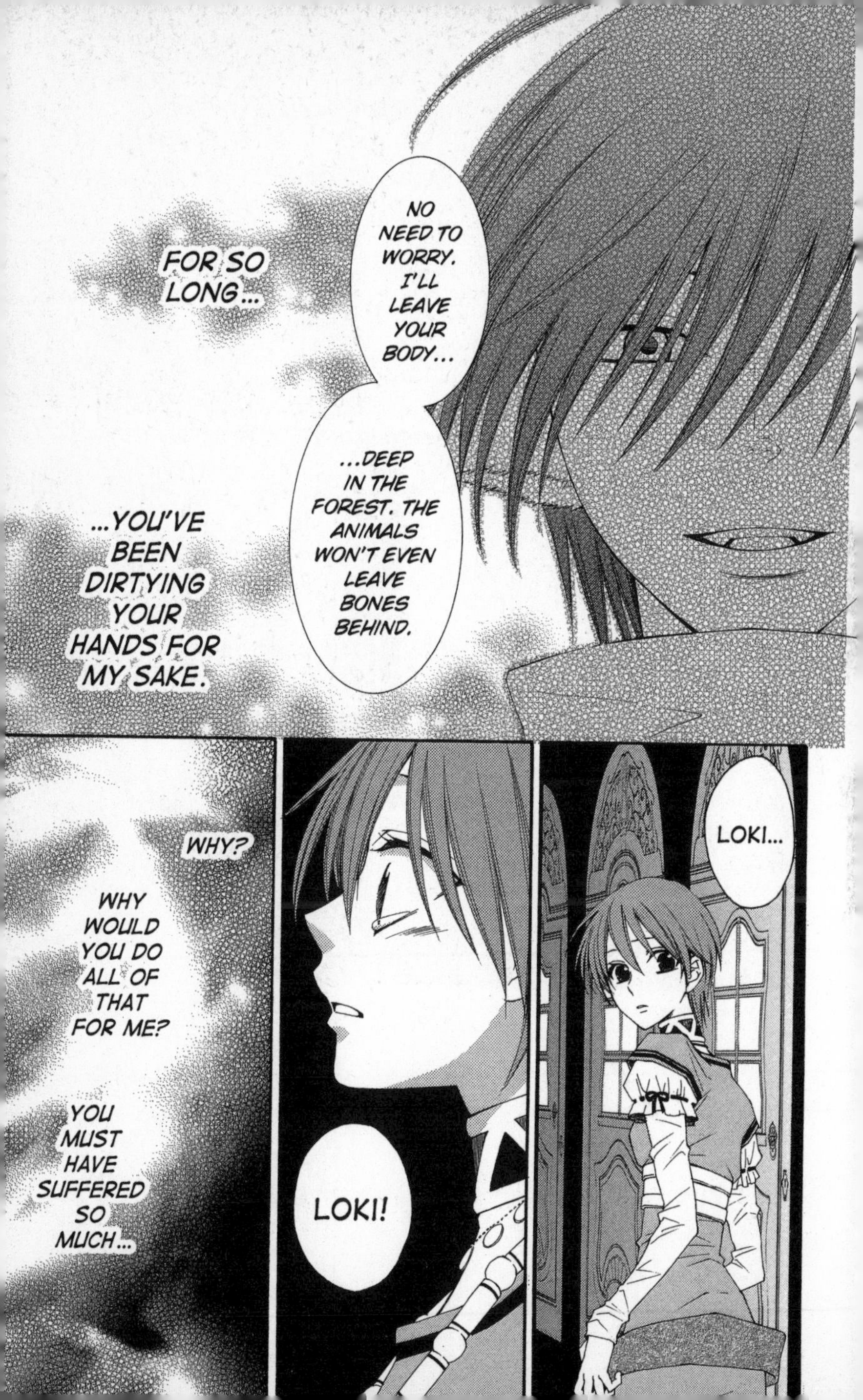
NO NEED TO WORRY. I'LL LEAVE YOUR BODY...
...DEEP IN THE FOREST. THE ANIMALS WON'T EVEN LEAVE BONES BEHIND.
FOR SO LONG...
...YOU'VE BEEN DIRTYING YOUR HANDS FOR MY SAKE.
LOKI...
LOKI!
WHY?
WHY WOULD YOU DO ALL OF THAT FOR ME?
YOU MUST HAVE SUFFERED SO MUCH...

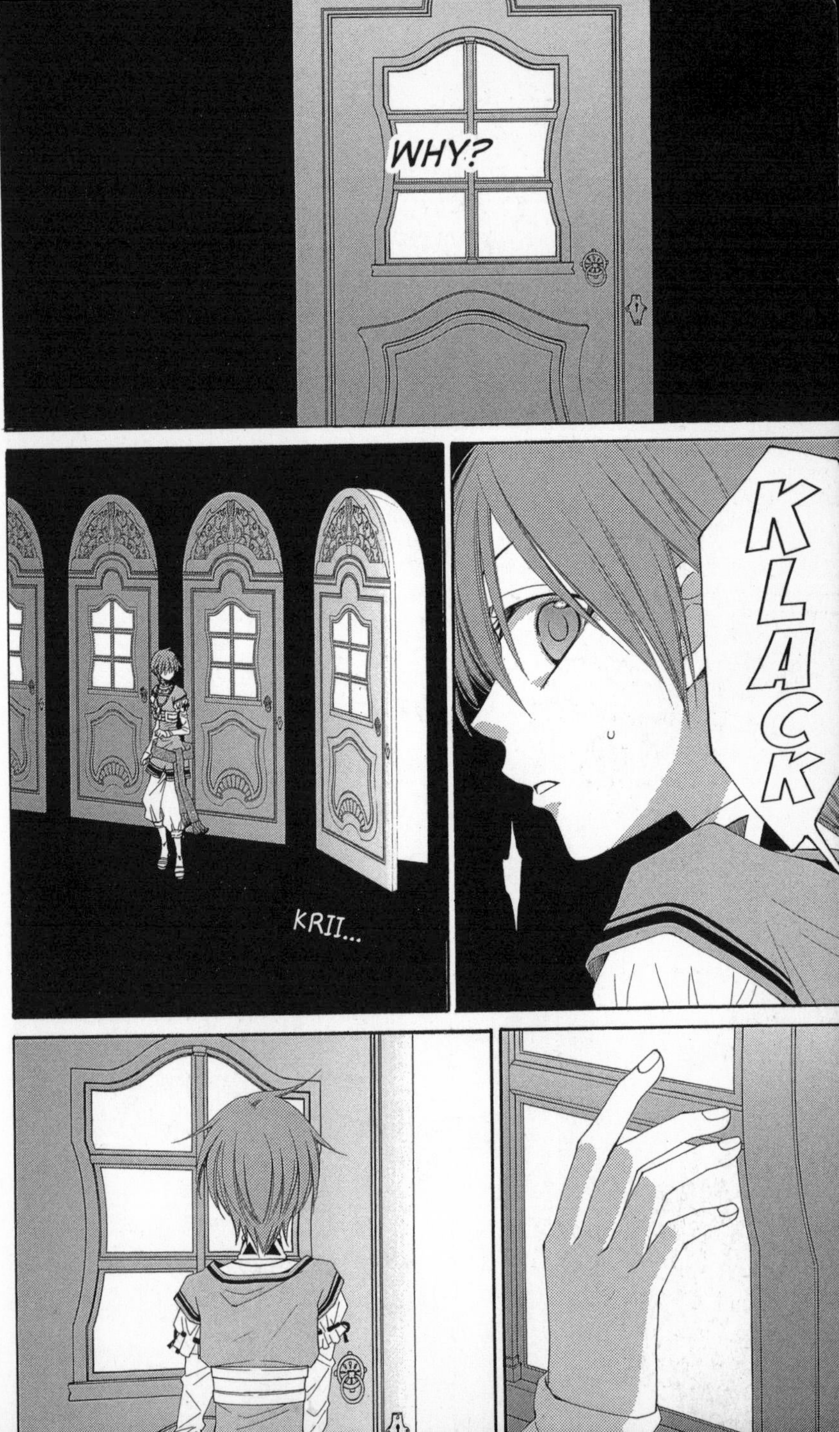
WHY?
KLACK
KRII...

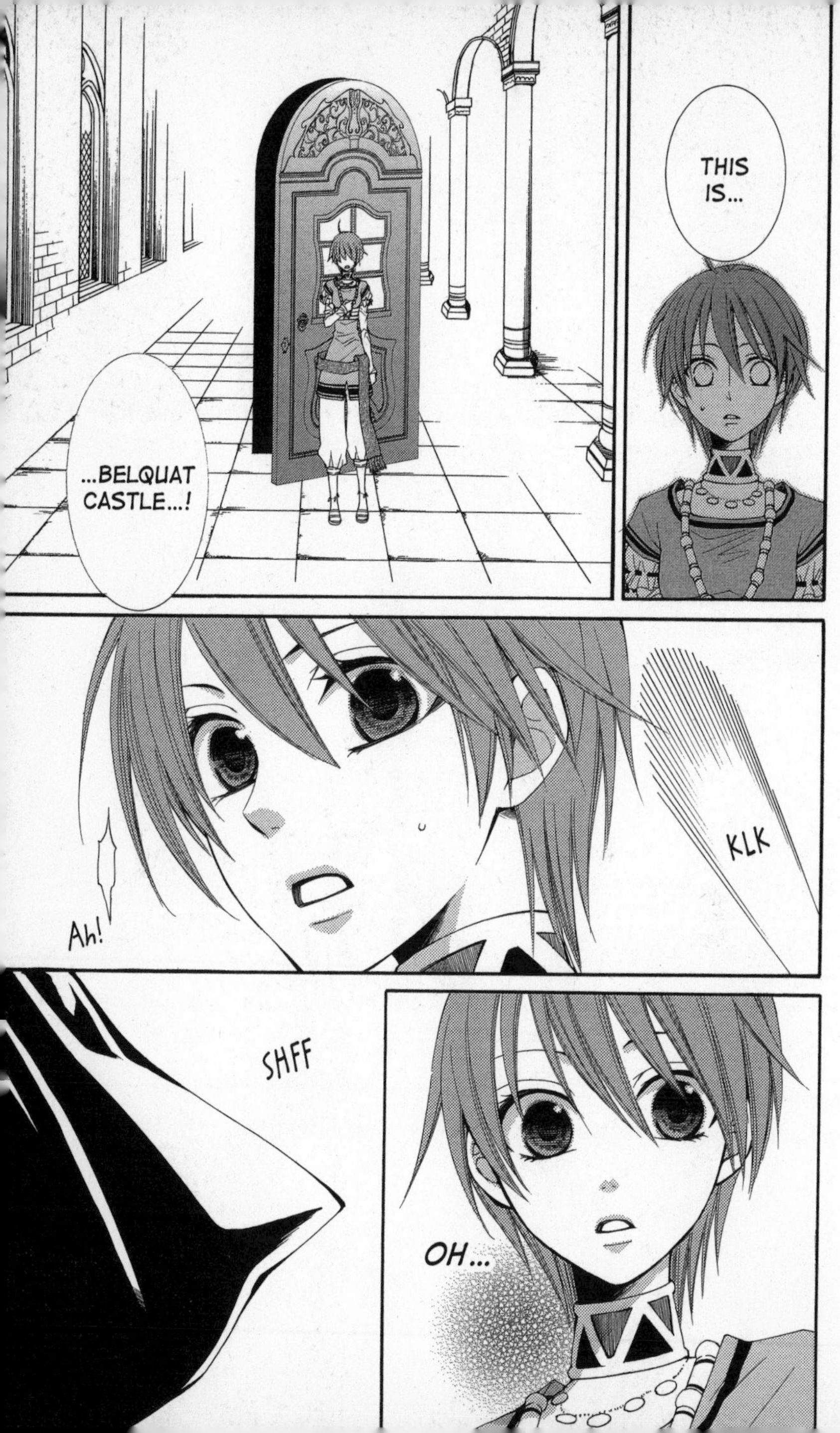
THIS IS...
...BELQUAT CASTLE...!
KLK
Ah!
OH...
SHFF

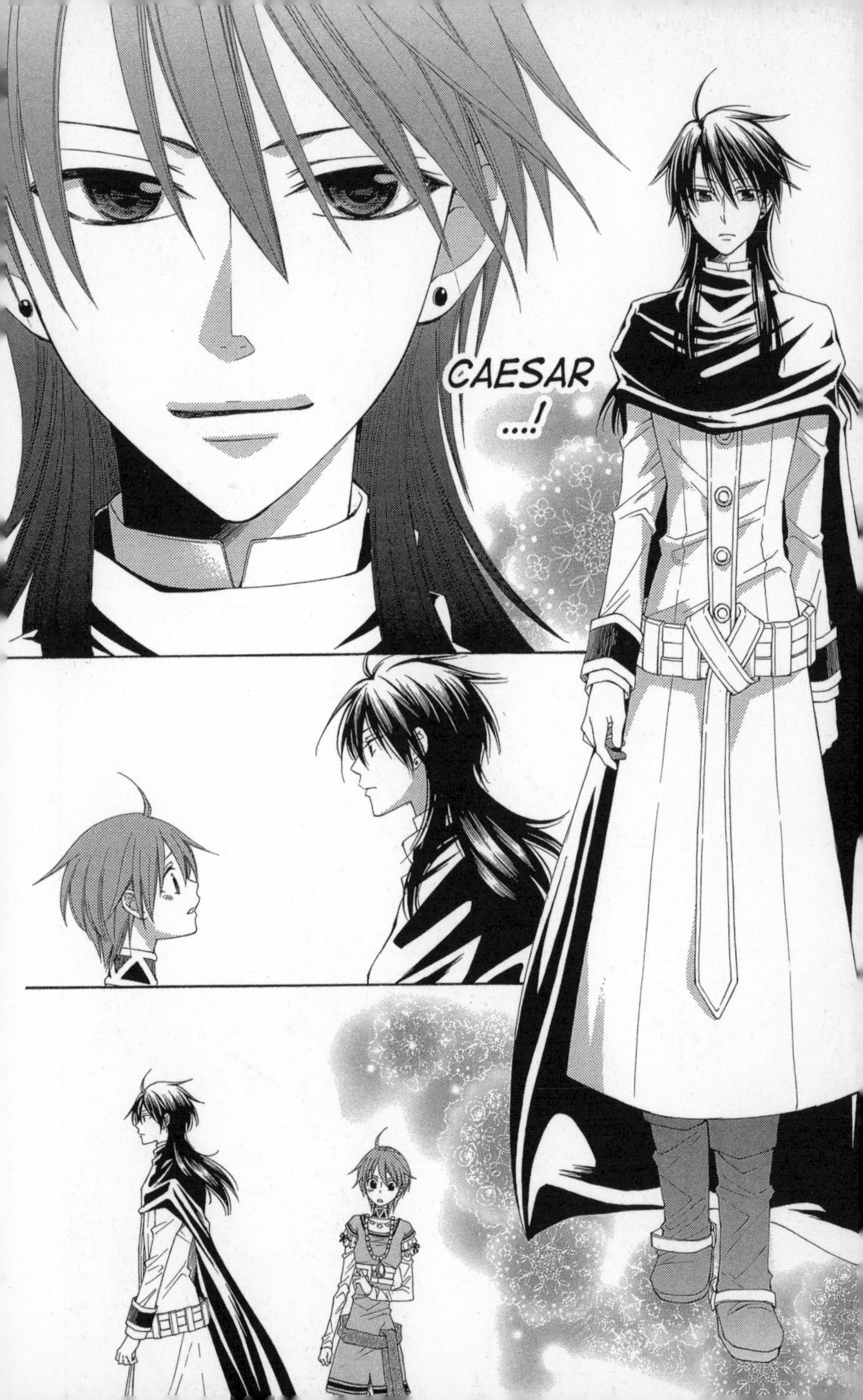
CAESAR
...!

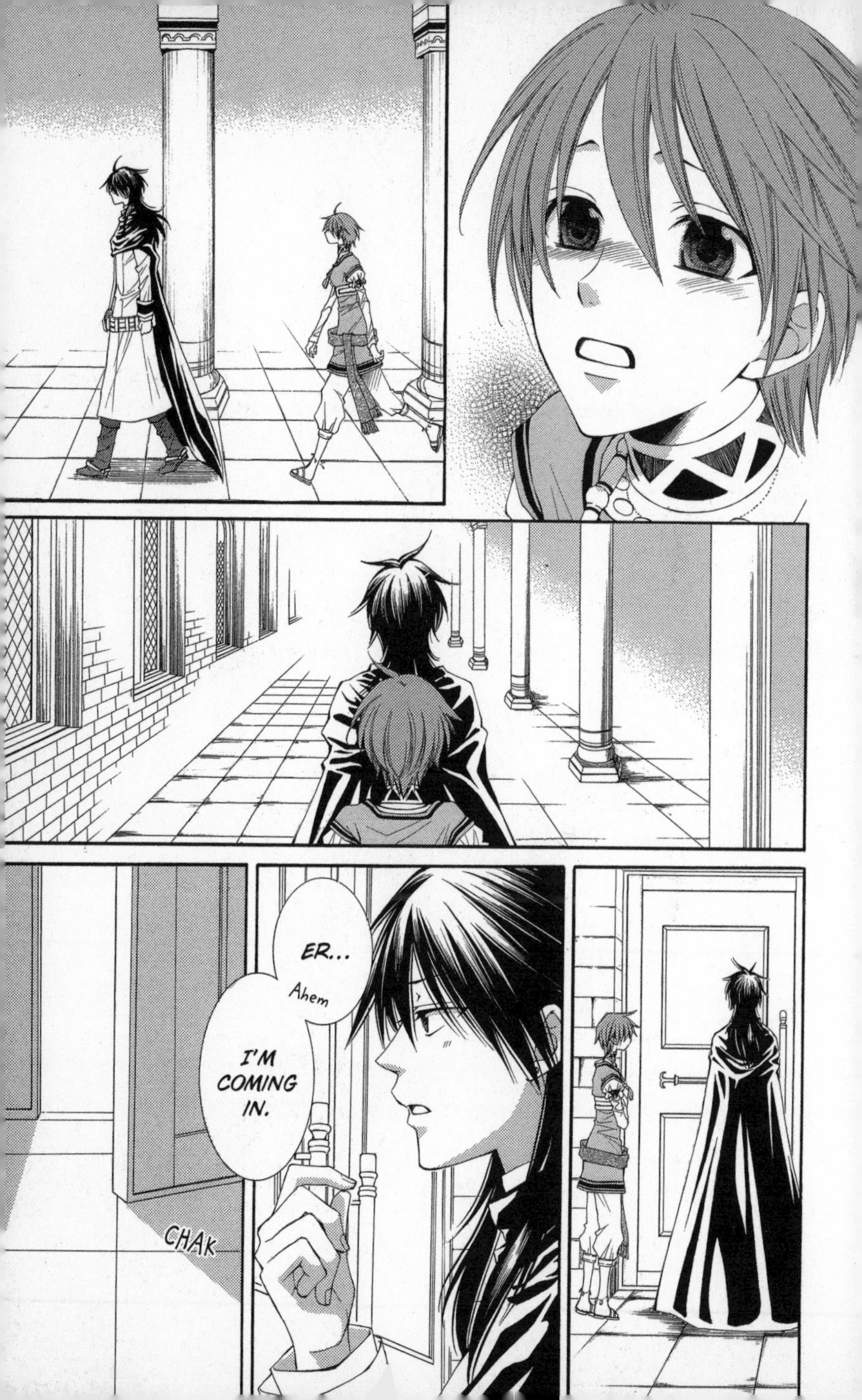
ER...
Ahem
I'M COMING IN.
CHAK

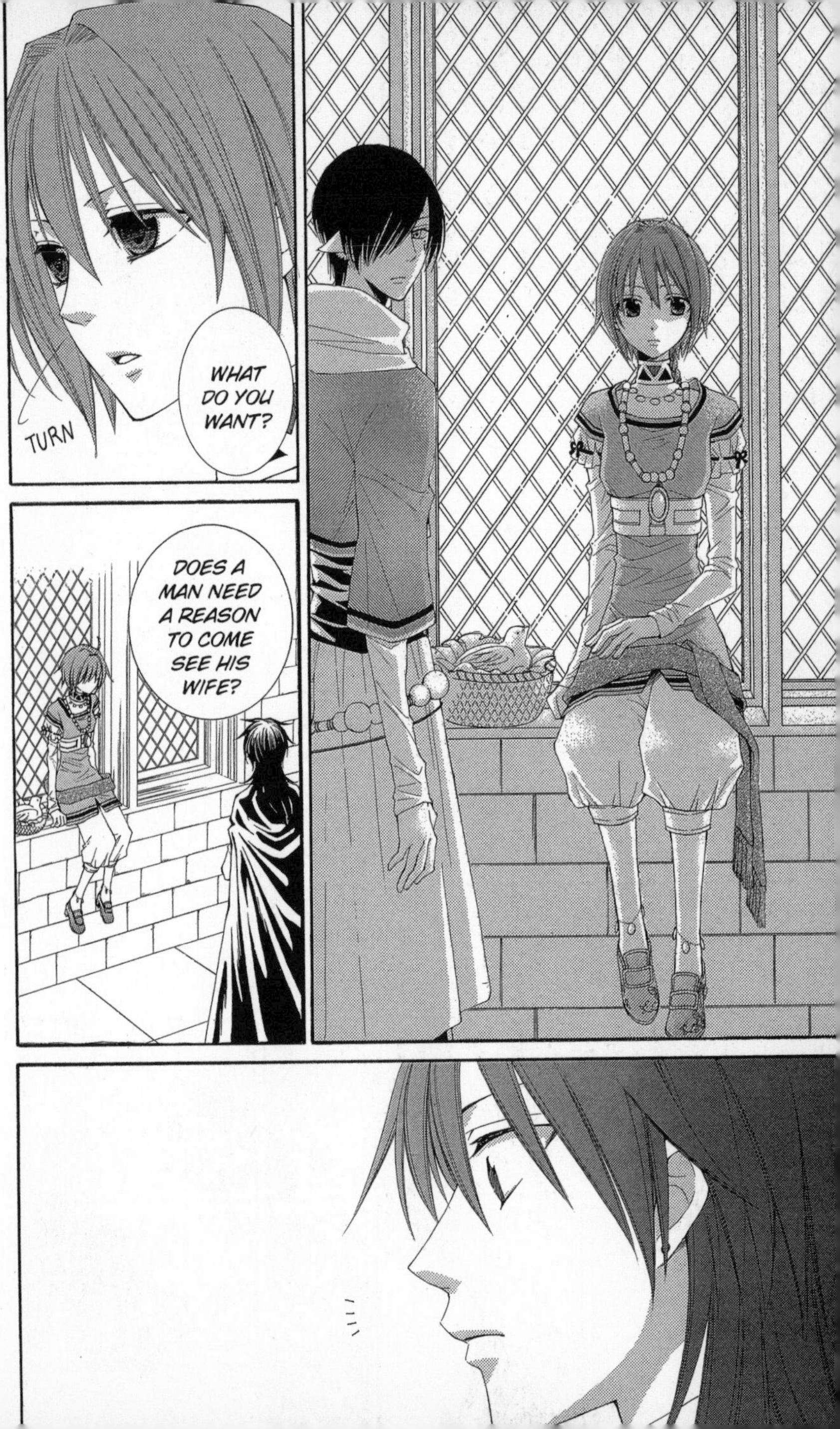
WHAT DO YOU WANT?
TURN
DOES A MAN NEED A REASON TO COME SEE HIS WIFE?

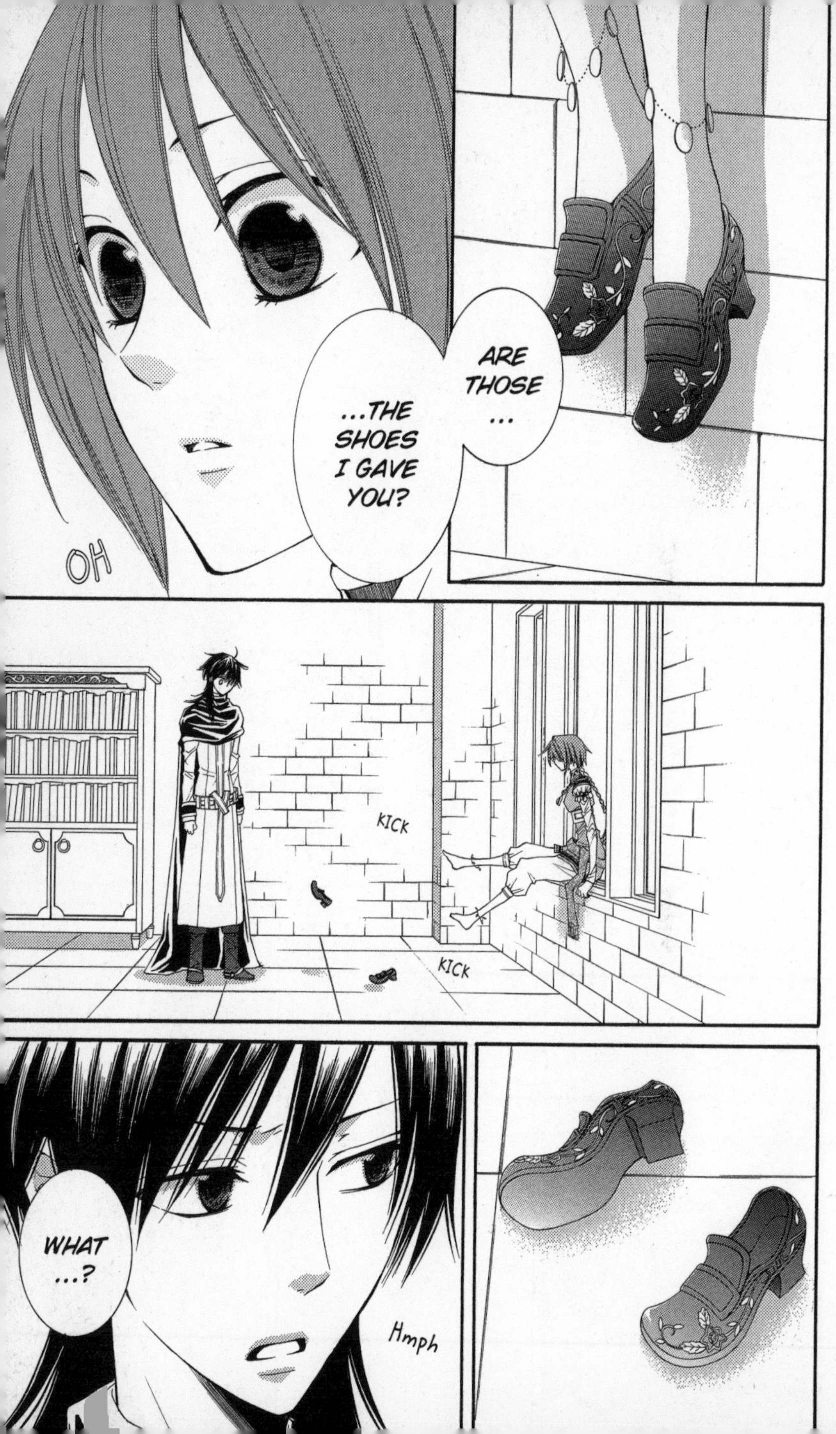
ARE THOSE ...
...THE SHOES I GAVE YOU?
OH
KICK
KICK
WHAT ...?
Hmph

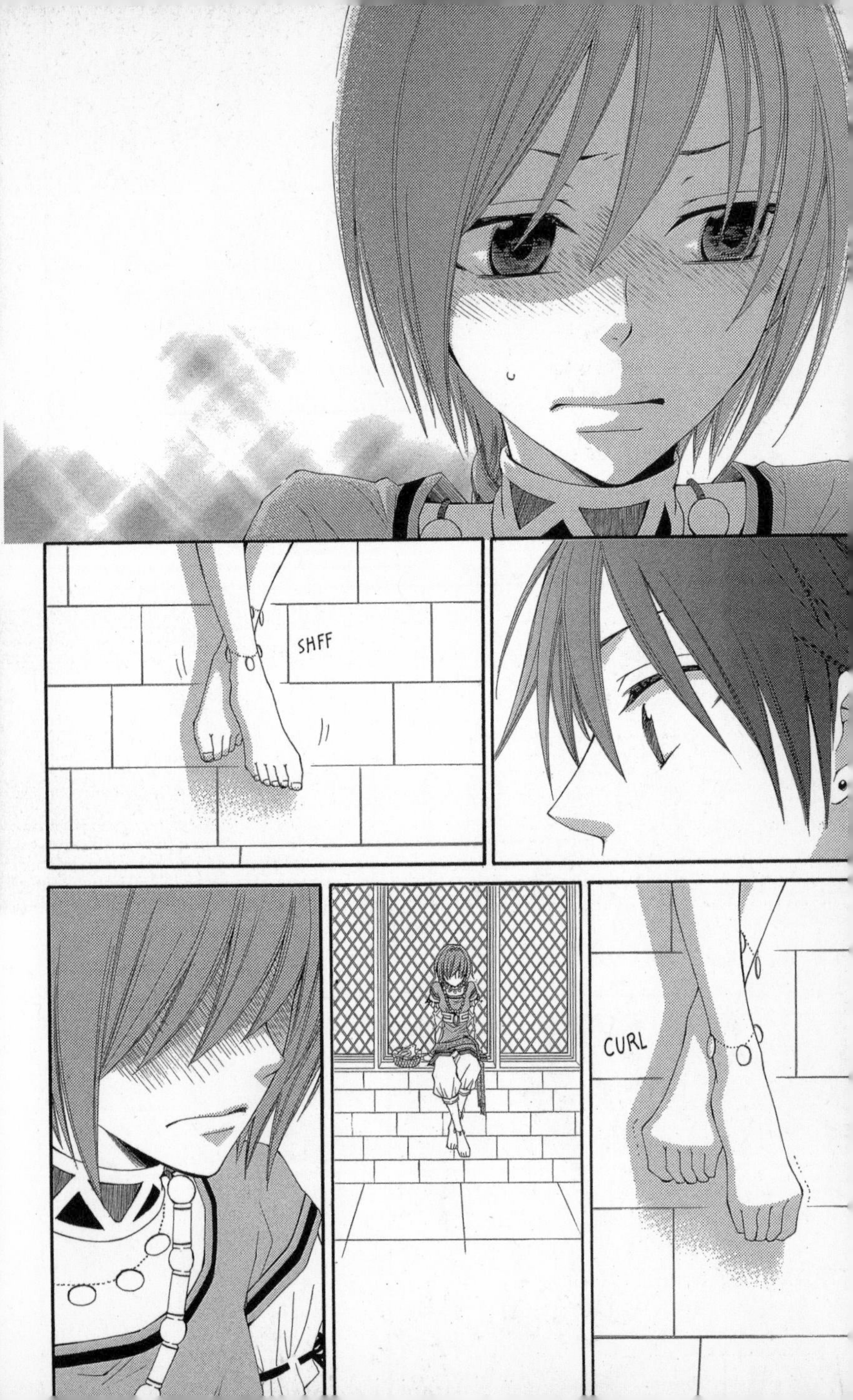
SHFF
CURL

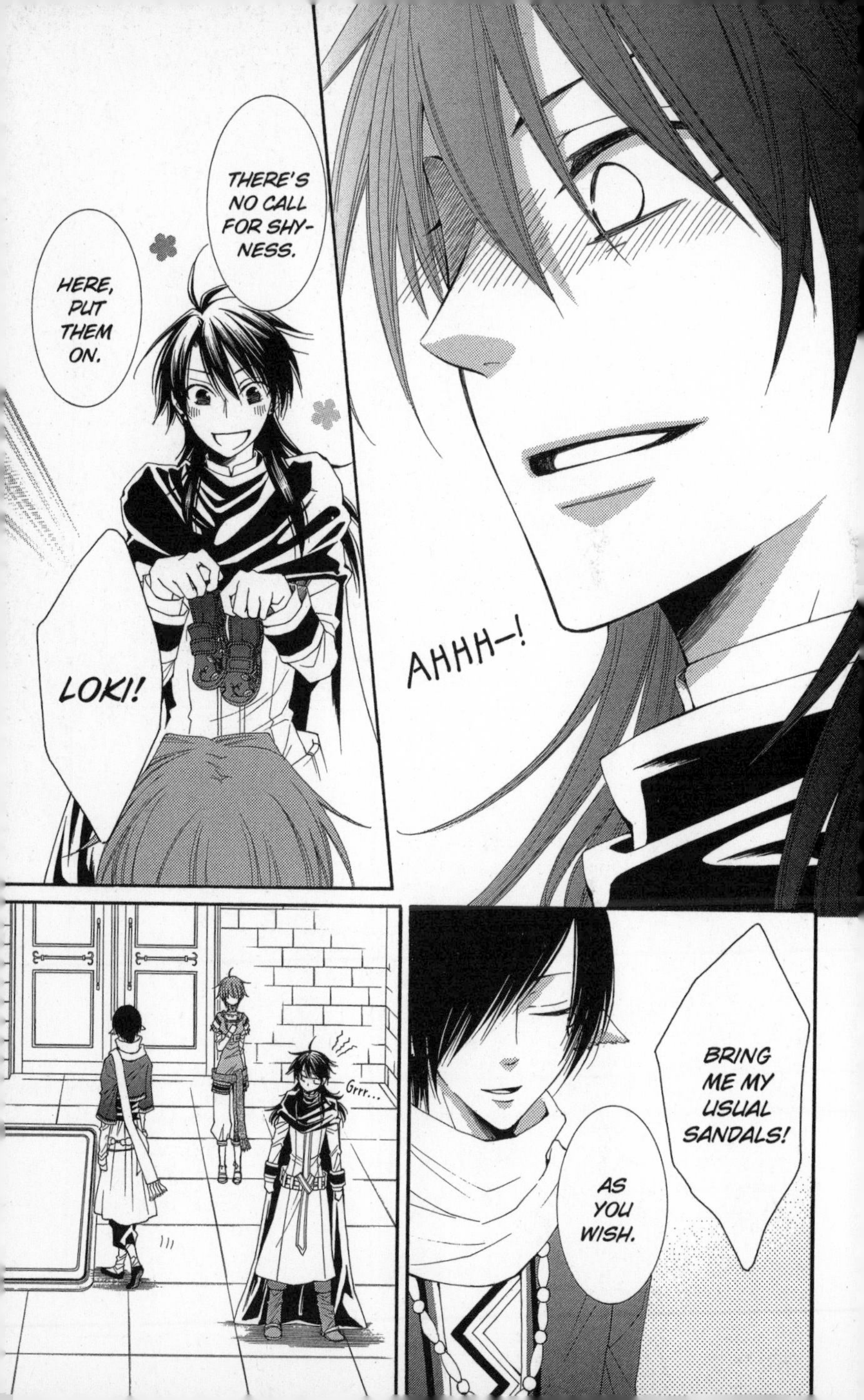
AHHH—!
THERE'S NO CALL FOR SHY-NESS.
HERE, PUT THEM ON.
LOKI!
BRING ME MY USUAL SANDALS!
AS YOU WISH.
Grrr...

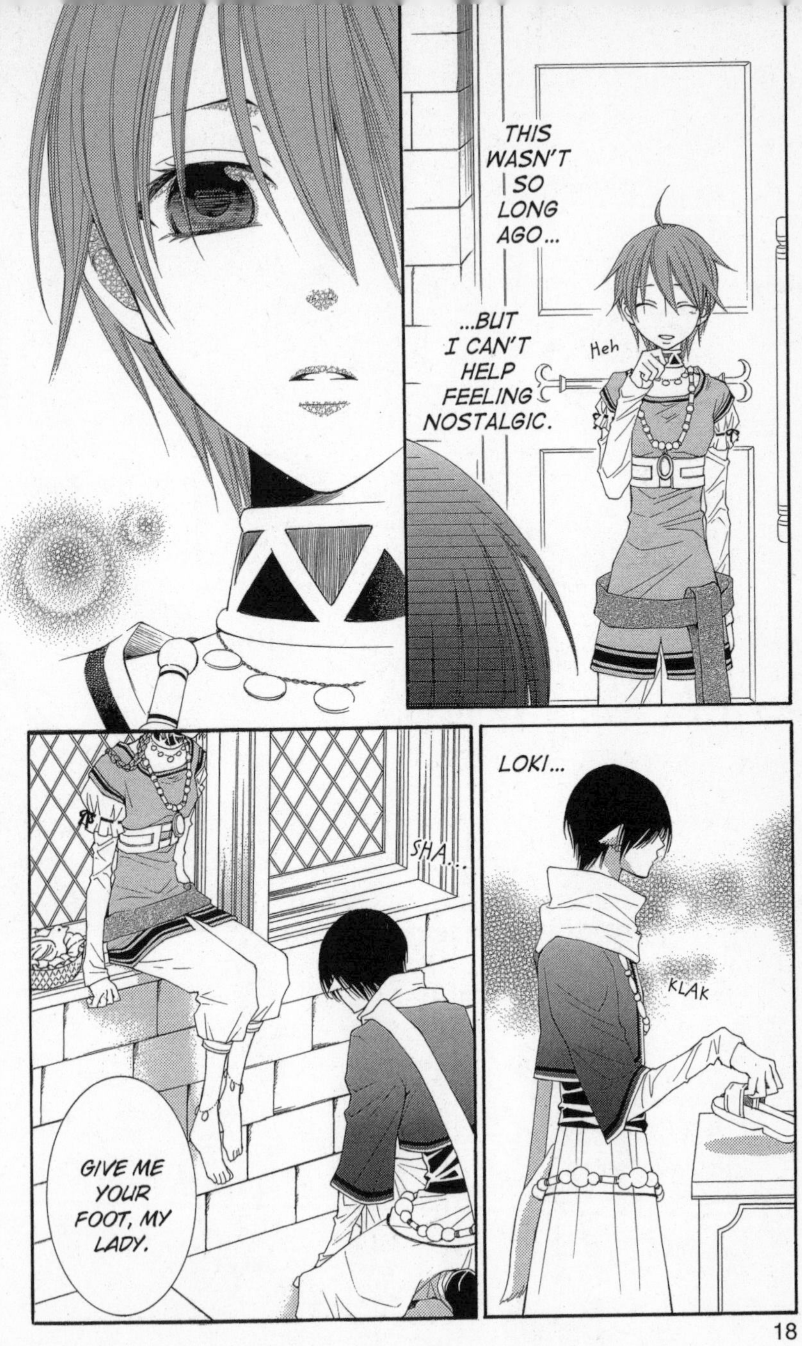
THIS WASN'T SO LONG AGO...
...BUT I CAN'T HELP FEELING NOSTALGIC.
Heh
LOKI...
KLAK
SHA...
GIVE ME YOUR FOOT, MY LADY.

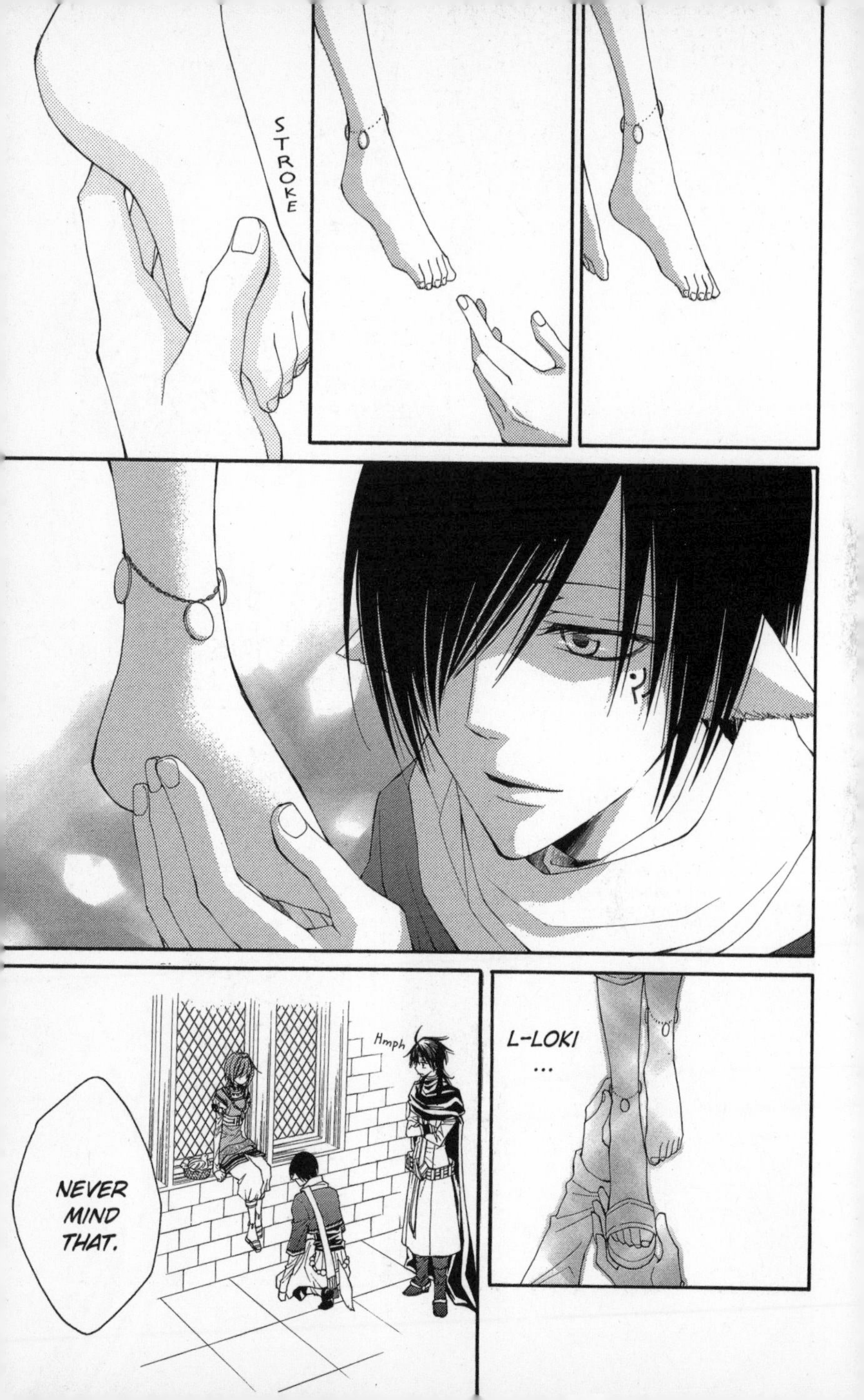
STROKE
L-LOKI ...
Hmph
NEVER MIND THAT.

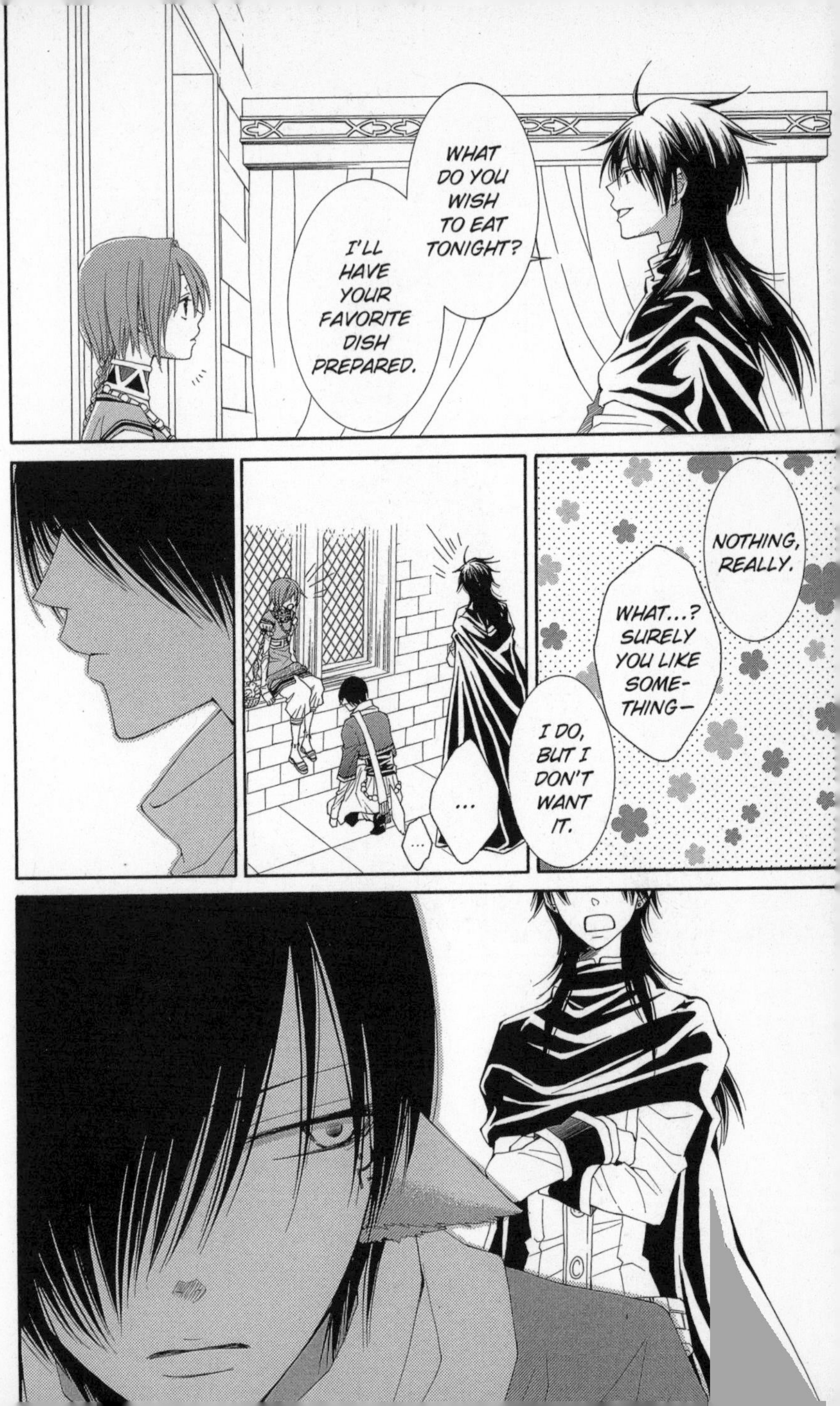
WHAT DO YOU WISH TO EAT TONIGHT?
I'LL HAVE YOUR FAVORITE DISH PREPARED.
NOTHING, REALLY.
WHAT...? SURELY YOU LIKE SOME-THING—
I DO, BUT I DON'T WANT IT.
...
...

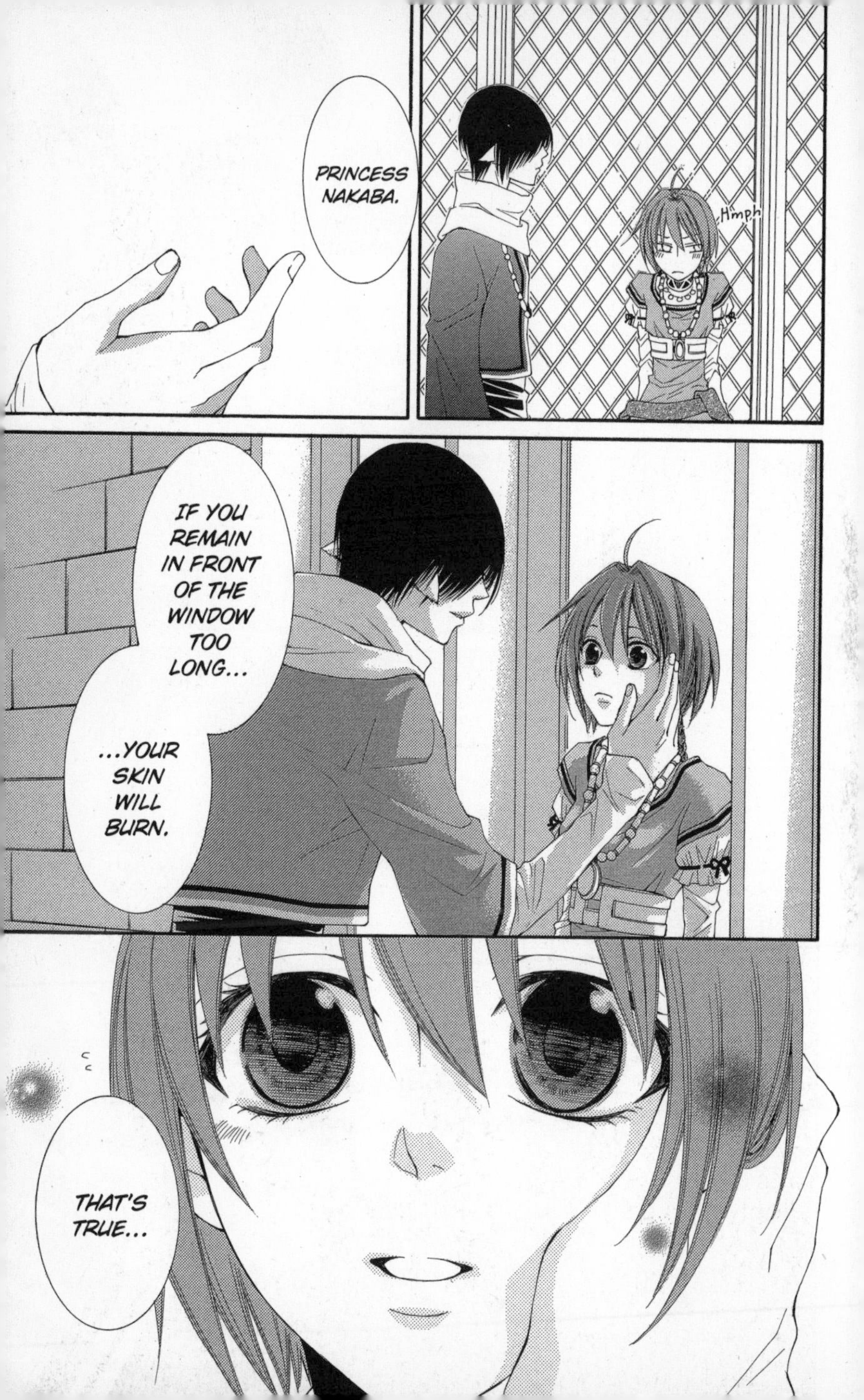
Hmph
PRINCESS NAKABA.
IF YOU REMAIN IN FRONT OF THE WINDOW TOO LONG...
...YOUR SKIN WILL BURN.
THAT'S TRUE...

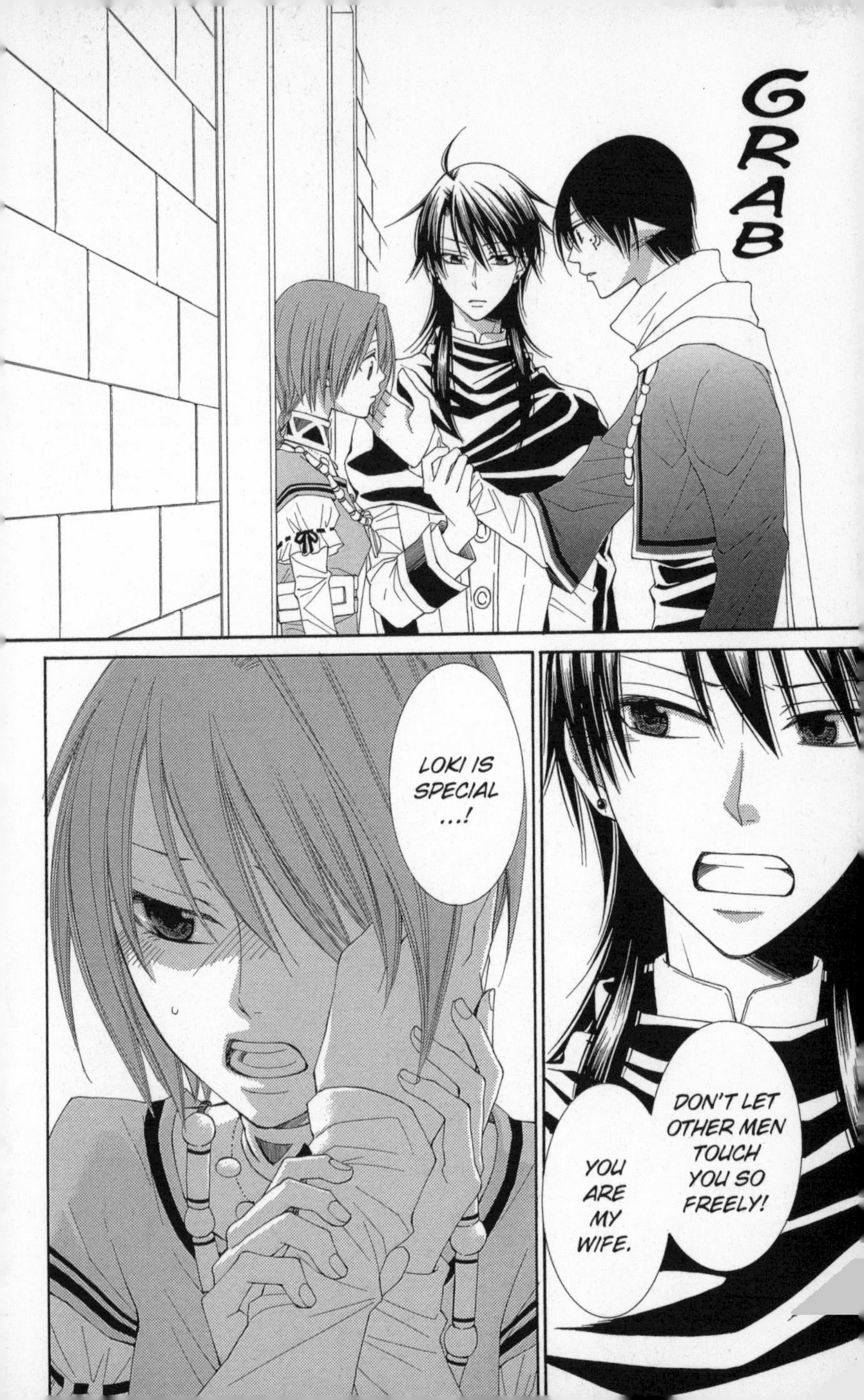
GRAB
DON'T LET OTHER MEN TOUCH YOU SO FREELY!
YOU ARE MY WIFE.
LOKI IS SPECIAL ...!

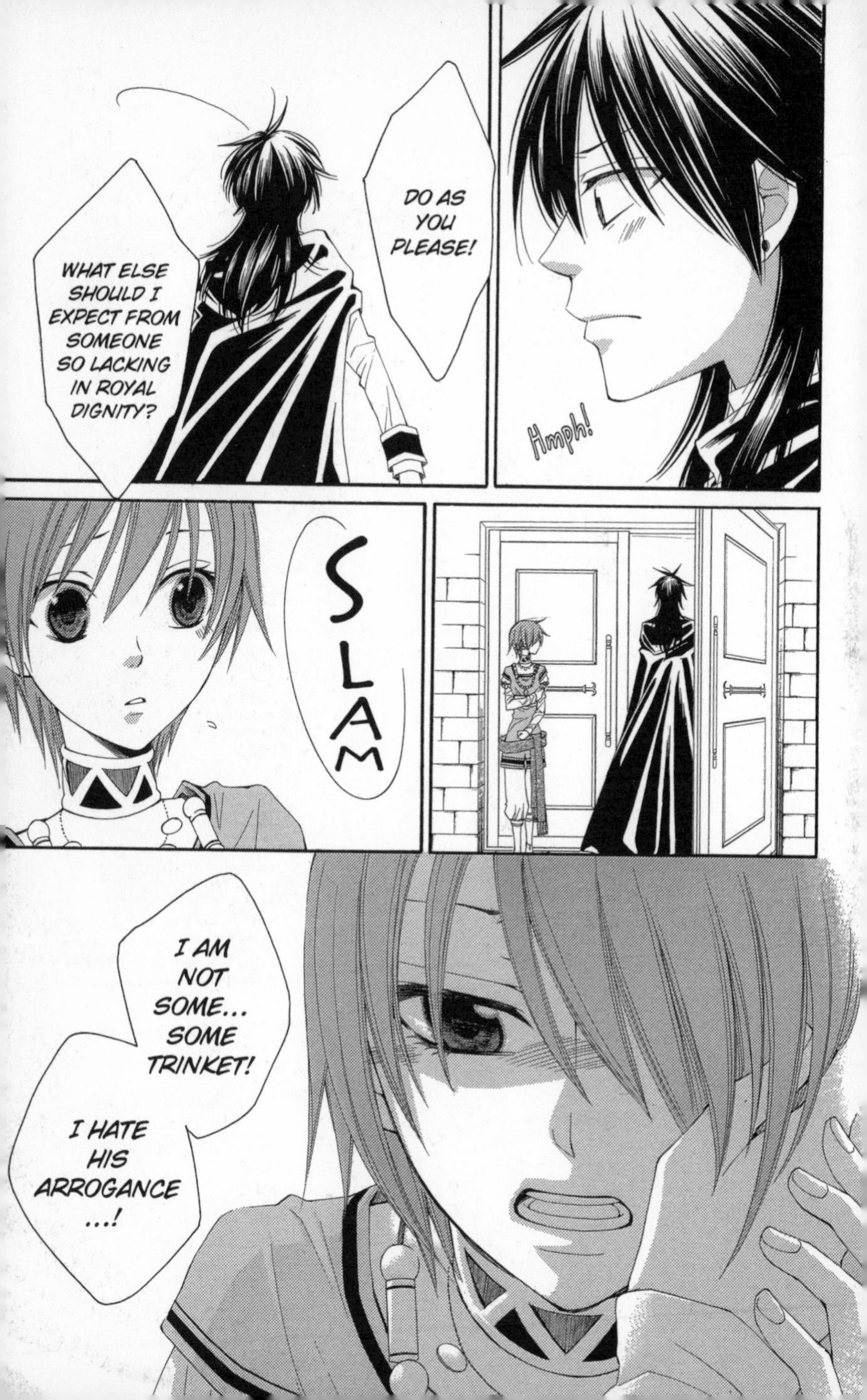
Hmph!
DO AS YOU PLEASE!
WHAT ELSE SHOULD I EXPECT FROM SOMEONE SO LACKING IN ROYAL DIGNITY?
SLAM
I AM NOT SOME... SOME TRINKET!
I HATE HIS ARROGANCE ...!

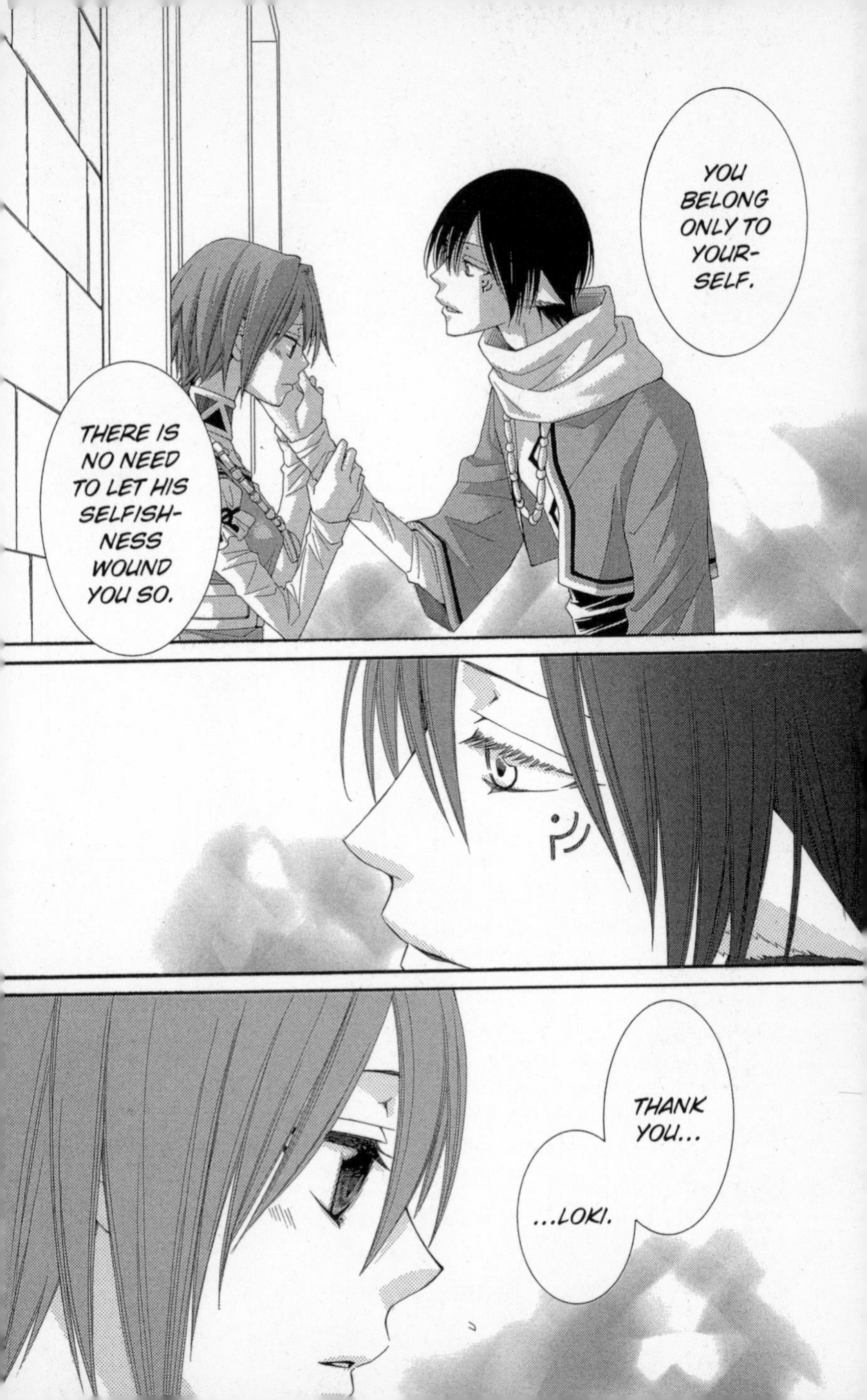
YOU BELONG ONLY TO YOUR-SELF.
THERE IS NO NEED TO LET HIS SELFISH-NESS WOUND YOU SO.
THANK YOU...
...LOKI.

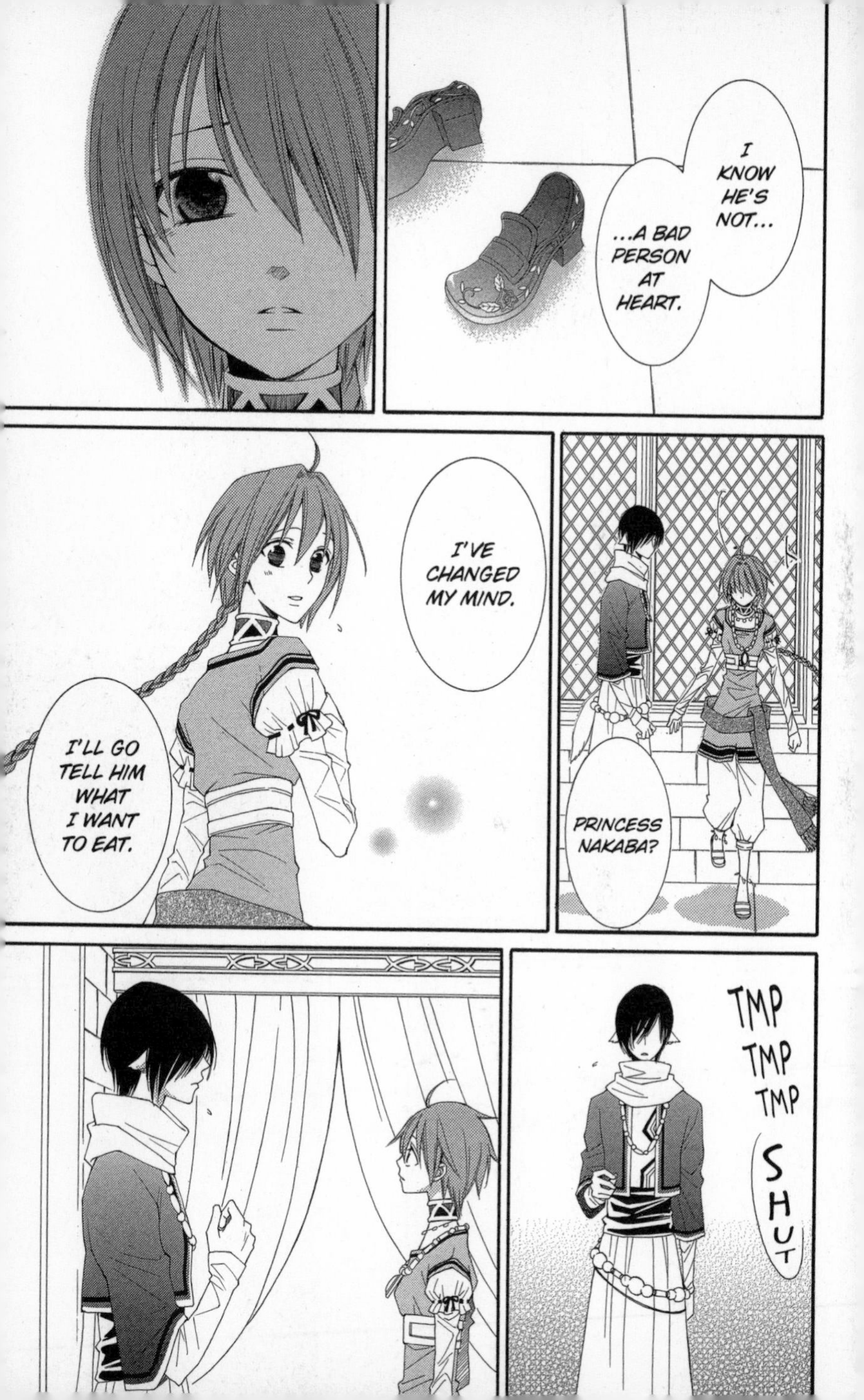
I KNOW HE'S NOT...
...A BAD PERSON AT HEART.
PRINCESS NAKABA?
I'VE CHANGED MY MIND.
I'LL GO TELL HIM WHAT I WANT TO EAT.
TMP TMP TMP
SHUT

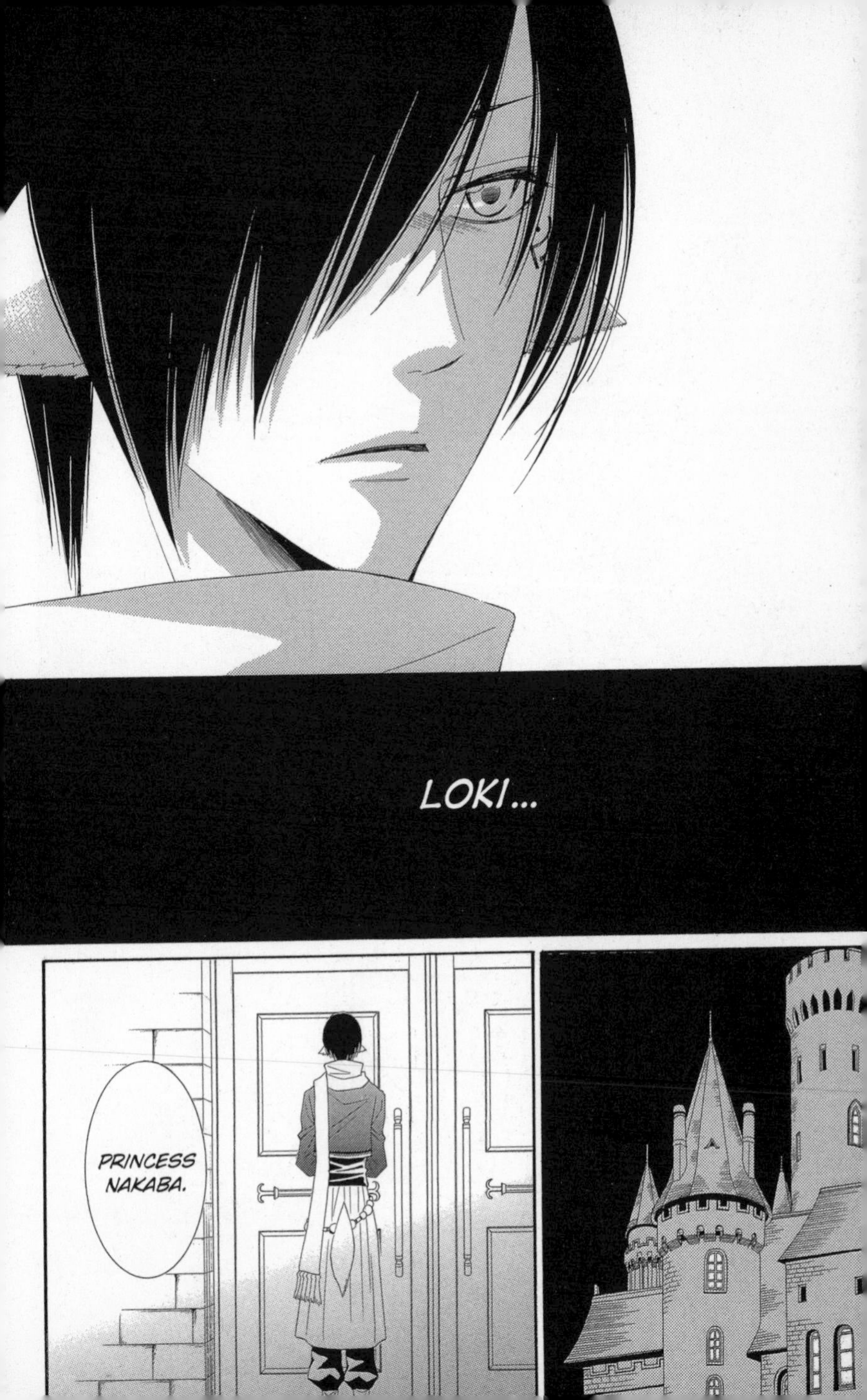
LOKI...
PRINCESS NAKABA.

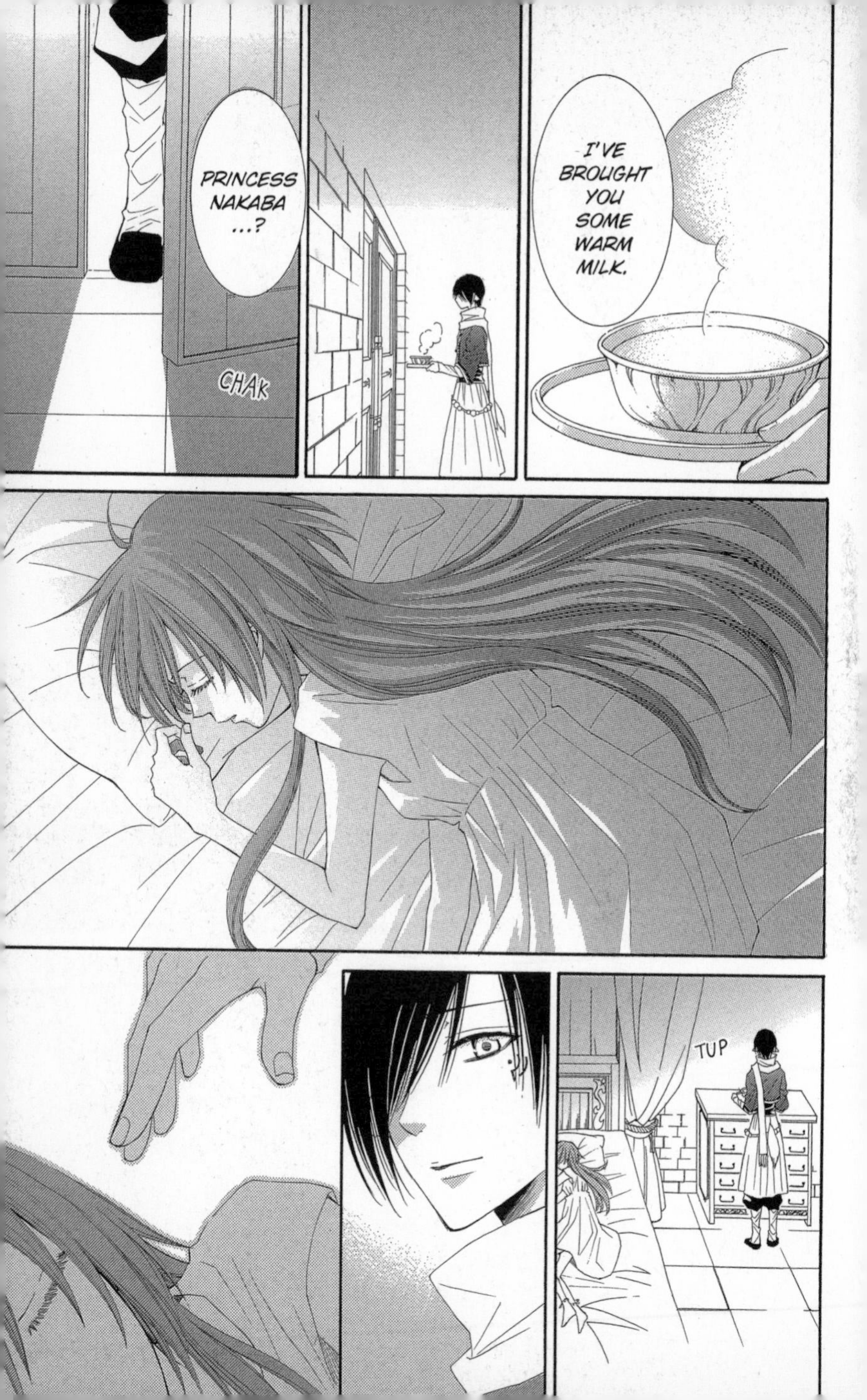
I'VE BROUGHT YOU SOME WARM MILK.
PRINCESS NAKABA ...?
CHAK
TUP

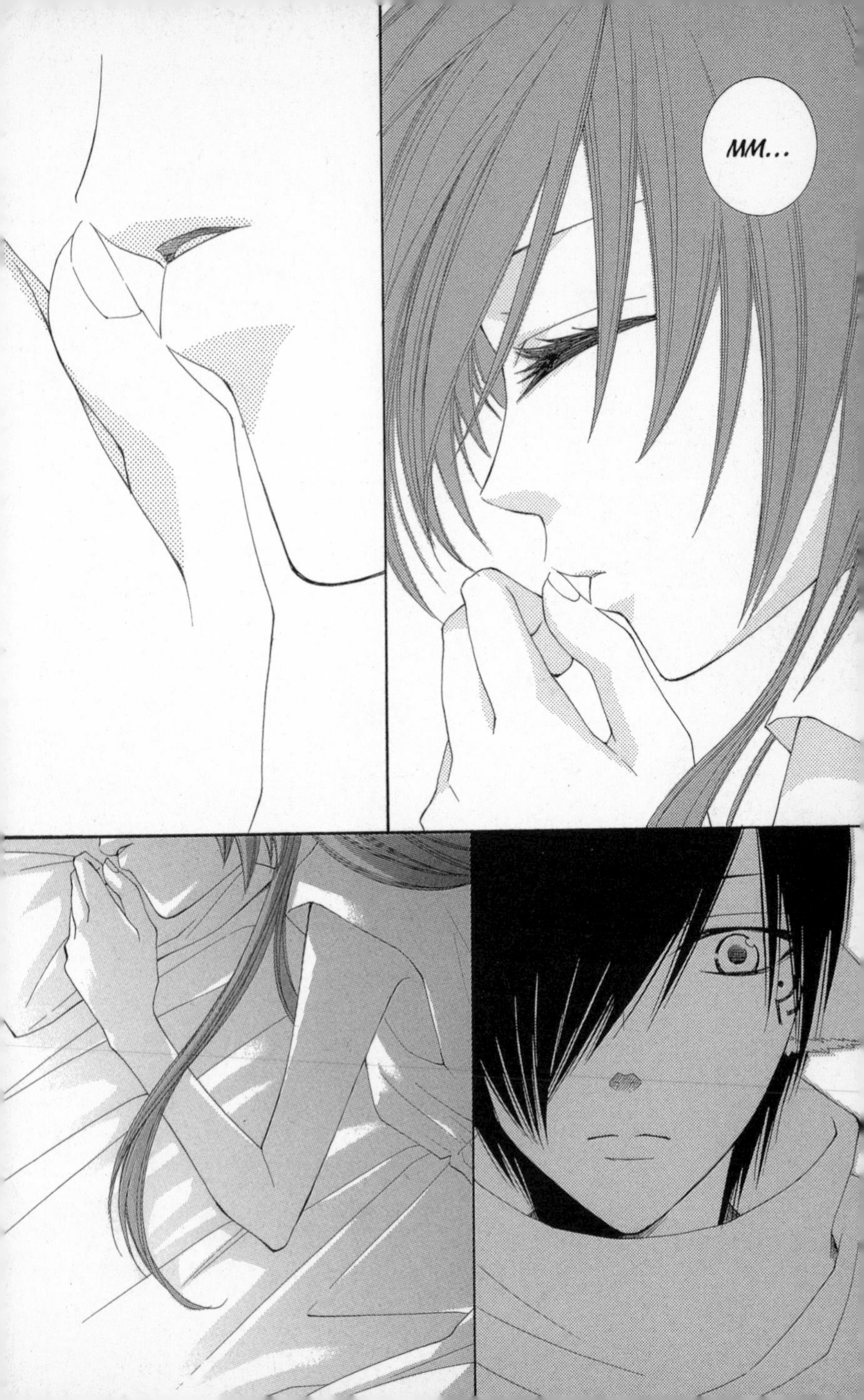
MM...

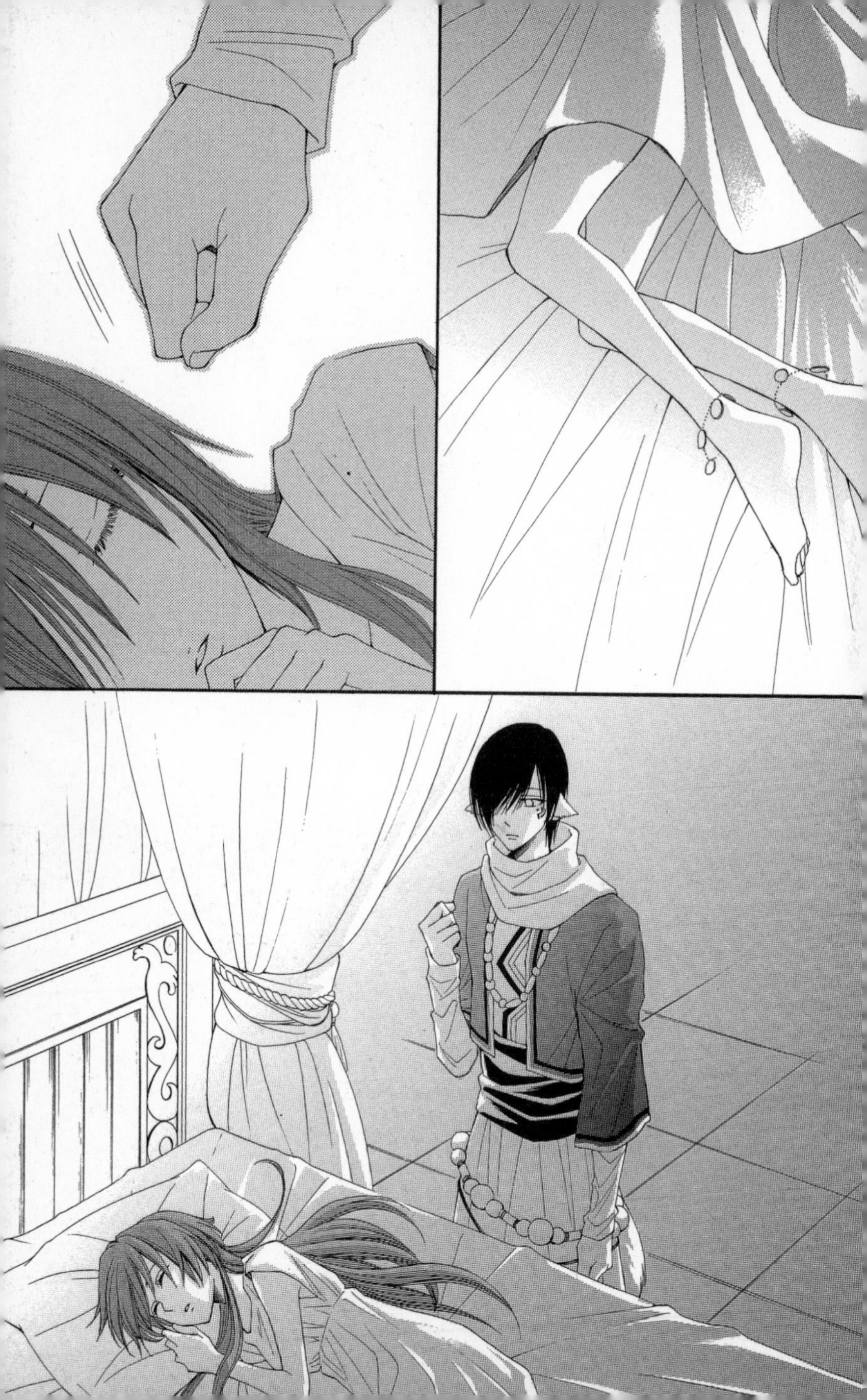

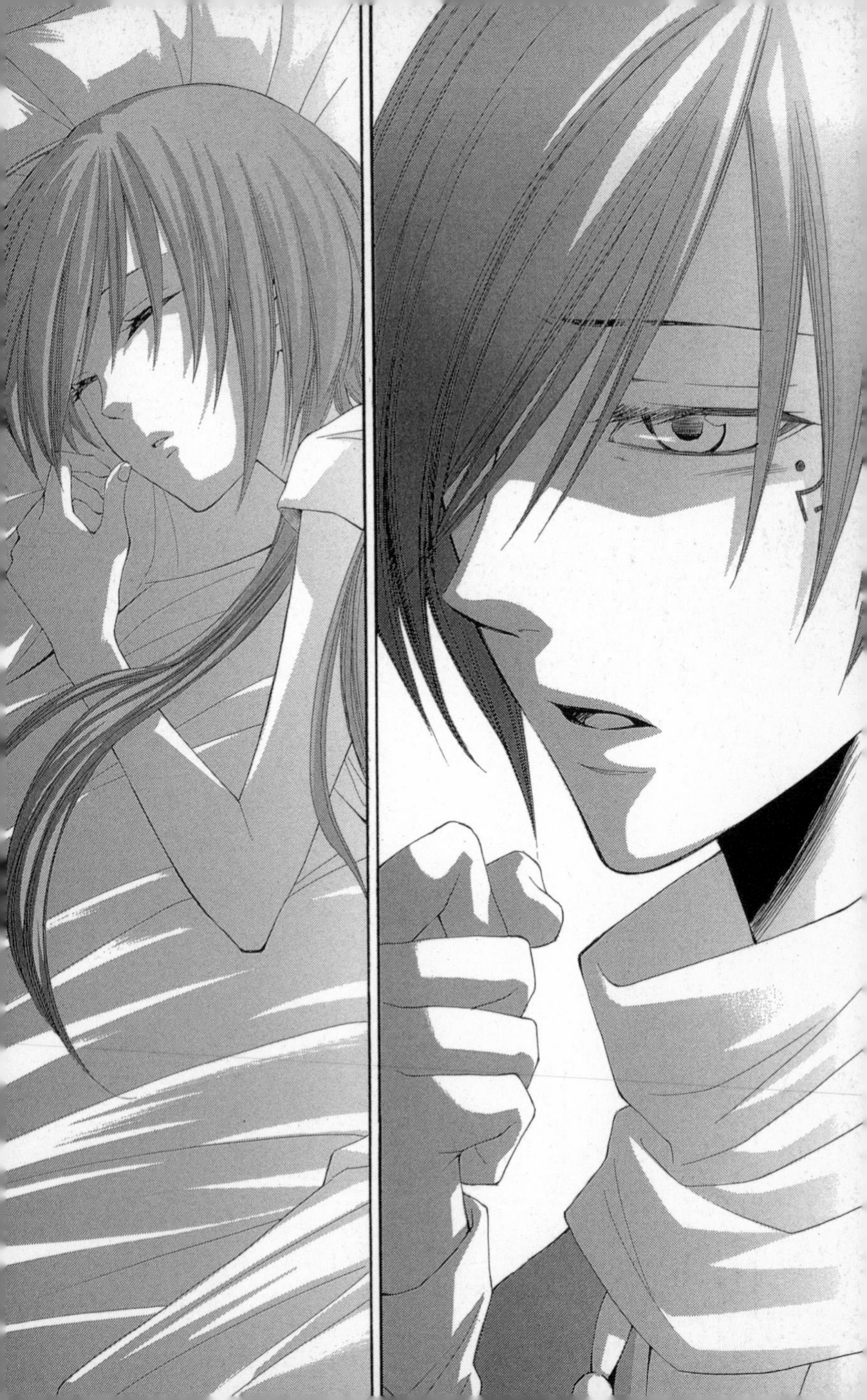

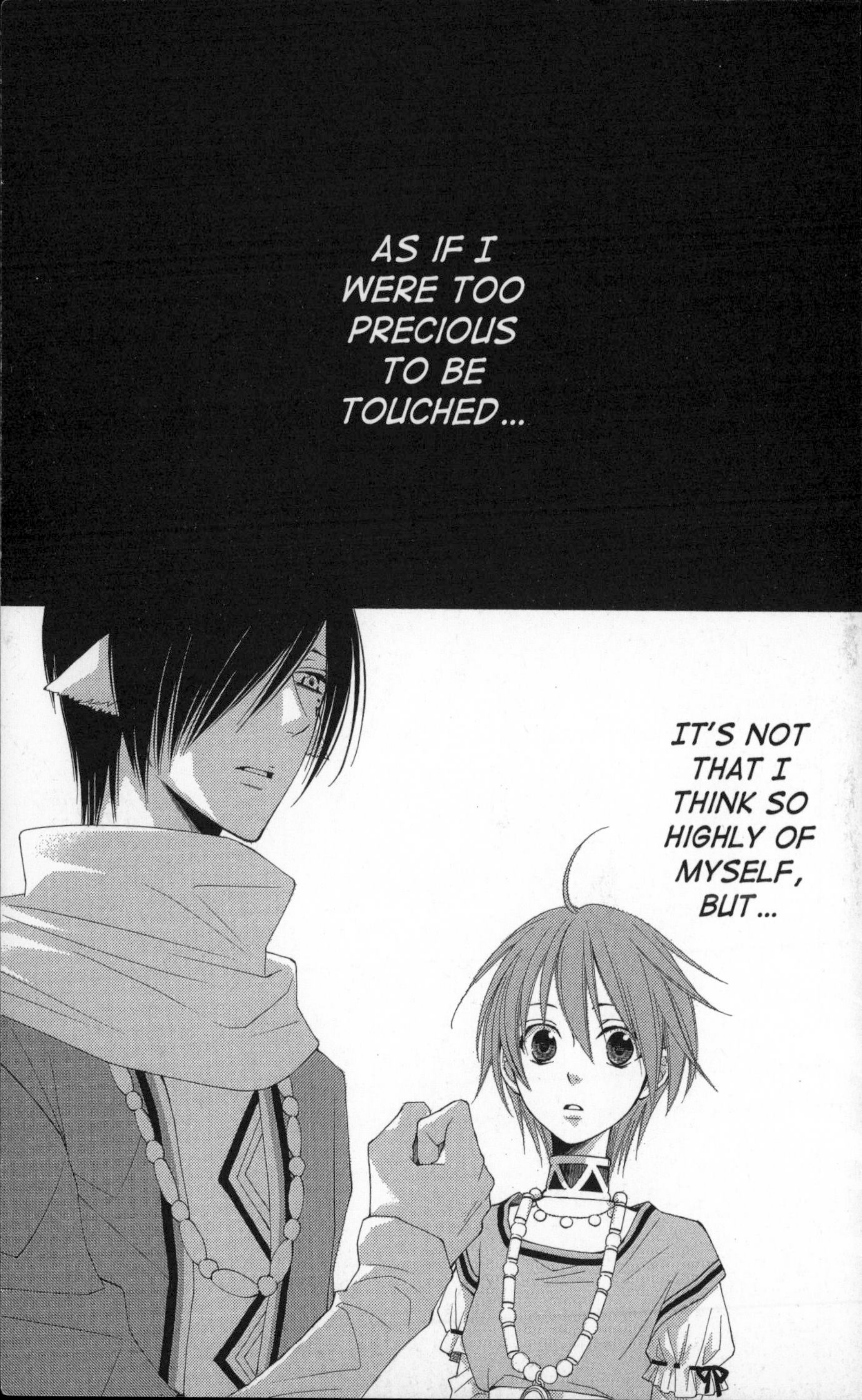
AS IF I WERE TOO PRECIOUS TO BE TOUCHED...
IT'S NOT THAT I THINK SO HIGHLY OF MYSELF, BUT...

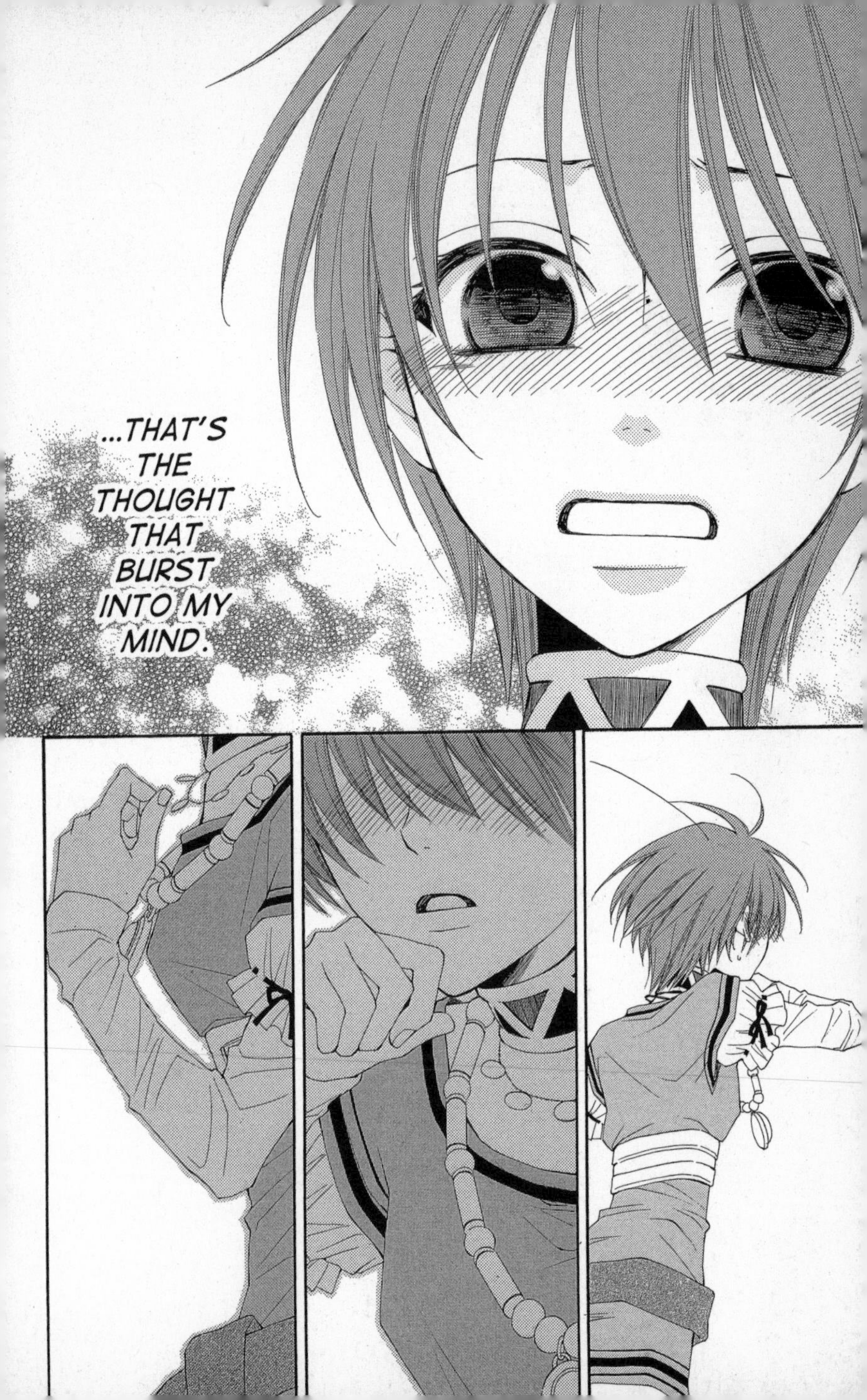
...THAT'S THE THOUGHT THAT BURST INTO MY MIND.

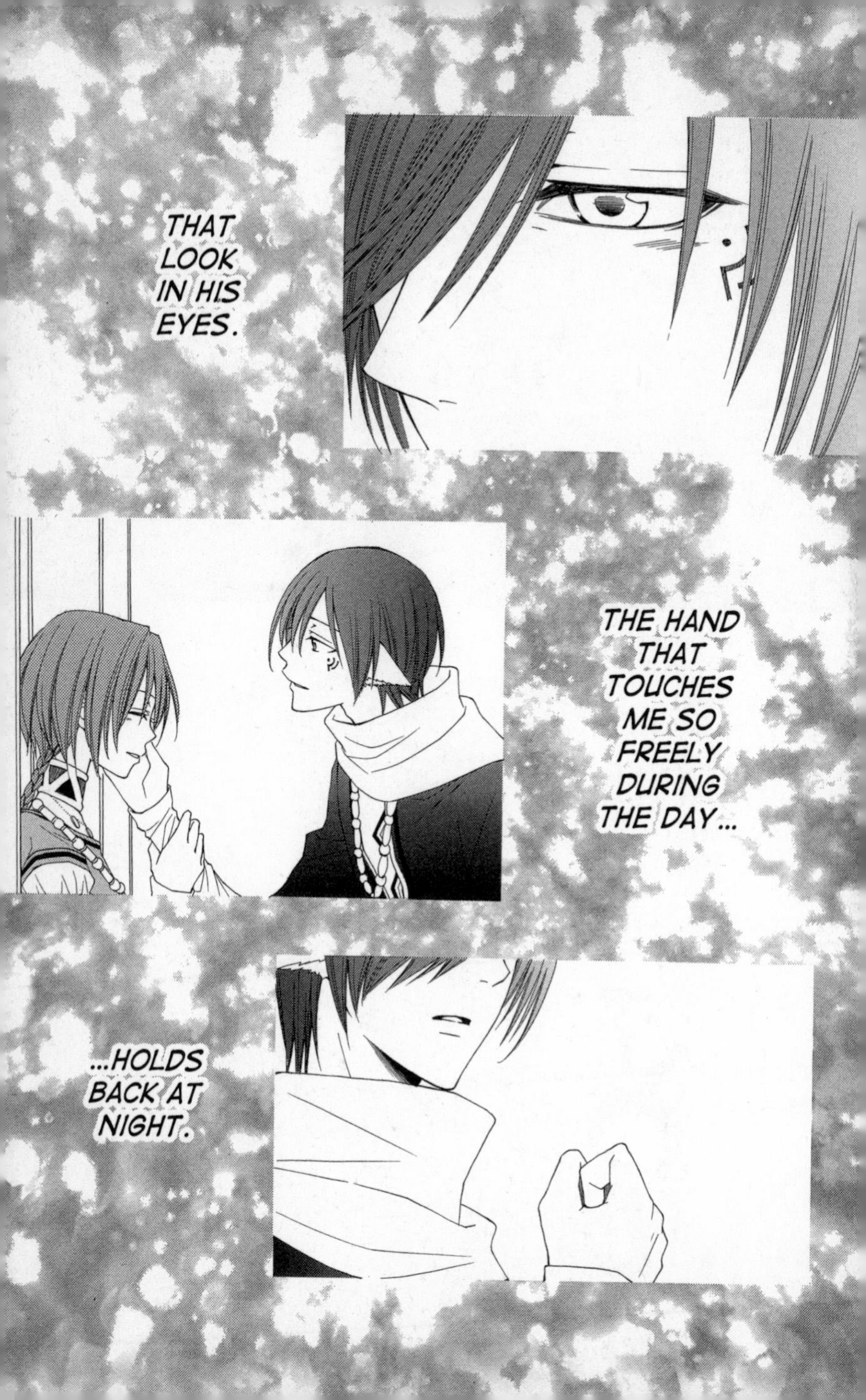
THAT LOOK IN HIS EYES.
THE HAND THAT TOUCHES ME SO FREELY DURING THE DAY...
...HOLDS BACK AT NIGHT.

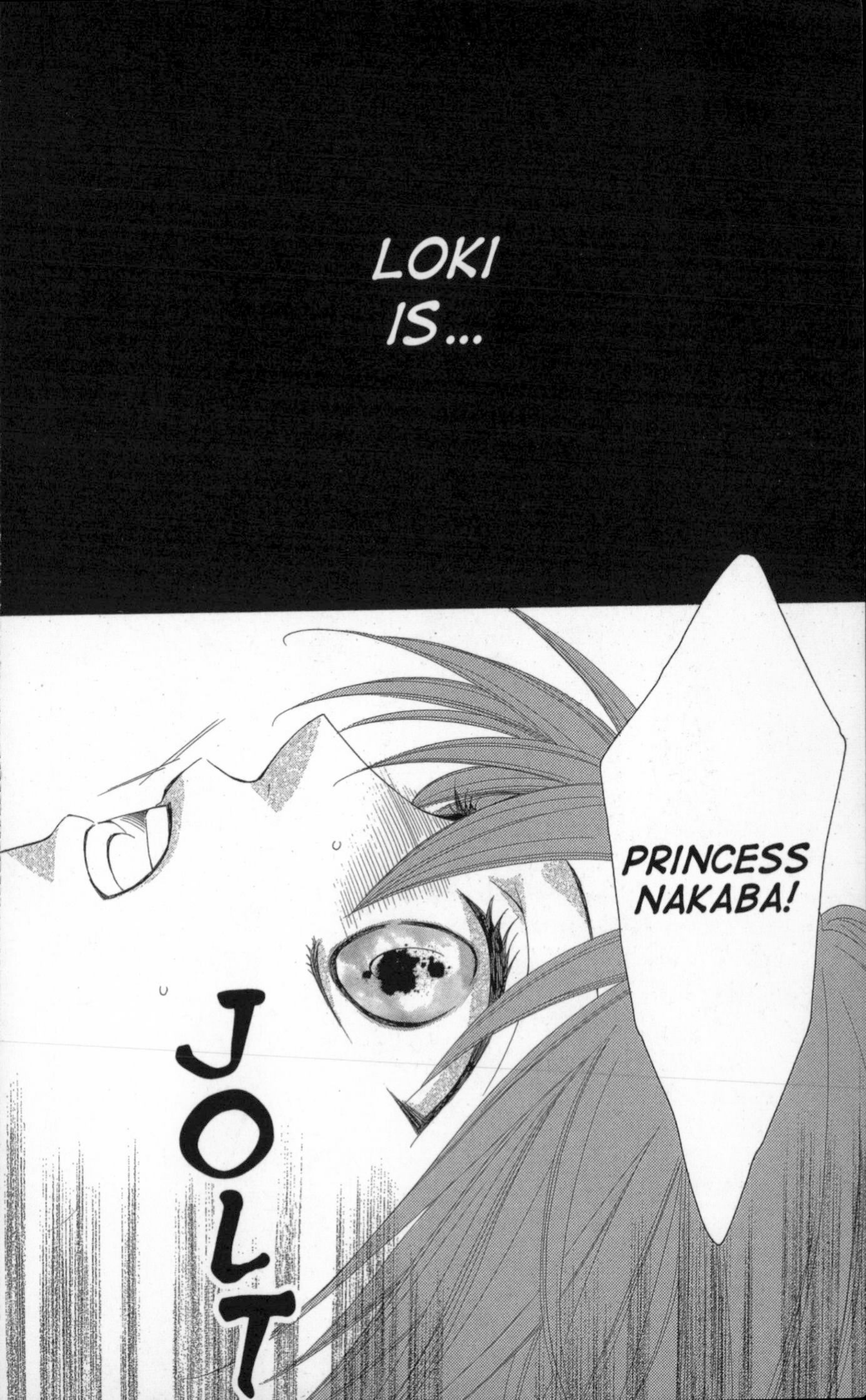
LOKI IS...
PRINCESS NAKABA!
JOLT

HUH....?

THIS IS...

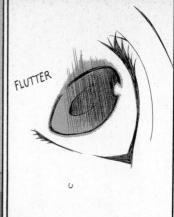

FLUTTER

...FROM THE LIKES OF AN **AJIN**.

GASP

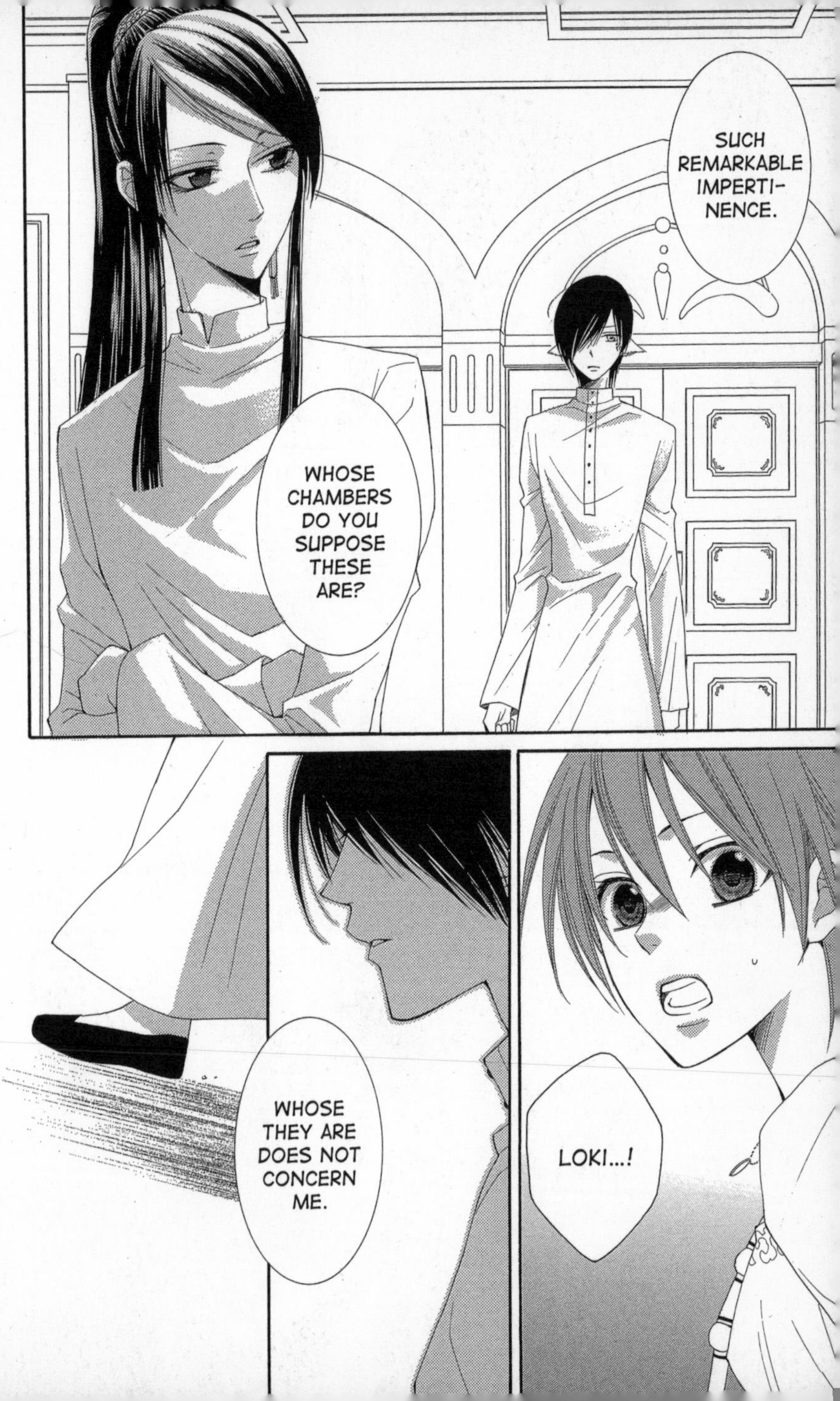
SUCH REMARKABLE IMPERTI- NENCE.
WHOSE CHAMBERS DO YOU SUPPOSE THESE ARE?
LOKI...!
WHOSE THEY ARE DOES NOT CONCERN ME.

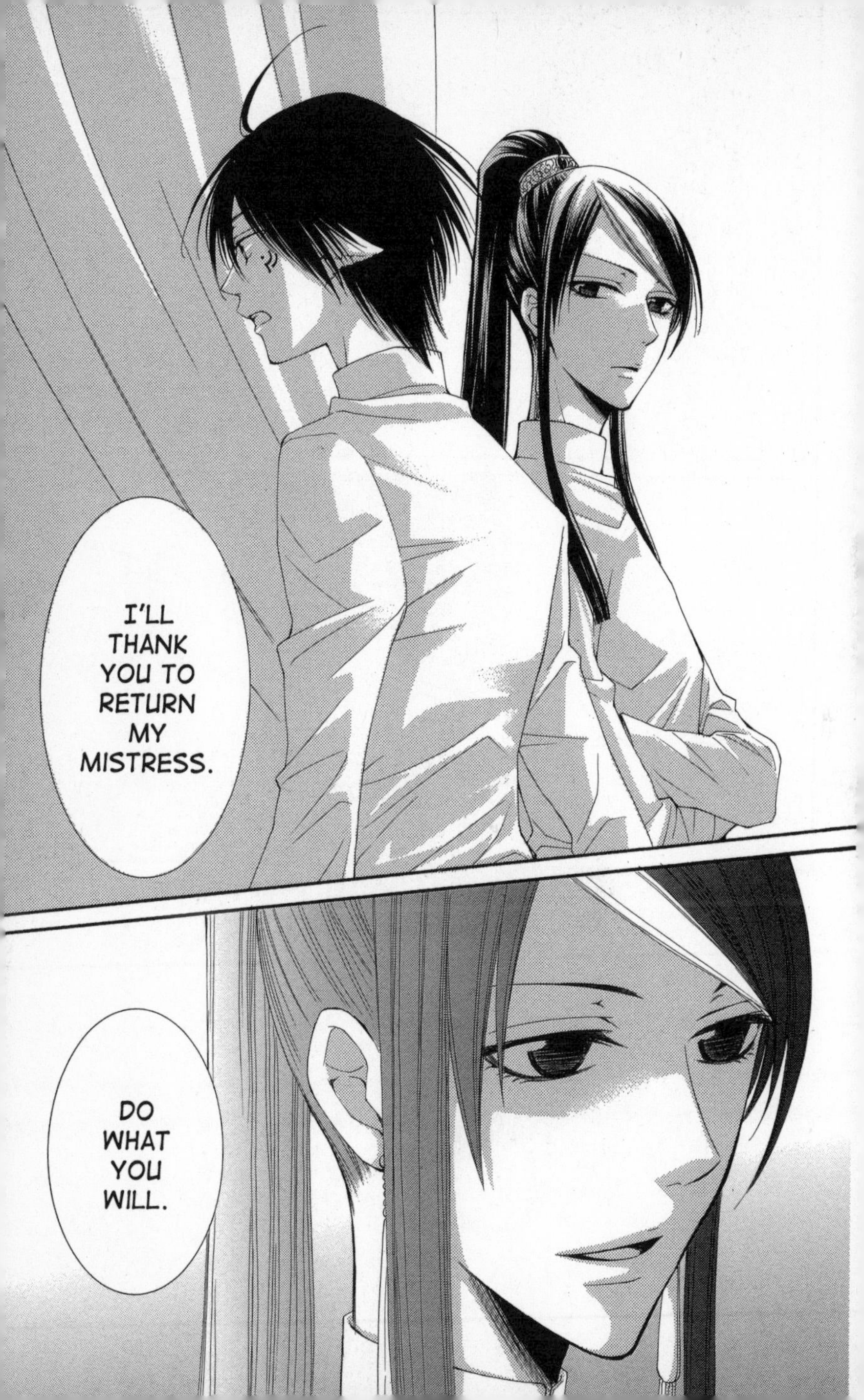
I'LL THANK YOU TO RETURN MY MISTRESS.
DO WHAT YOU WILL.

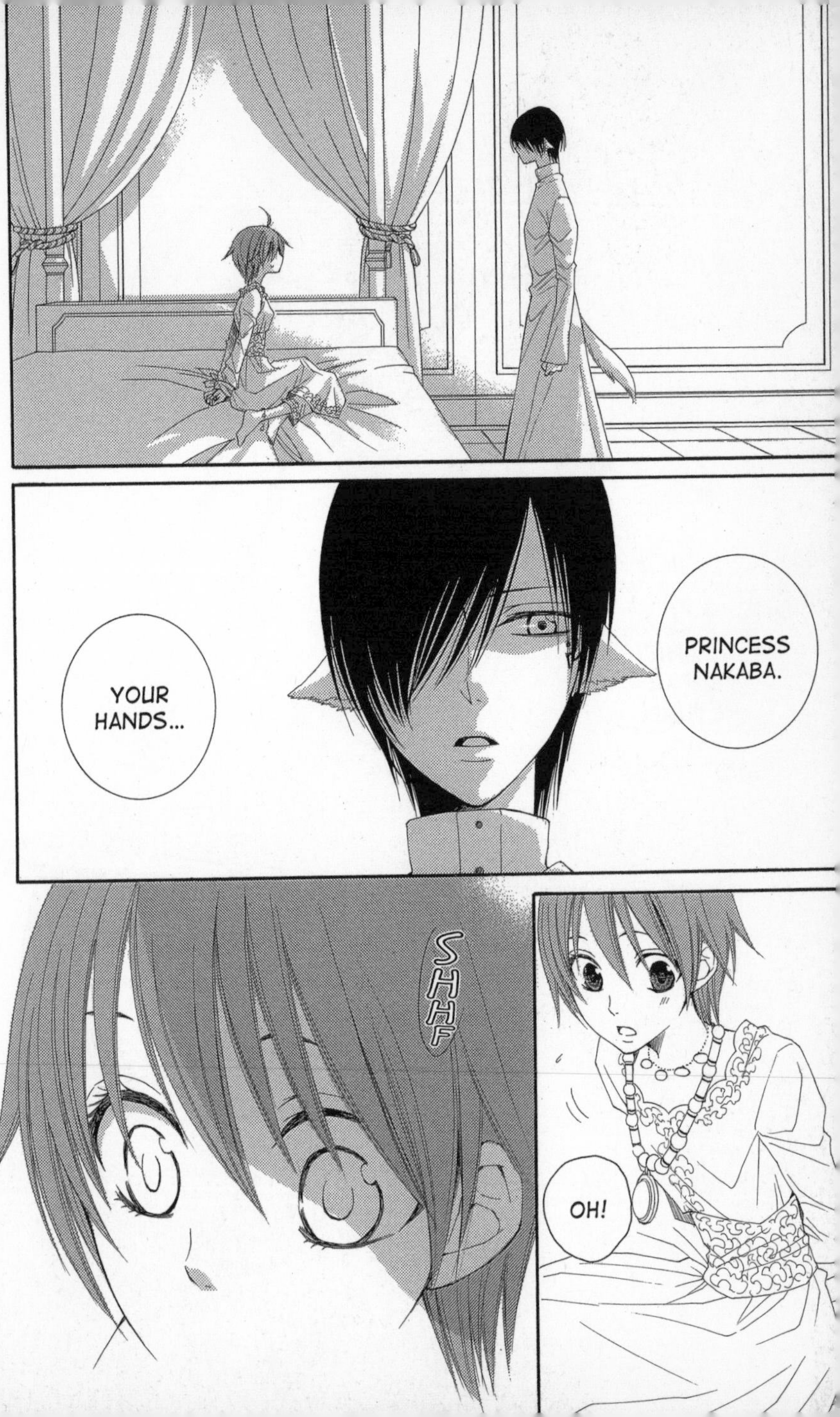
PRINCESS NAKABA.
YOUR HANDS...
OH!
SHHF

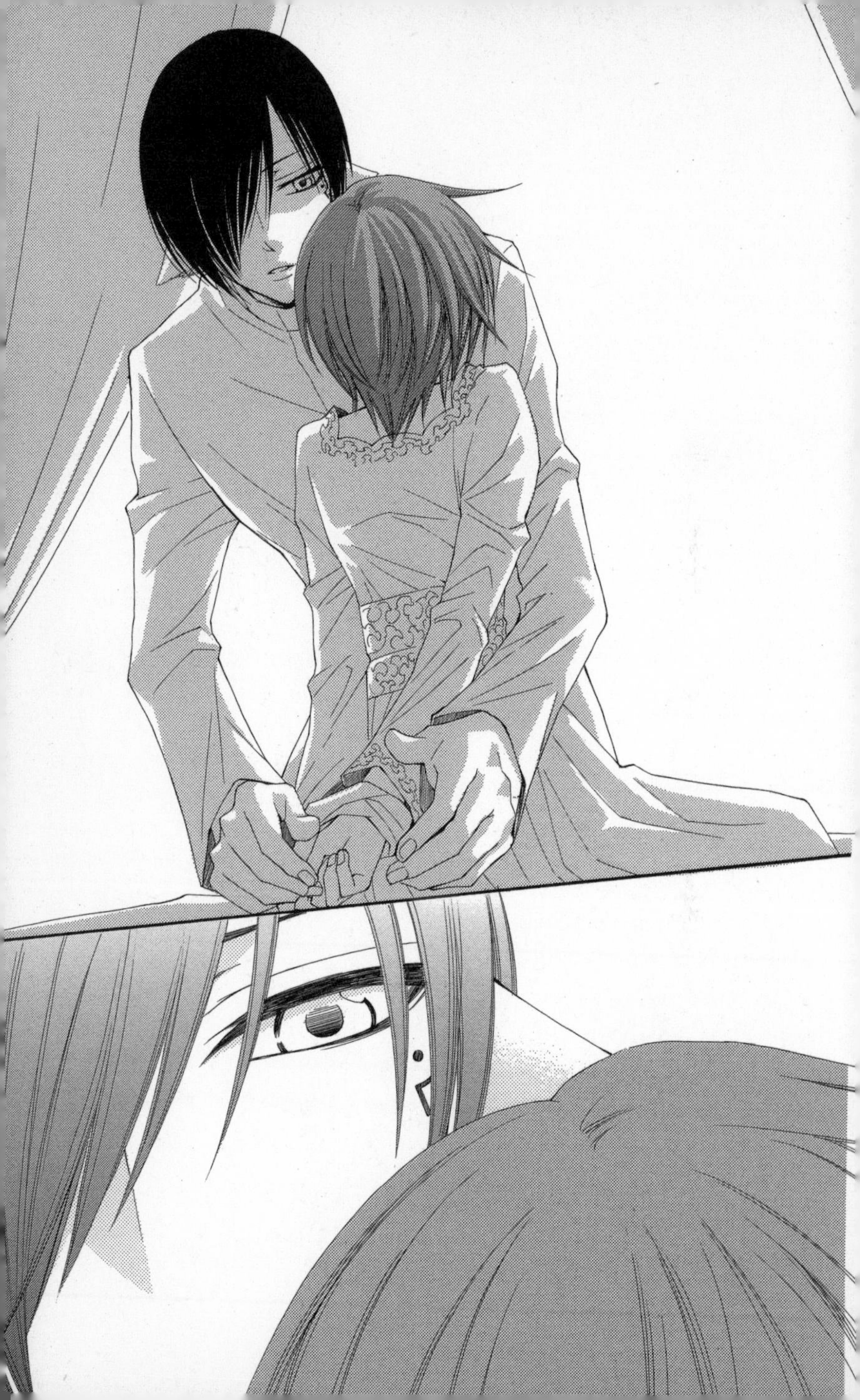

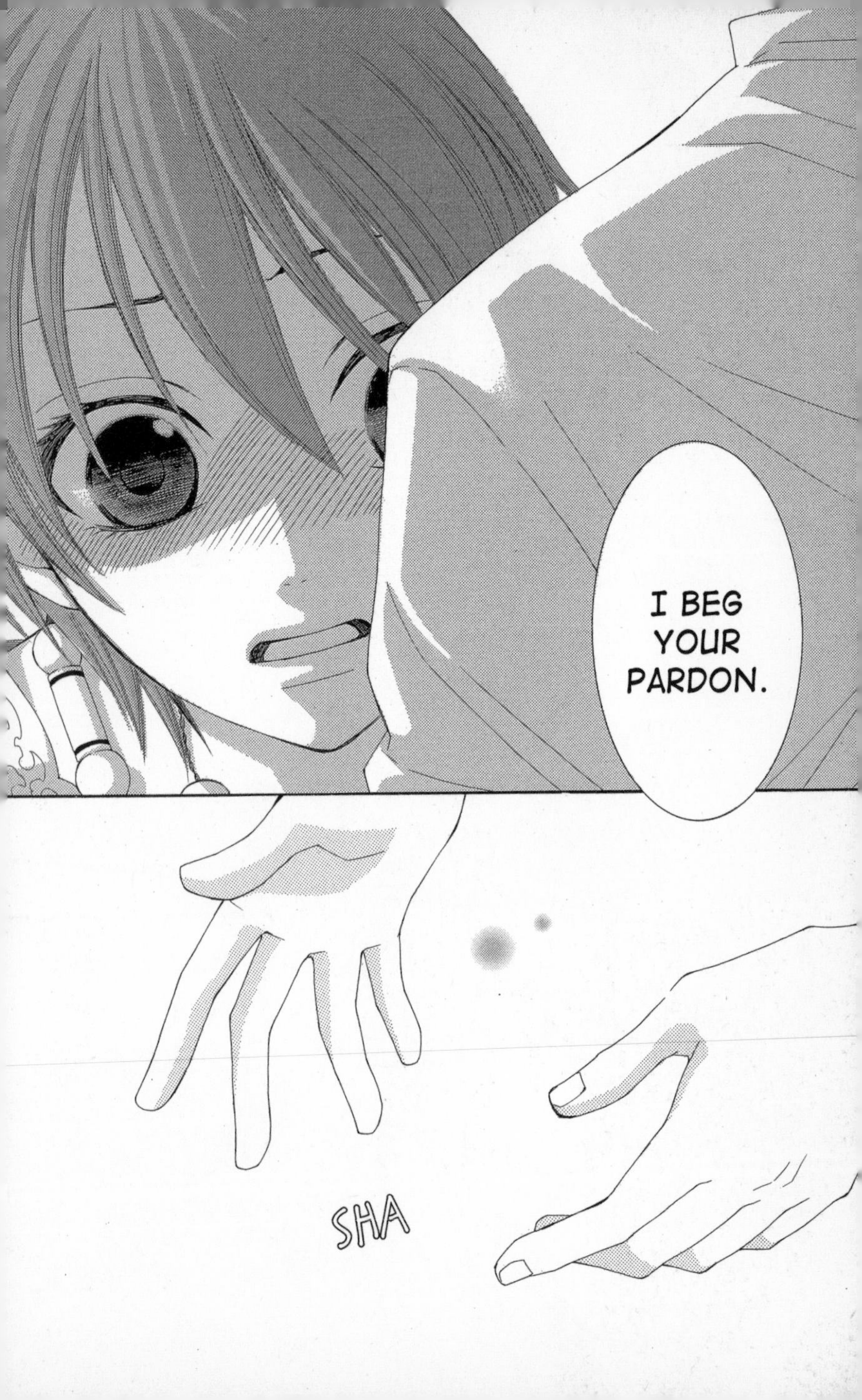
I BEG YOUR PARDON.
SHA

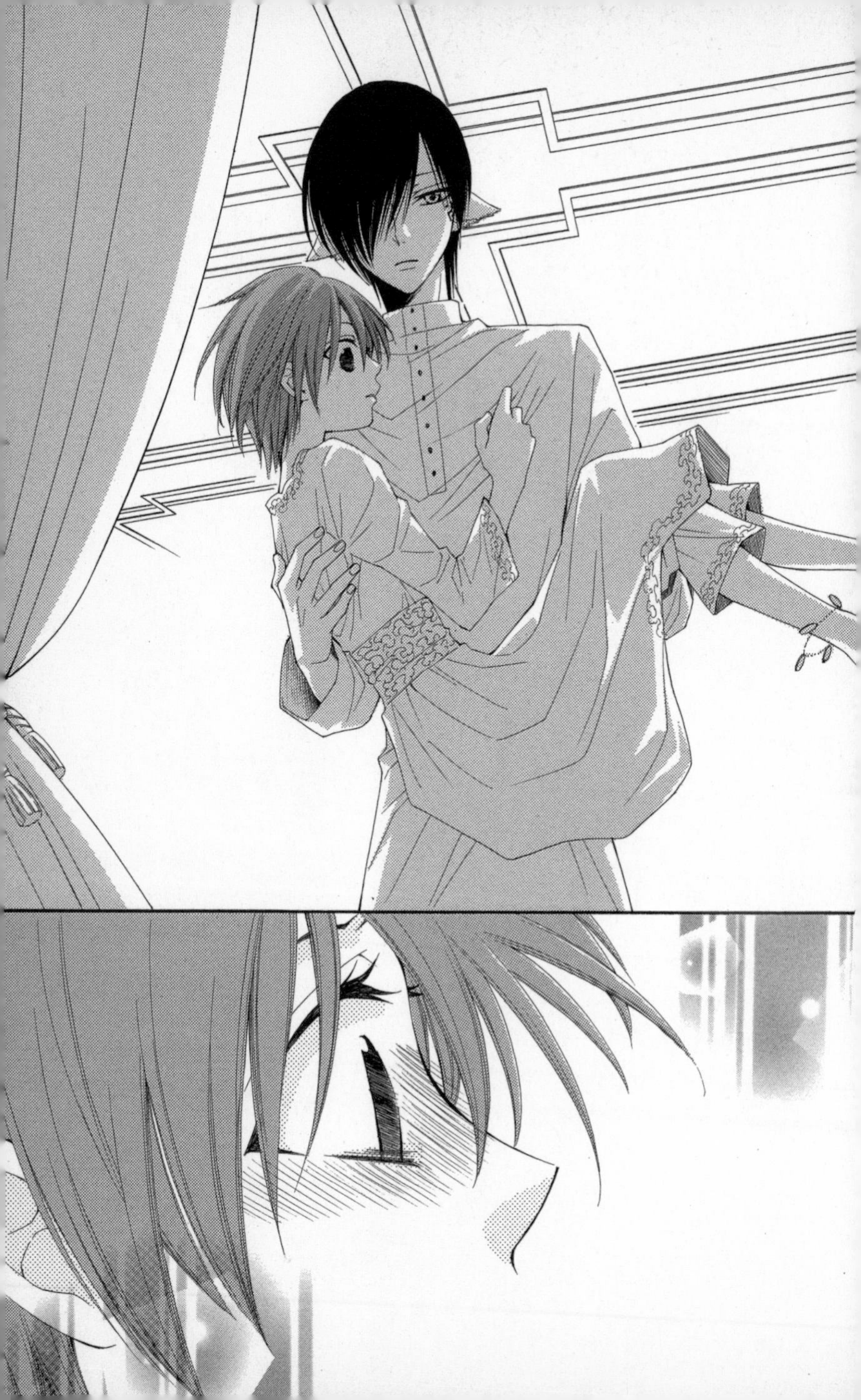

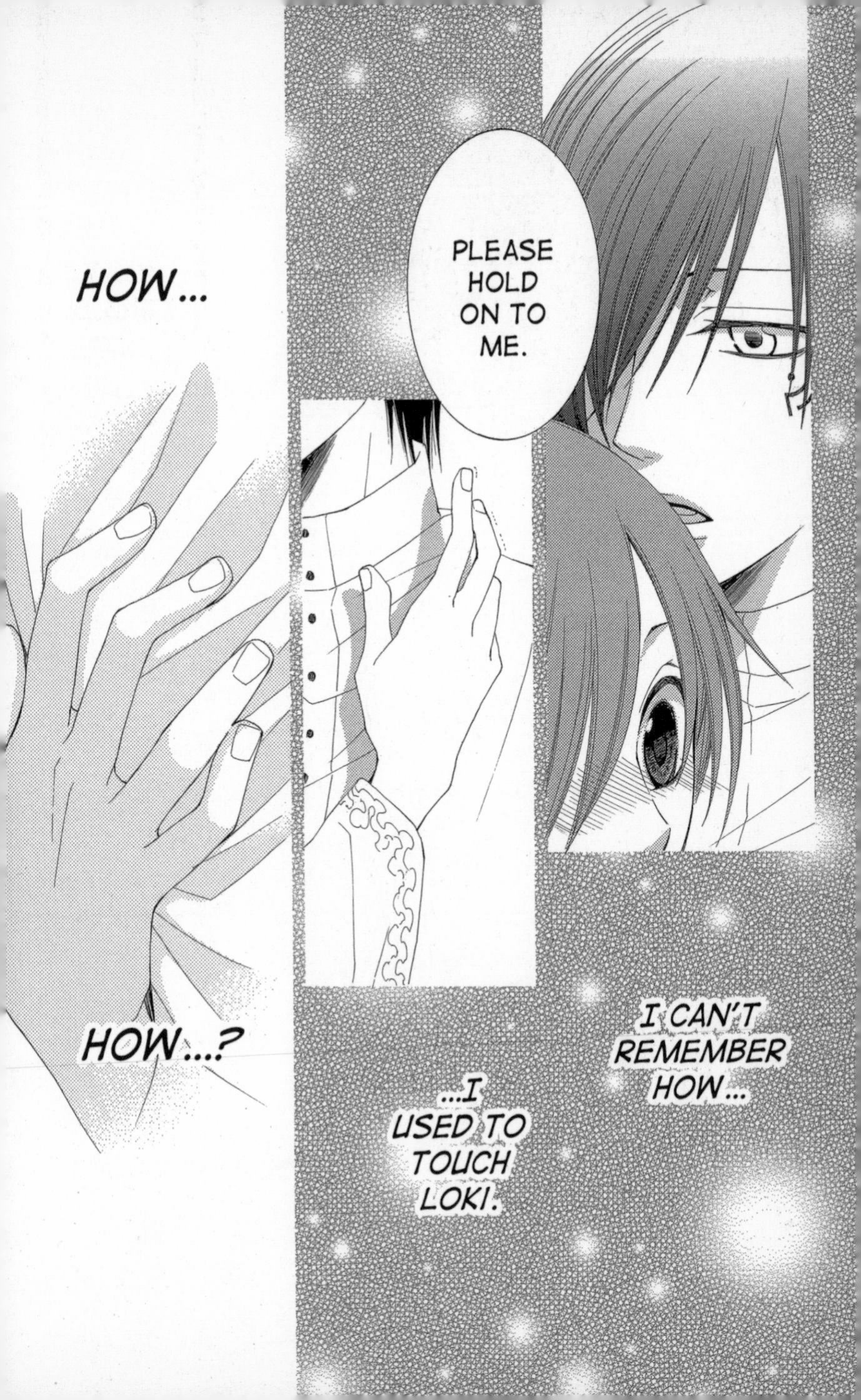
PLEASE HOLD ON TO ME.
I CAN'T REMEMBER HOW...
...I USED TO TOUCH LOKI.
HOW...
HOW...?

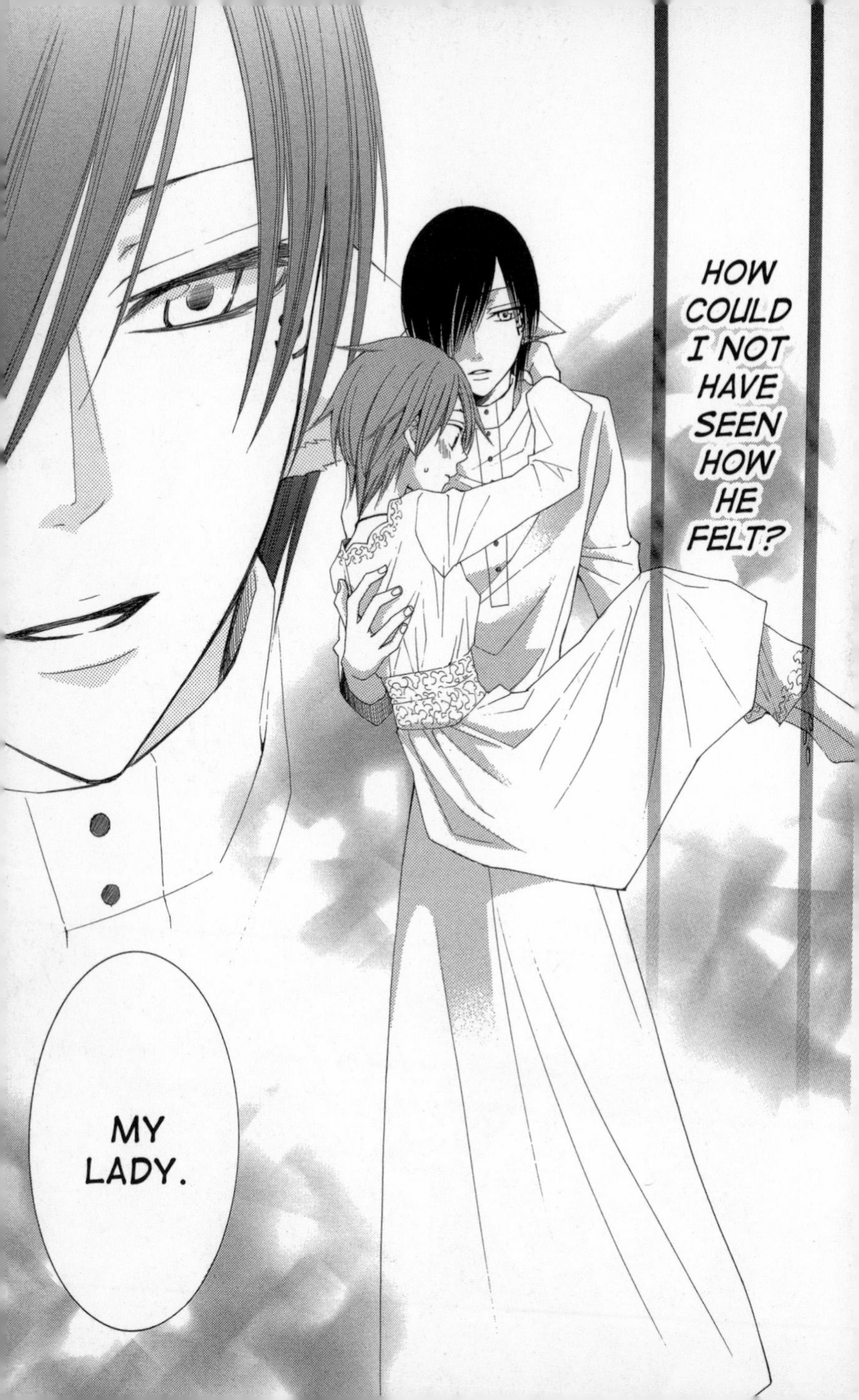
HOW COULD I NOT HAVE SEEN HOW HE FELT?
MY LADY.

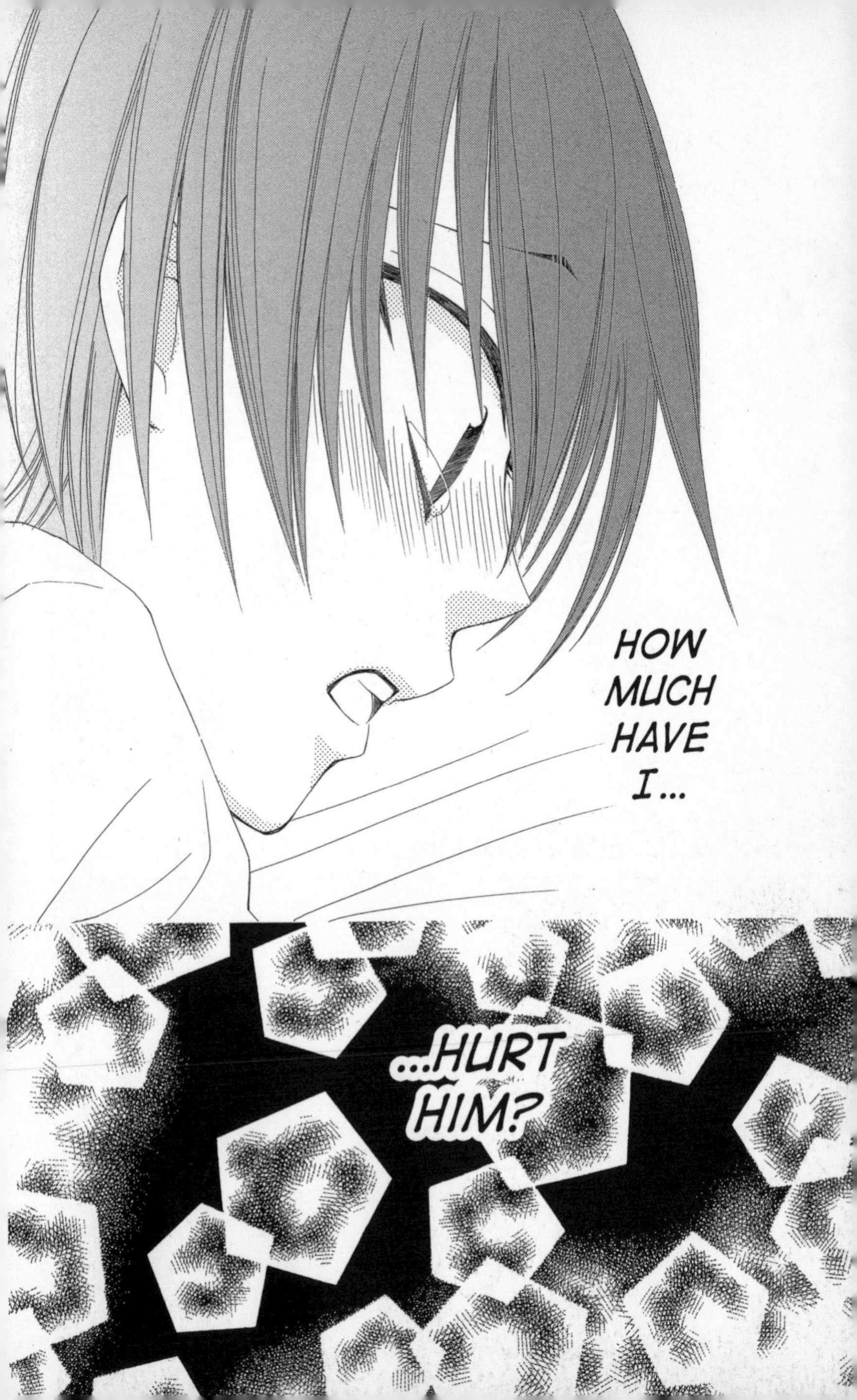
HOW MUCH HAVE I...
...HURT HIM?

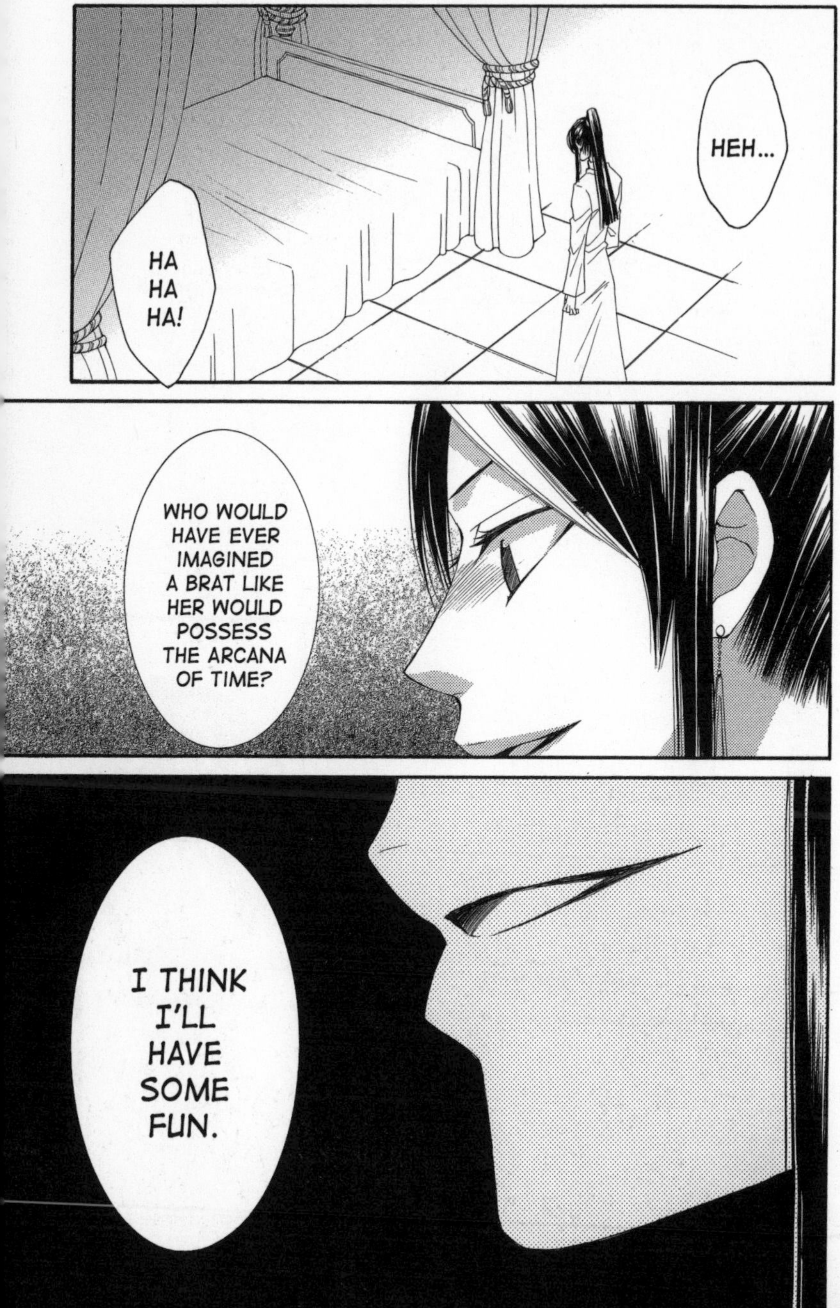
HEH...
HA HA HA!
WHO WOULD HAVE EVER IMAGINED A BRAT LIKE HER WOULD POSSESS THE ARCANA OF TIME?
I THINK I'LL HAVE SOME FUN.

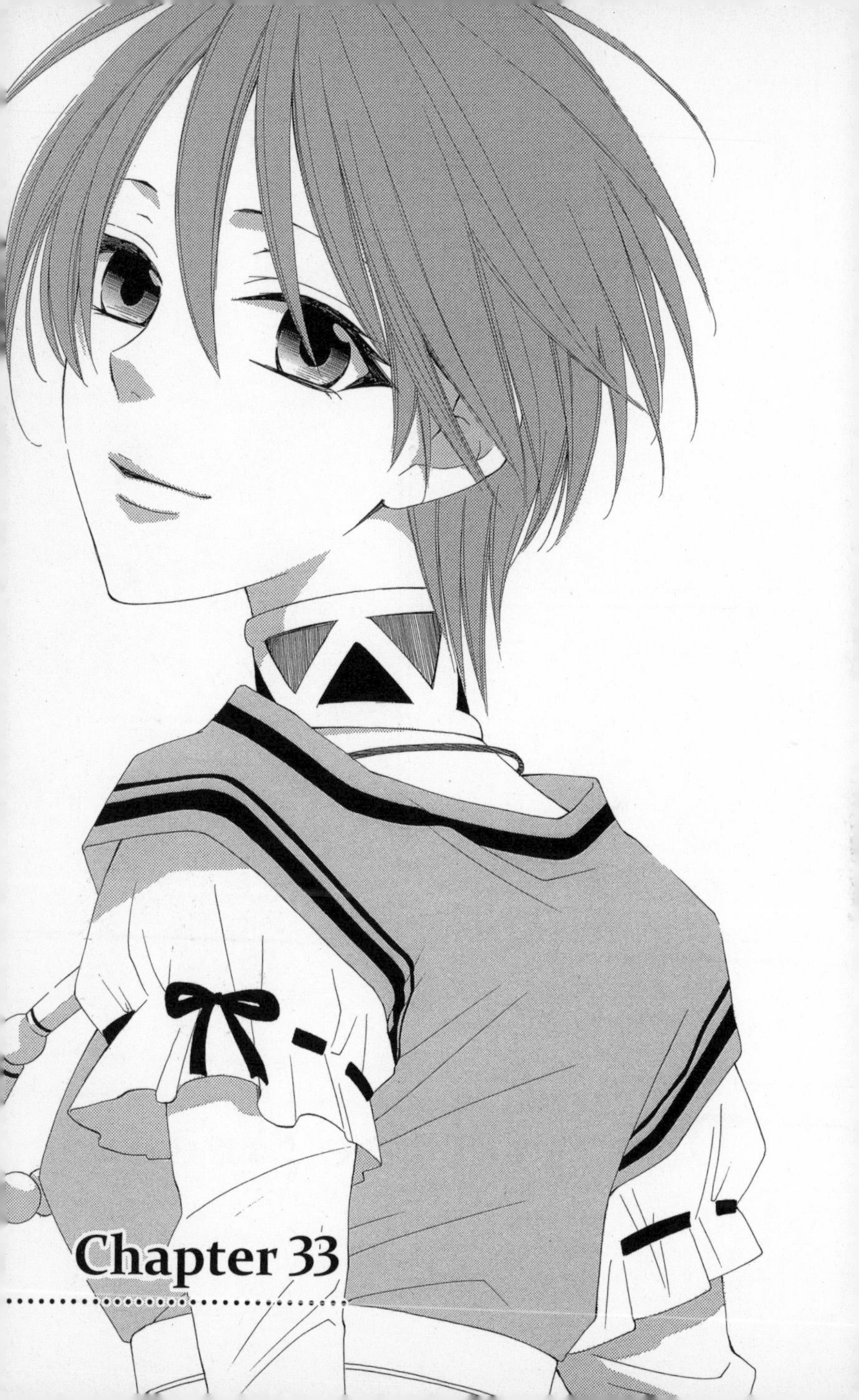

Chapter 33

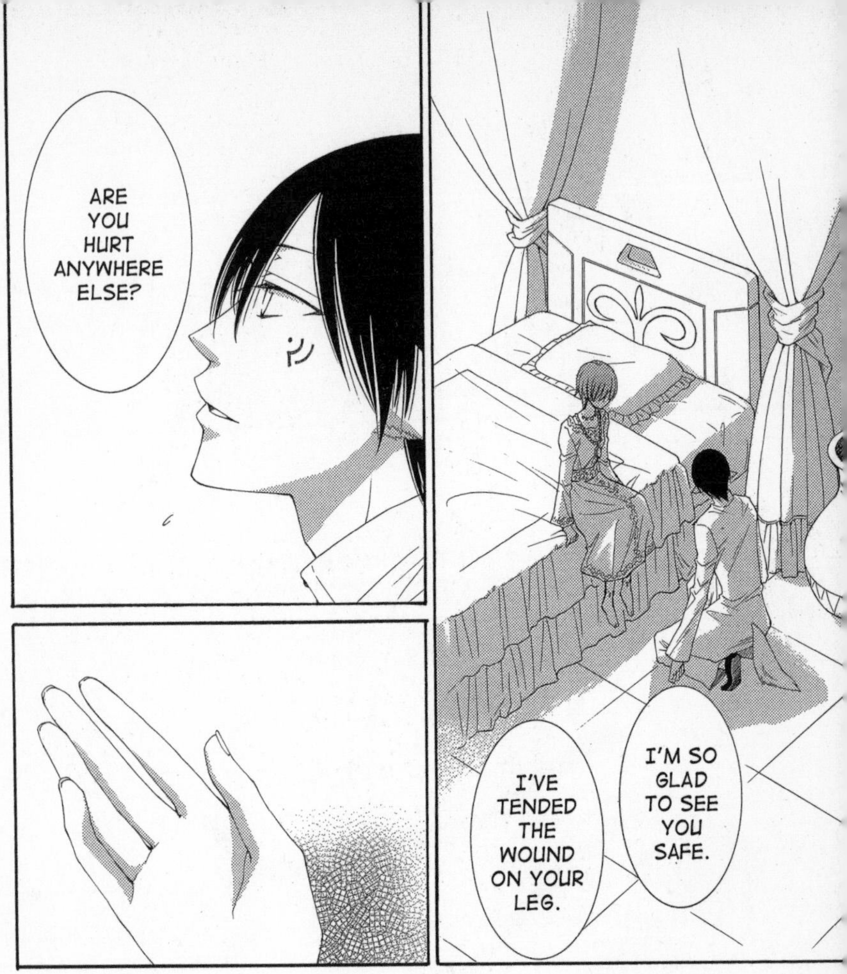
I'M SO GLAD TO SEE YOU SAFE.
I'VE TENDED THE WOUND ON YOUR LEG.
ARE YOU HURT ANYWHERE ELSE?

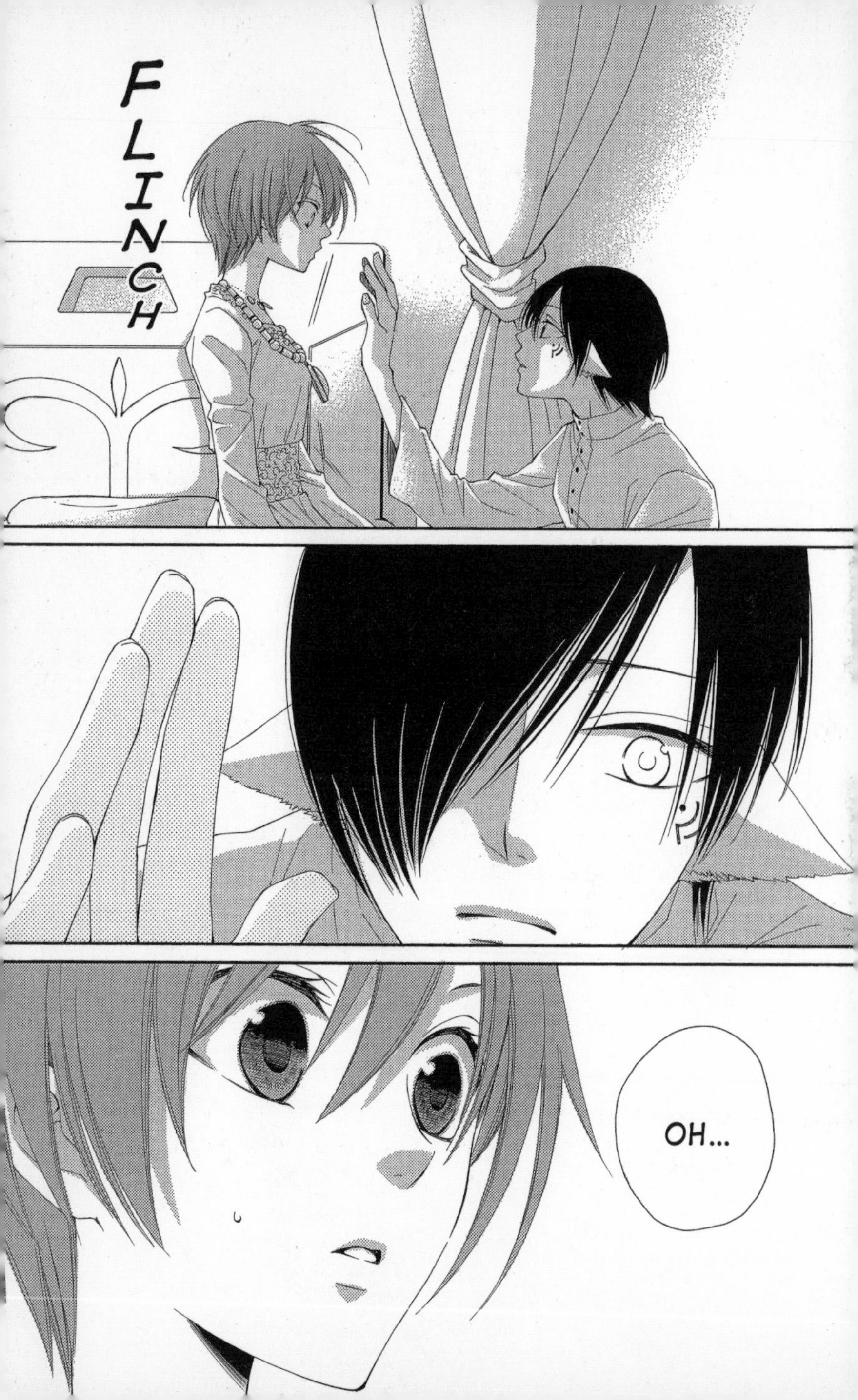
FLINCH
OH...

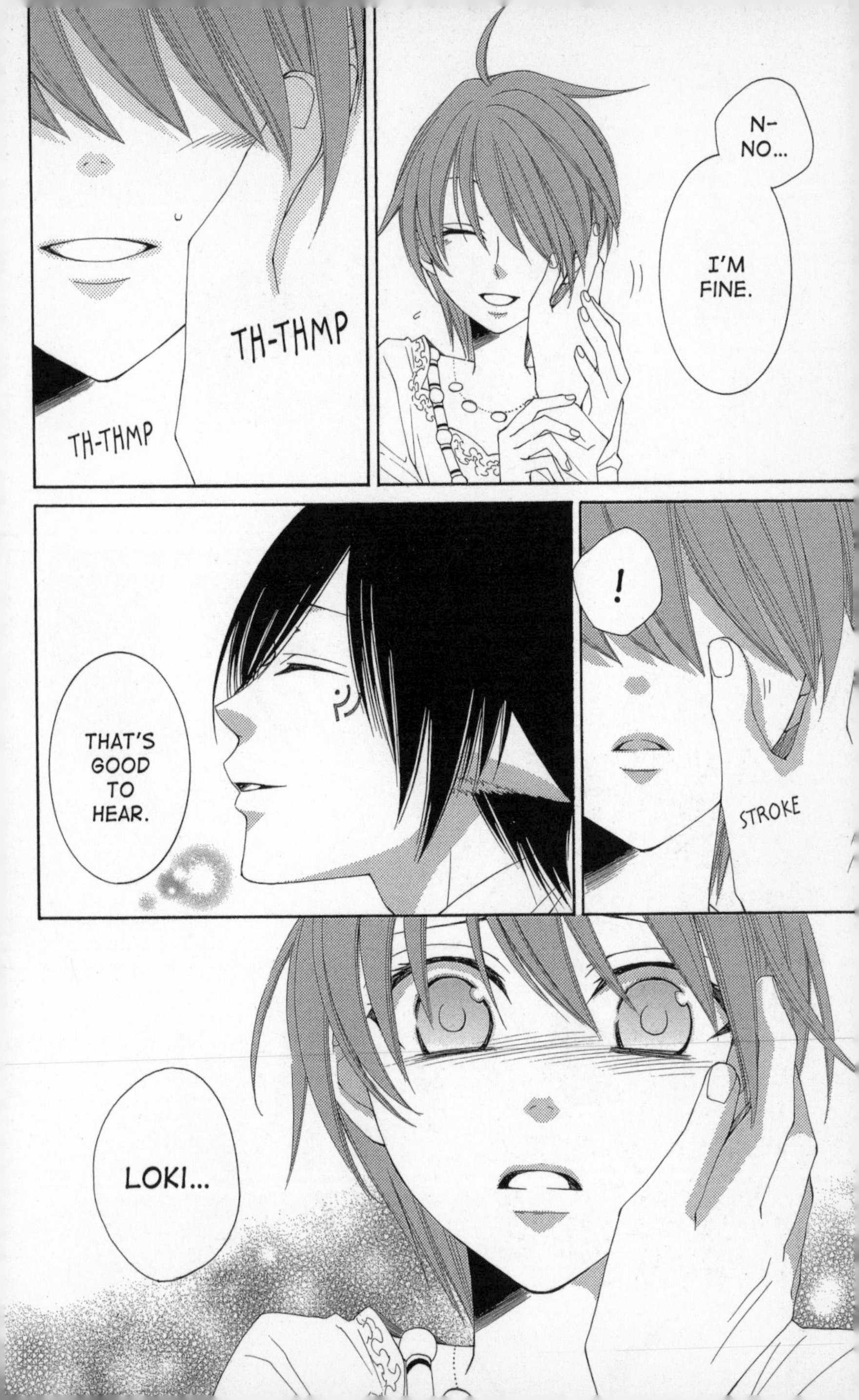
N- NO...
I'M FINE.
TH-THMP
TH-THMP
!
STROKE
THAT'S GOOD TO HEAR.
LOKI...

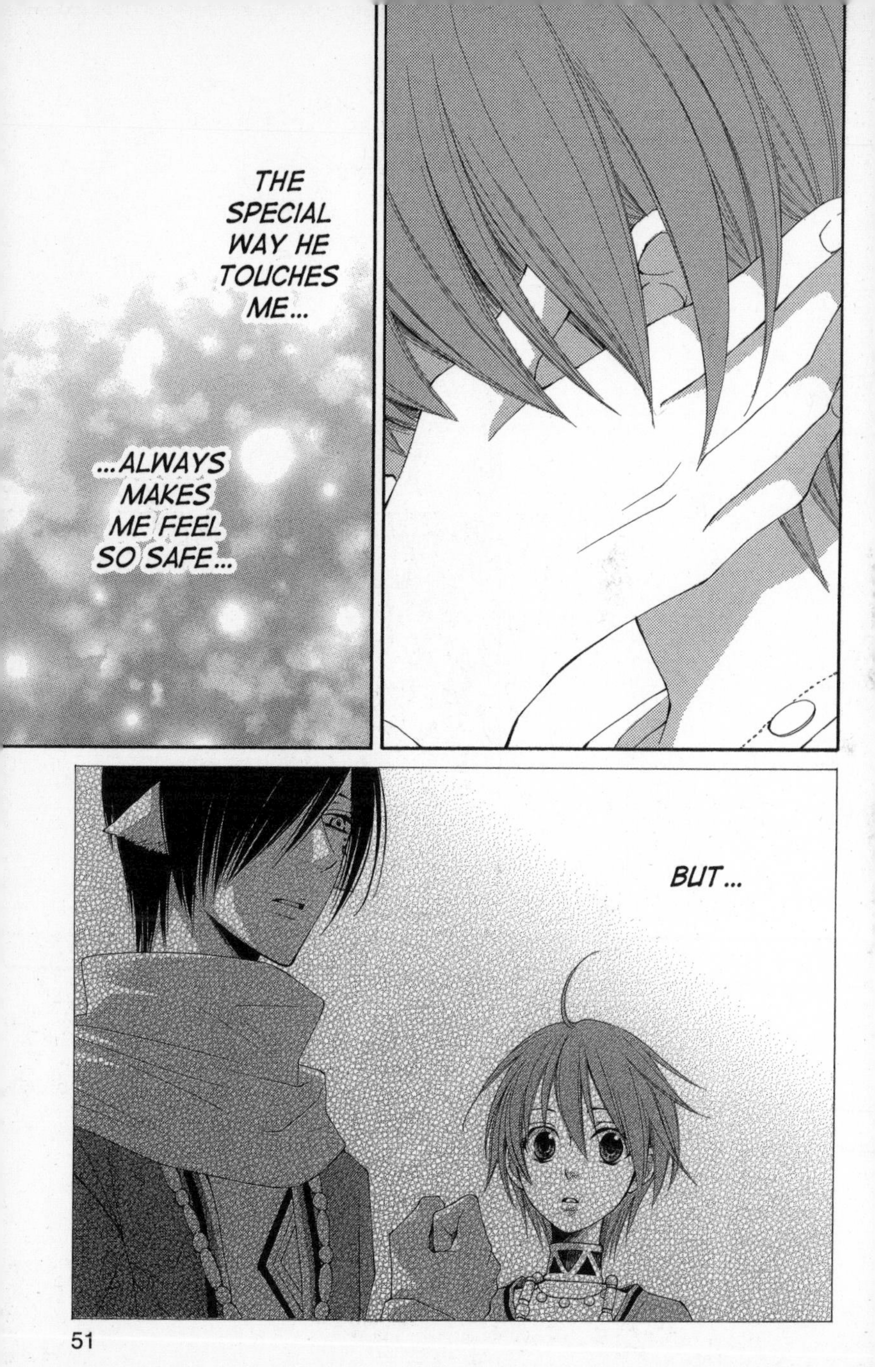
THE SPECIAL WAY HE TOUCHES ME...
...ALWAYS MAKES ME FEEL SO SAFE...
BUT...

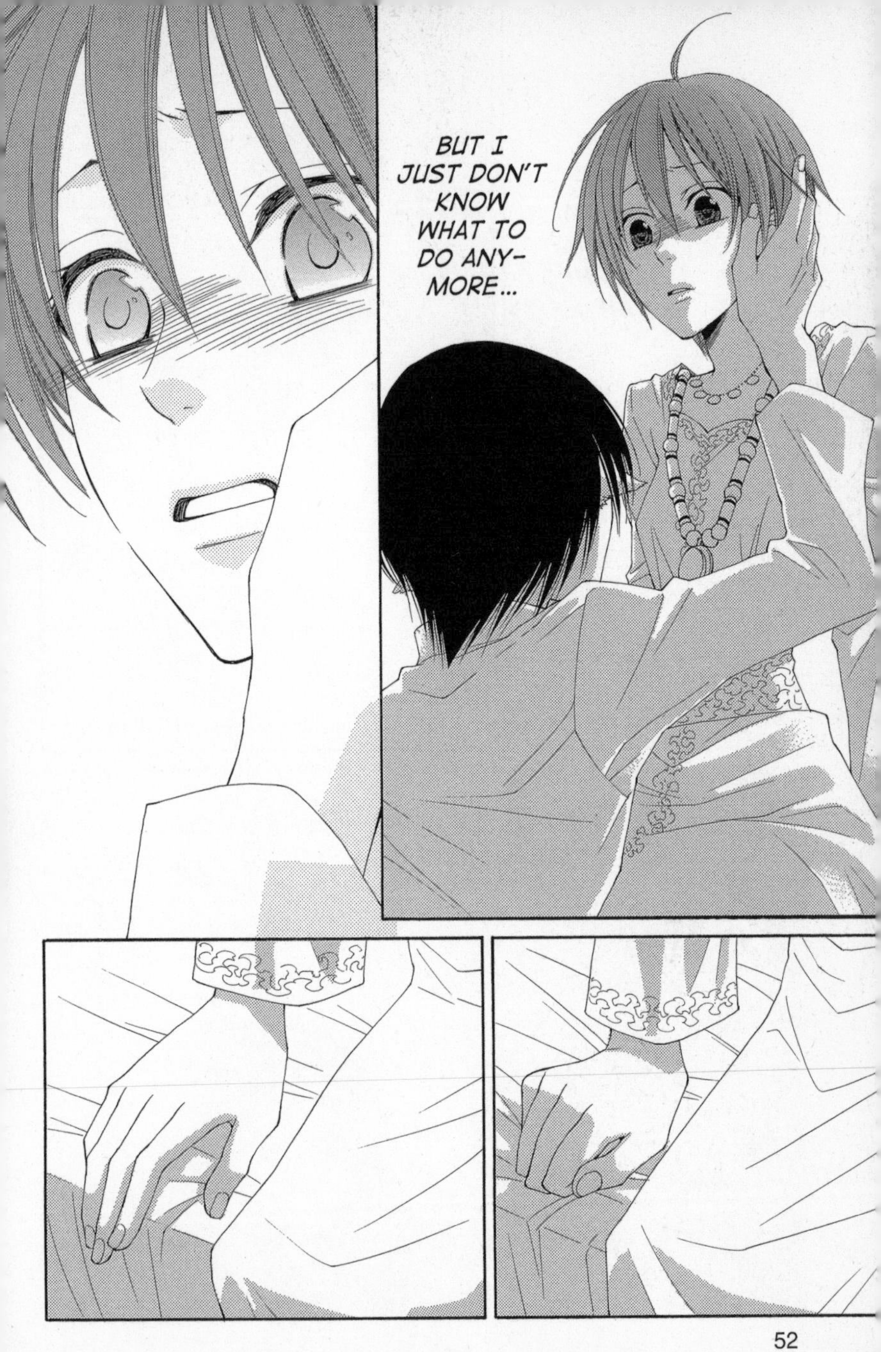
BUT I JUST DON'T KNOW WHAT TO DO ANY-MORE...

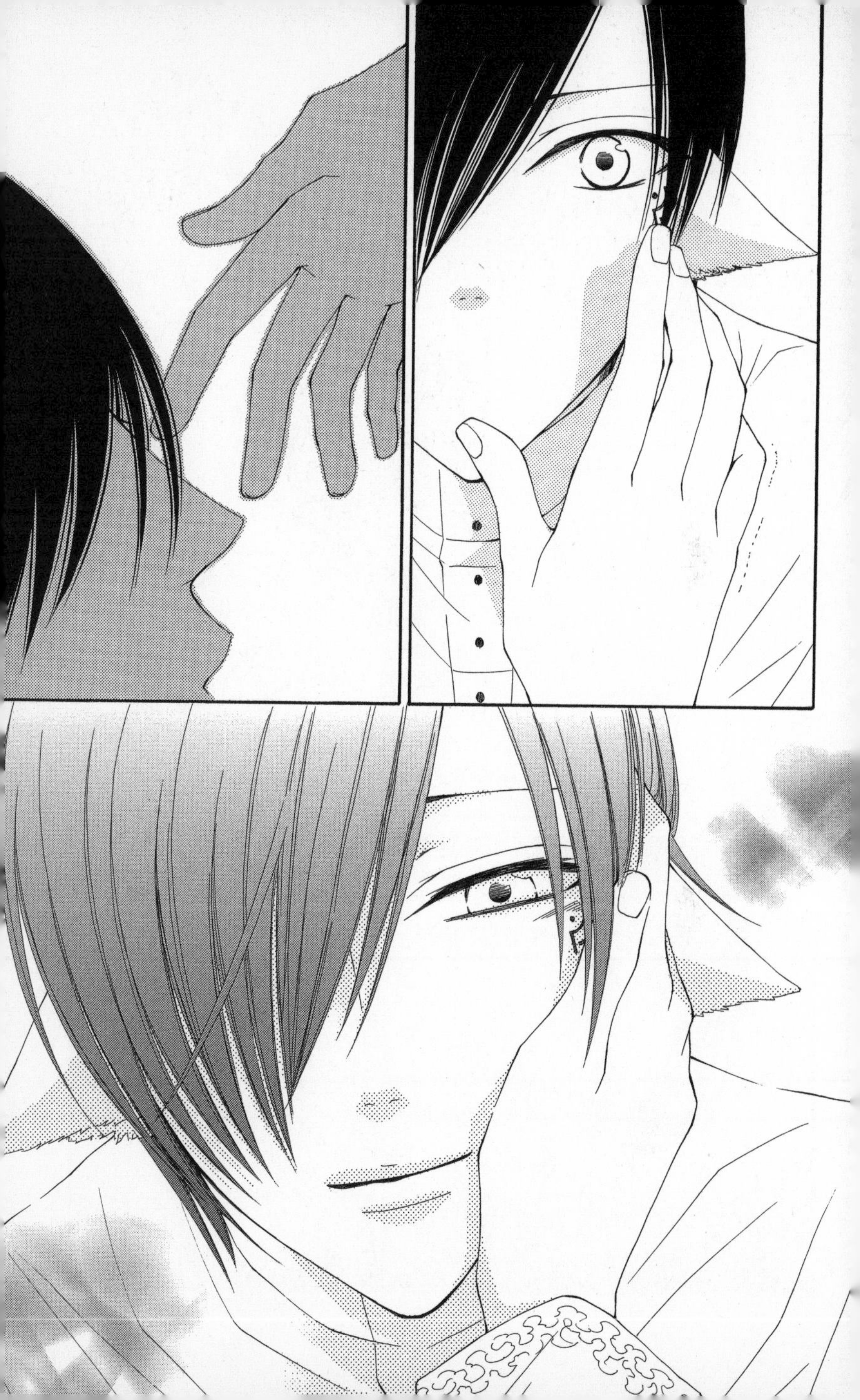

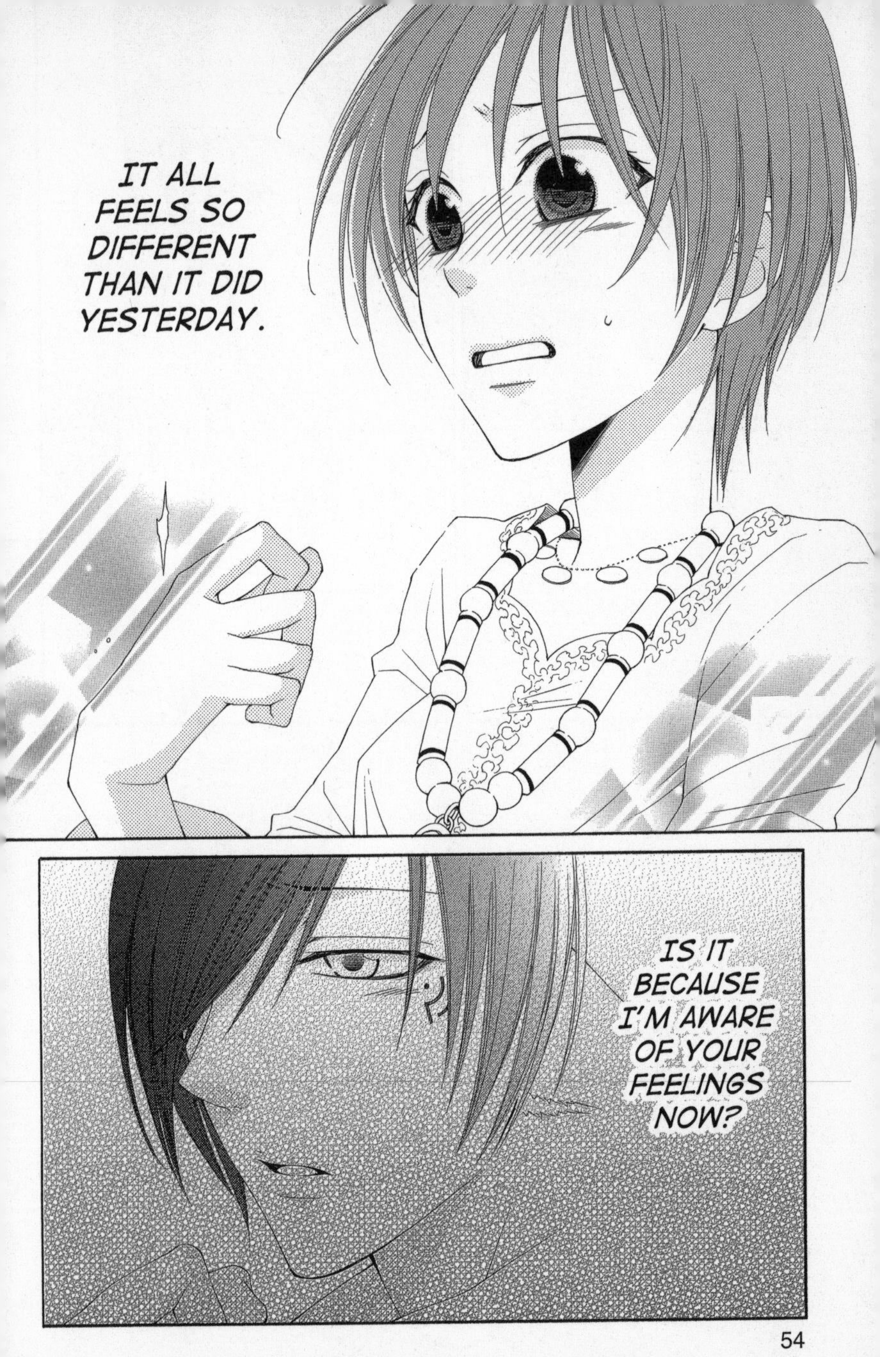
IT ALL FEELS SO DIFFERENT THAN IT DID YESTERDAY.
IS IT BECAUSE I'M AWARE OF YOUR FEELINGS NOW?

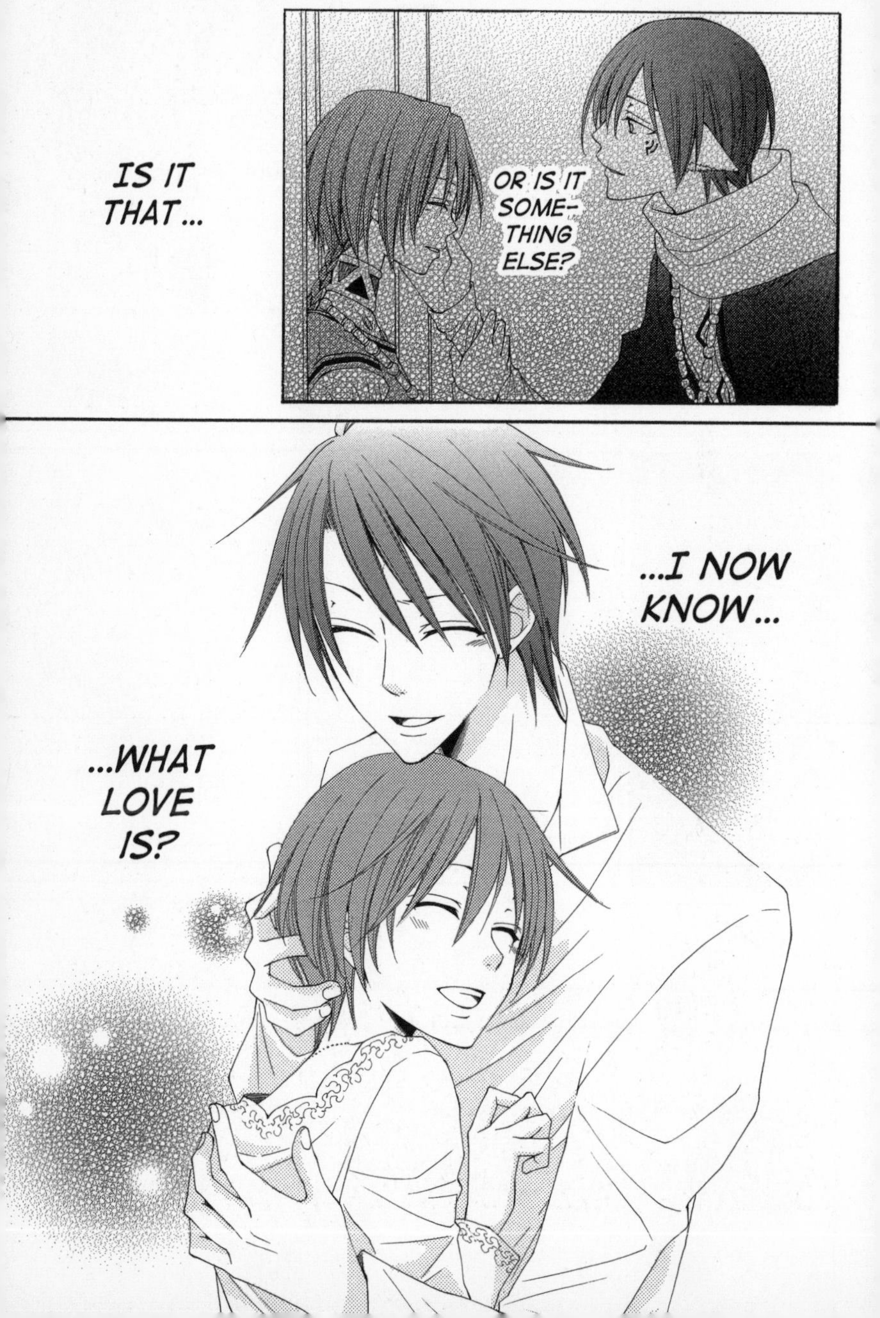
OR IS IT SOMETHING-THING ELSE?
IS IT THAT...
...I NOW KNOW...
...WHAT LOVE IS?

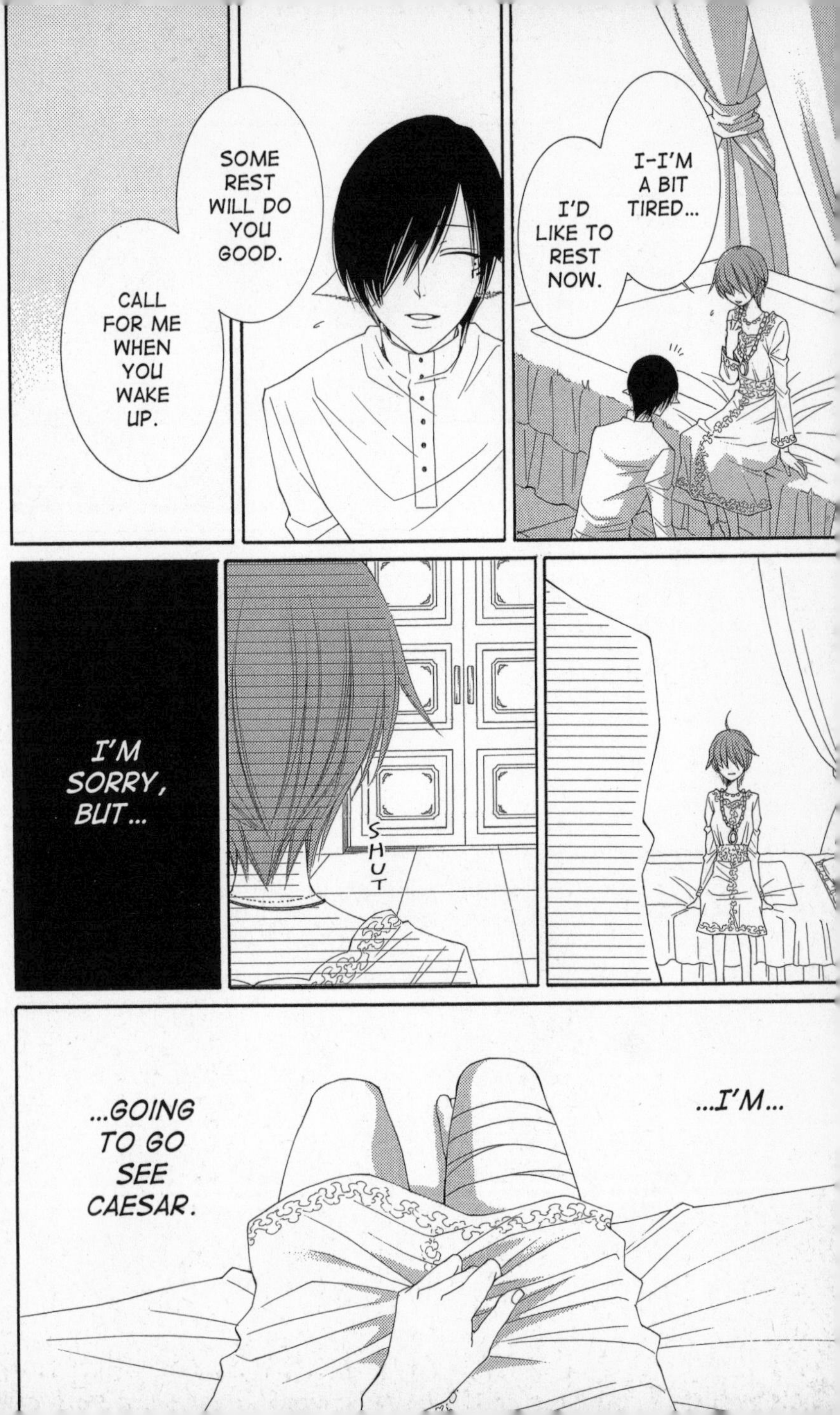
I-I'M A BIT TIRED...
I'D LIKE TO REST NOW.
SOME REST WILL DO YOU GOOD.
CALL FOR ME WHEN YOU WAKE UP.
SHUT
I'M SORRY, BUT...
...I'M...
...GOING TO GO SEE CAESAR.

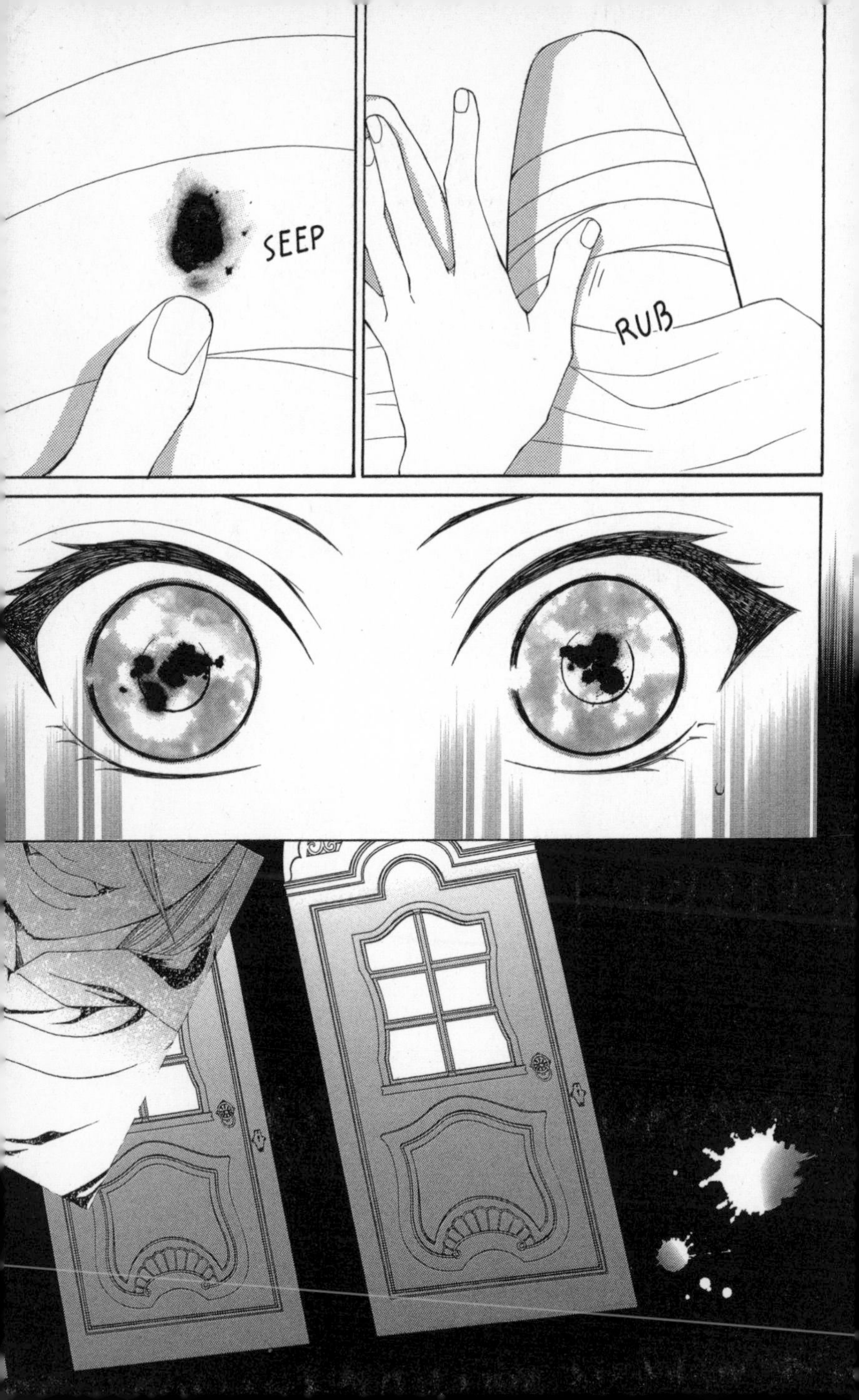
RUB
SEEP

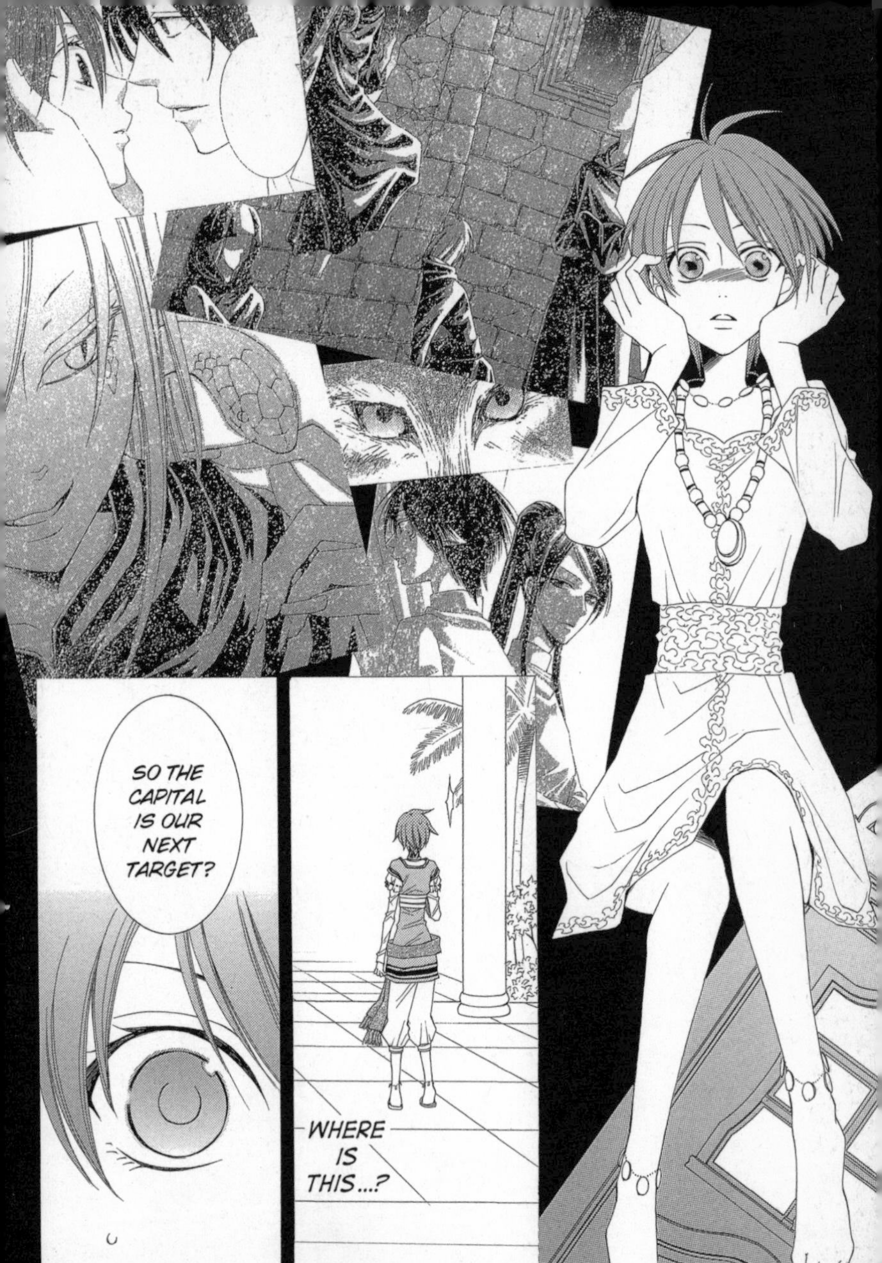
WHERE IS THIS...?
SO THE CAPITAL IS OUR NEXT TARGET?

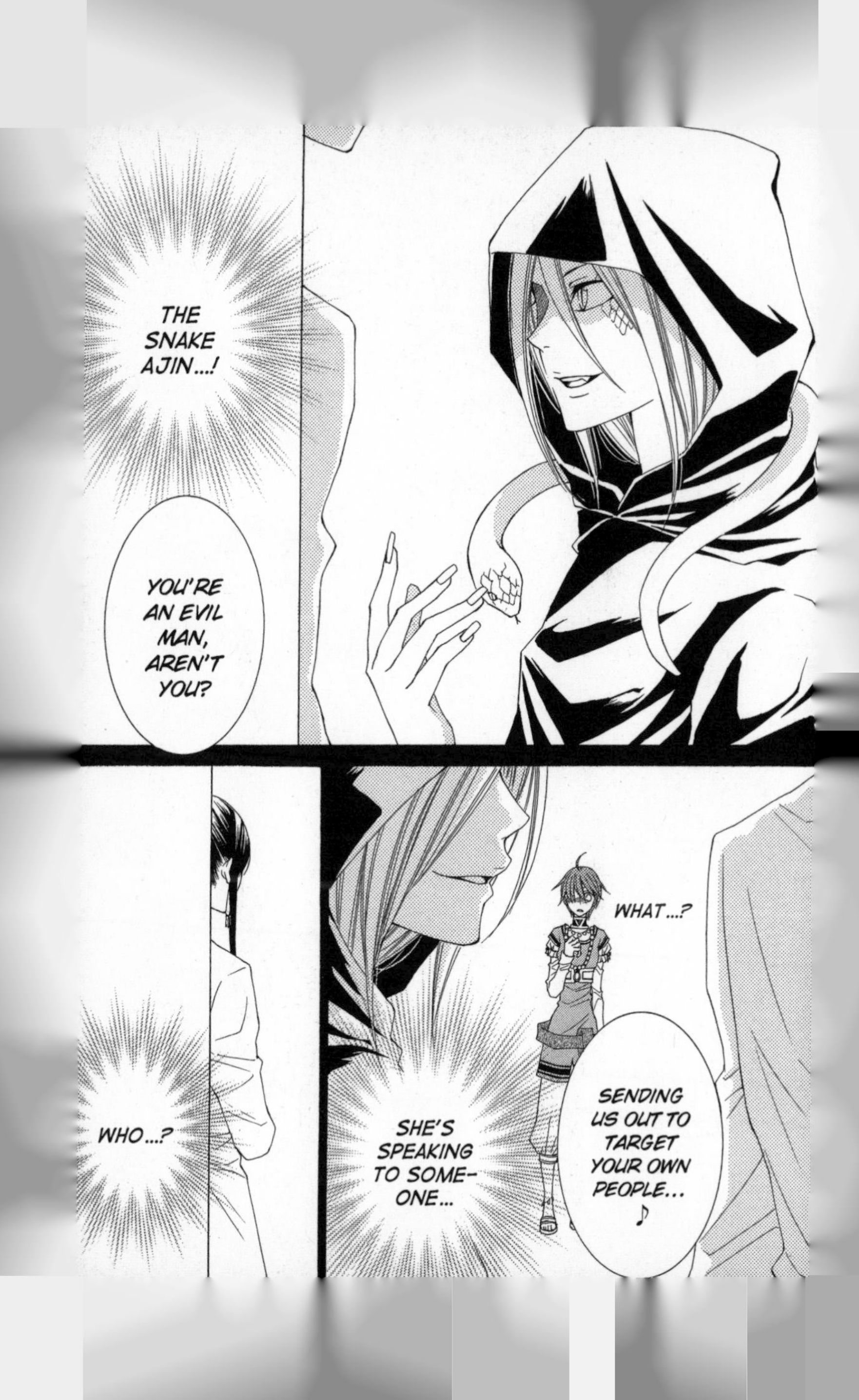
THE SNAKE AJIN...!
YOU'RE AN EVIL MAN, AREN'T YOU?
WHAT...?
SENDING US OUT TO TARGET YOUR OWN PEOPLE... ♪
SHE'S SPEAKING TO SOME-ONE...
WHO...?

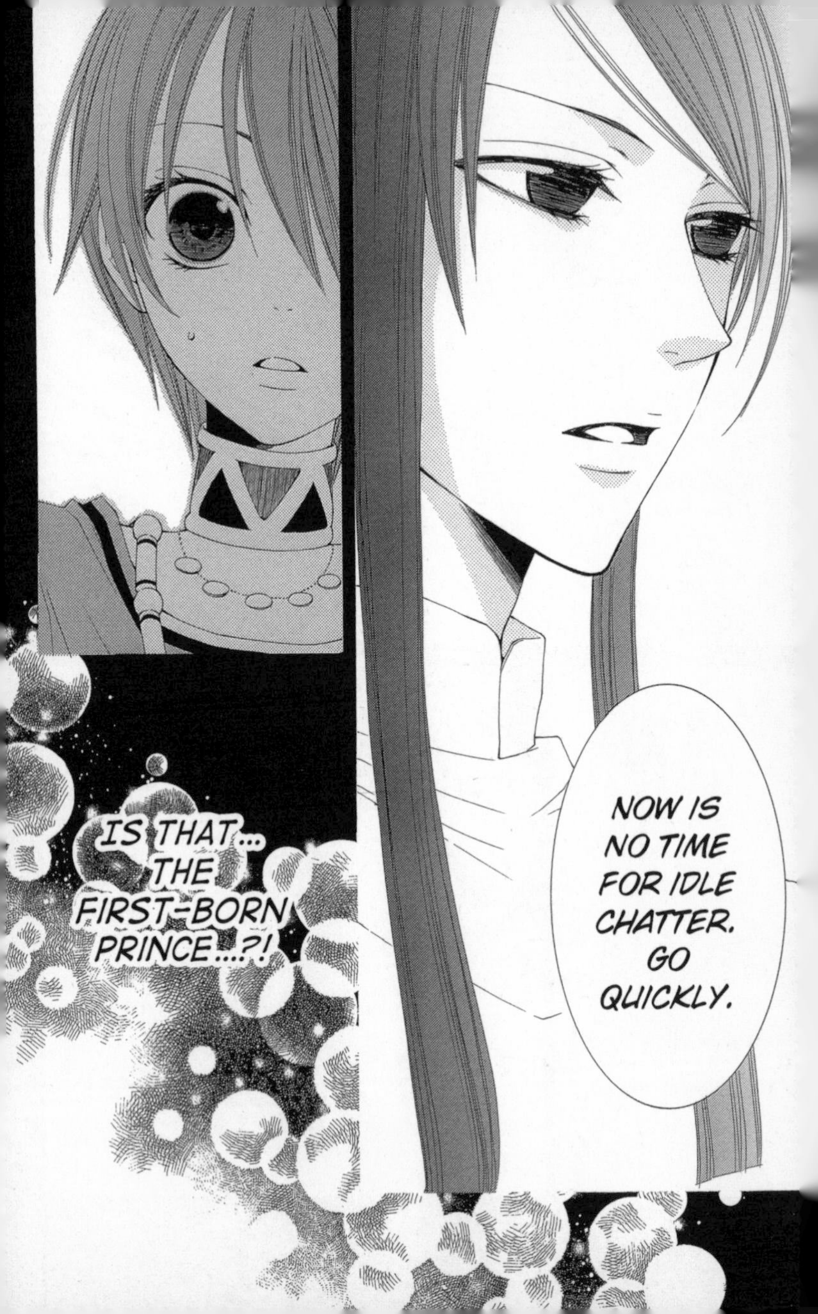
NOW IS NO TIME FOR IDLE CHATTER. GO QUICKLY.
IS THAT... THE FIRST-BORN PRINCE...?!

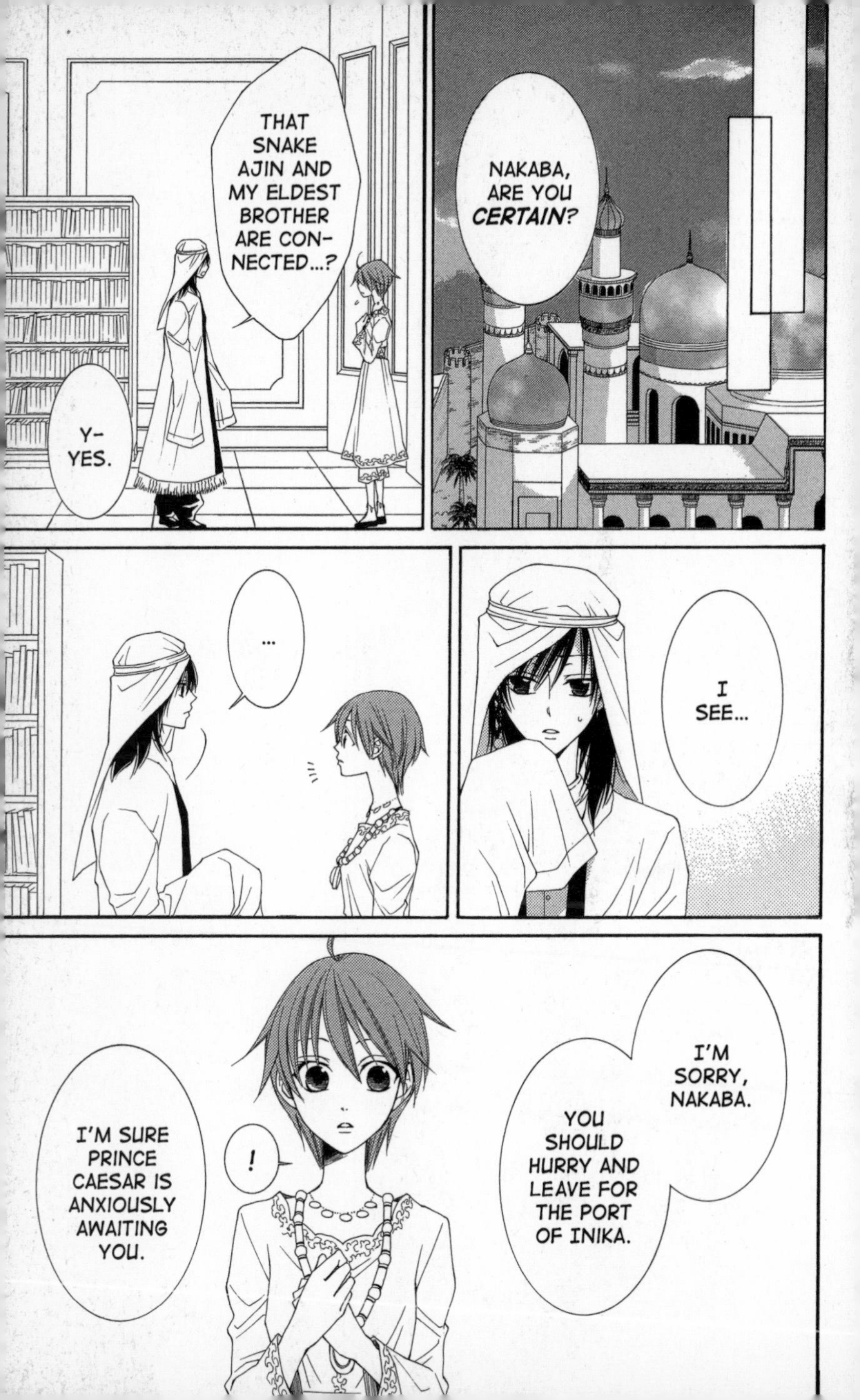
NAKABA, ARE YOU *CERTAIN*?
THAT SNAKE AJIN AND MY ELDEST BROTHER ARE CON-NECTED...?
Y-YES.
I SEE...
...
I'M SORRY, NAKABA.
YOU SHOULD HURRY AND LEAVE FOR THE PORT OF INIKA.
!
I'M SURE PRINCE CAESAR IS ANXIOUSLY AWAITING YOU.

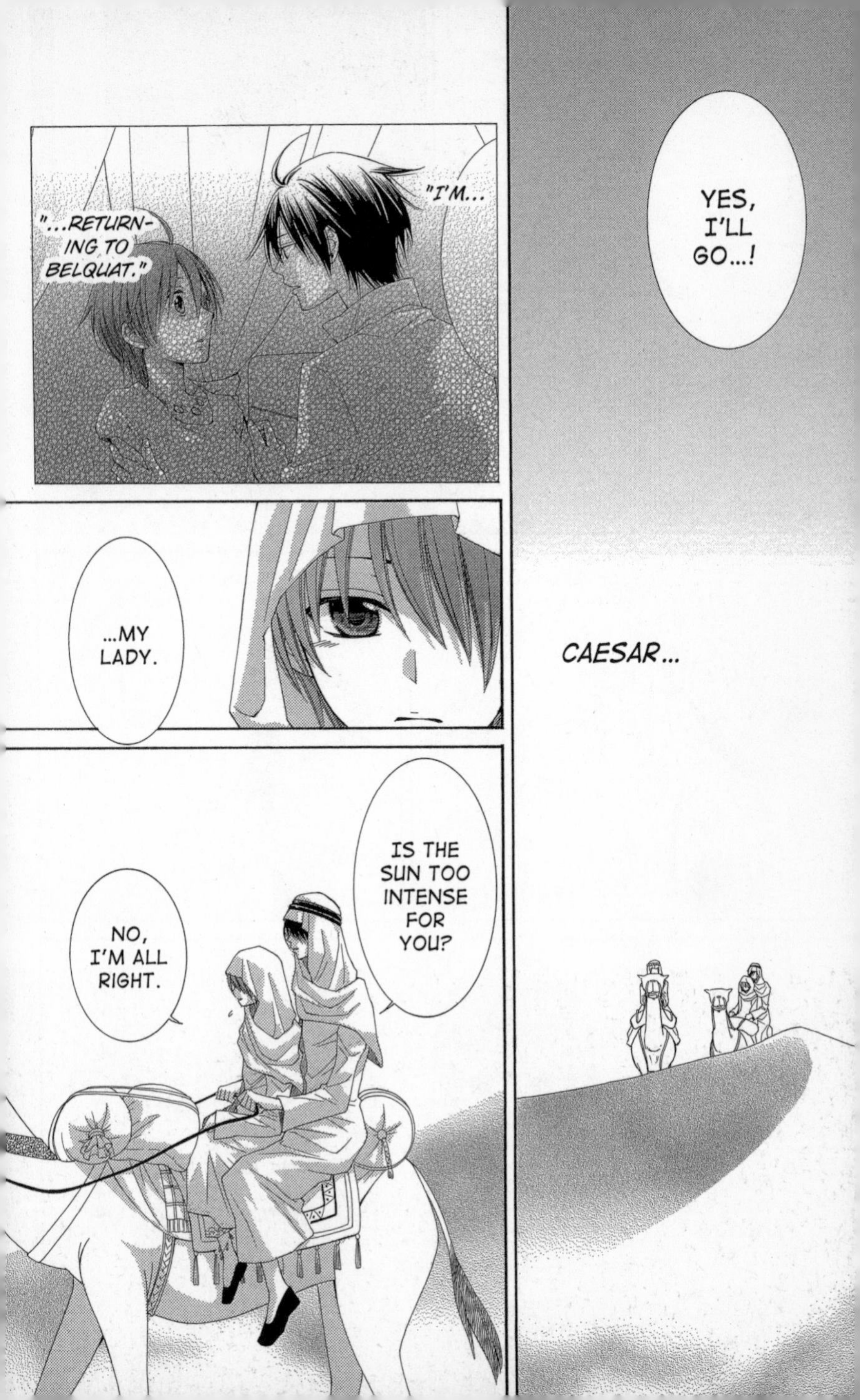
YES, I'LL GO...!
CAESAR...
"I'M...
"...RETURNING TO BELQUAT."
...MY LADY.
IS THE SUN TOO INTENSE FOR YOU?
NO, I'M ALL RIGHT.

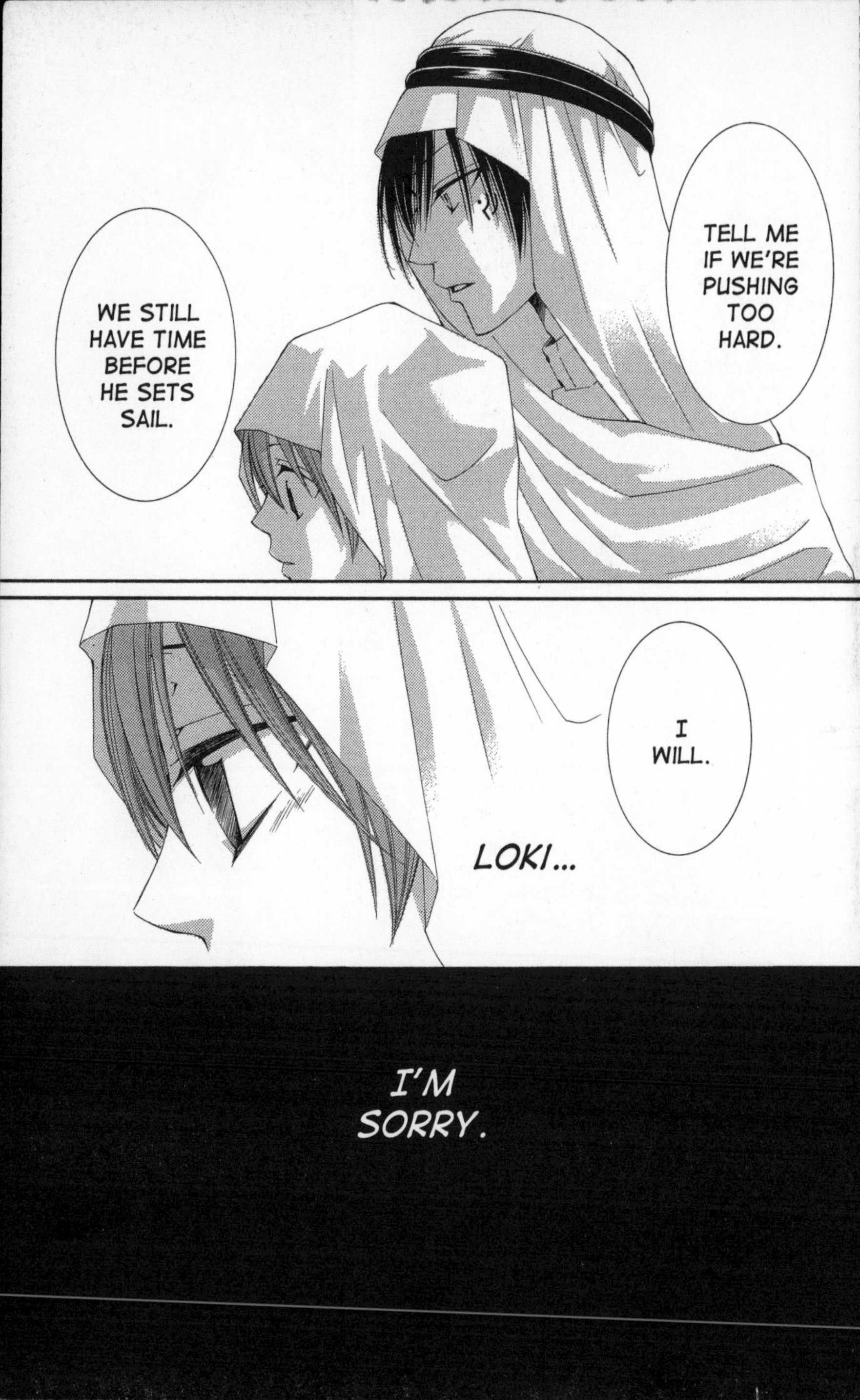
TELL ME IF WE'RE PUSHING TOO HARD.
WE STILL HAVE TIME BEFORE HE SETS SAIL.
I WILL.
LOKI...
I'M SORRY.

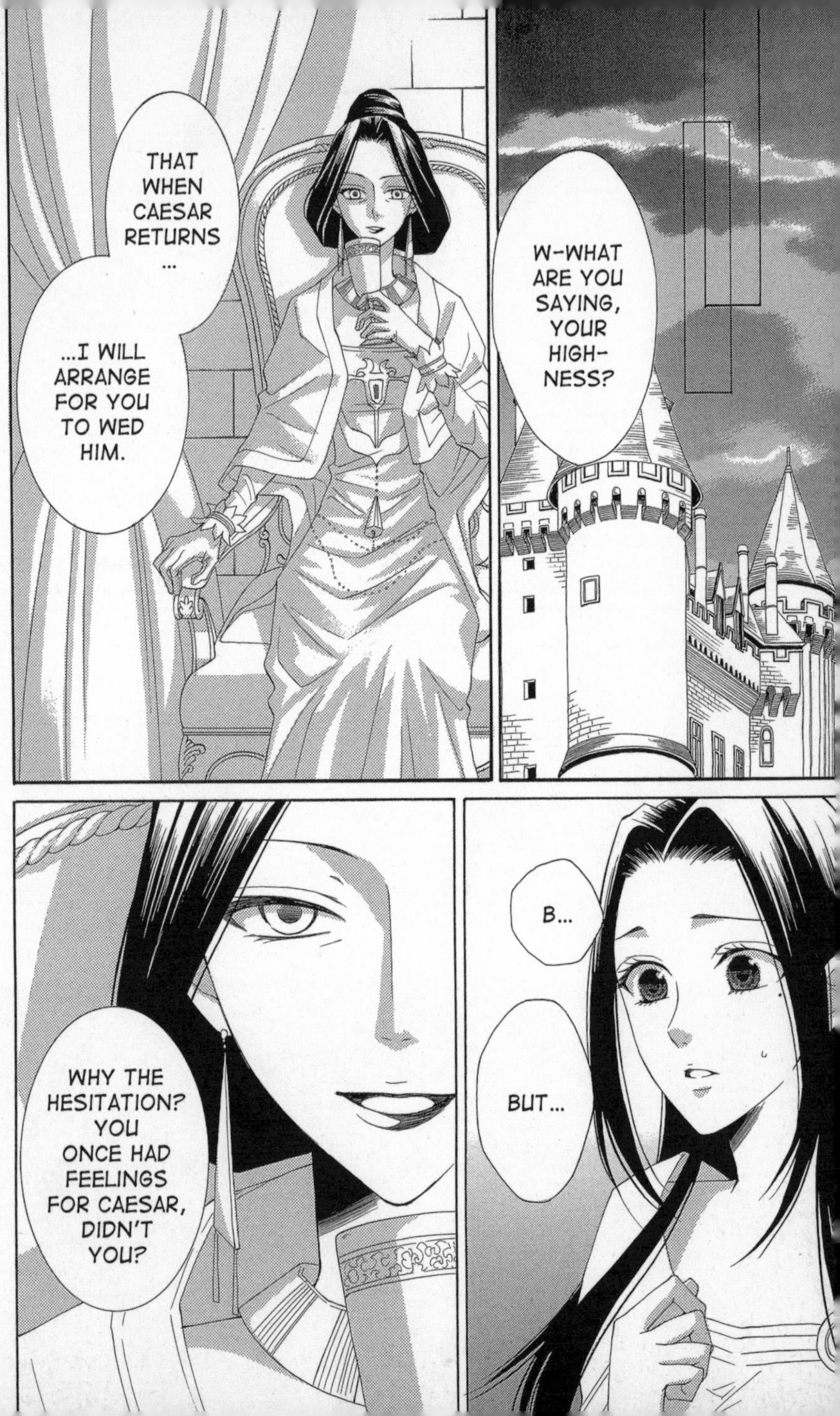
W-WHAT ARE YOU SAYING, YOUR HIGHNESS?
THAT WHEN CAESAR RETURNS...
...I WILL ARRANGE FOR YOU TO WED HIM.
B...
BUT...
WHY THE HESITATION? YOU ONCE HAD FEELINGS FOR CAESAR, DIDN'T YOU?

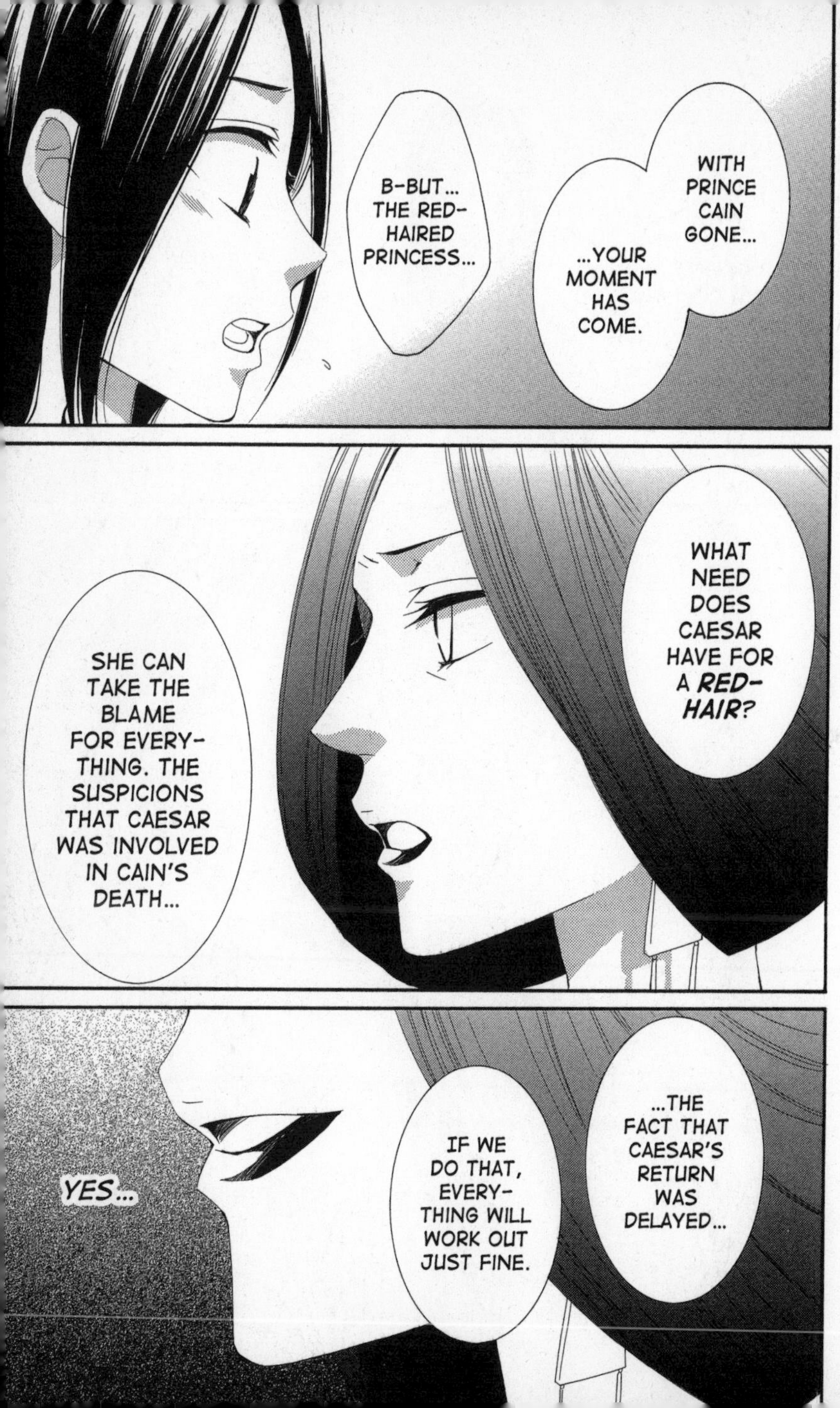
WITH PRINCE CAIN GONE...
...YOUR MOMENT HAS COME.
B-BUT... THE RED-HAIRED PRINCESS...
WHAT NEED DOES CAESAR HAVE FOR A *RED-HAIR*?
SHE CAN TAKE THE BLAME FOR EVERYTHING. THE SUSPICIONS THAT CAESAR WAS INVOLVED IN CAIN'S DEATH...
...THE FACT THAT CAESAR'S RETURN WAS DELAYED...
IF WE DO THAT, EVERYTHING WILL WORK OUT JUST FINE.
YES...

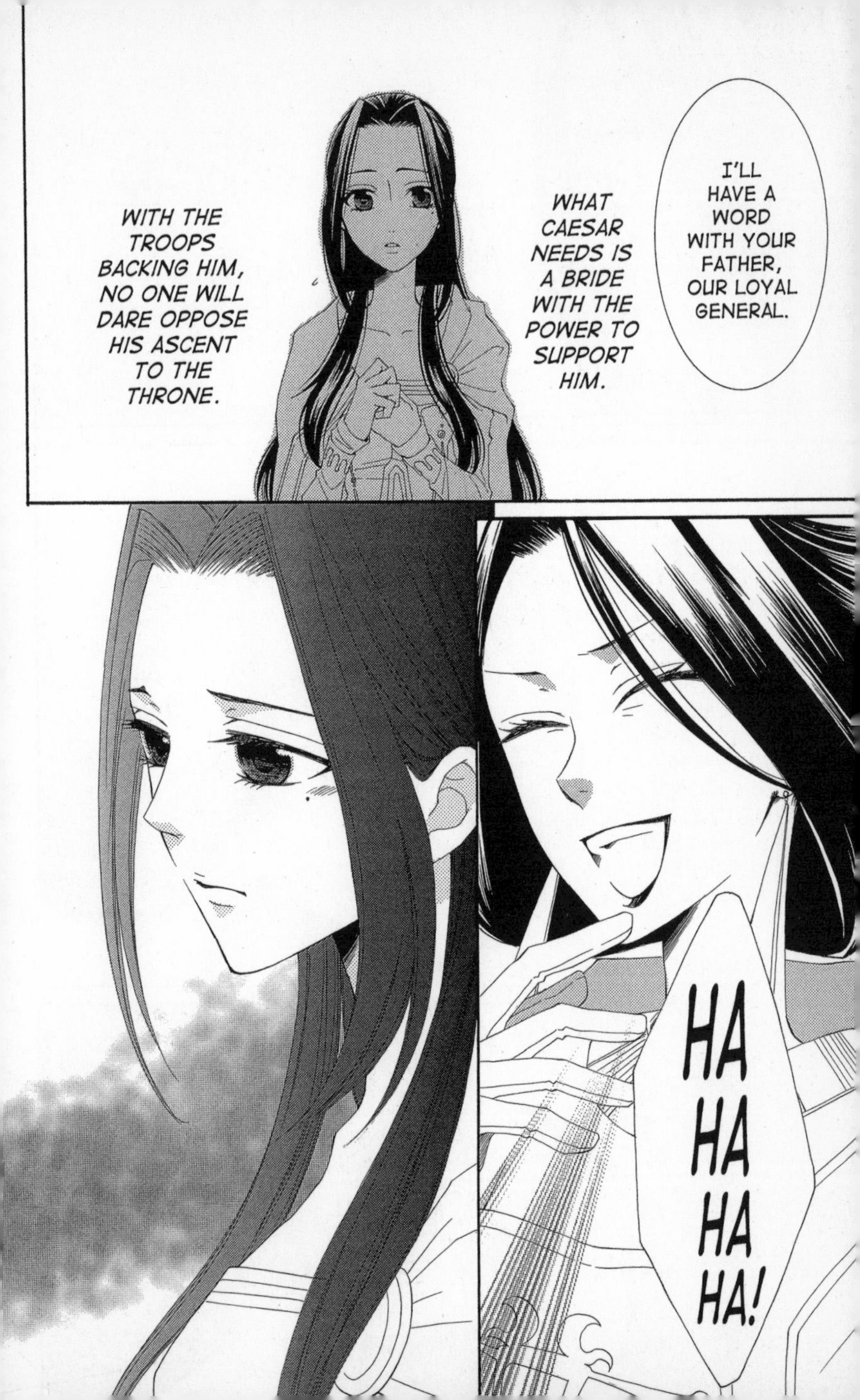
I'LL HAVE A WORD WITH YOUR FATHER, OUR LOYAL GENERAL.
WHAT CAESAR NEEDS IS A BRIDE WITH THE POWER TO SUPPORT HIM.
WITH THE TROOPS BACKING HIM, NO ONE WILL DARE OPPOSE HIS ASCENT TO THE THRONE.
HA HA HA HA!

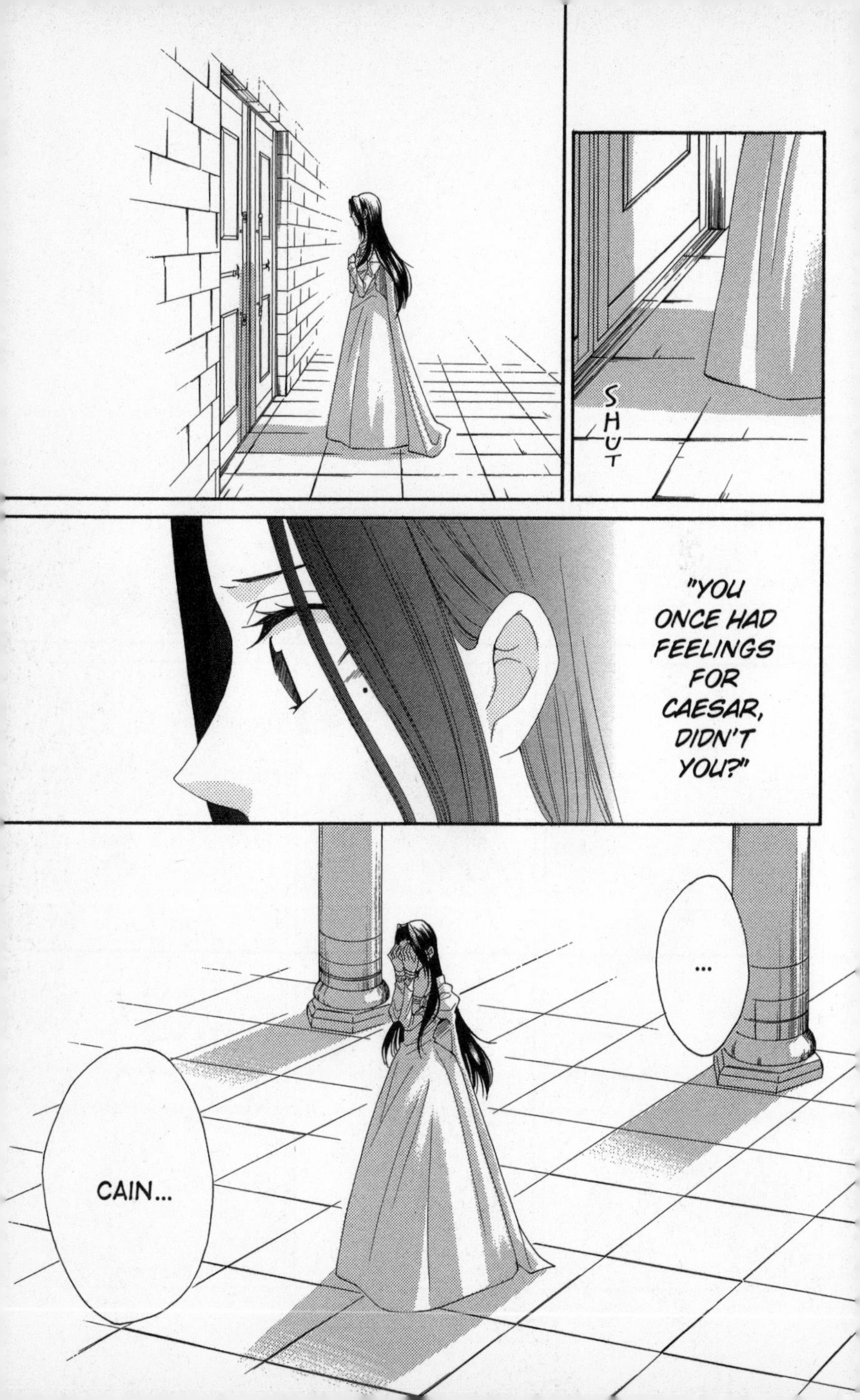
SHUT
"YOU ONCE HAD FEELINGS FOR CAESAR, DIDN'T YOU?"
...
CAIN...

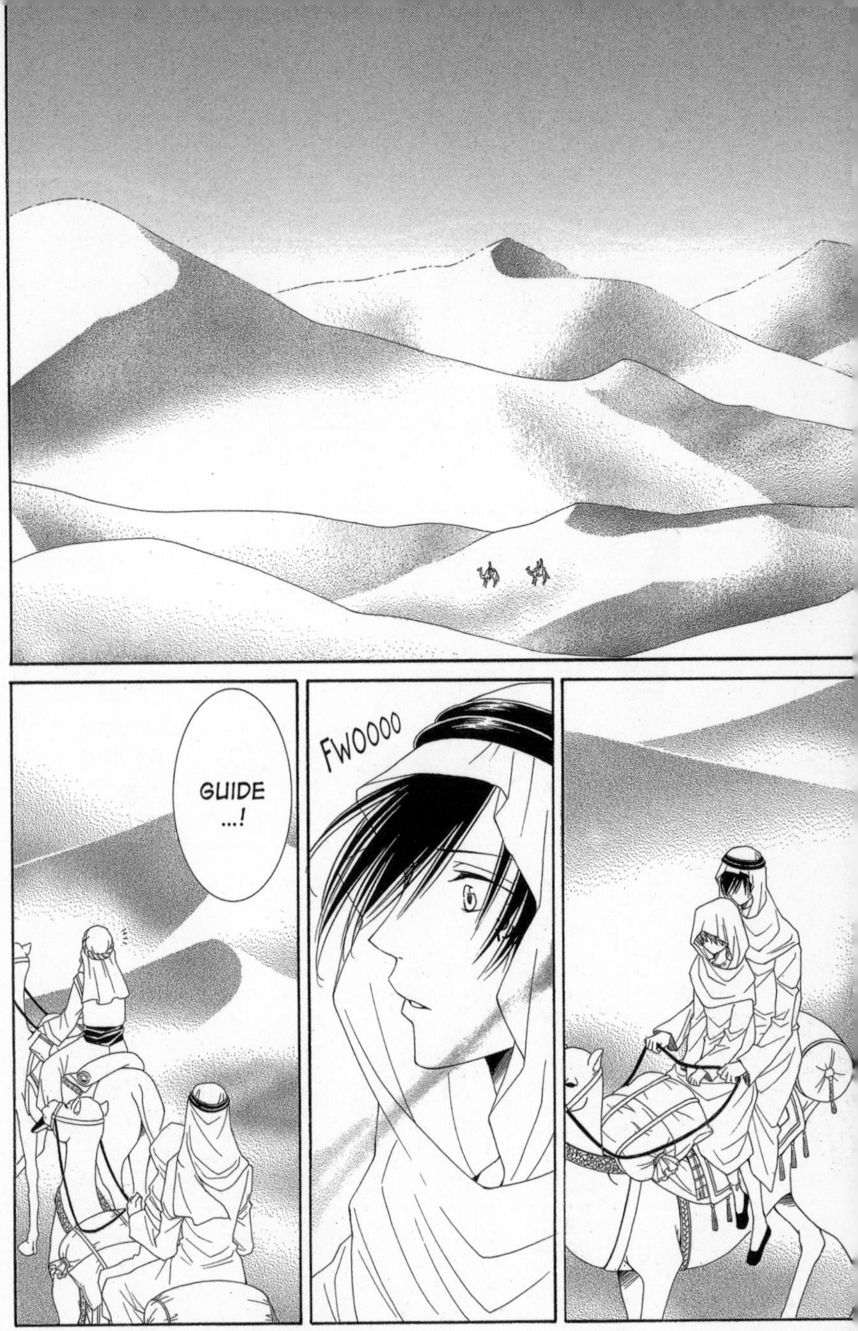
FWOOOO
GUIDE ...!

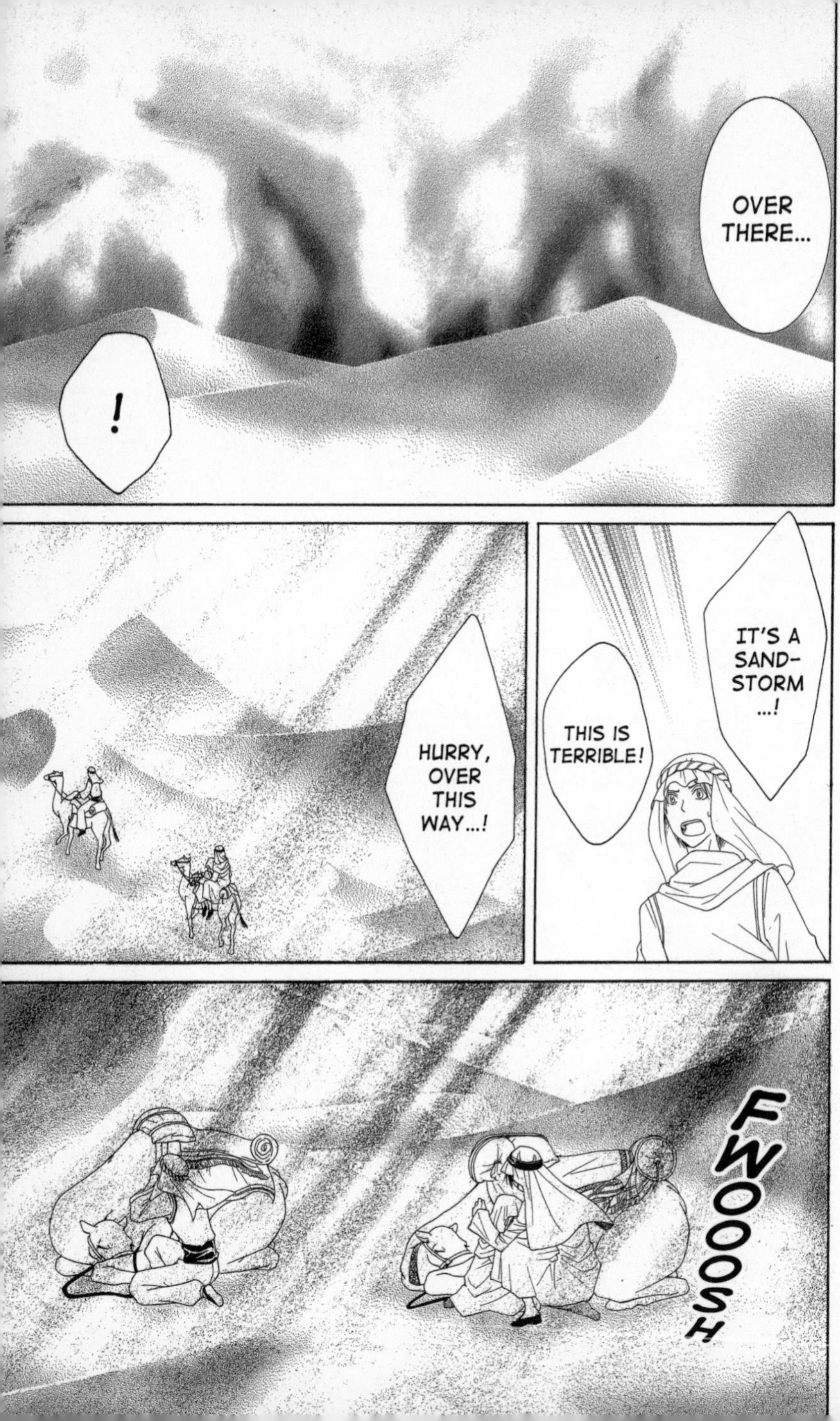
OVER THERE...
!
IT'S A SAND-STORM ...!
THIS IS TERRIBLE!
HURRY, OVER THIS WAY...!
FWOOOSH

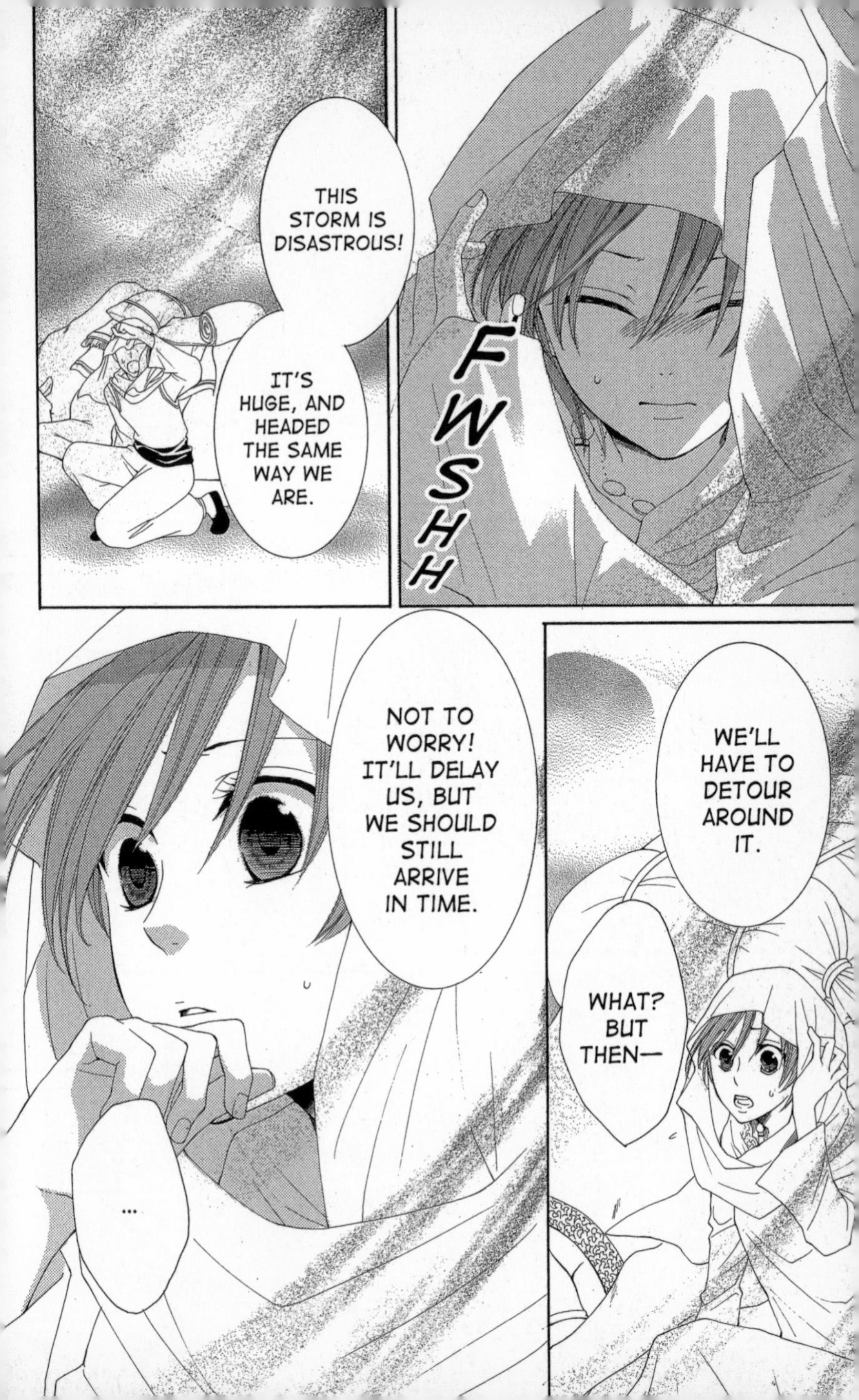
FWSHH
THIS STORM IS DISASTROUS!
IT'S HUGE, AND HEADED THE SAME WAY WE ARE.
WE'LL HAVE TO DETOUR AROUND IT.
WHAT? BUT THEN—
NOT TO WORRY! IT'LL DELAY US, BUT WE SHOULD STILL ARRIVE IN TIME.
...

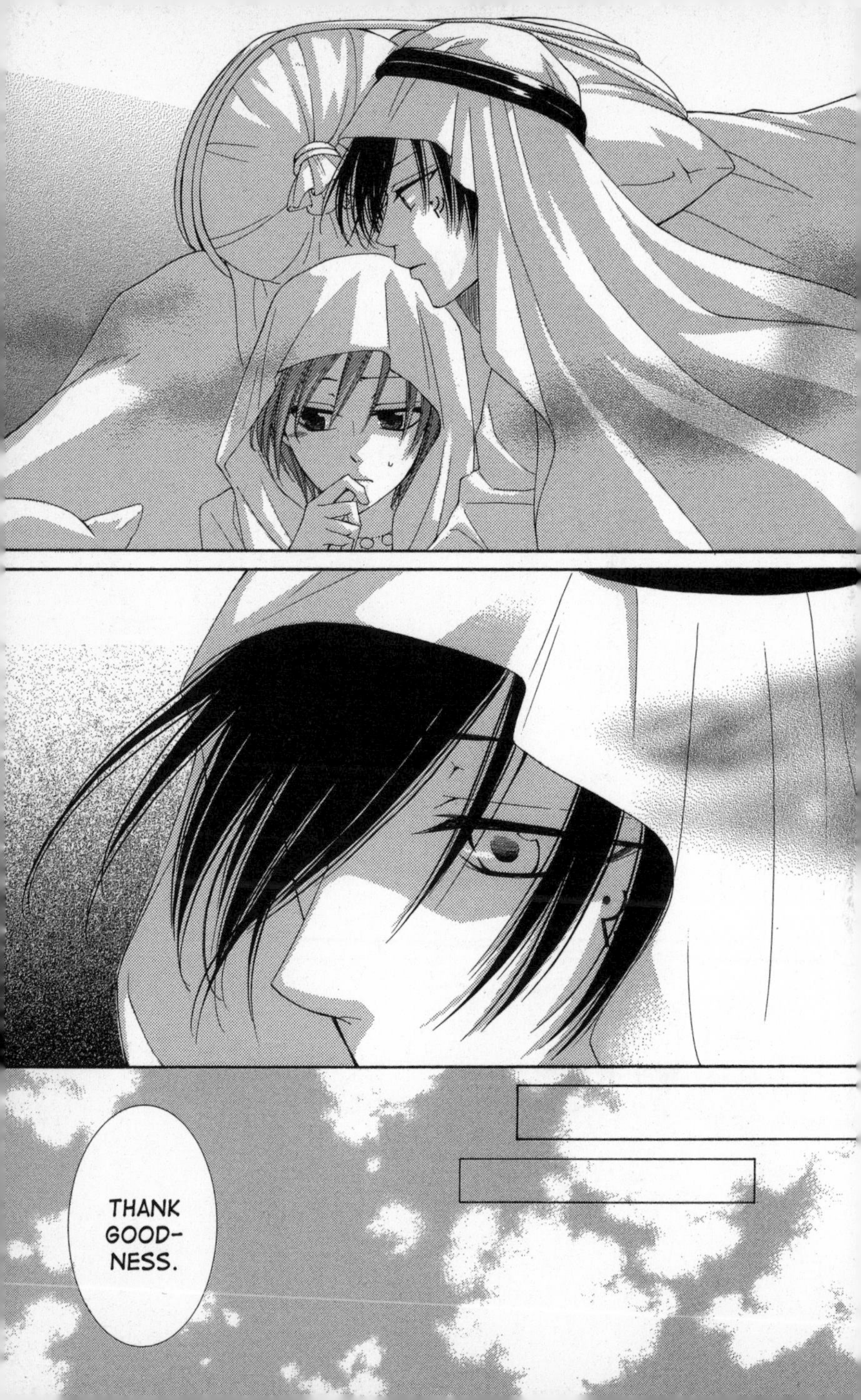
THANK GOOD-NESS.

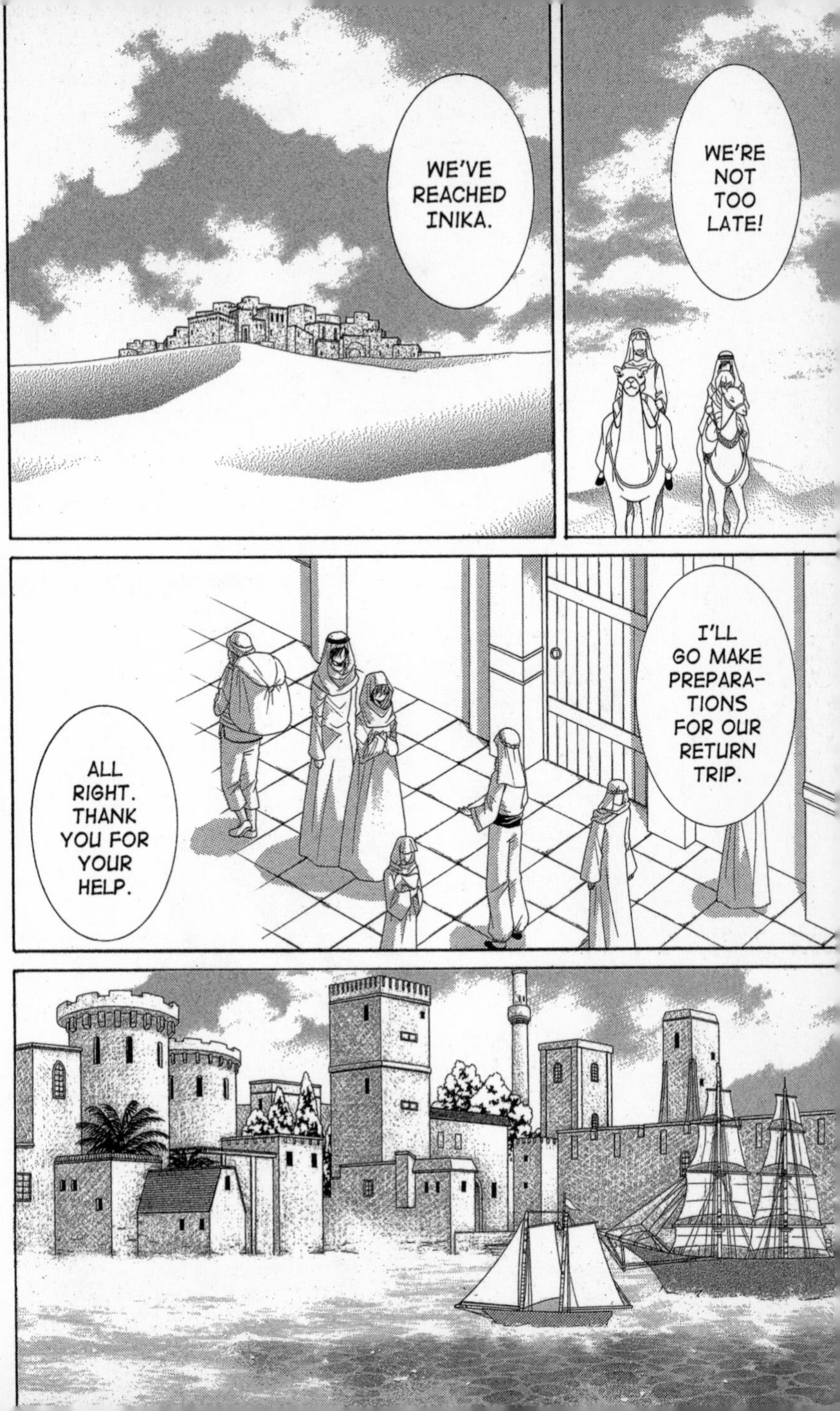
WE'RE NOT TOO LATE!
WE'VE REACHED INIKA.
I'LL GO MAKE PREPARA-TIONS FOR OUR RETURN TRIP.
ALL RIGHT. THANK YOU FOR YOUR HELP.

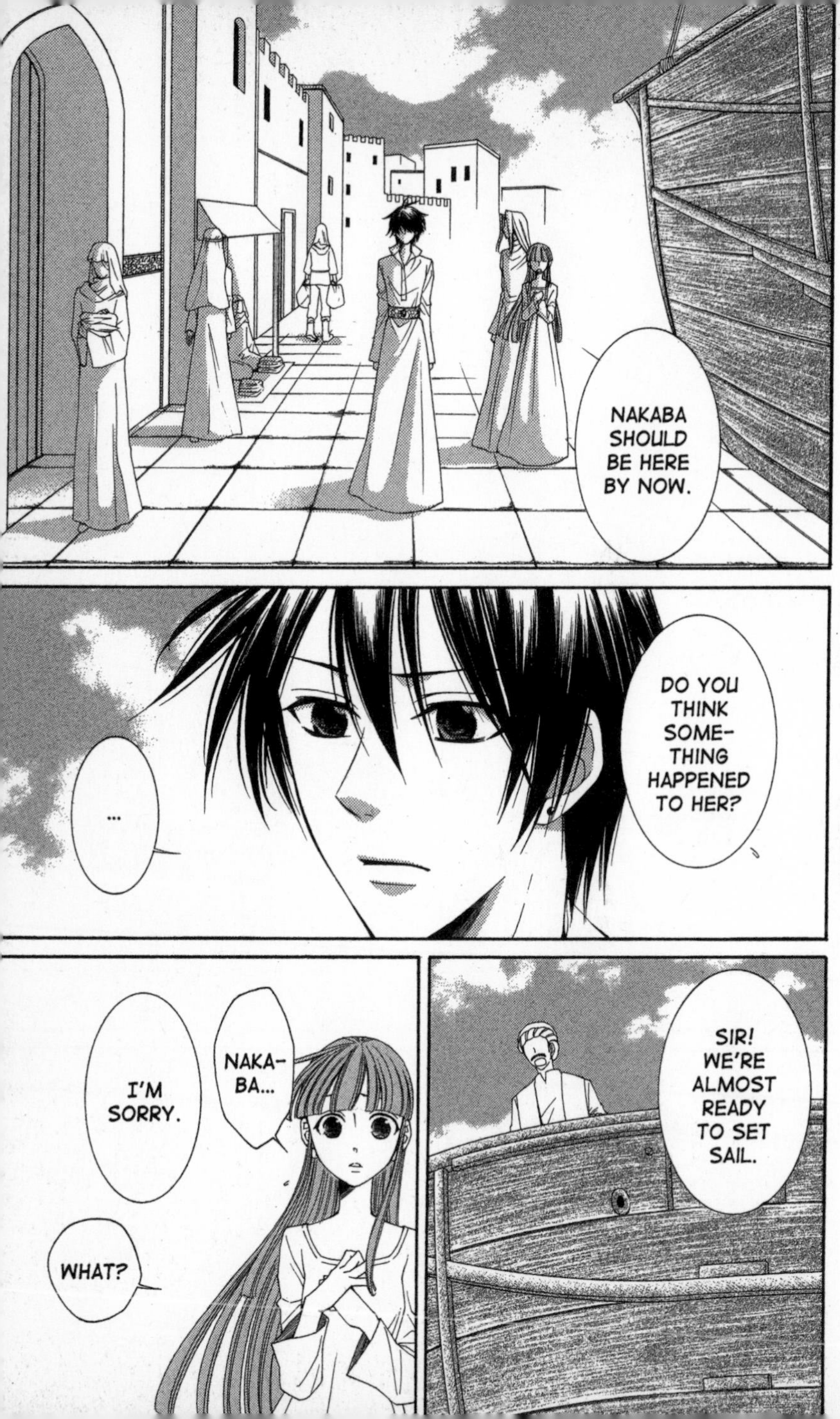
NAKABA SHOULD BE HERE BY NOW.
DO YOU THINK SOME-THING HAPPENED TO HER?
...
SIR! WE'RE ALMOST READY TO SET SAIL.
NAKA-BA...
I'M SORRY.
WHAT?

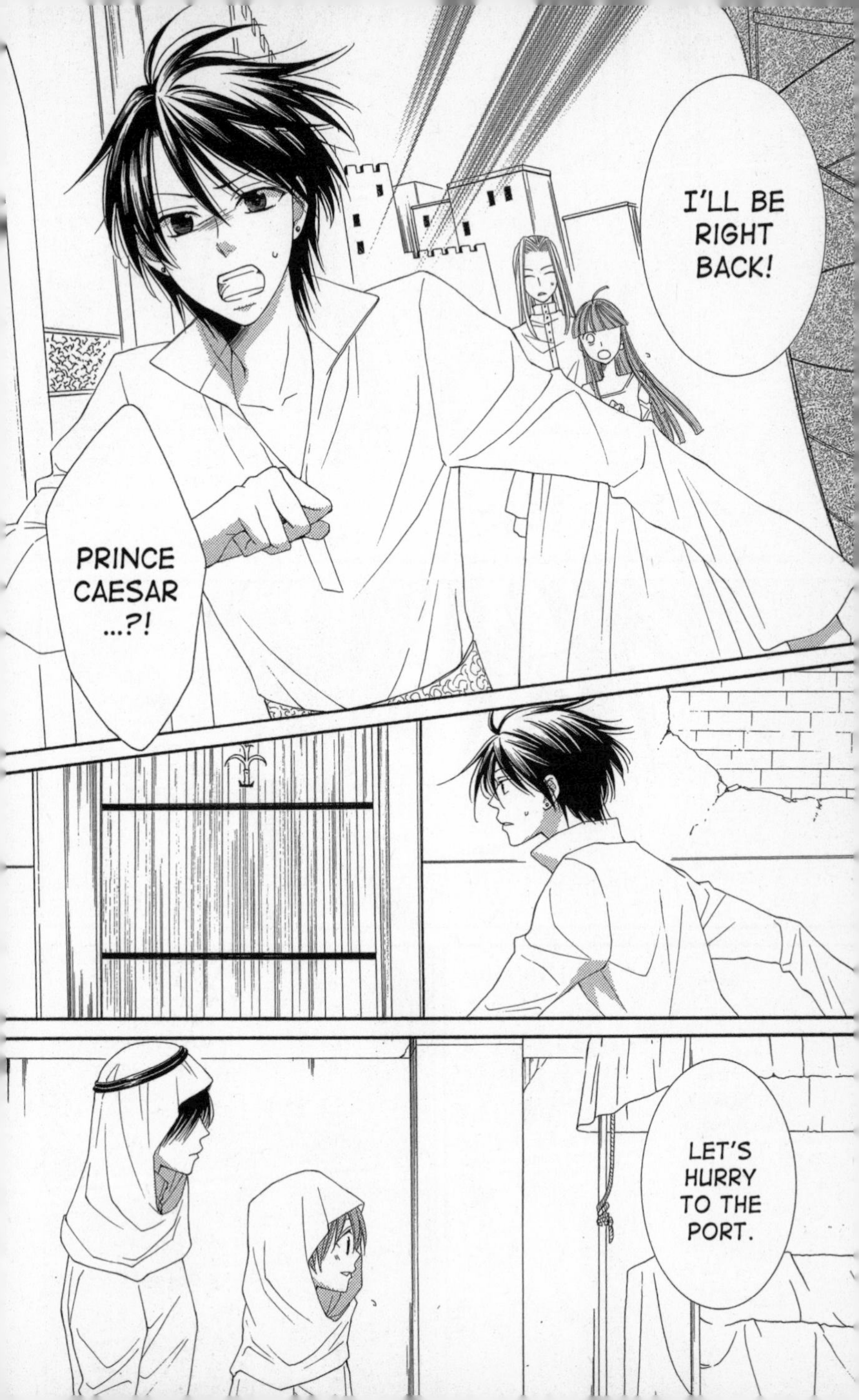
I'LL BE RIGHT BACK!
PRINCE CAESAR ...?!
LET'S HURRY TO THE PORT.

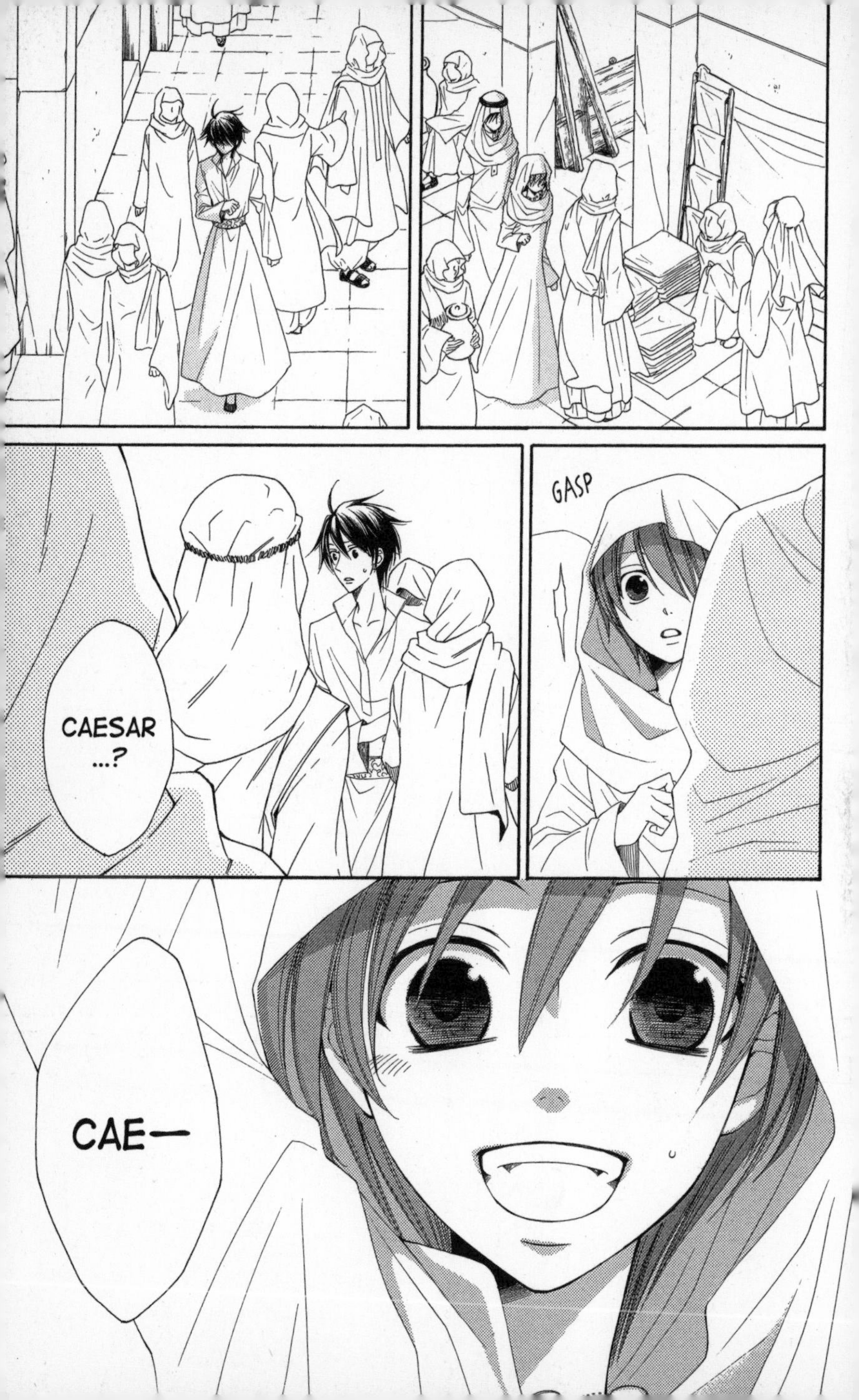
GASP
CAESAR ...?
CAE—

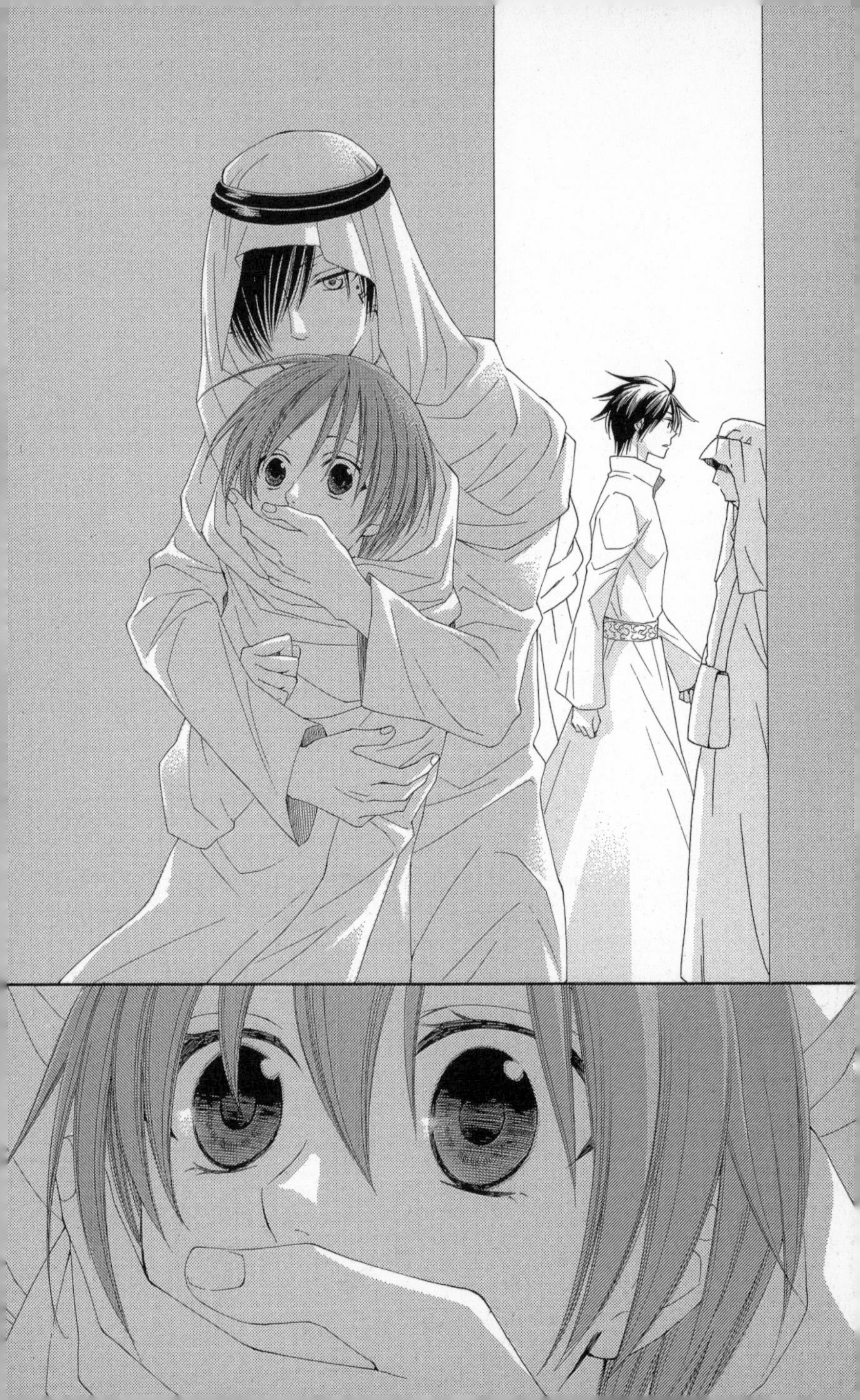

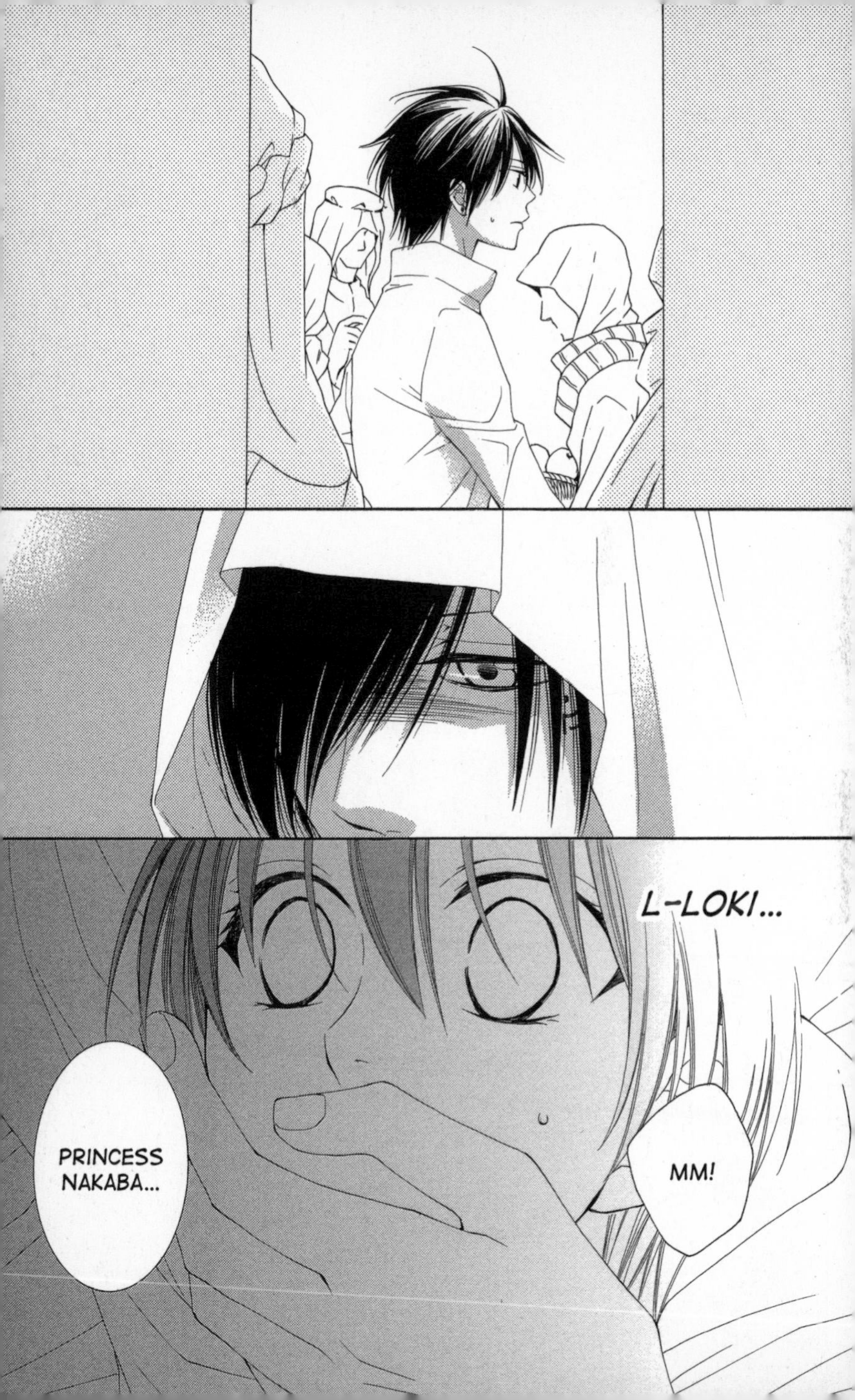
L-LOKI...
MM!
PRINCESS NAKABA...

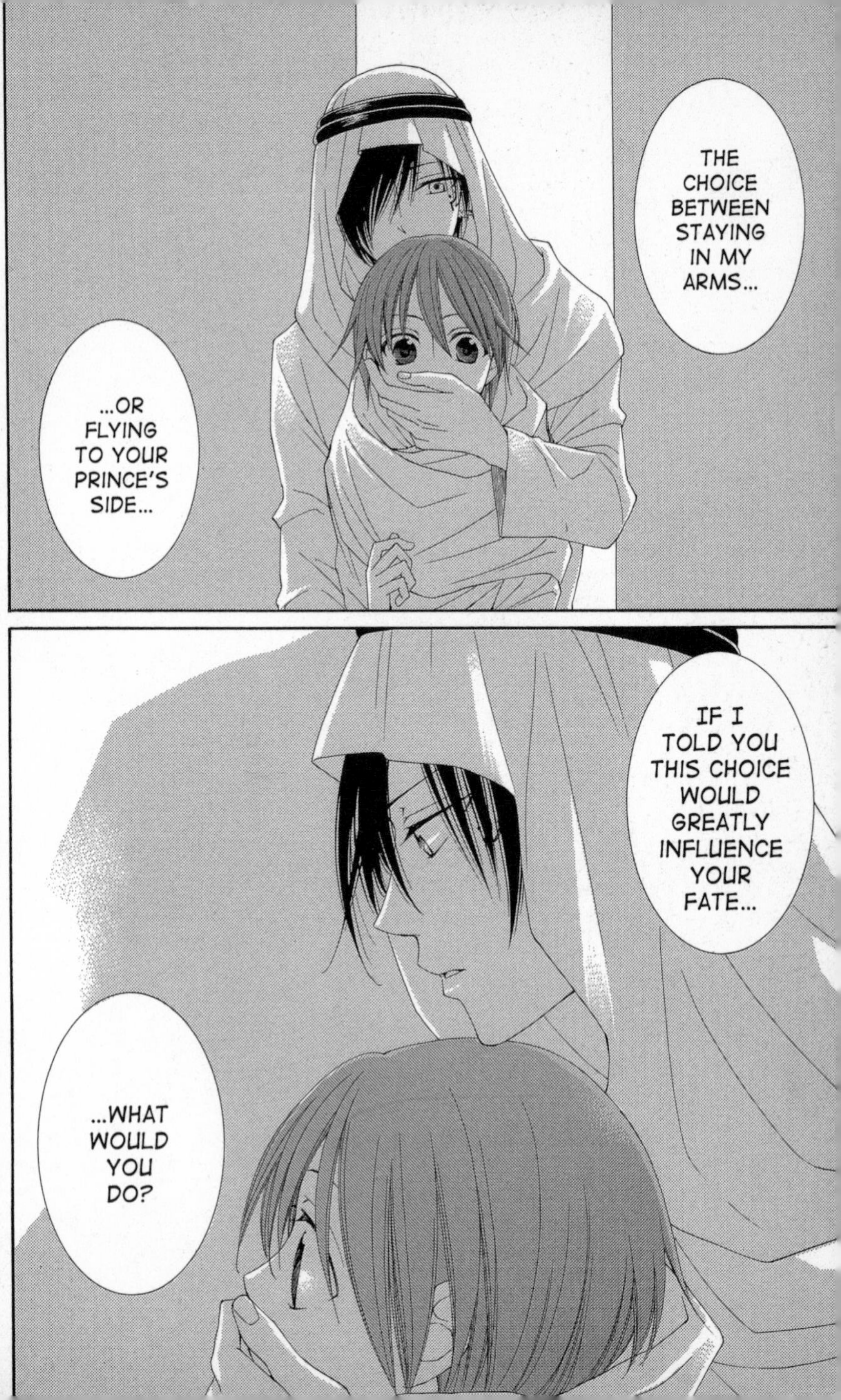
THE CHOICE BETWEEN STAYING IN MY ARMS...
...OR FLYING TO YOUR PRINCE'S SIDE...
IF I TOLD YOU THIS CHOICE WOULD GREATLY INFLUENCE YOUR FATE...
...WHAT WOULD YOU DO?

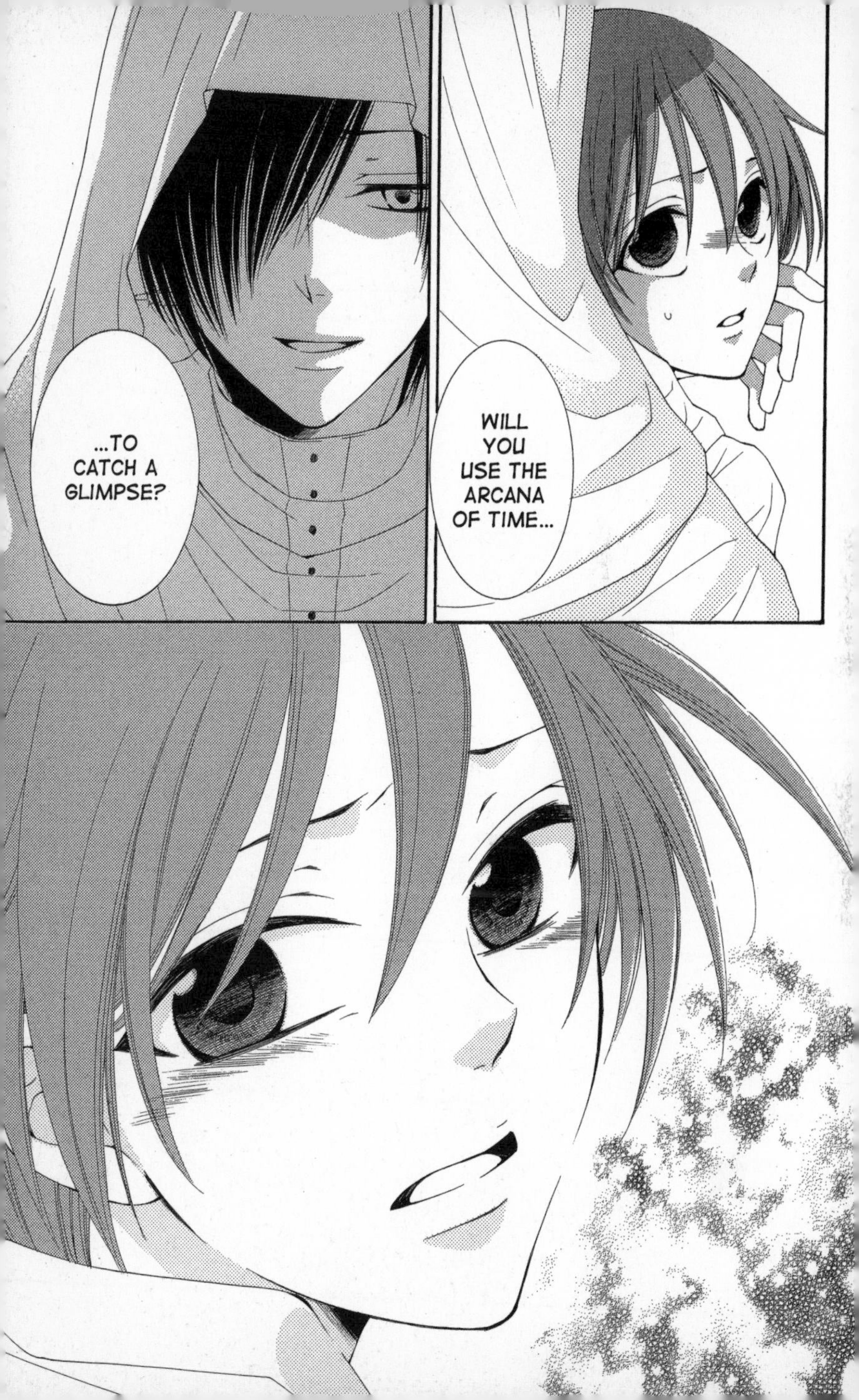
WILL YOU USE THE ARCANA OF TIME...
...TO CATCH A GLIMPSE?

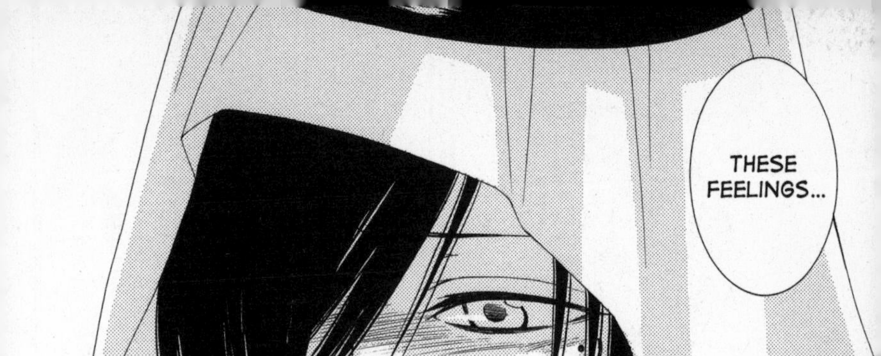
THESE FEELINGS...
THE UGLY FEELINGS IN MY HEART...
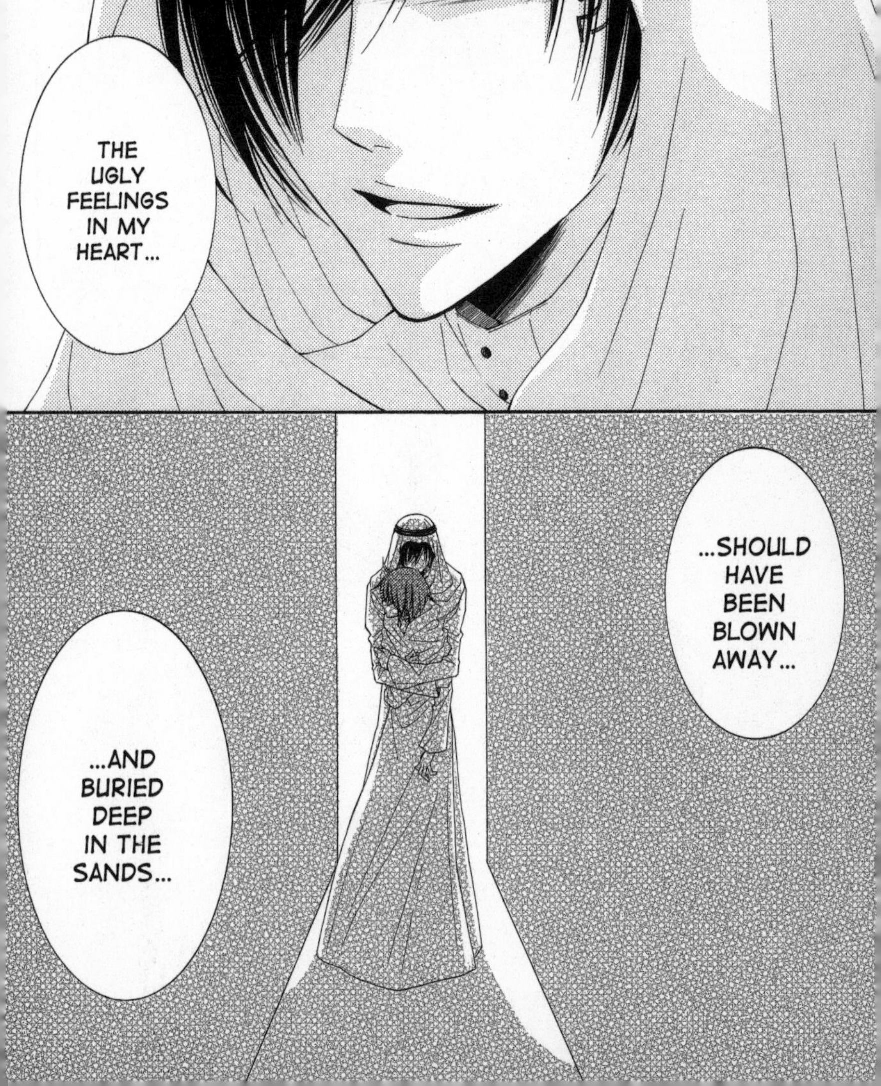
...SHOULD HAVE BEEN BLOWN AWAY...
...AND BURIED DEEP IN THE SANDS...

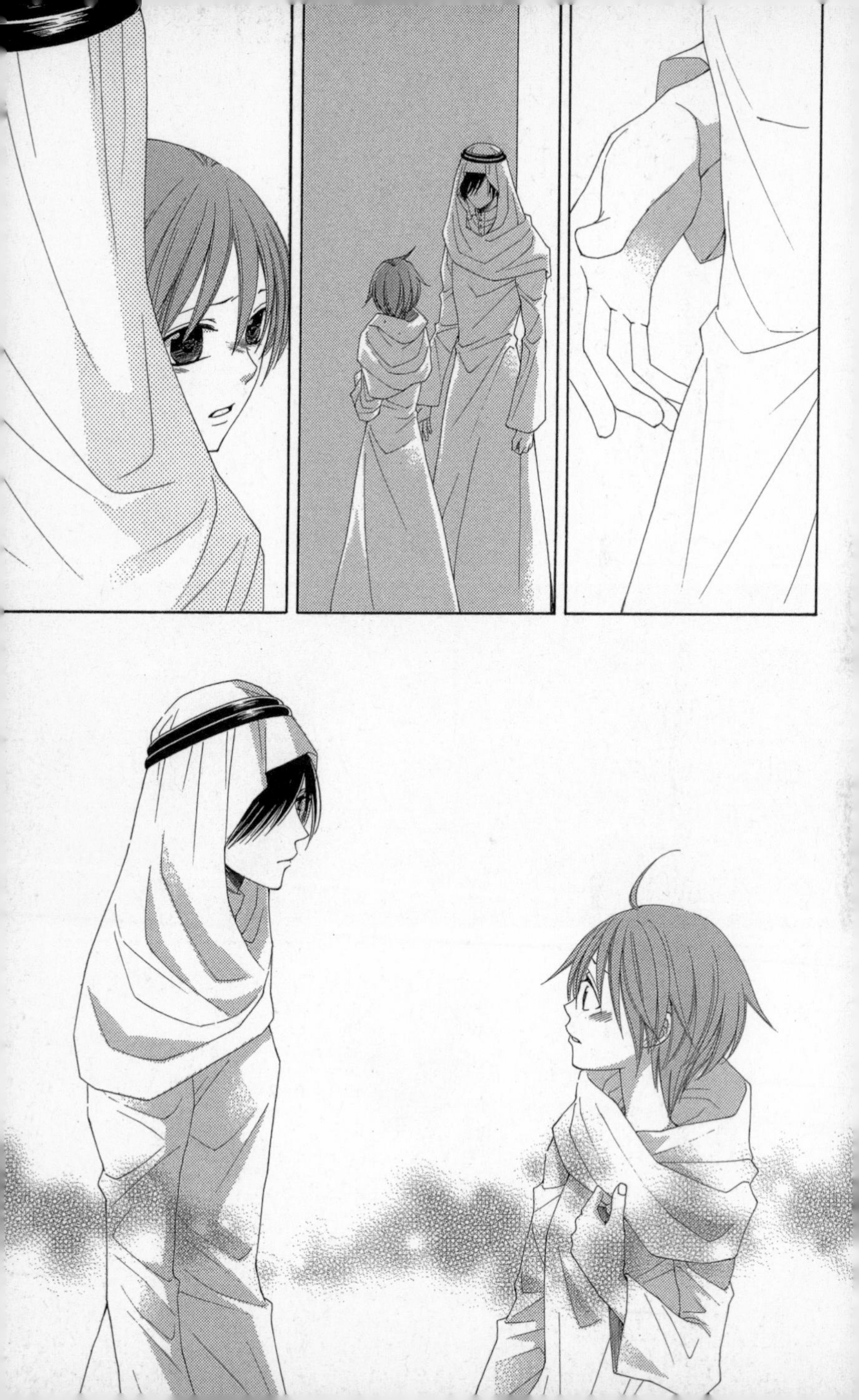

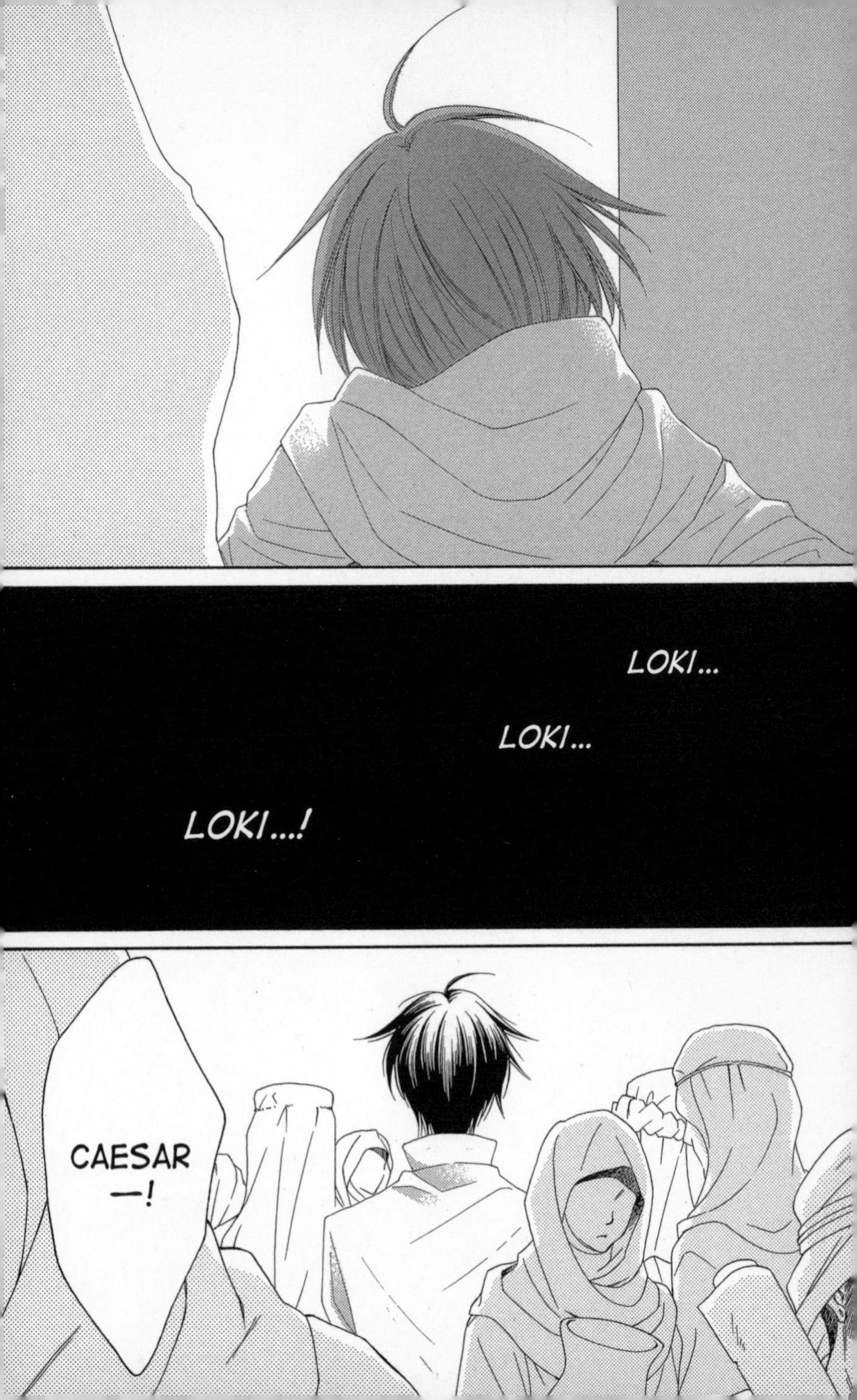
LOKI...
LOKI...
LOKI...!
CAESAR —!

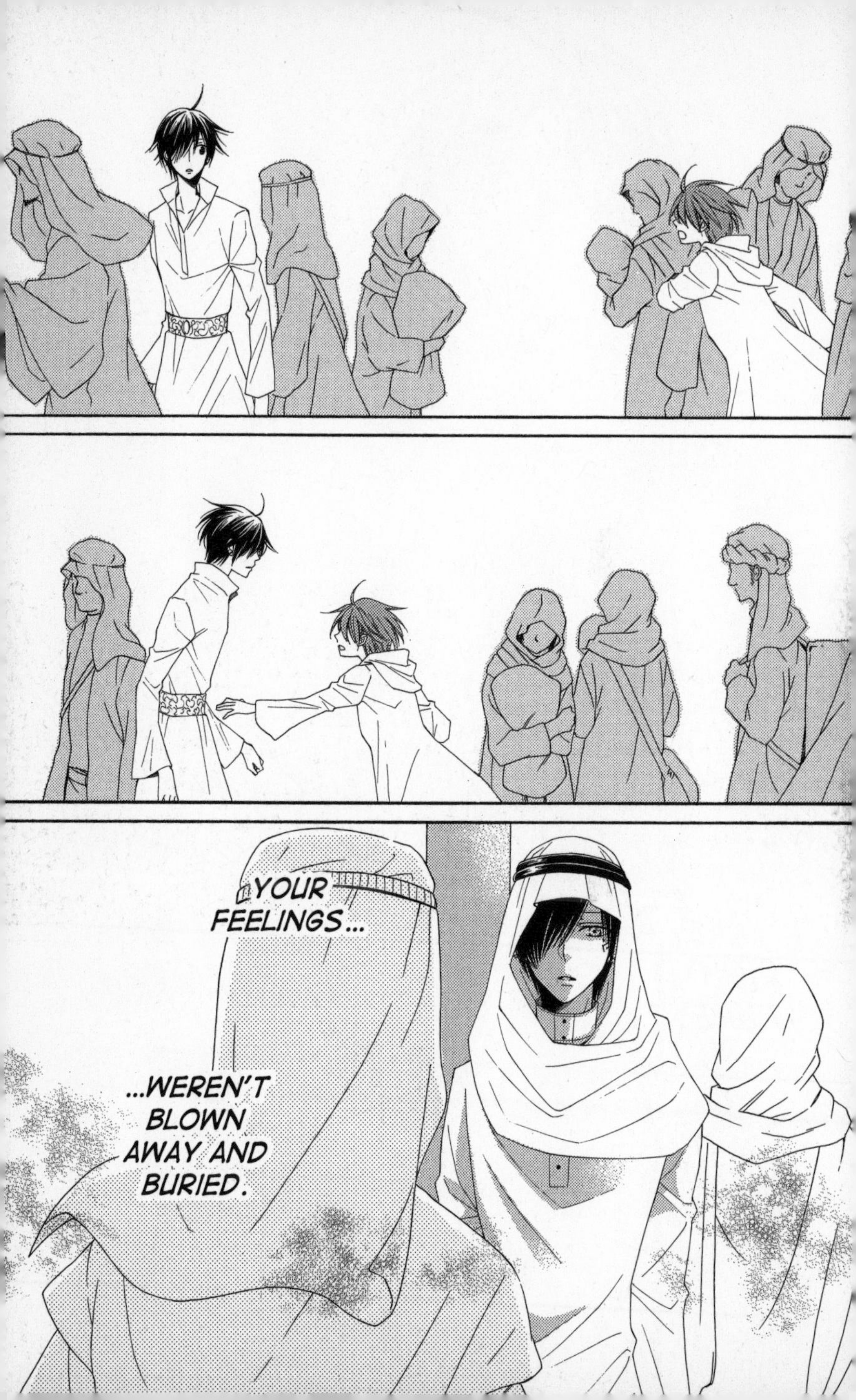
YOUR FEELINGS...
...WEREN'T BLOWN AWAY AND BURIED.

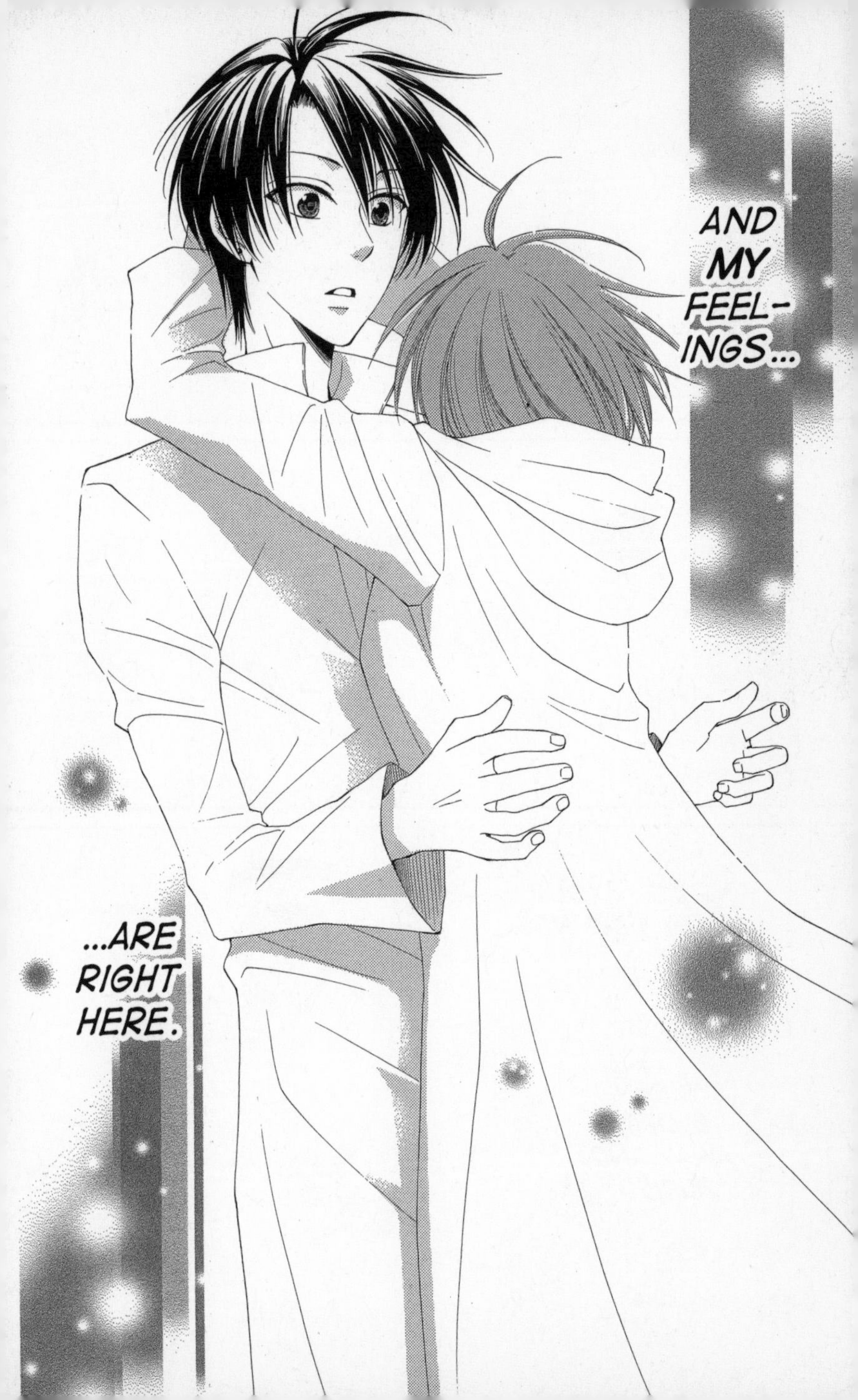
AND MY FEEL-INGS...
...ARE RIGHT HERE.

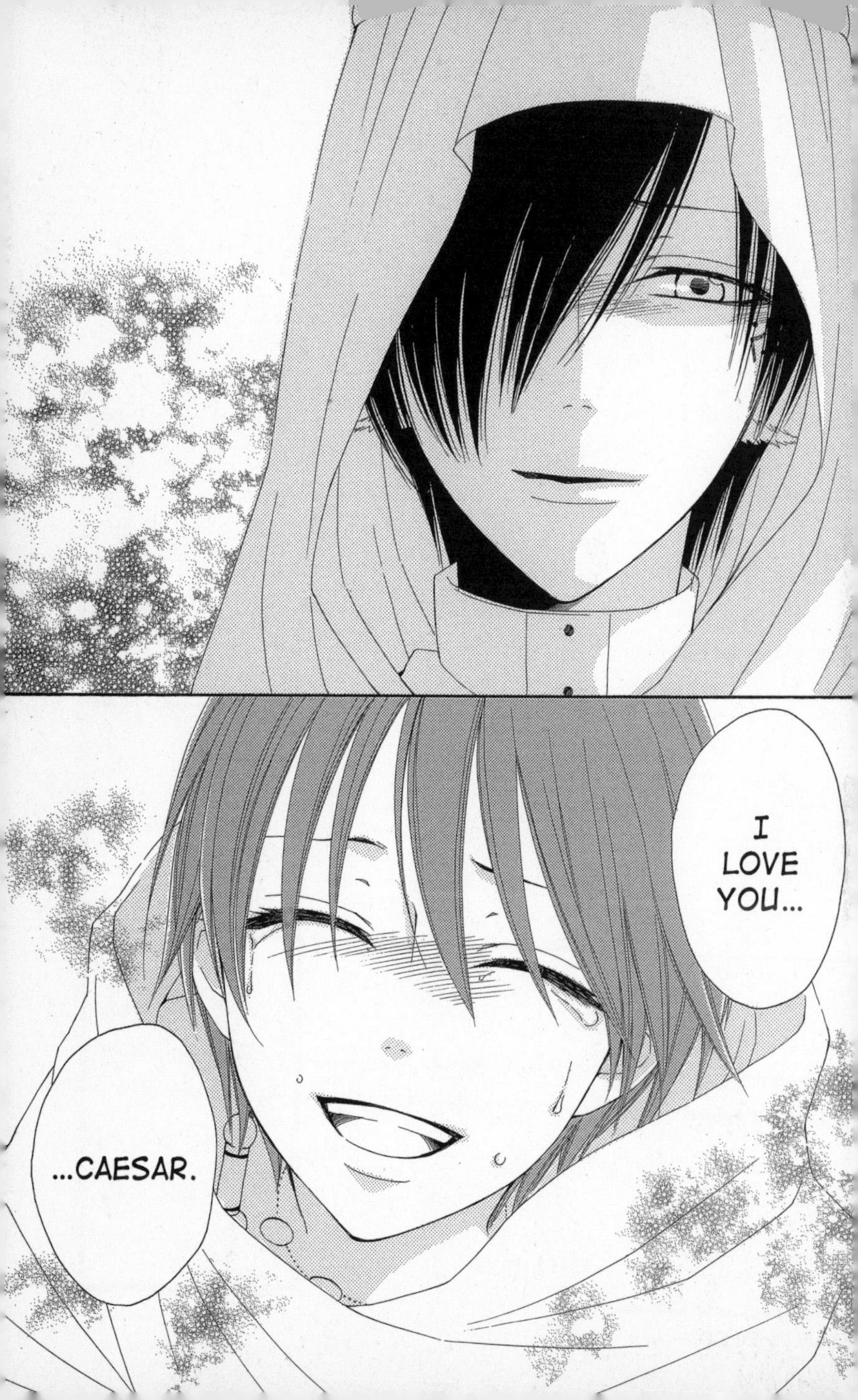
I LOVE YOU...
...CAESAR.

Chapter 34

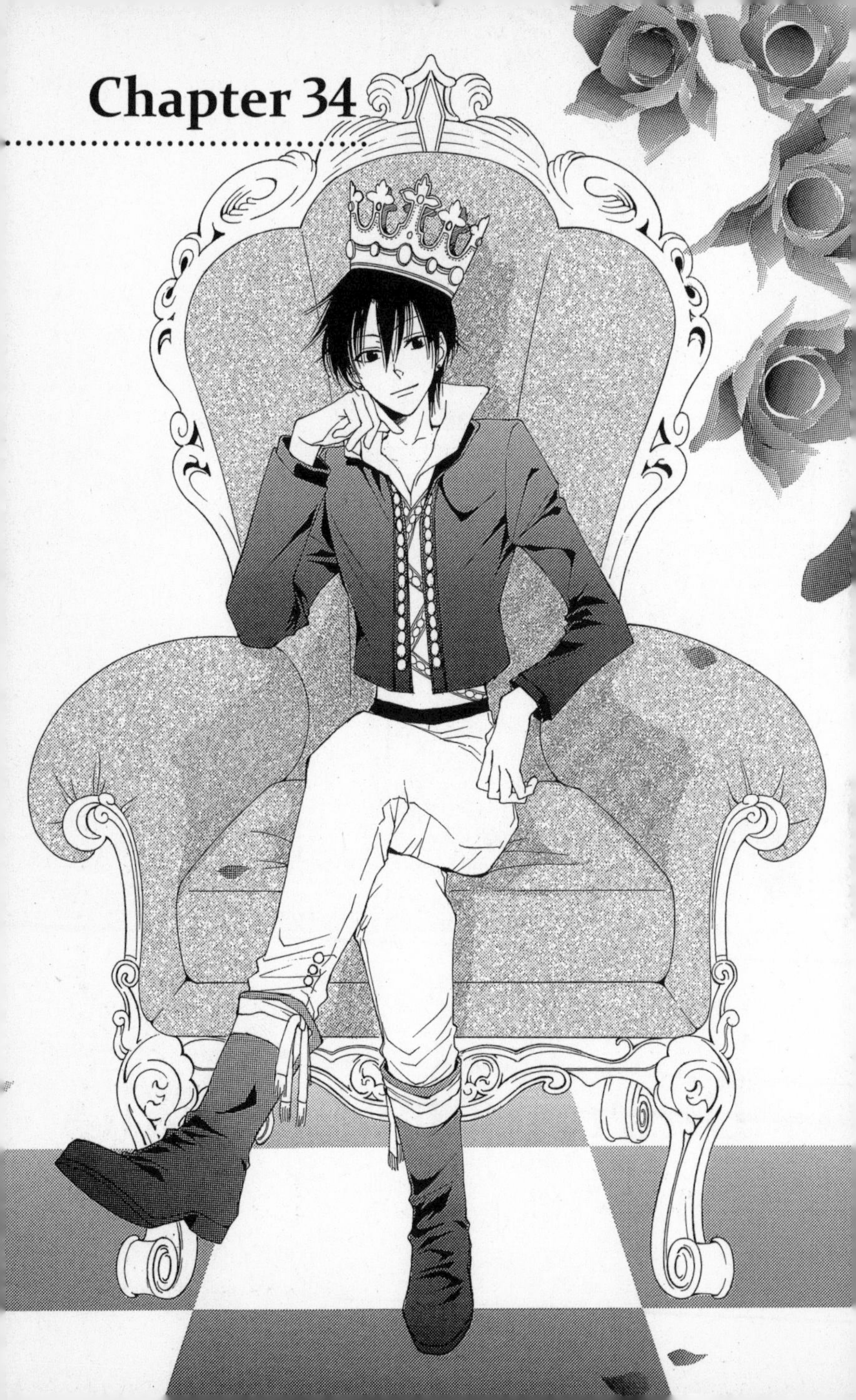

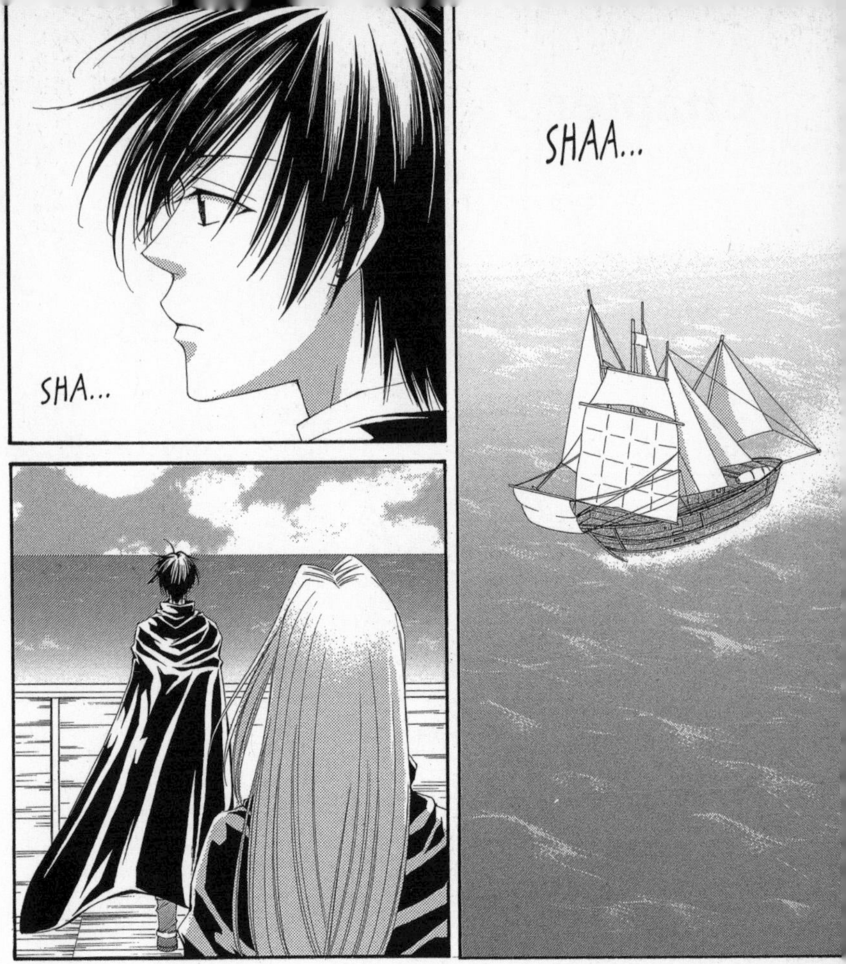
SHAA...
SHA...

Dawn of the Arcana

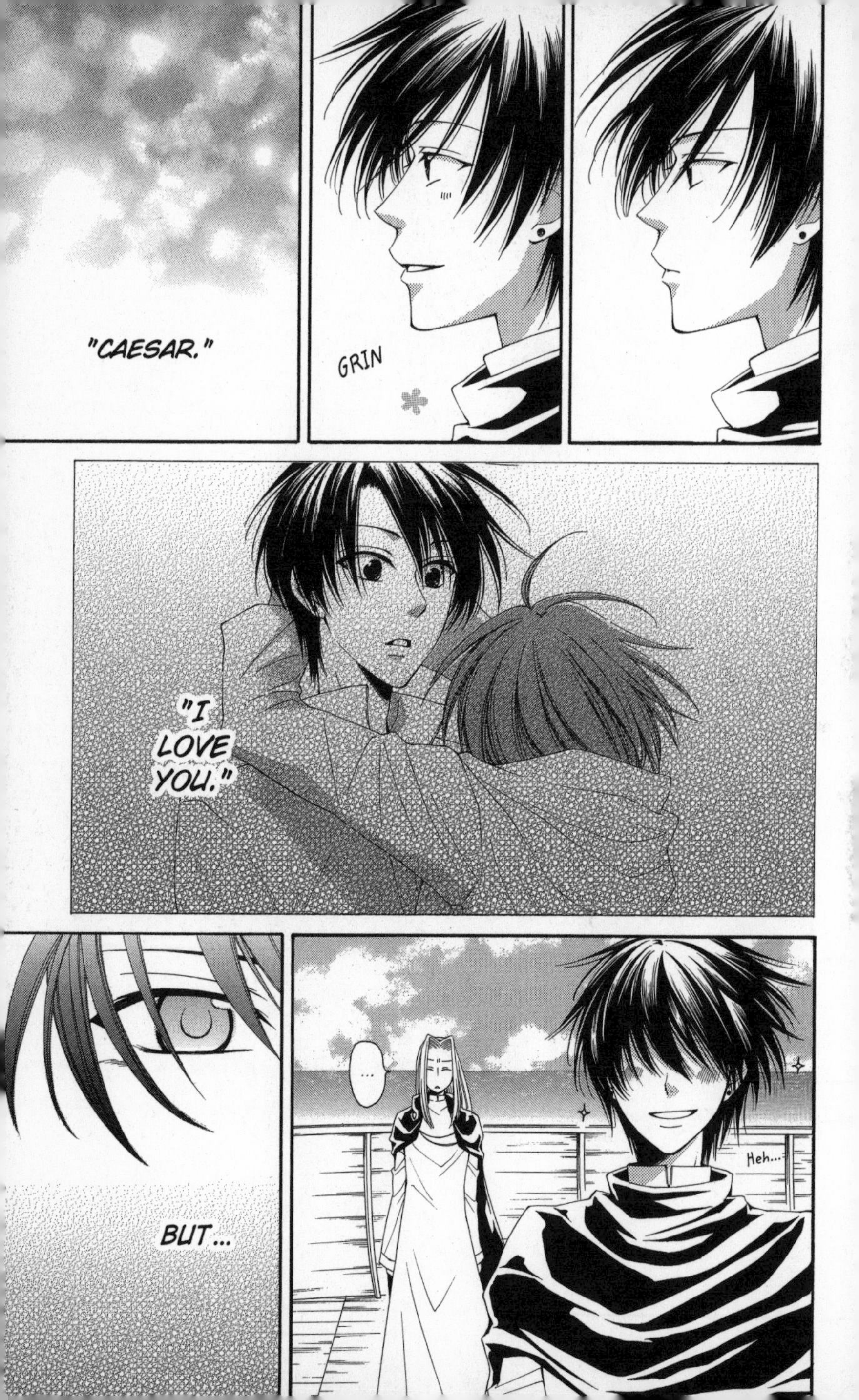
GRIN
"CAESAR."
"I LOVE YOU."
...
Heh...
BUT...

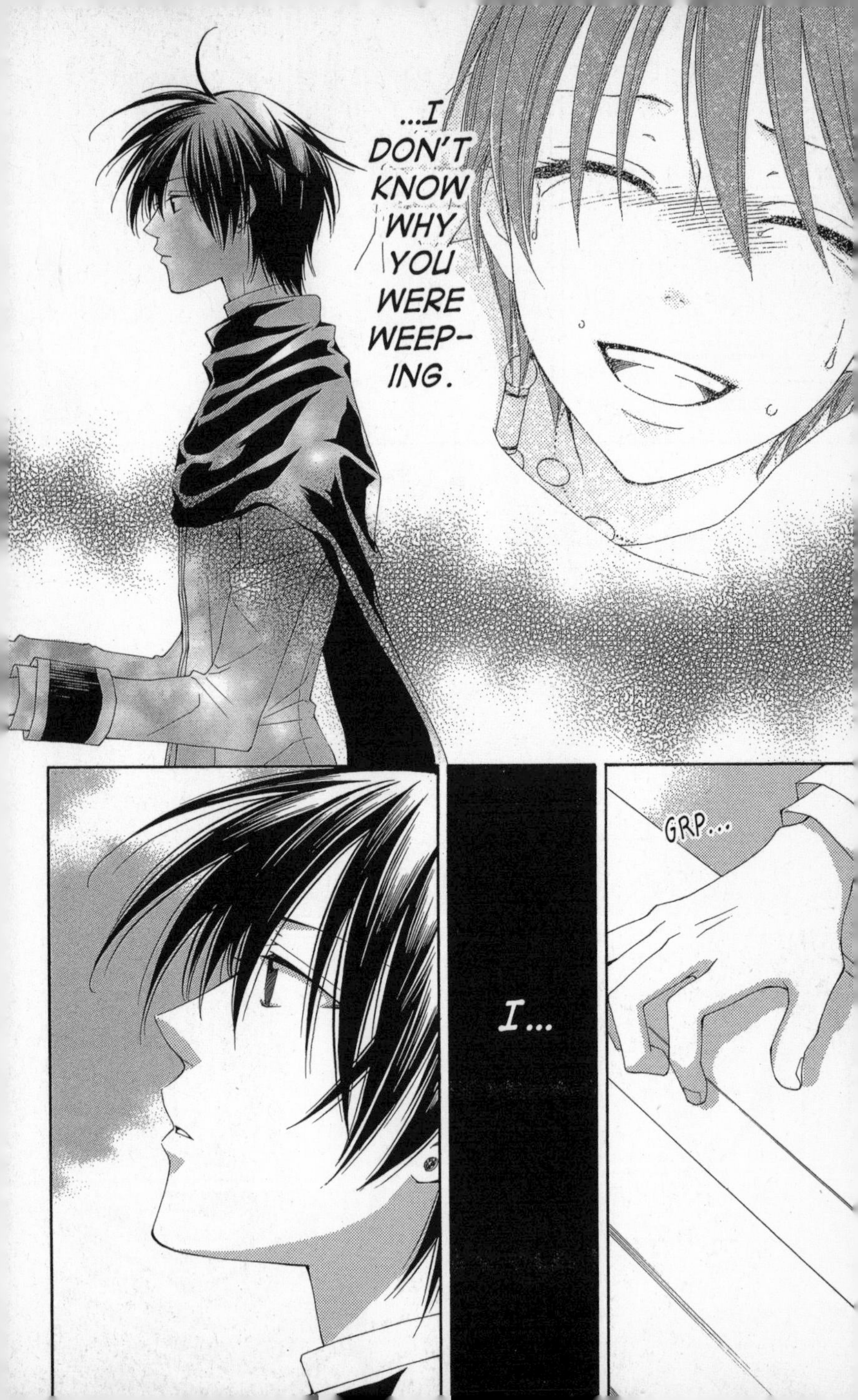
...I DON'T KNOW WHY YOU WERE WEEP-ING.
GRP...
I...

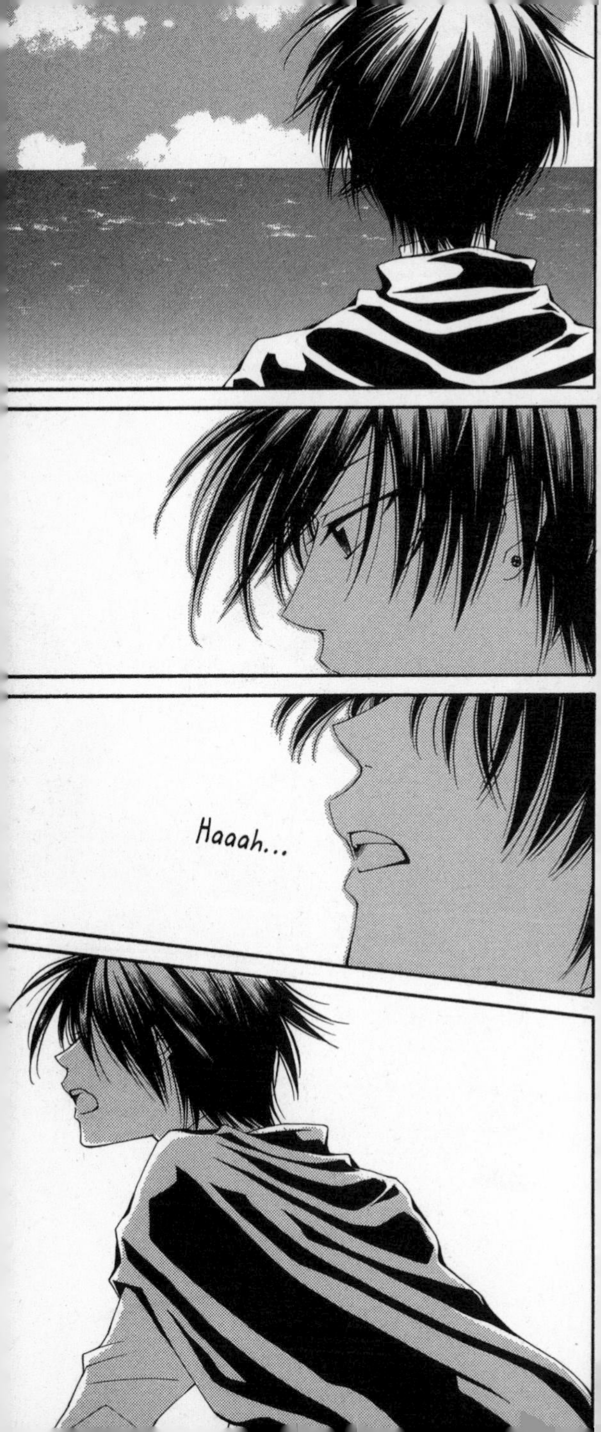
Haaah...

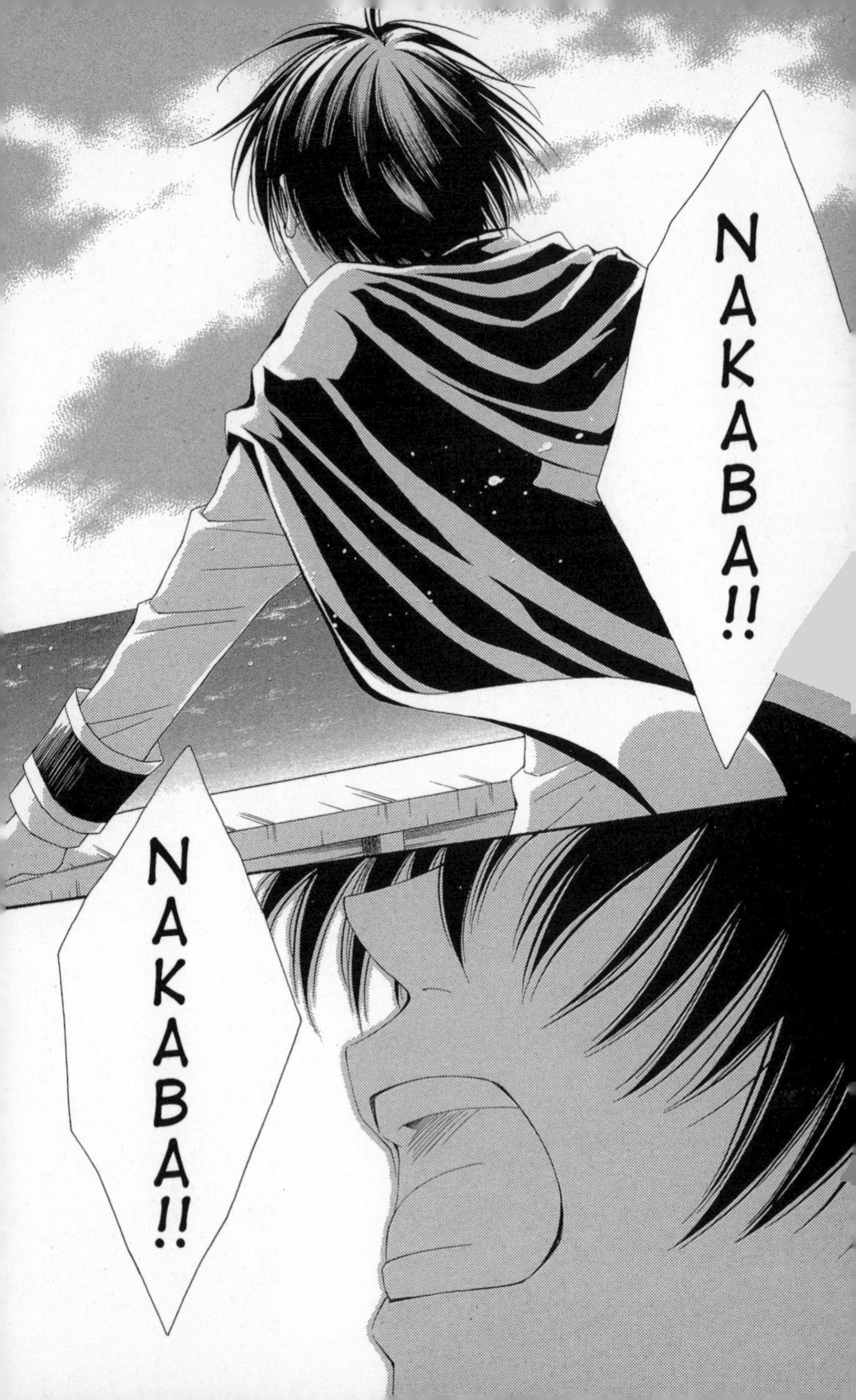
NAKABA!!
NAKABA!!

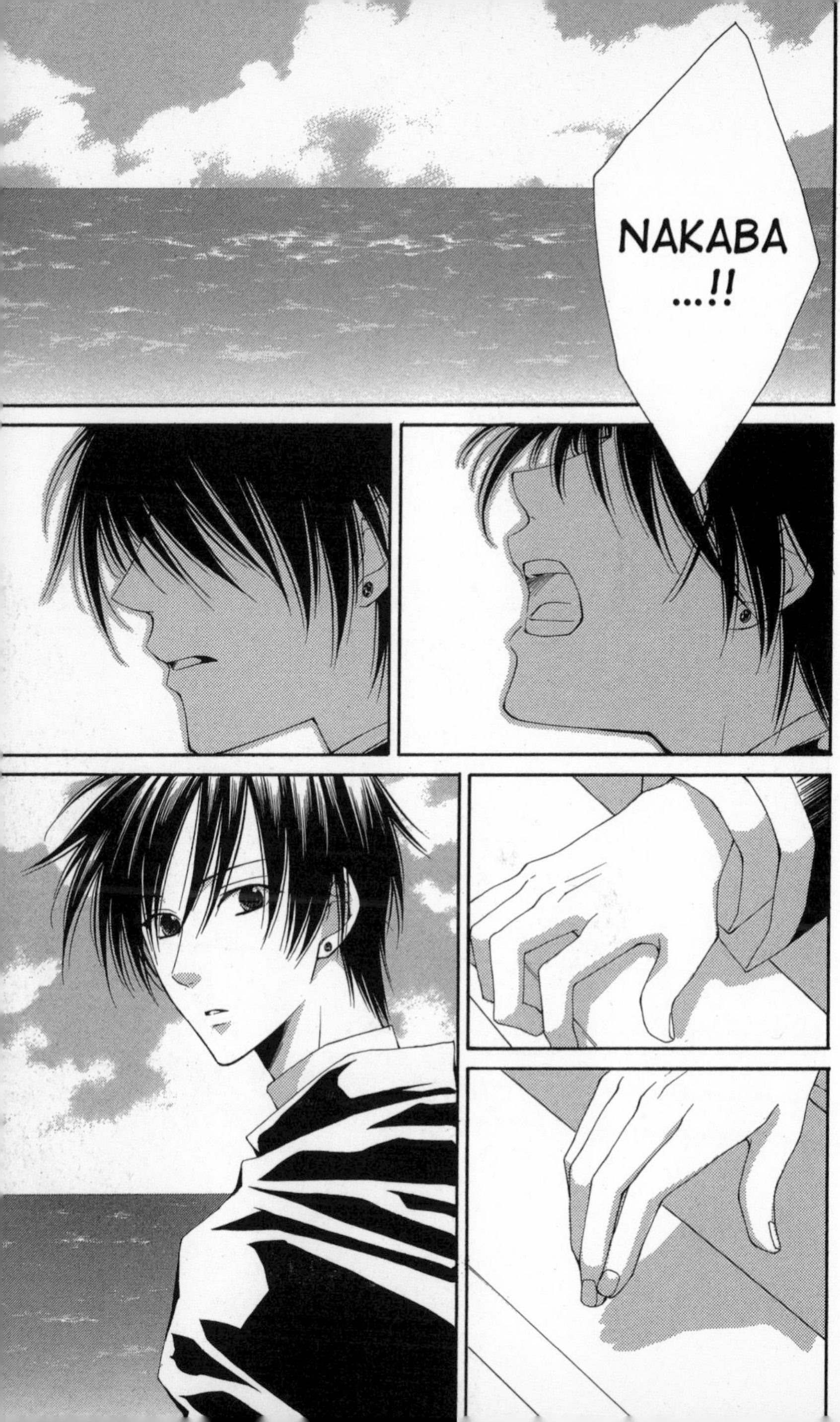
NAKABA ...!!

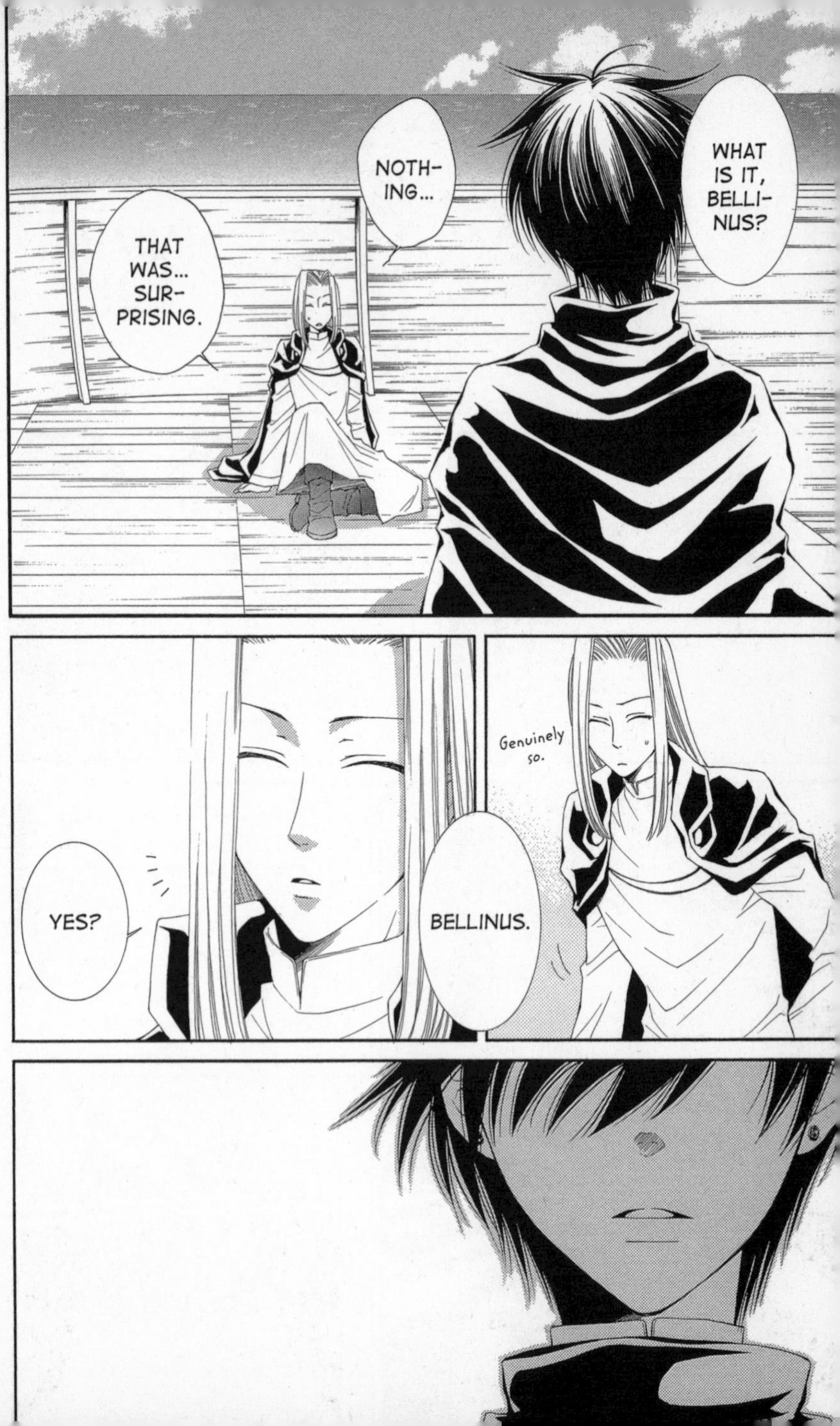
WHAT IS IT, BELLINUS?
NOTH-ING...
THAT WAS... SUR-PRISING.
Genuinely so.
BELLINUS.
YES?

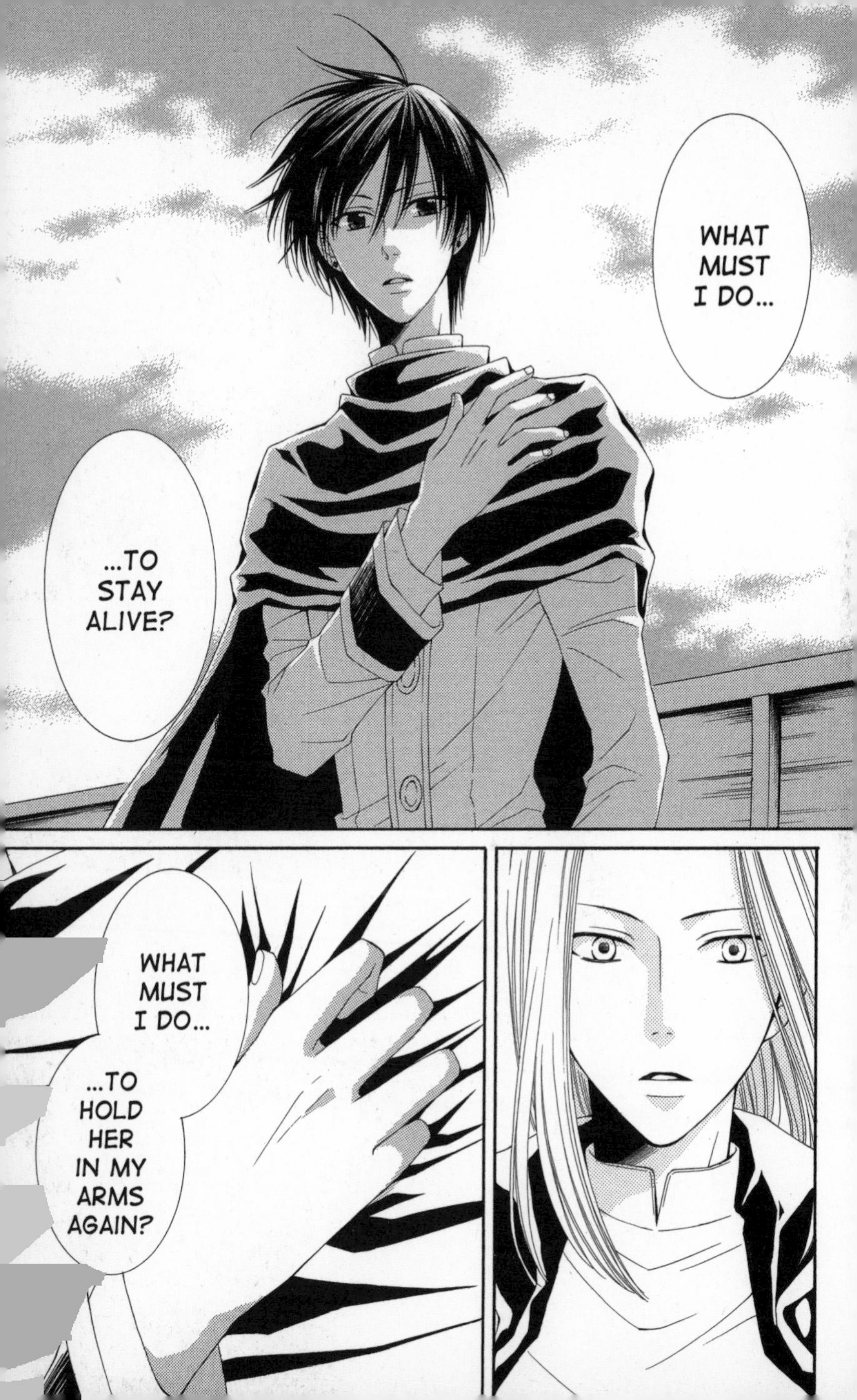
WHAT MUST I DO...
...TO STAY ALIVE?
WHAT MUST I DO...
...TO HOLD HER IN MY ARMS AGAIN?

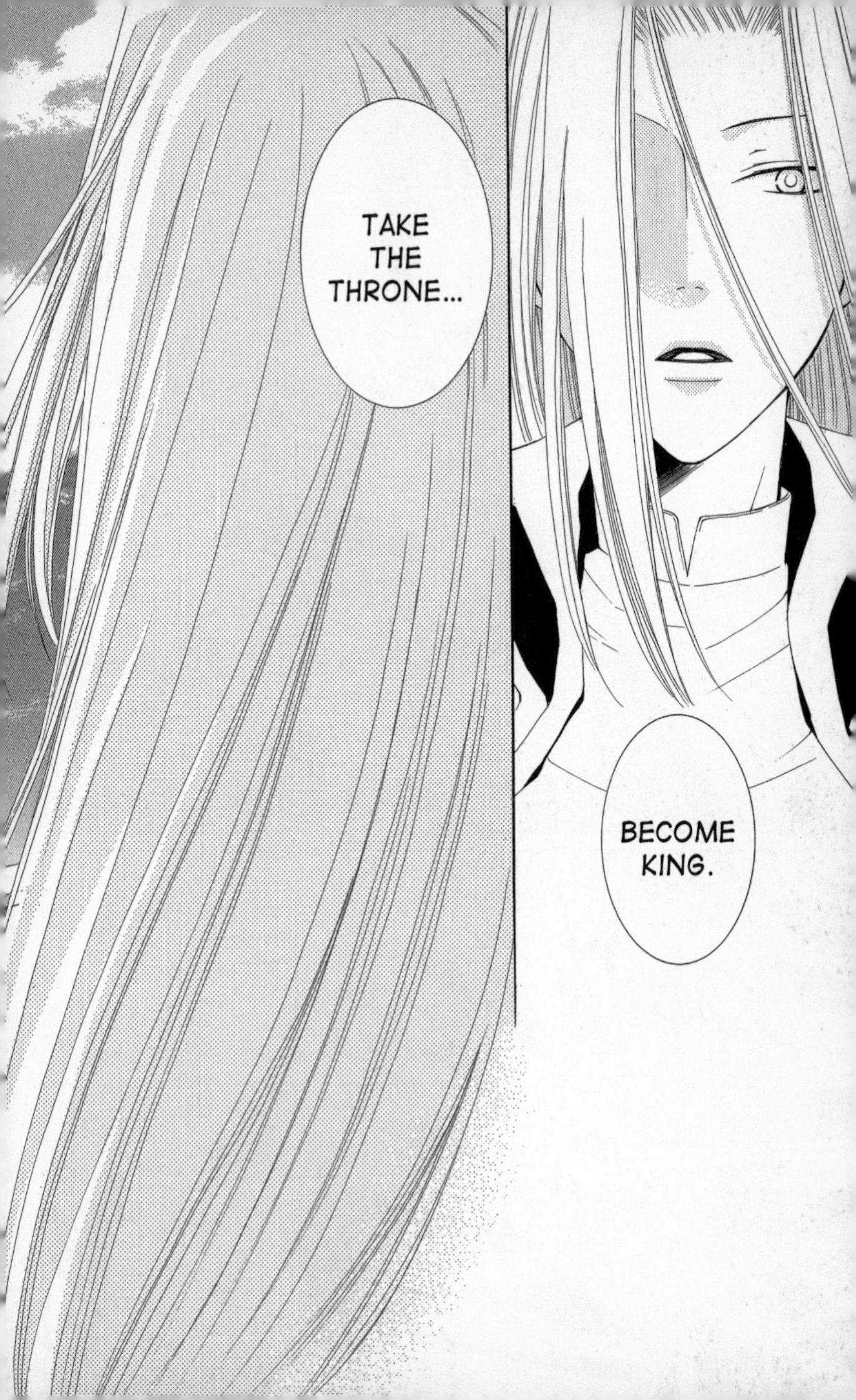
TAKE THE THRONE...
BECOME KING.

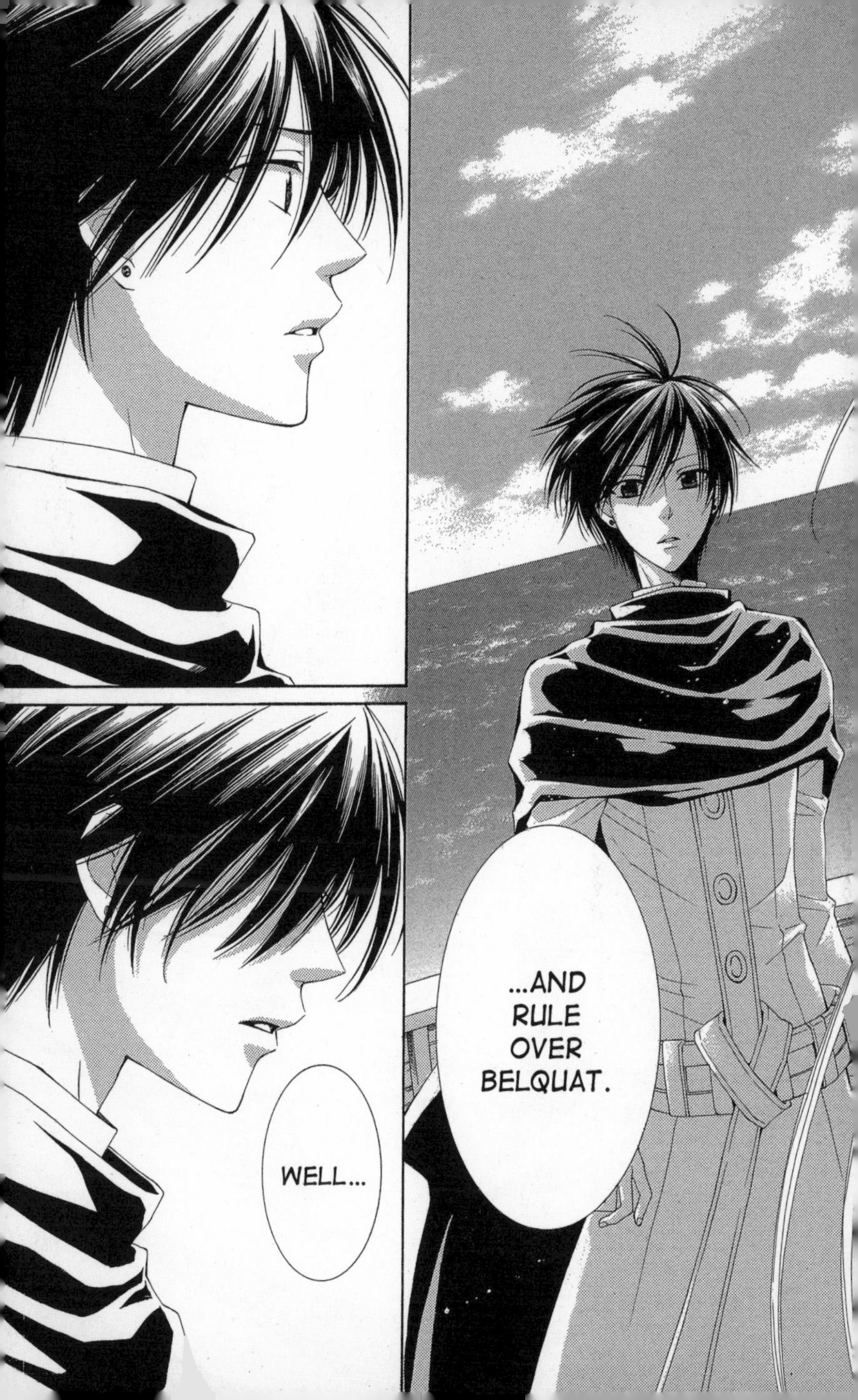
...AND RULE OVER BELQUAT.
WELL...

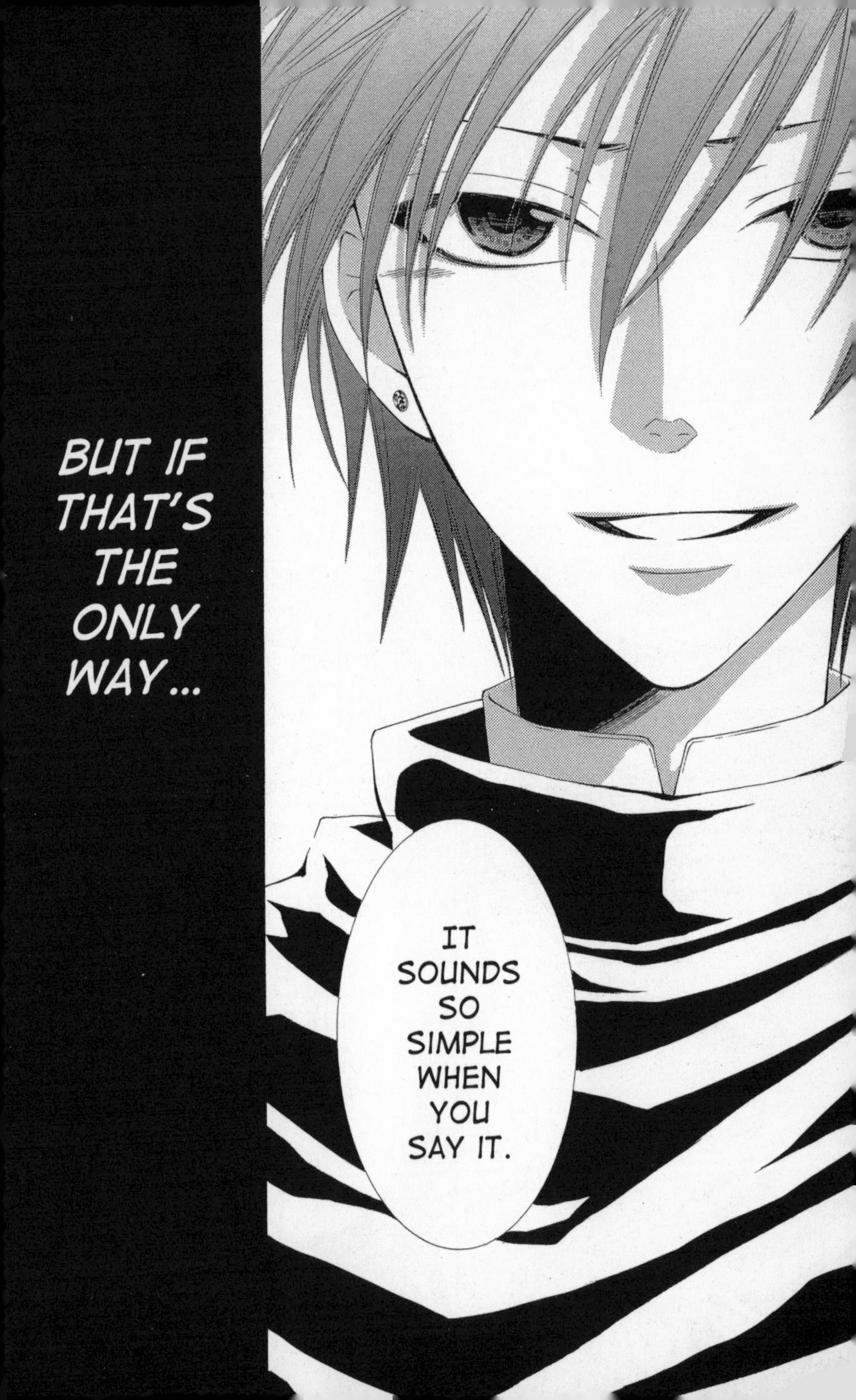
IT SOUNDS SO SIMPLE WHEN YOU SAY IT.
BUT IF THAT'S THE ONLY WAY...

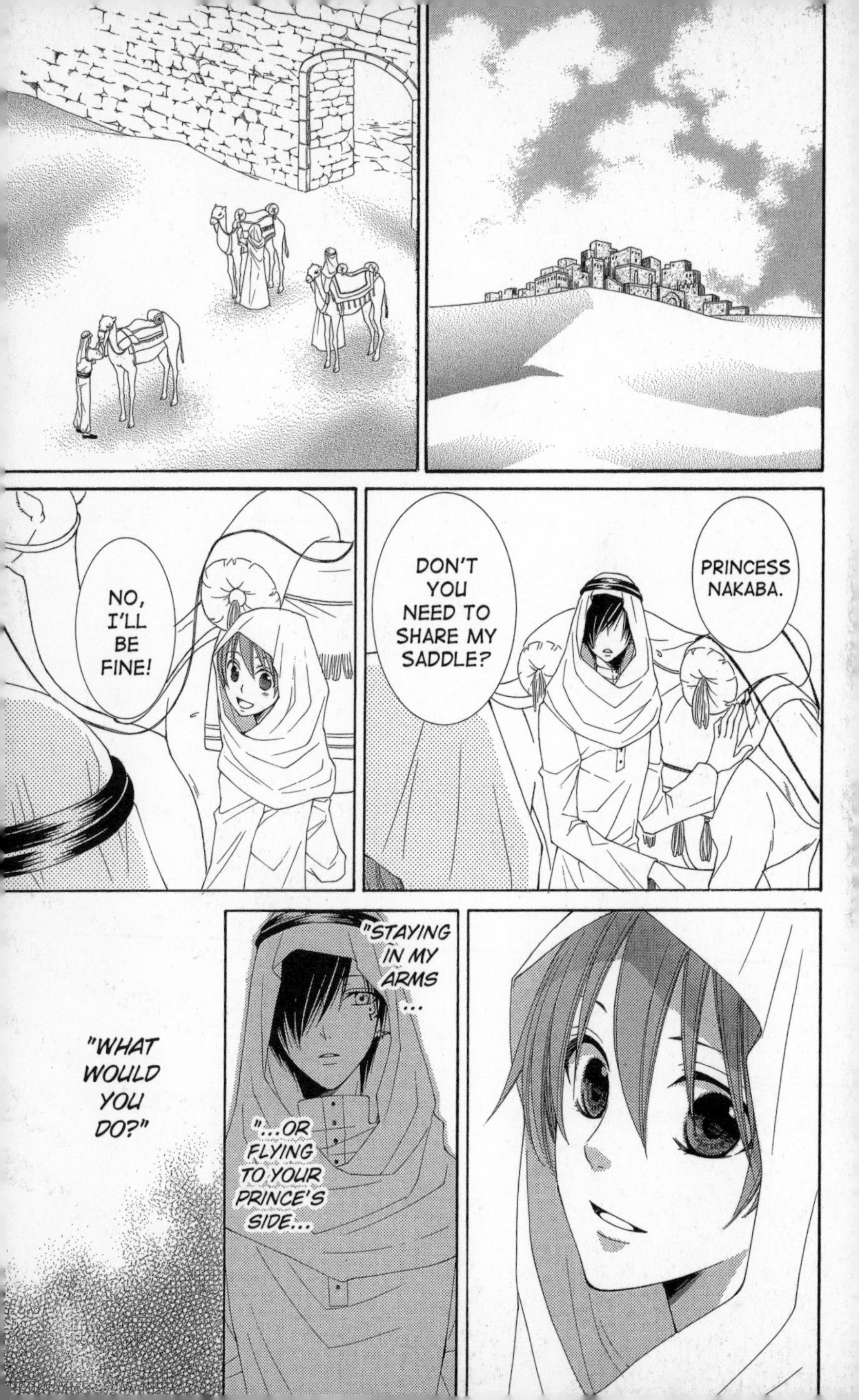
PRINCESS NAKABA.
DON'T YOU NEED TO SHARE MY SADDLE?
NO, I'LL BE FINE!
"STAYING IN MY ARMS ...
"...OR FLYING TO YOUR PRINCE'S SIDE...
"WHAT WOULD YOU DO?"

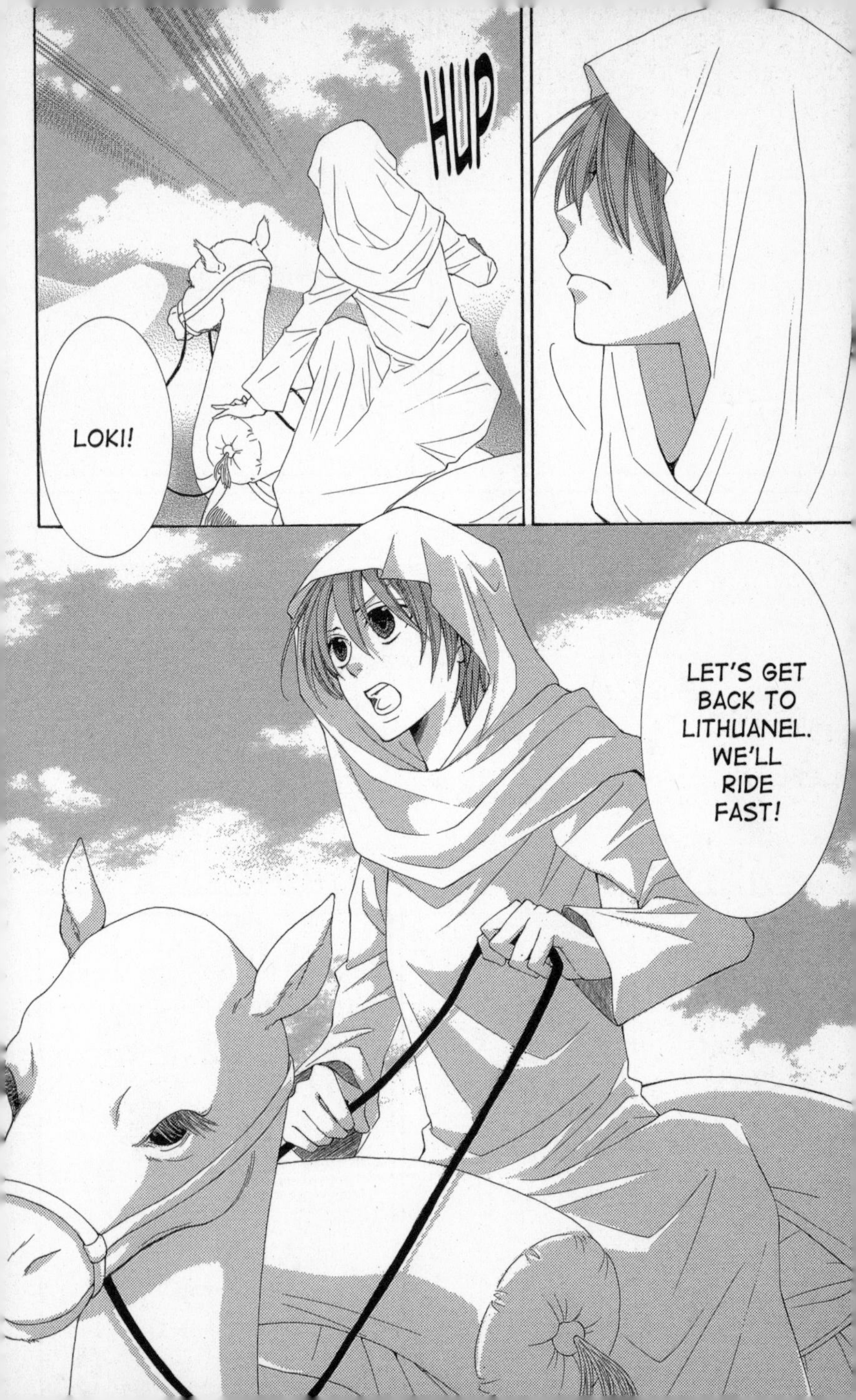
HUP
LOKI!
LET'S GET BACK TO LITHUANEL. WE'LL RIDE FAST!

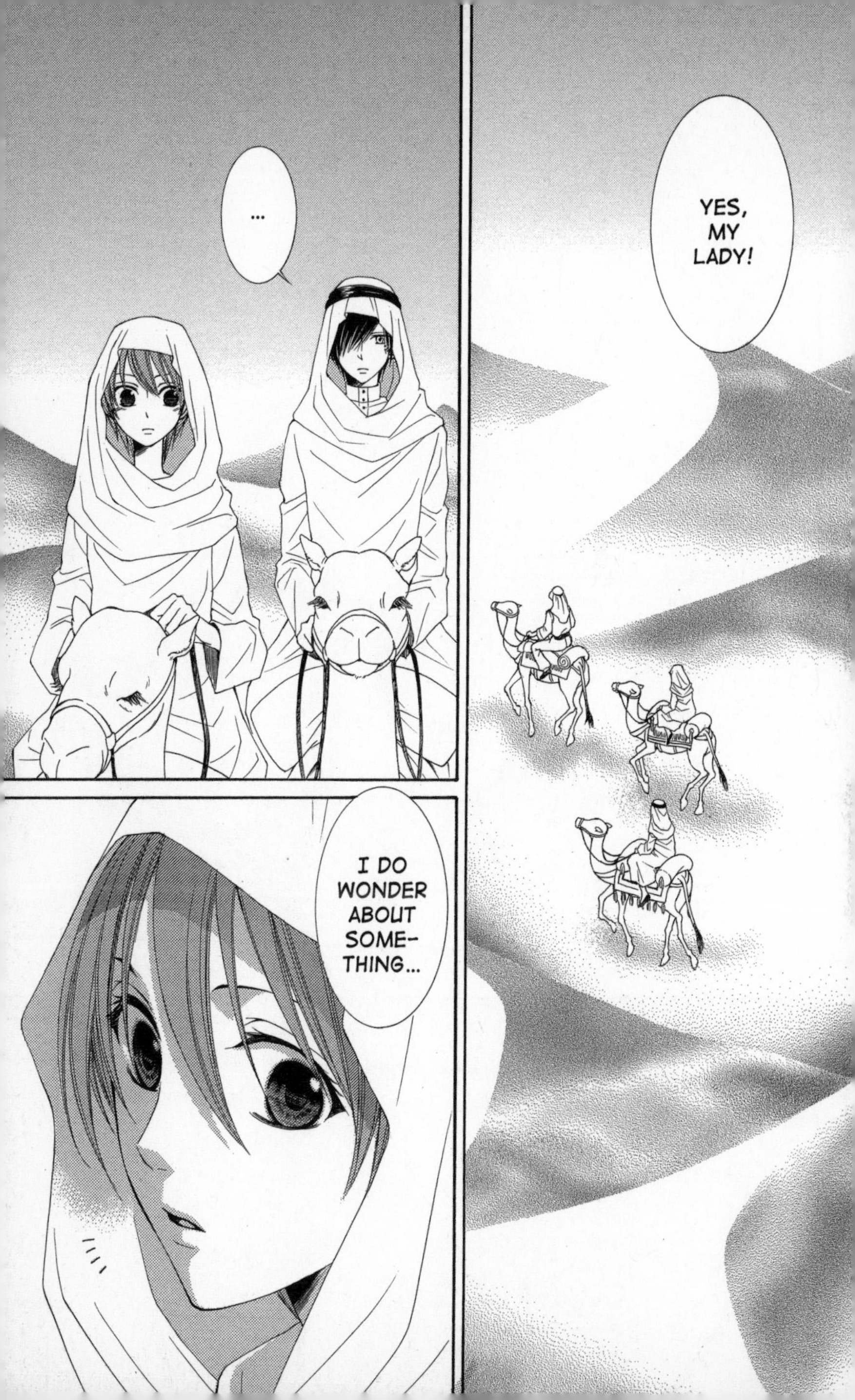
YES, MY LADY!
...
I DO WONDER ABOUT SOME-THING...

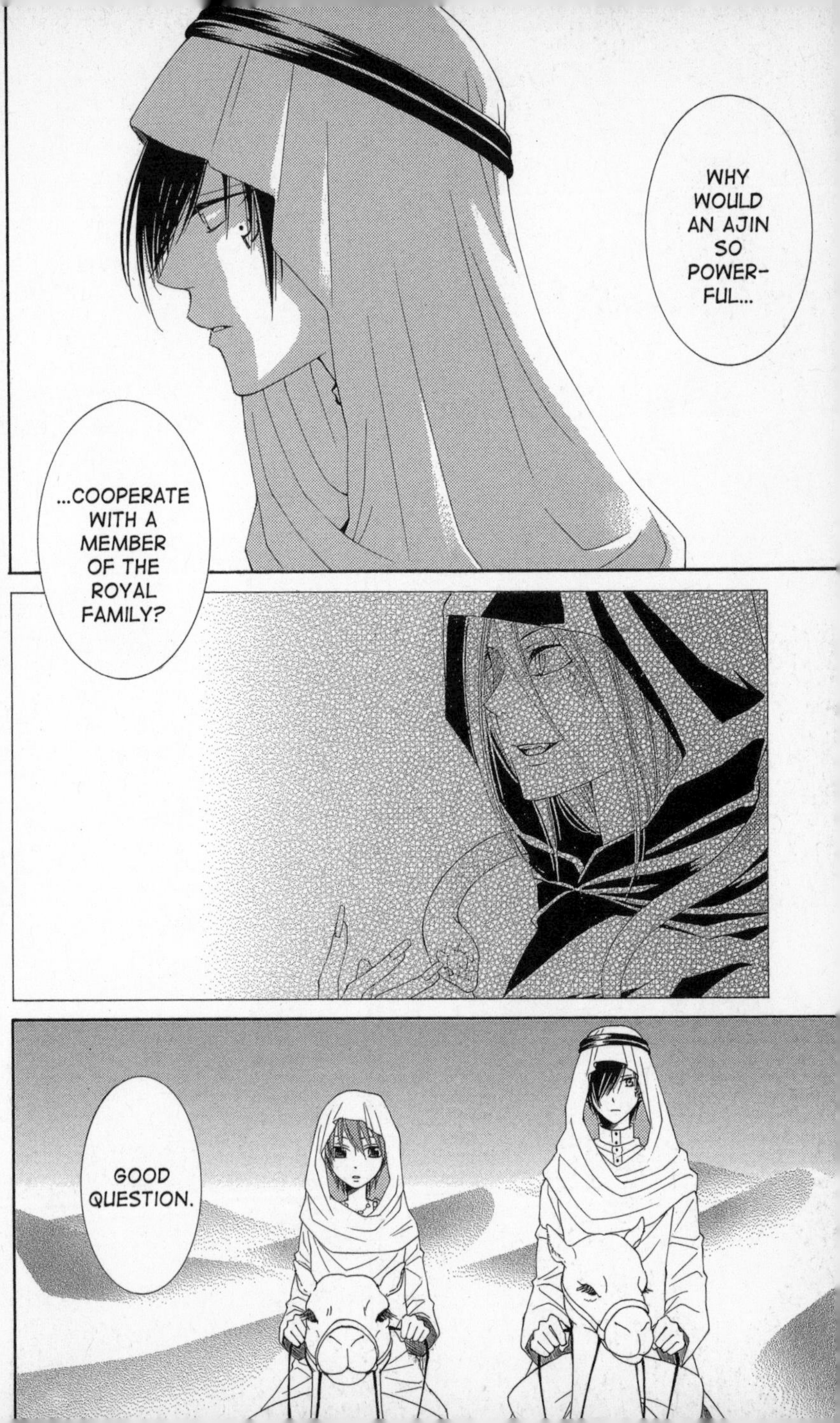
WHY WOULD AN AJIN SO POWER-FUL...
...COOPERATE WITH A MEMBER OF THE ROYAL FAMILY?
GOOD QUESTION.

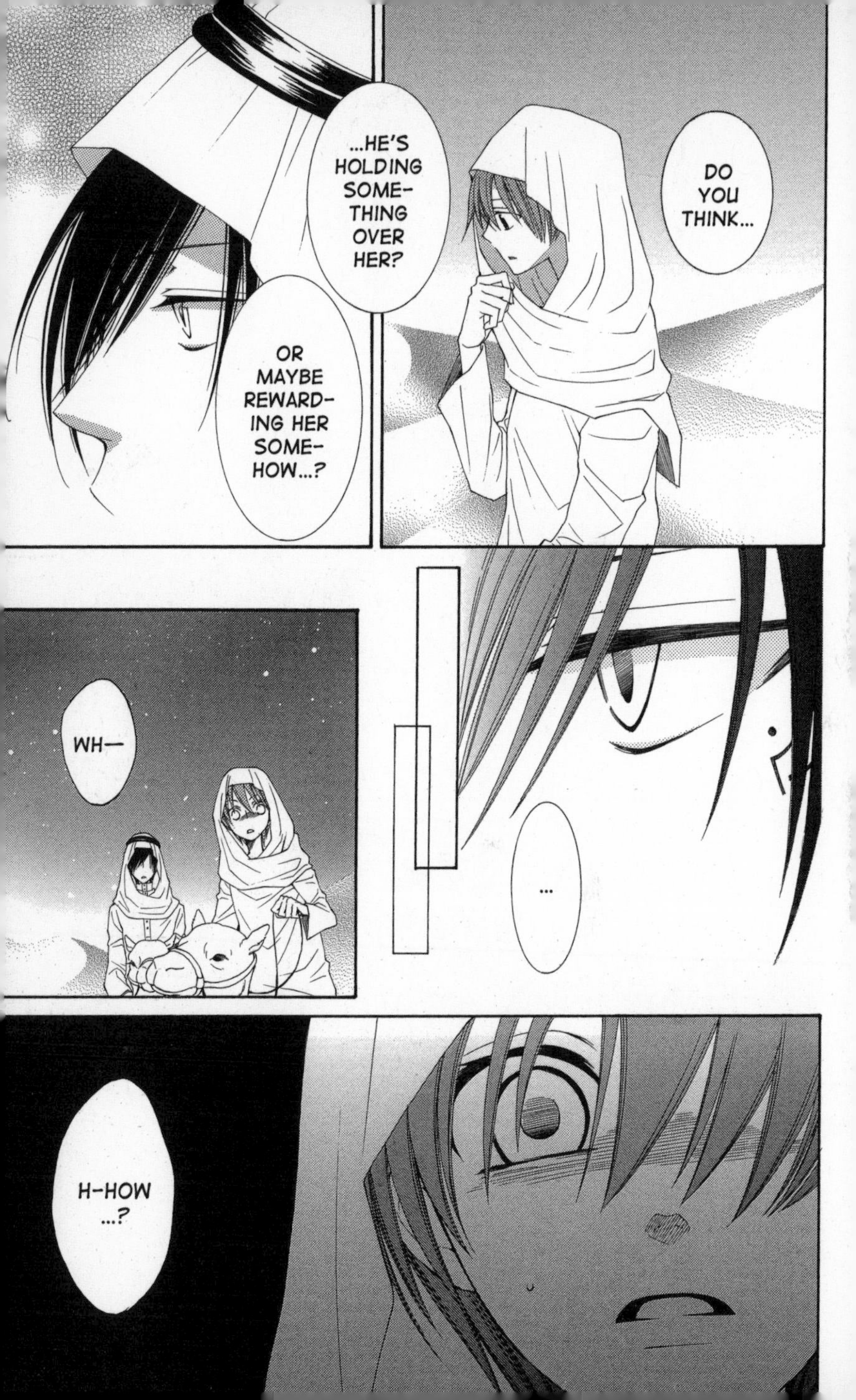
DO YOU THINK...
...HE'S HOLDING SOME-THING OVER HER?
OR MAYBE REWARD-ING HER SOME-HOW...?
...
WH—
H-HOW ...?

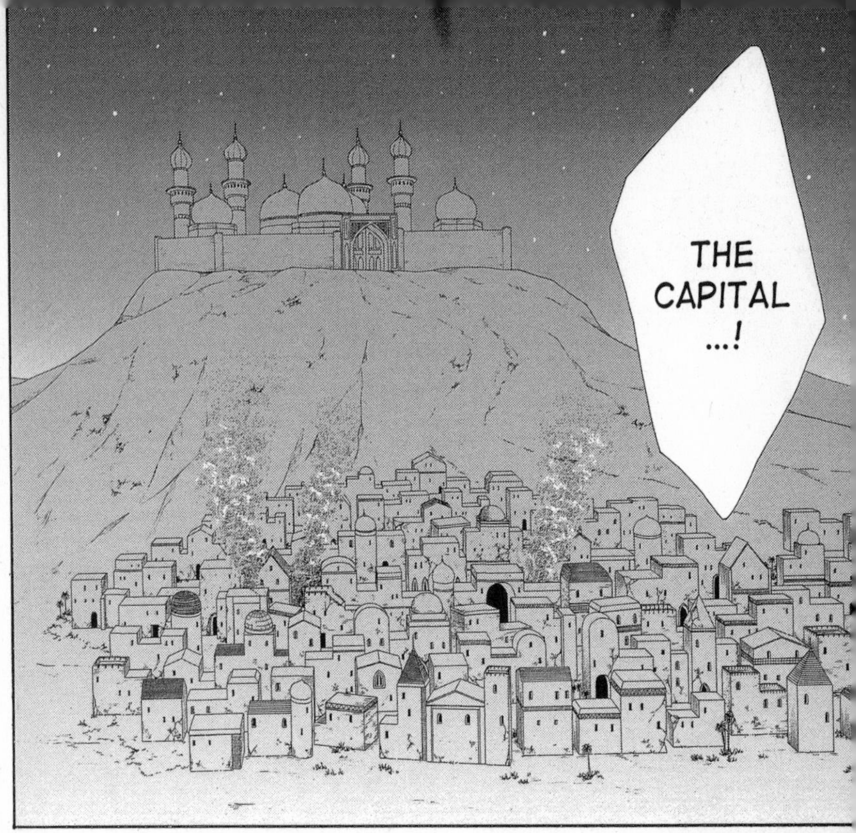
THE CAPITAL ...!
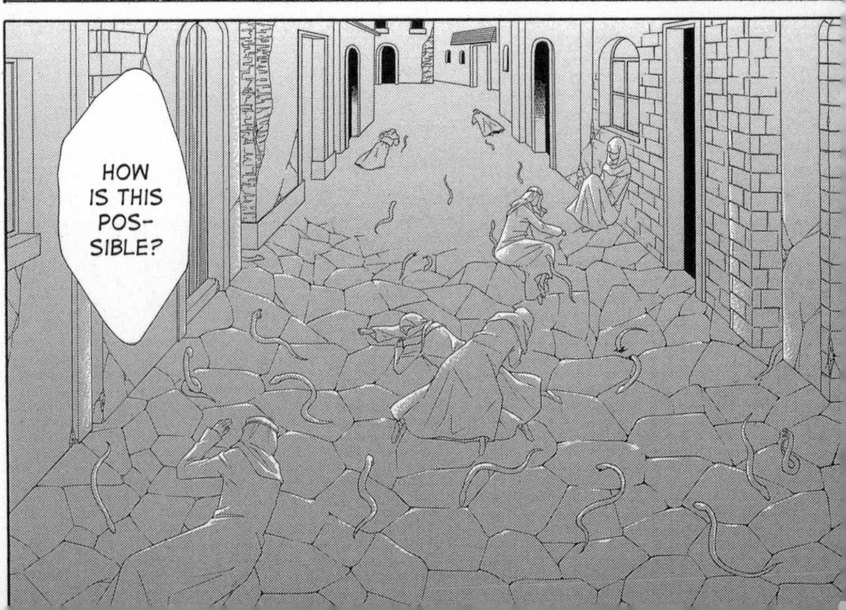
HOW IS THIS POS-SIBLE?

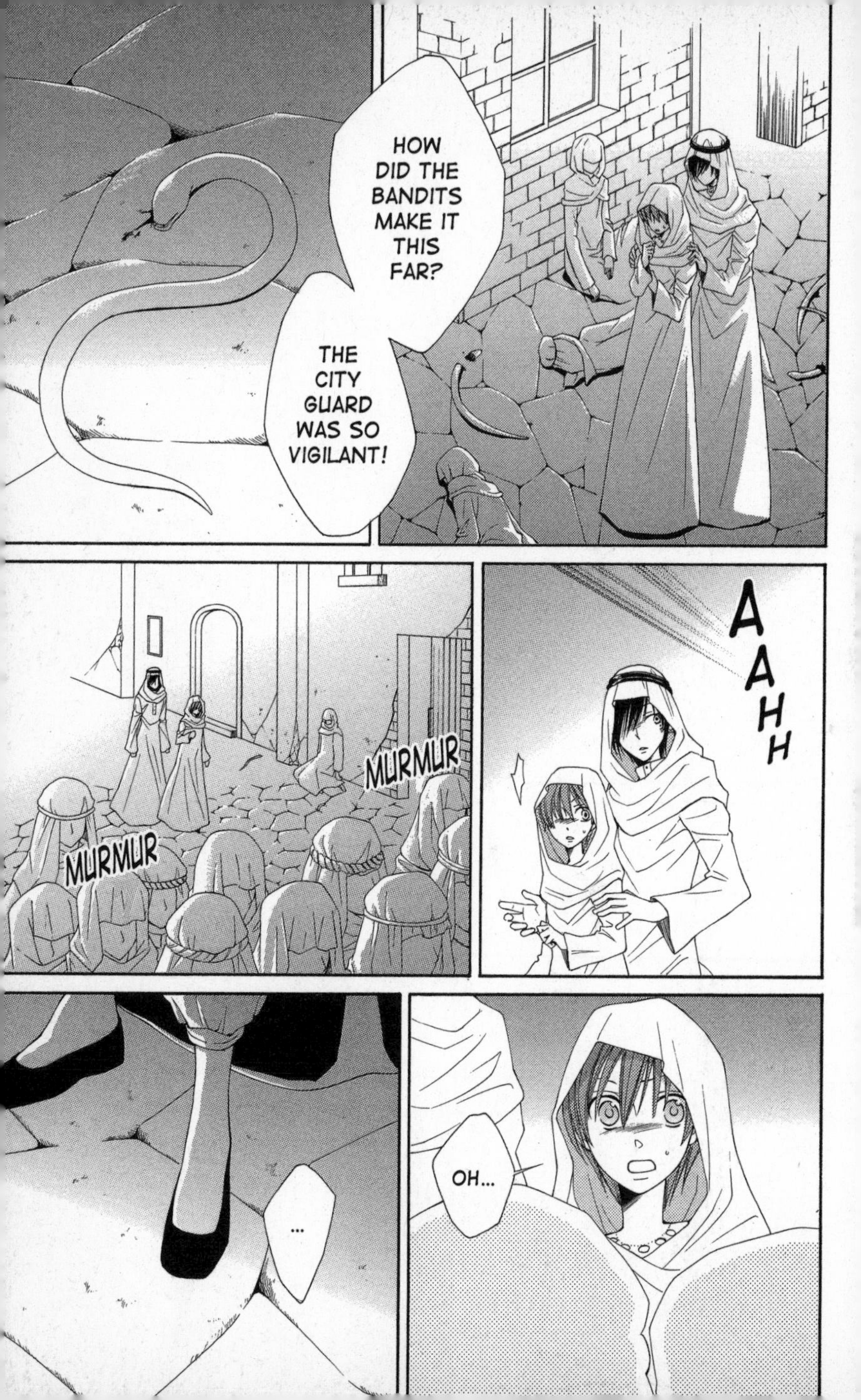
HOW DID THE BANDITS MAKE IT THIS FAR?
THE CITY GUARD WAS SO VIGILANT!
AAHH
MURMUR
MURMUR
OH...
...

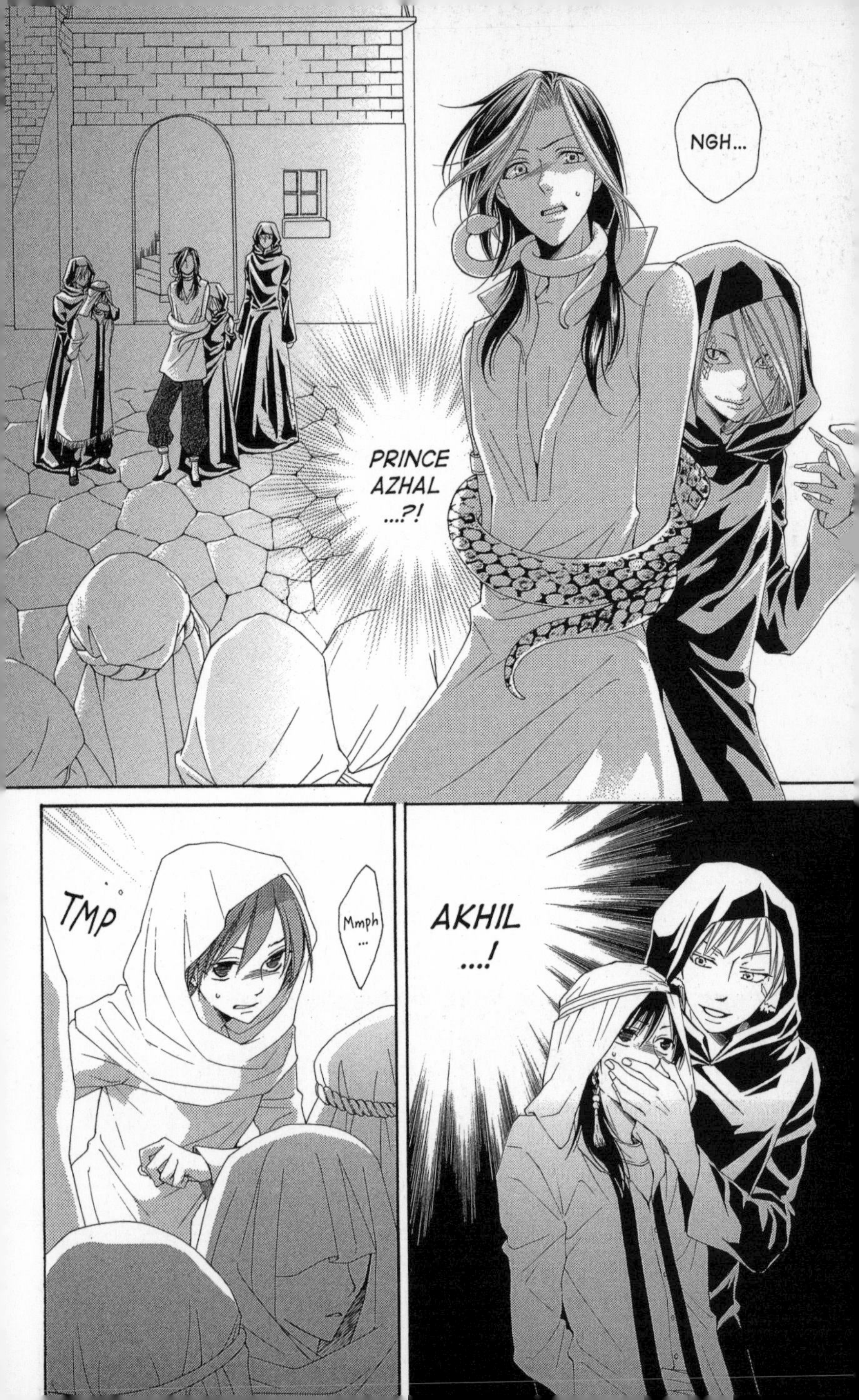
NGH...
PRINCE AZHAL ...?!
AKHIL ...!
Mmph ...
TMP

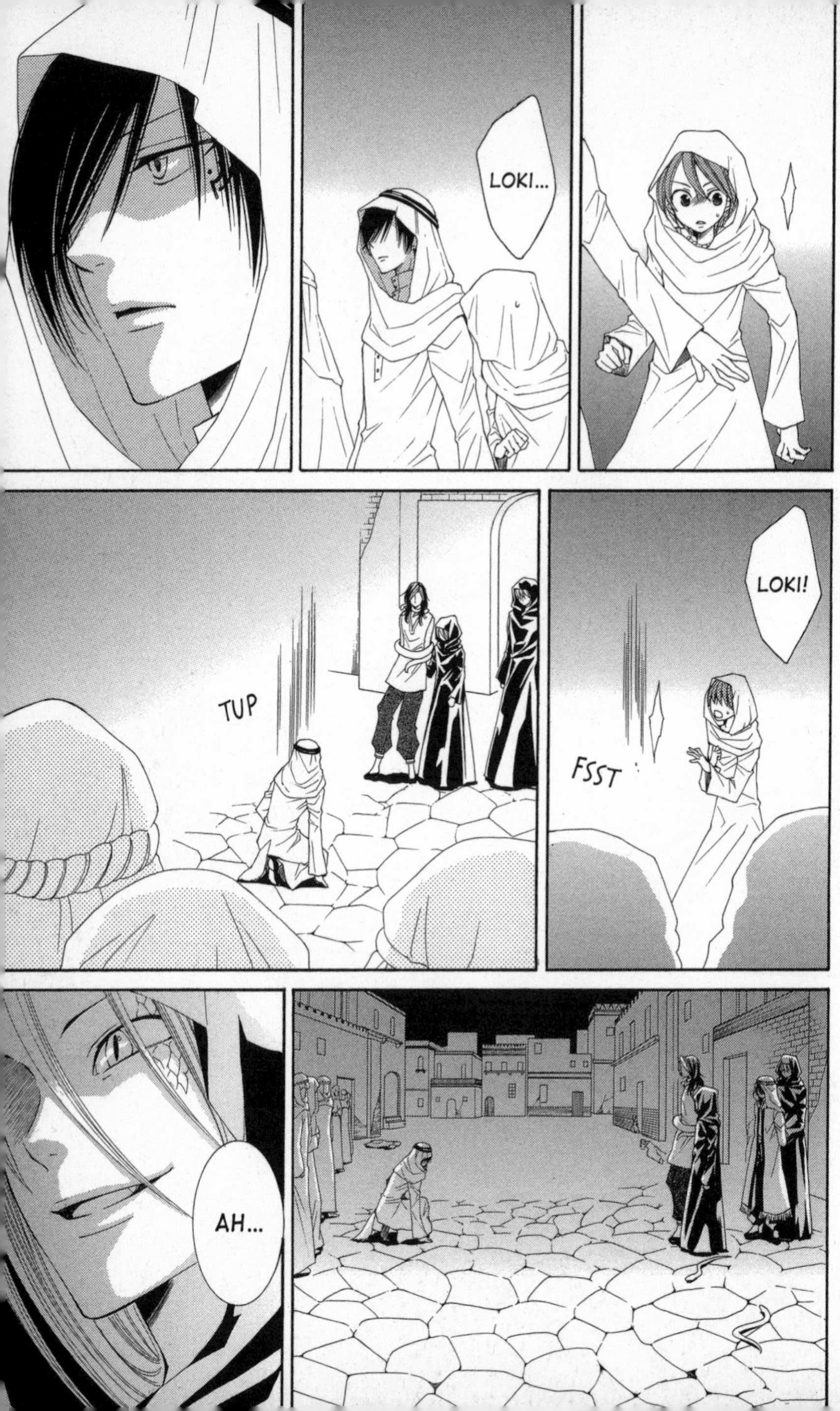
LOKI...
LOKI!
FSST
TUP
AH...

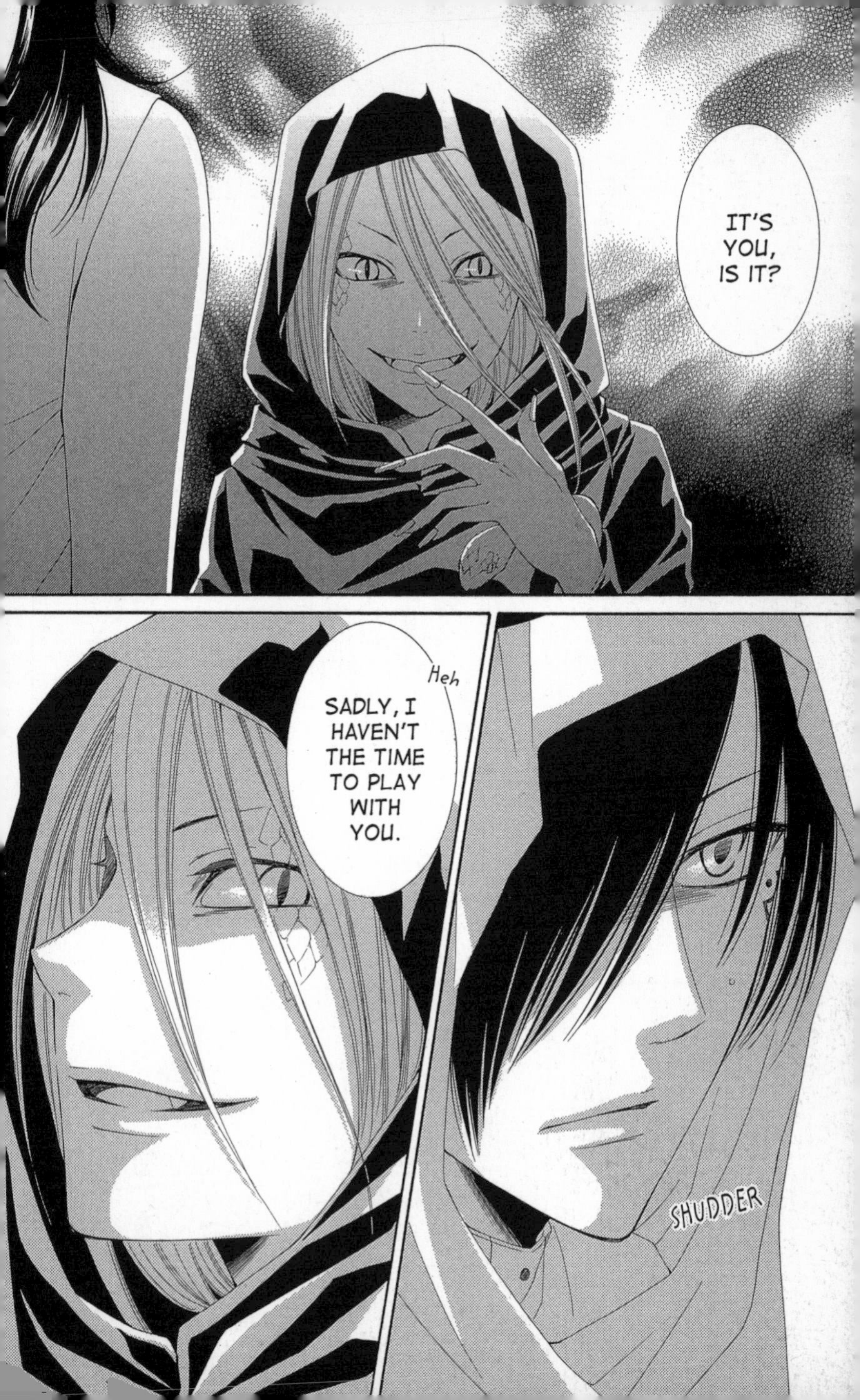
IT'S YOU, IS IT?
Heh
SADLY, I HAVEN'T THE TIME TO PLAY WITH YOU.
SHUDDER

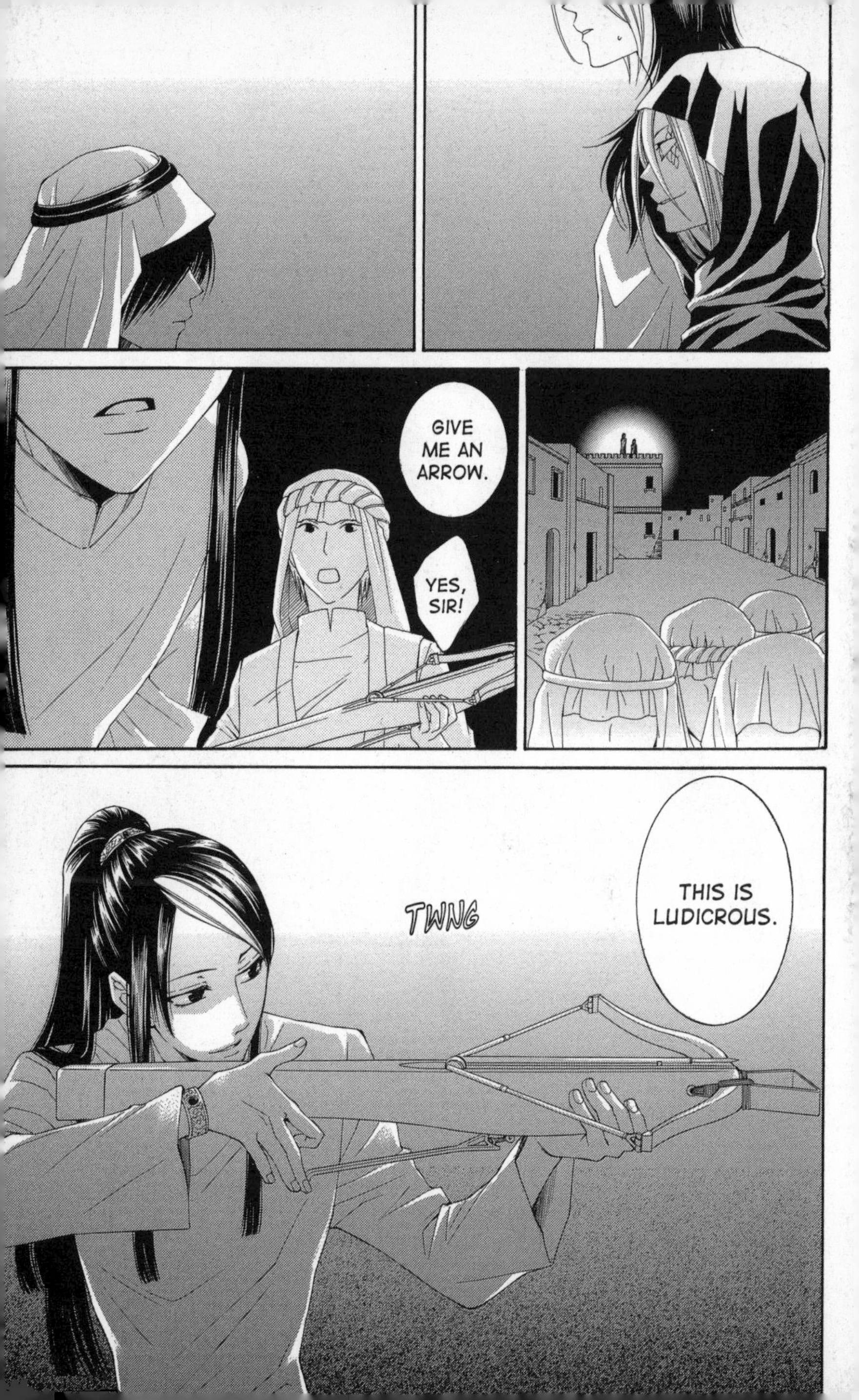
GIVE ME AN ARROW.
YES, SIR!
THIS IS LUDICROUS.
TWNG

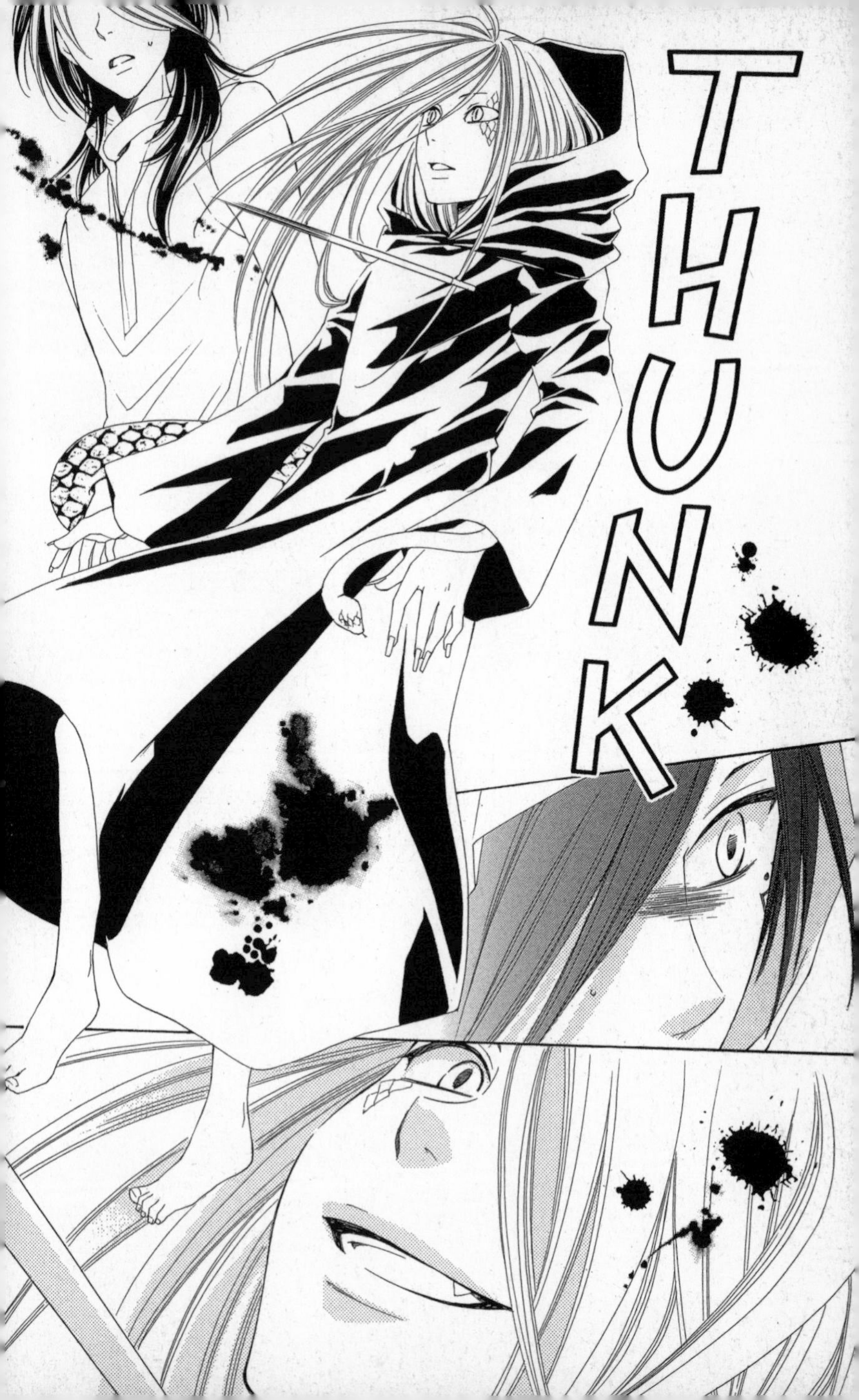
THUNK

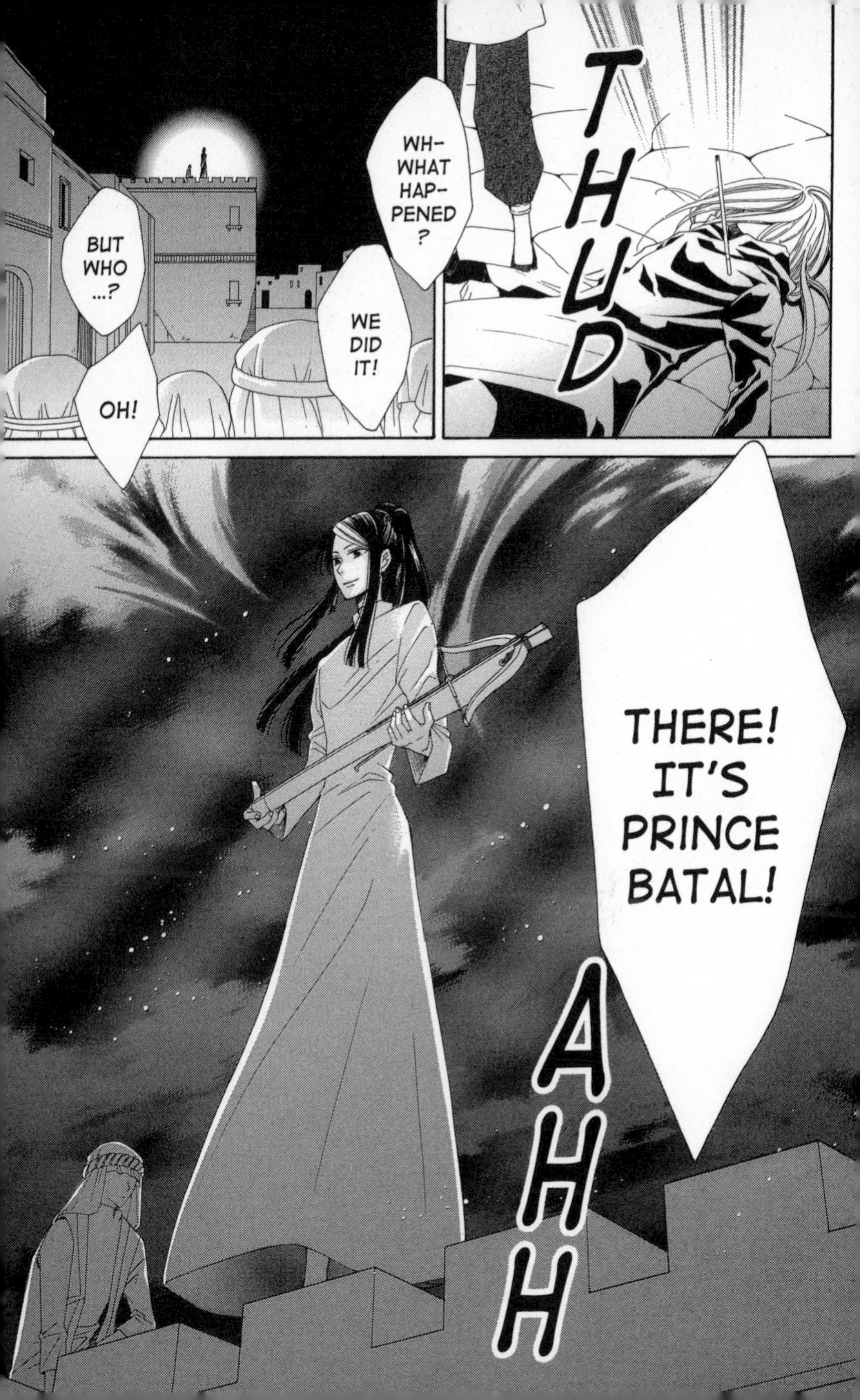
THUD
WH-WHAT HAP-PENED?
BUT WHO ...?
WE DID IT!
OH!
THERE! IT'S PRINCE BATAL!
AHHH

エラーヘア
Elaheh

I rather like her.

Chapter 35

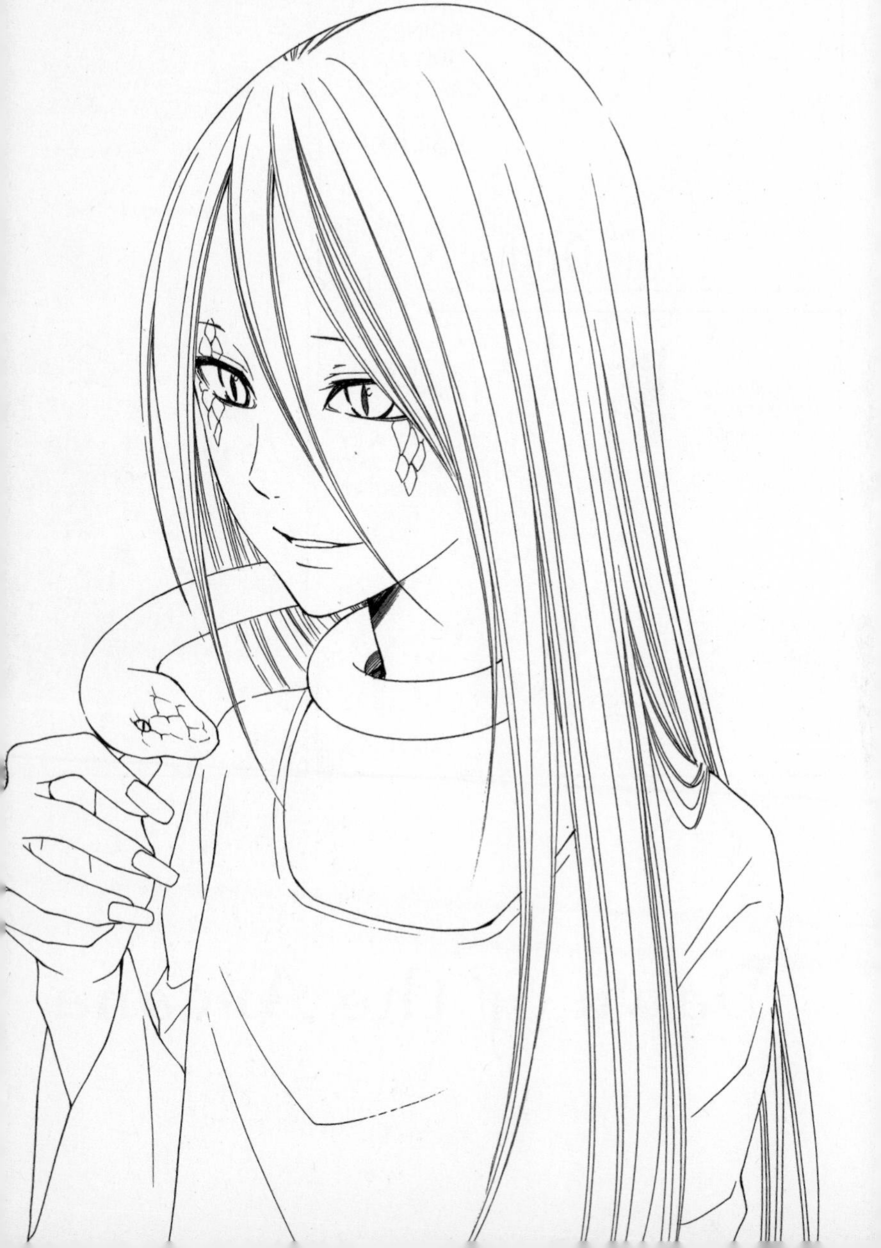

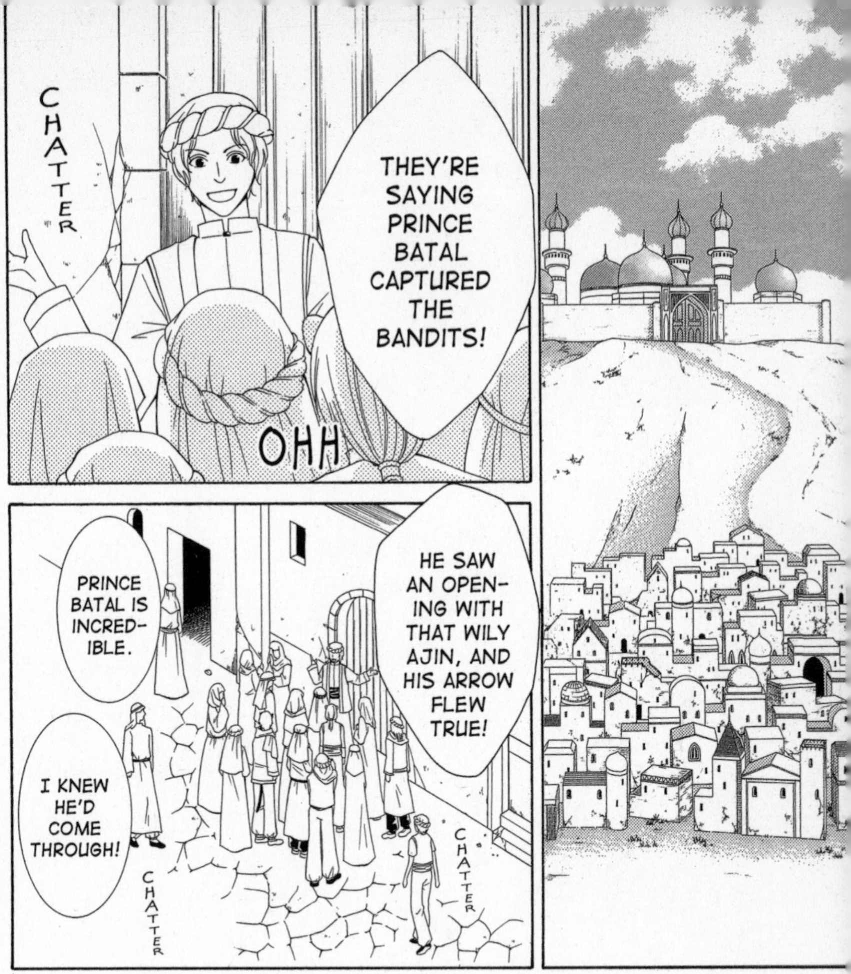
THEY'RE SAYING PRINCE BATAL CAPTURED THE BANDITS!
CHATTER
OHH
HE SAW AN OPEN-ING WITH THAT WILY AJIN, AND HIS ARROW FLEW TRUE!
PRINCE BATAL IS INCRED-IBLE.
CHATTER
I KNEW HE'D COME THROUGH!
CHATTER

Dawn of the Arcana

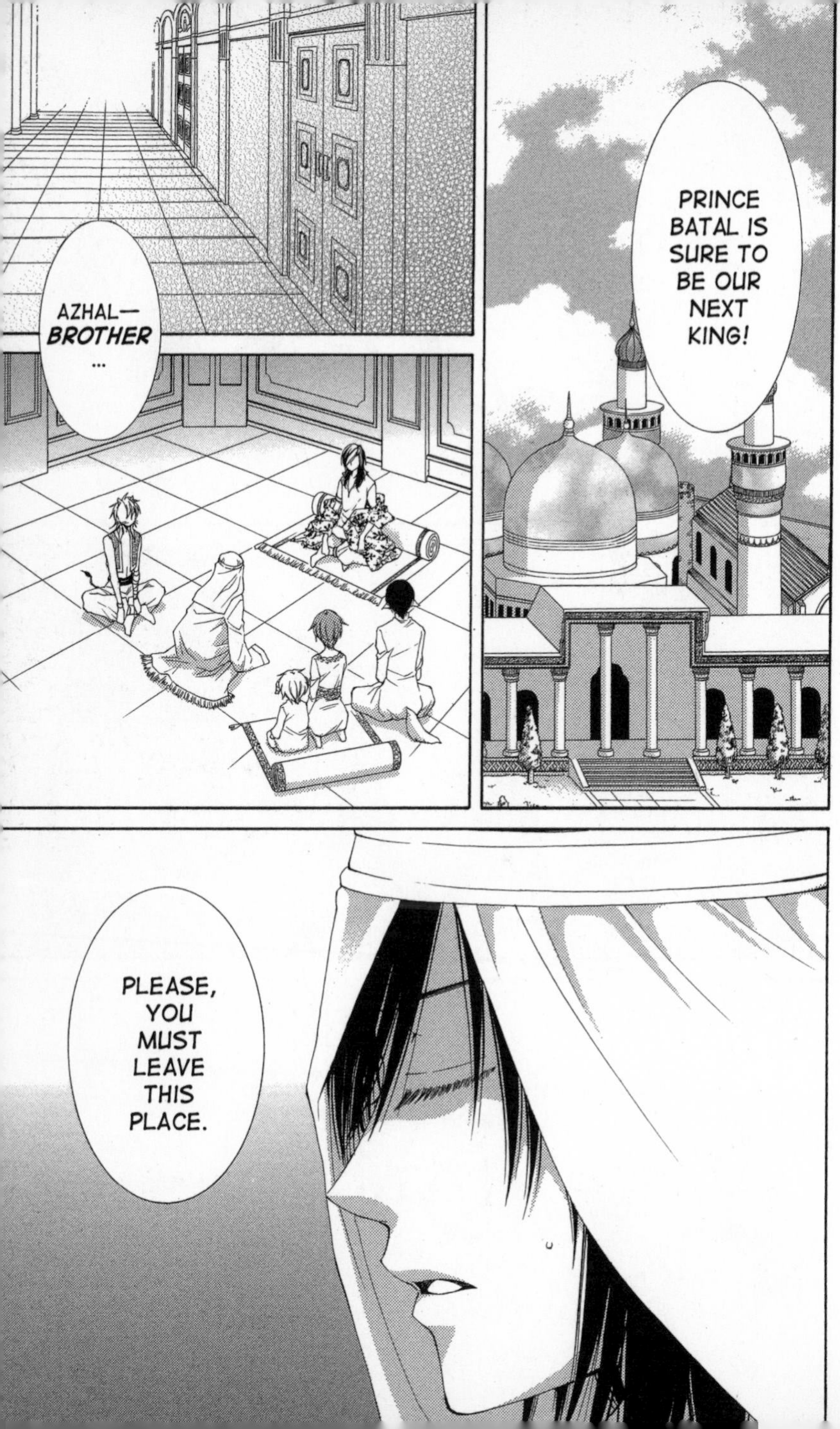
PRINCE BATAL IS SURE TO BE OUR NEXT KING!
AZHAL—BROTHER...
PLEASE, YOU MUST LEAVE THIS PLACE.

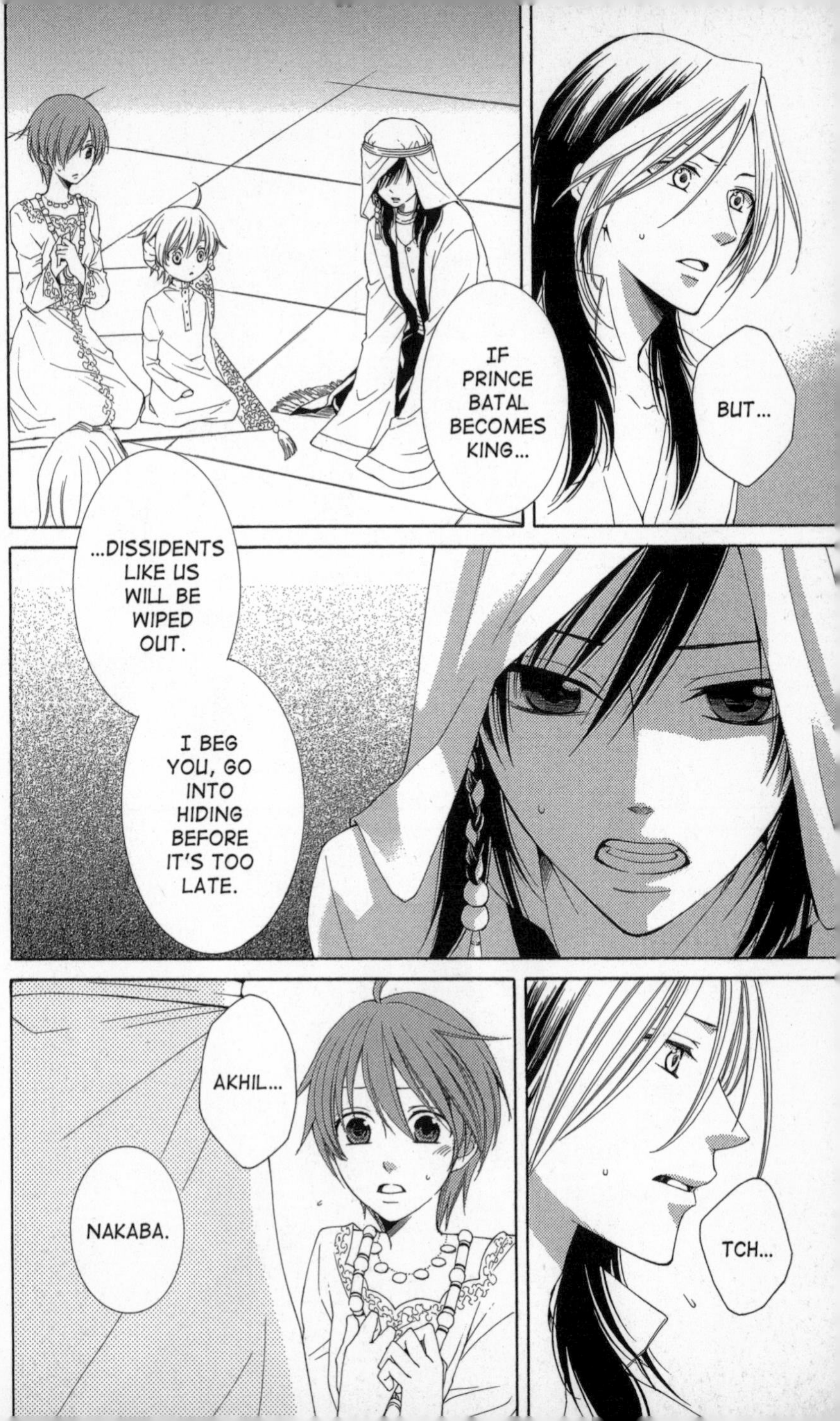
BUT...
IF PRINCE BATAL BECOMES KING...
...DISSIDENTS LIKE US WILL BE WIPED OUT.
I BEG YOU, GO INTO HIDING BEFORE IT'S TOO LATE.
TCH...
AKHIL...
NAKABA.

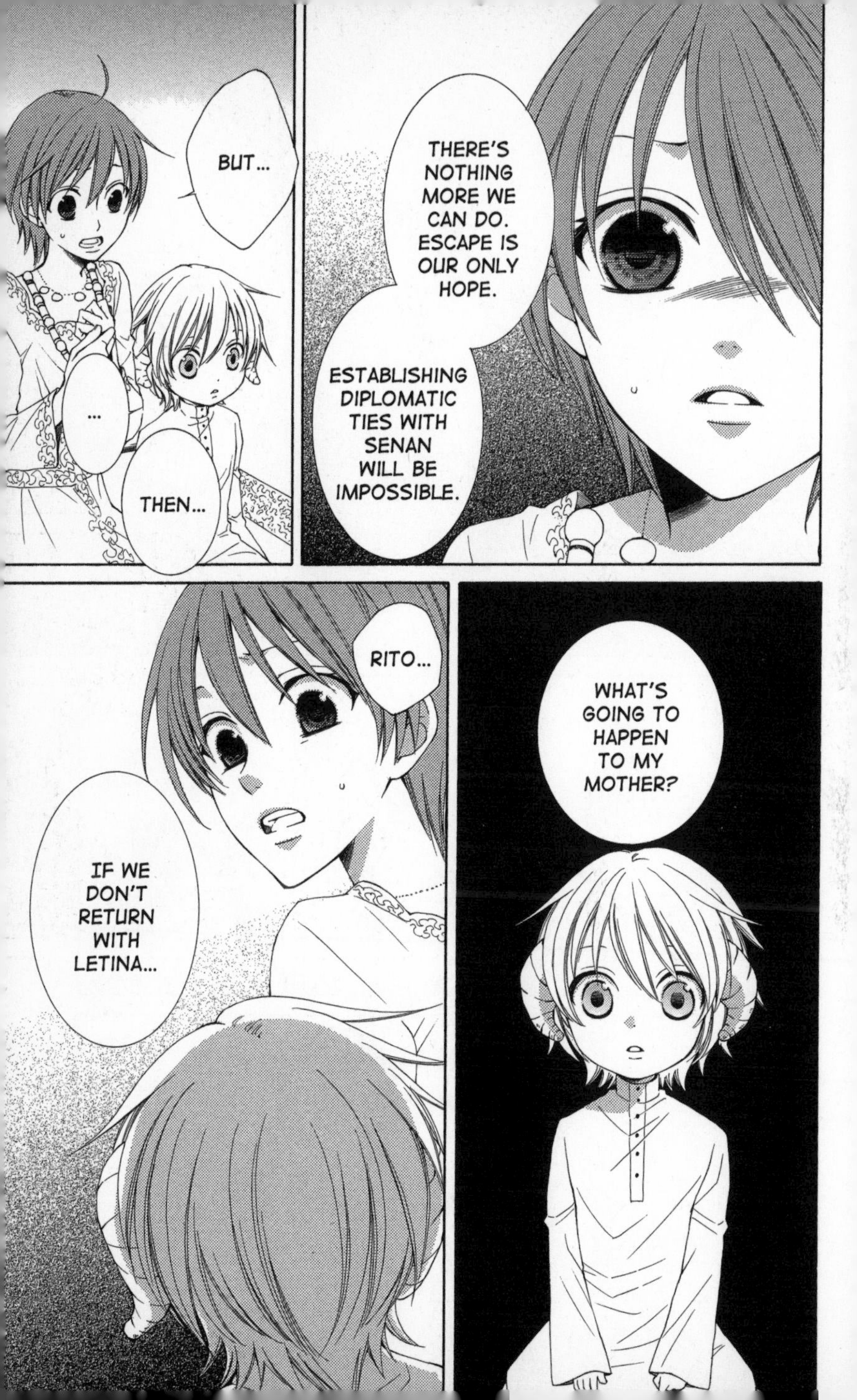
THERE'S NOTHING MORE WE CAN DO. ESCAPE IS OUR ONLY HOPE.
ESTABLISHING DIPLOMATIC TIES WITH SENAN WILL BE IMPOSSIBLE.
BUT...
...
THEN...
WHAT'S GOING TO HAPPEN TO MY MOTHER?
RITO...
IF WE DON'T RETURN WITH LETINA...

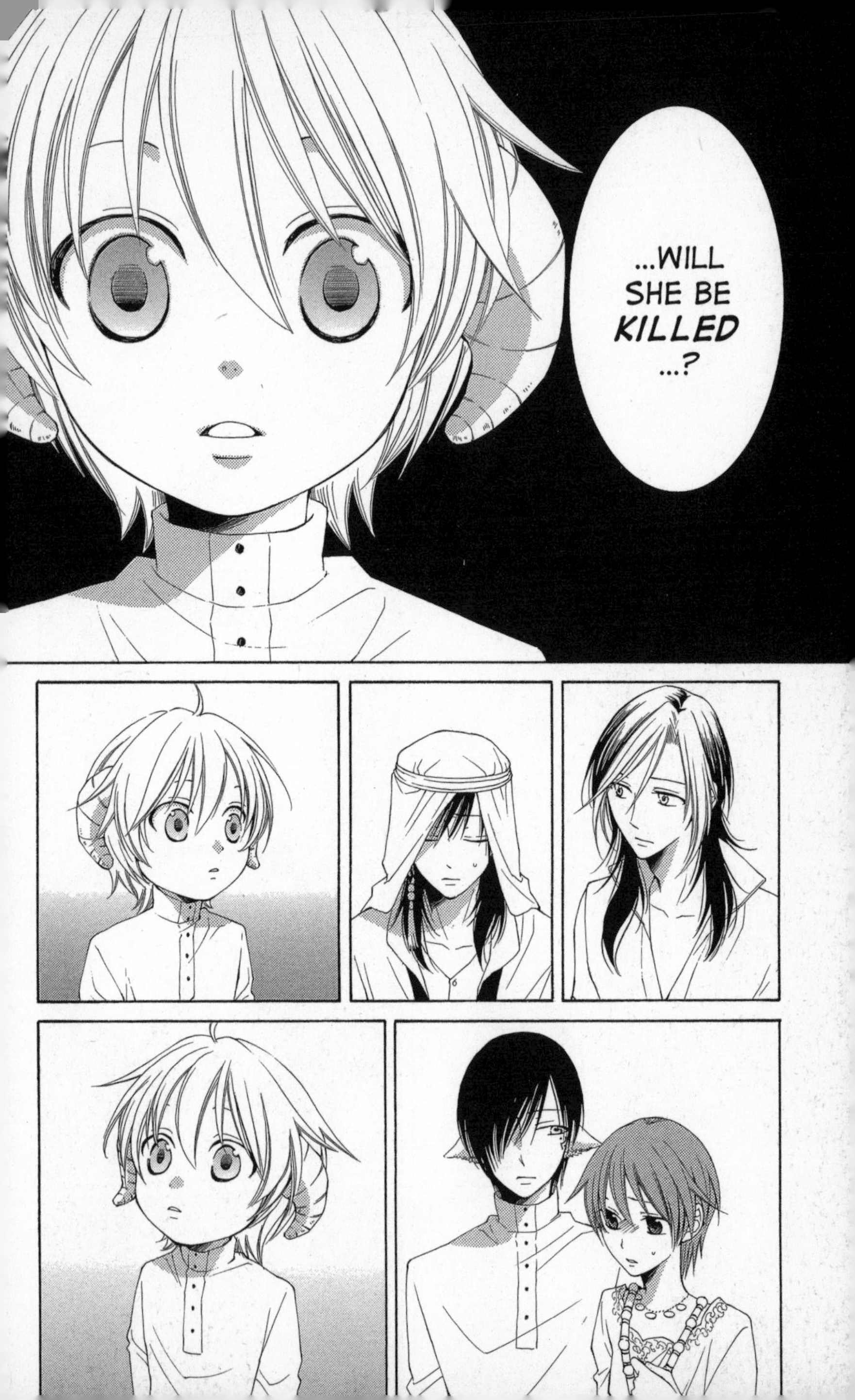
...WILL SHE BE *KILLED* ...?

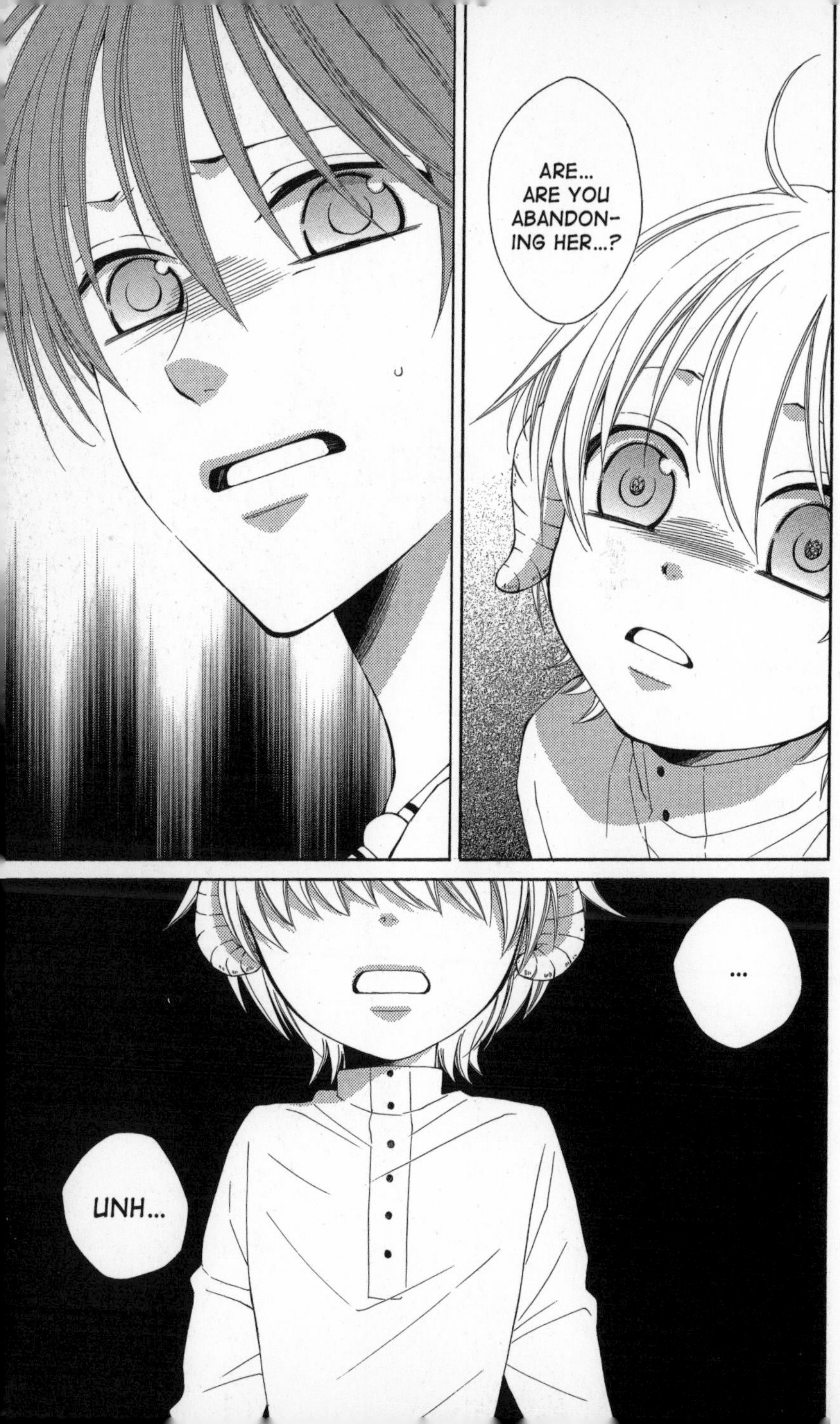
ARE... ARE YOU ABANDONING HER...?
...
UNH...

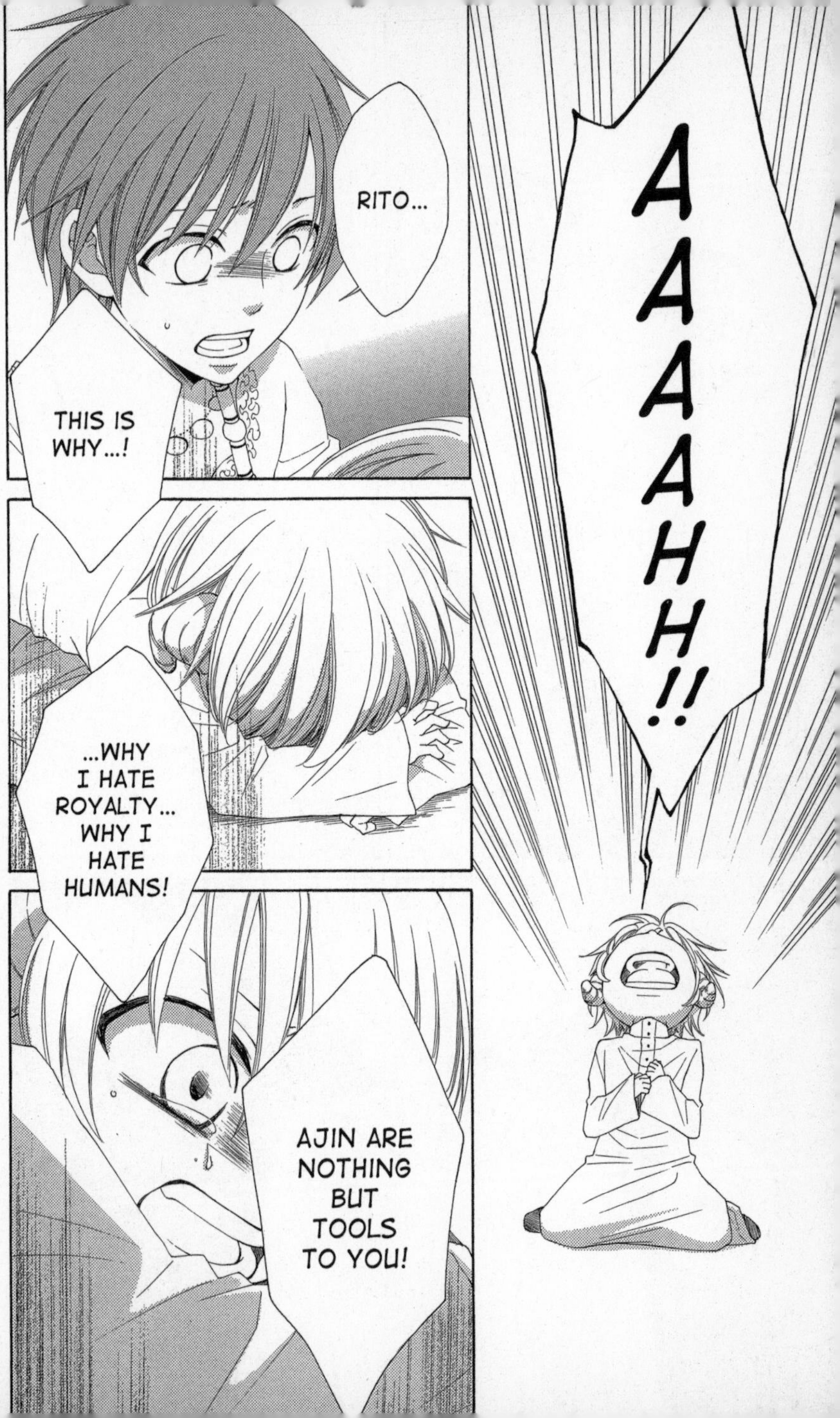
AAAAHH!!
RITO...
THIS IS WHY...!
...WHY I HATE ROYALTY... WHY I HATE HUMANS!
AJIN ARE NOTHING BUT TOOLS TO YOU!

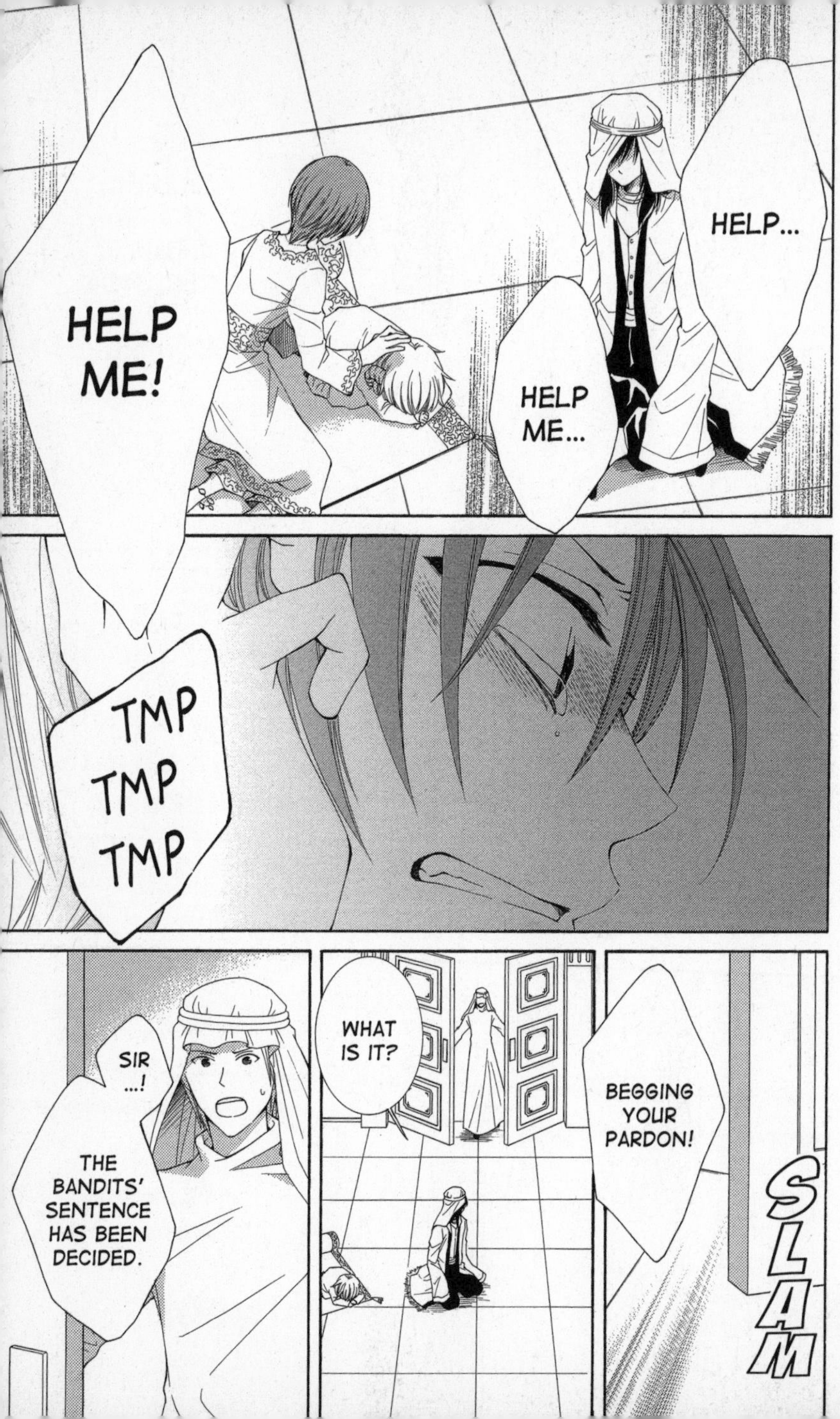
HELP...
HELP ME...
HELP ME!
TMP TMP TMP
BEGGING YOUR PARDON!
SLAM
WHAT IS IT?
SIR ...!
THE BANDITS' SENTENCE HAS BEEN DECIDED.

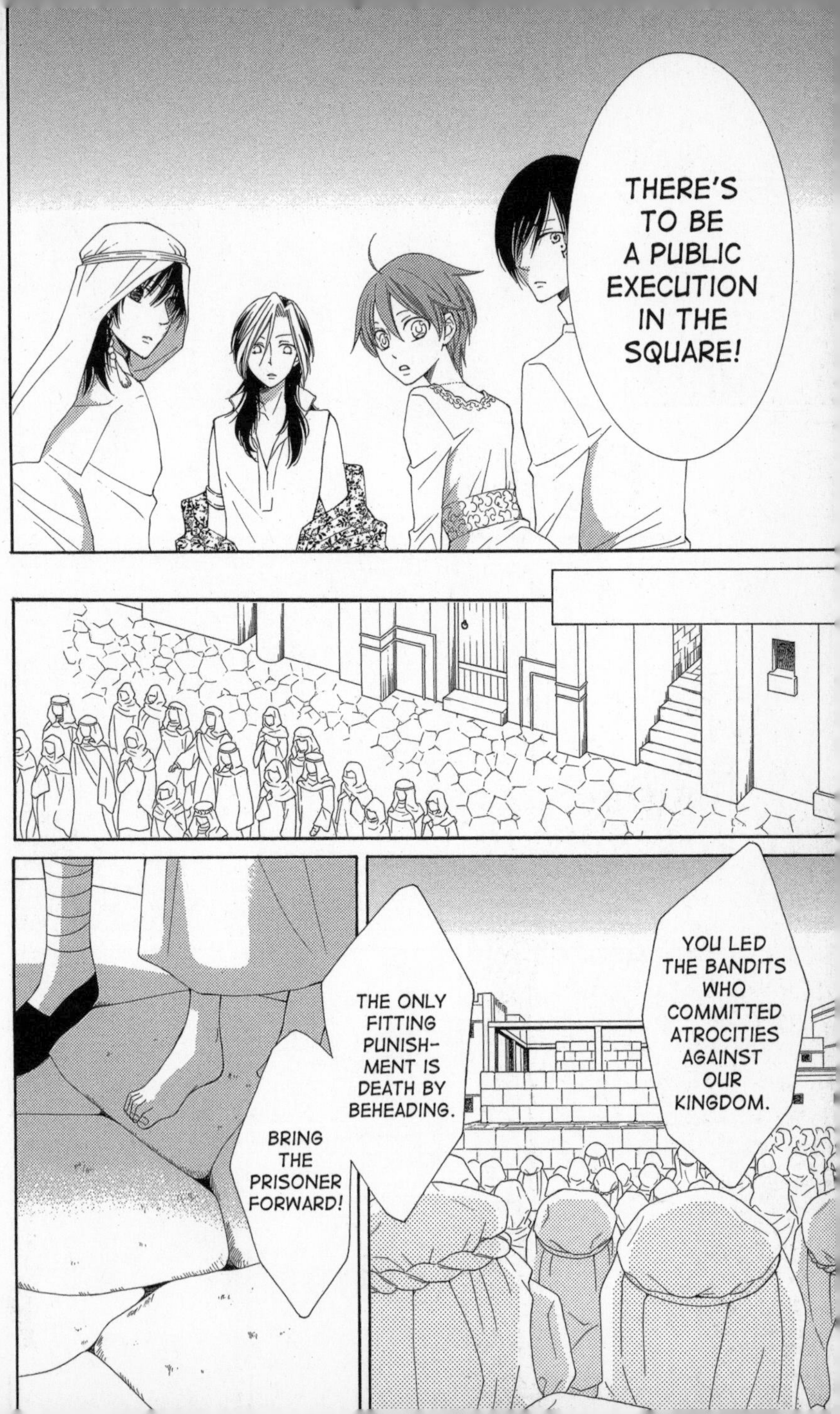
THERE'S TO BE A PUBLIC EXECUTION IN THE SQUARE!
YOU LED THE BANDITS WHO COMMITTED ATROCITIES AGAINST OUR KINGDOM.
THE ONLY FITTING PUNISH-MENT IS DEATH BY BEHEADING.
BRING THE PRISONER FORWARD!

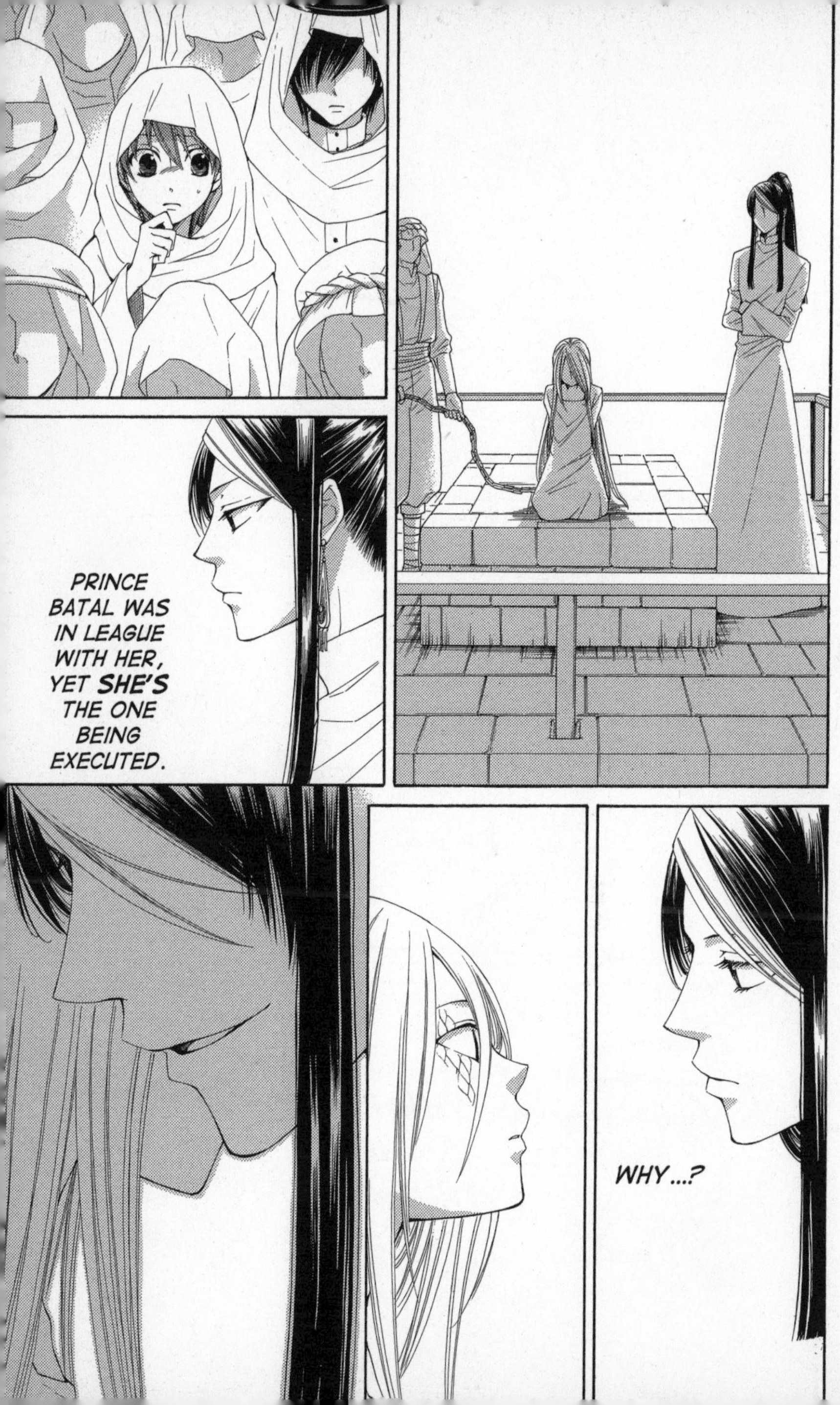
PRINCE BATAL WAS IN LEAGUE WITH HER, YET **SHE'S** THE ONE BEING EXECUTED.
WHY...?

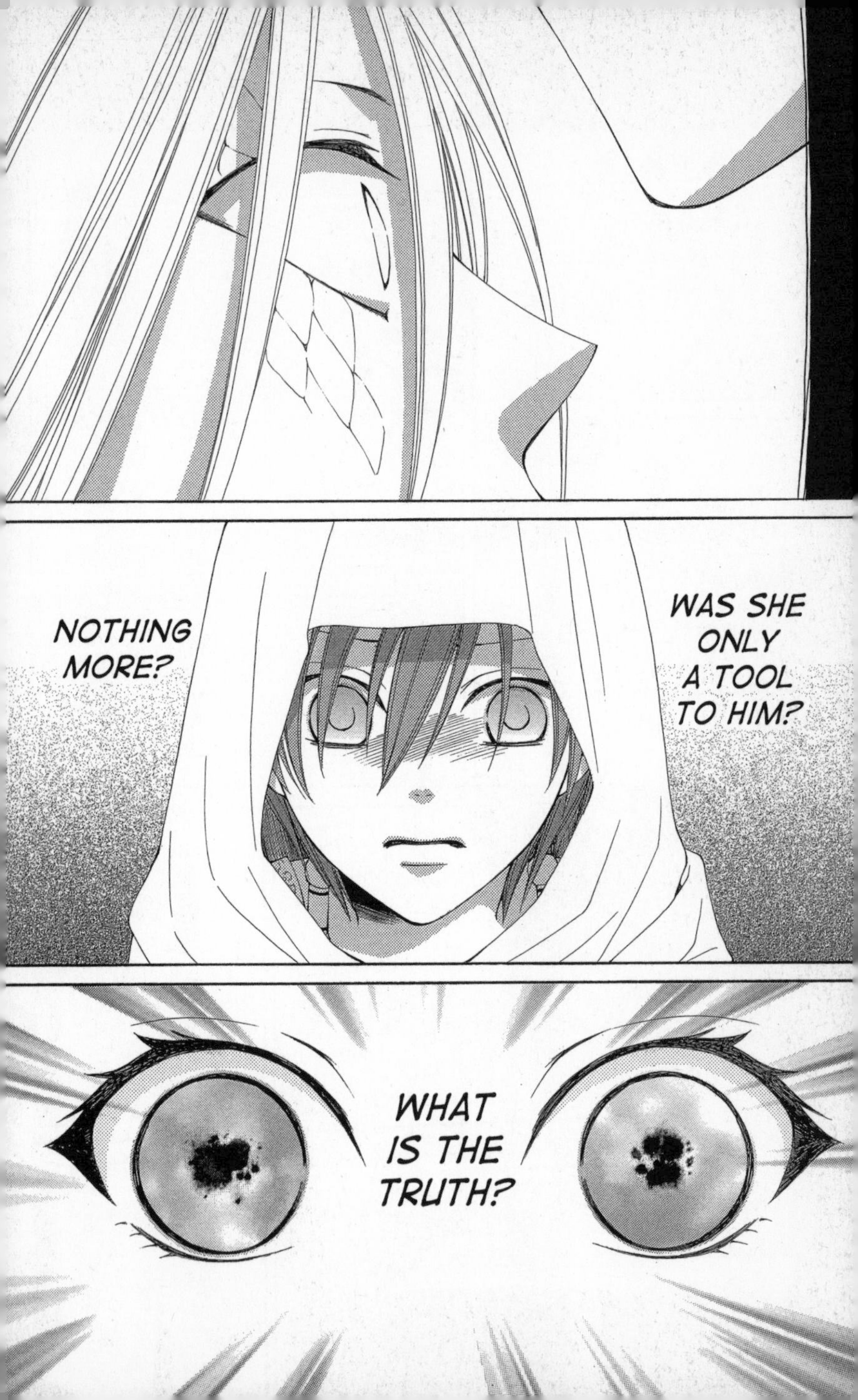
WAS SHE ONLY A TOOL TO HIM?
NOTHING MORE?
WHAT IS THE TRUTH?

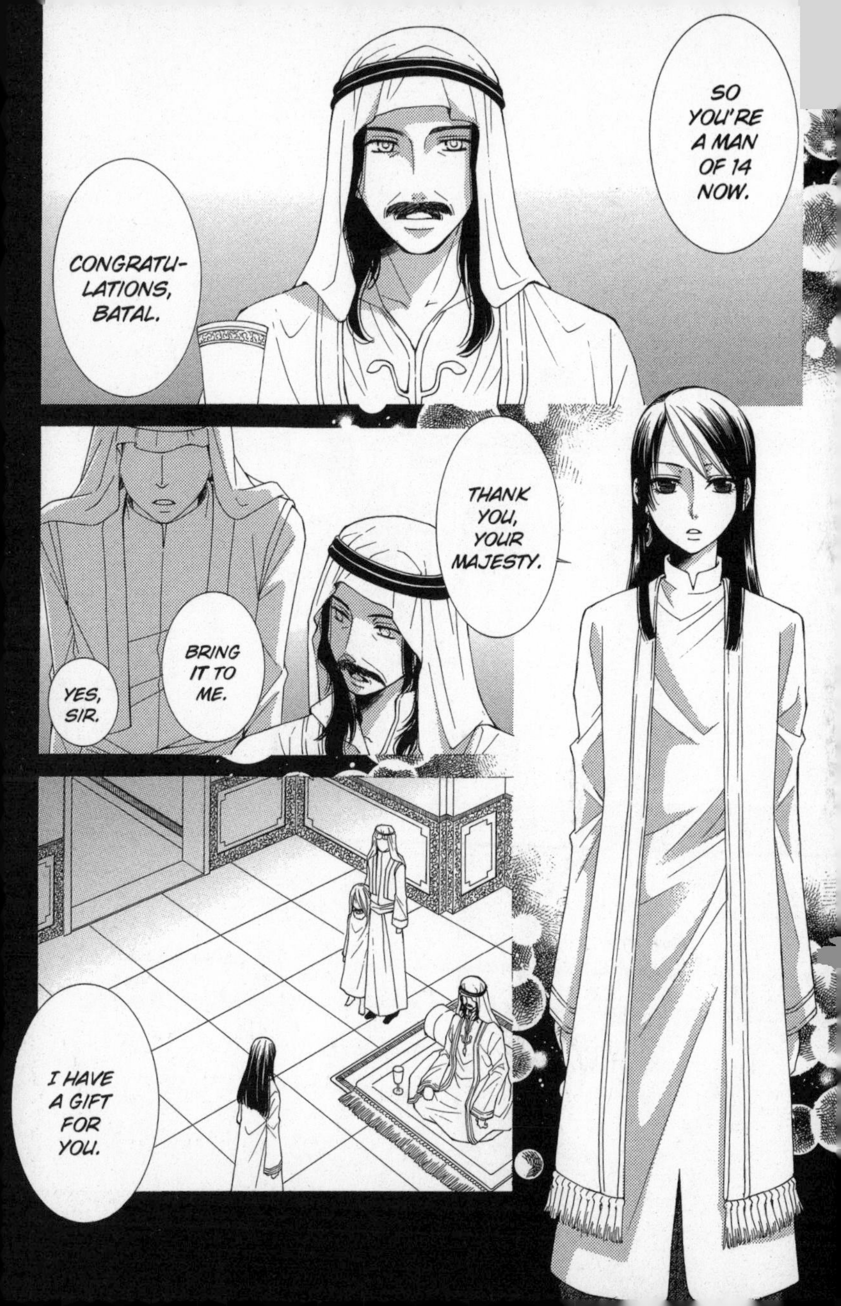
SO YOU'RE A MAN OF 14 NOW.
CONGRATU-LATIONS, BATAL.
THANK YOU, YOUR MAJESTY.
BRING IT TO ME.
YES, SIR.
I HAVE A GIFT FOR YOU.

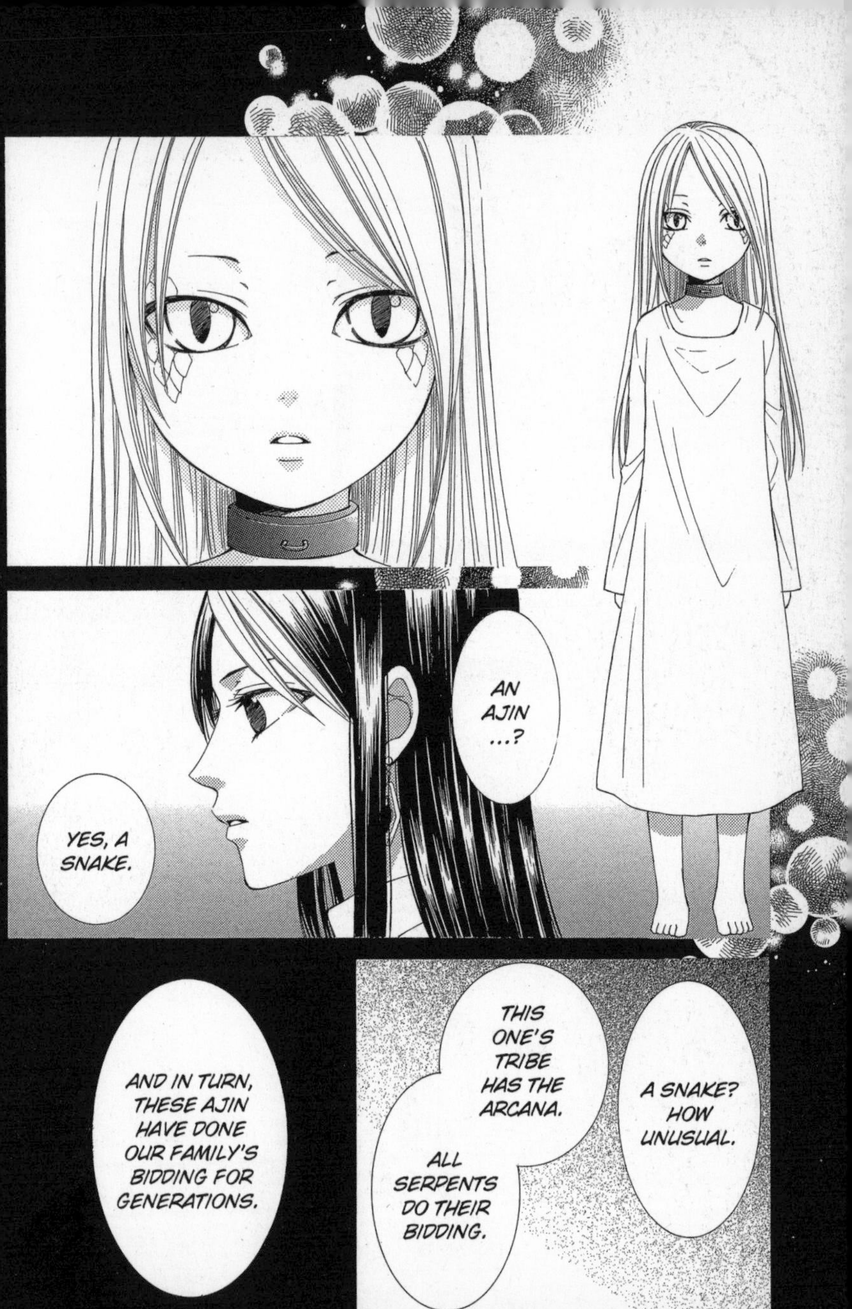
AN AJIN ...?
YES, A SNAKE.
A SNAKE? HOW UNUSUAL.
THIS ONE'S TRIBE HAS THE ARCANA.
ALL SERPENTS DO THEIR BIDDING.
AND IN TURN, THESE AJIN HAVE DONE OUR FAMILY'S BIDDING FOR GENERATIONS.

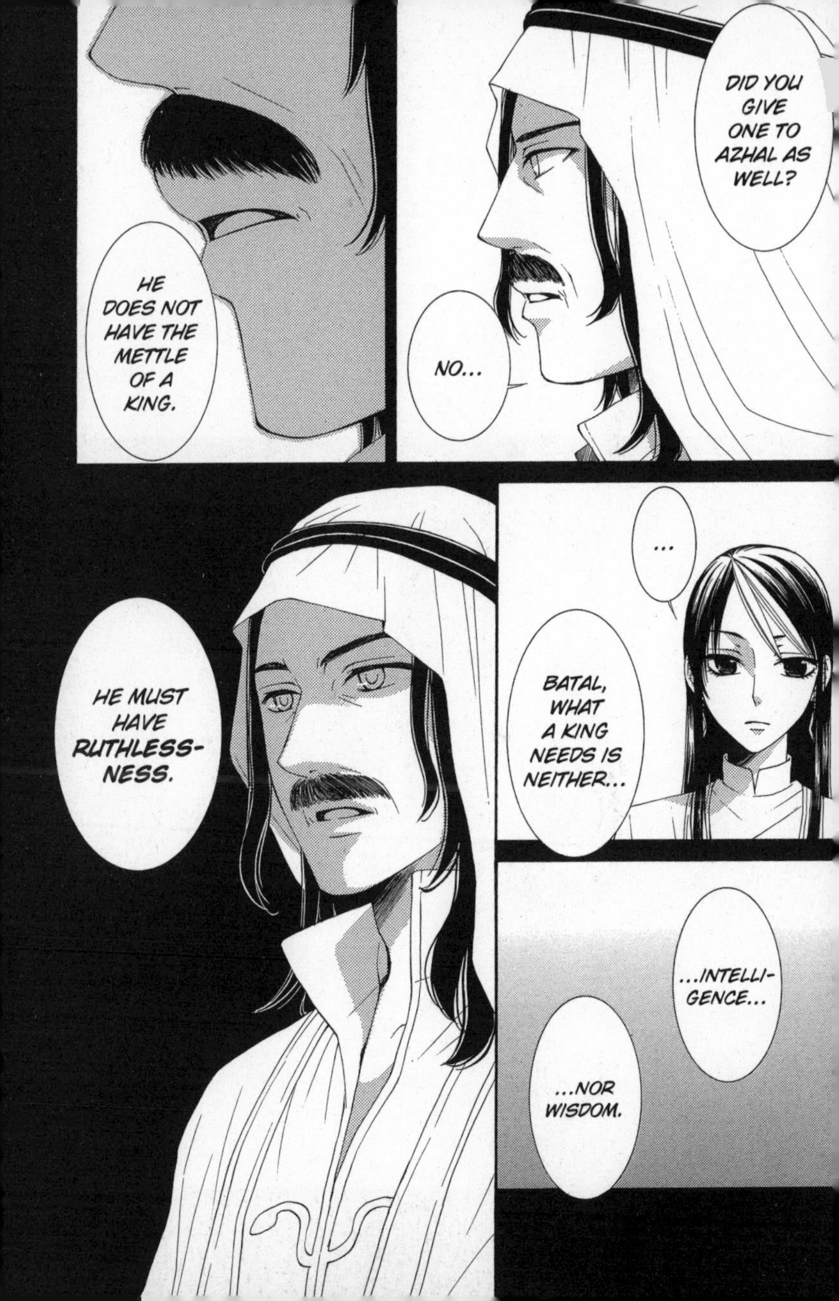
DID YOU GIVE ONE TO AZHAL AS WELL?
NO...
HE DOES NOT HAVE THE METTLE OF A KING.
...
BATAL, WHAT A KING NEEDS IS NEITHER...
...INTELLIGENCE...
...NOR WISDOM.
HE MUST HAVE RUTHLESSNESS.

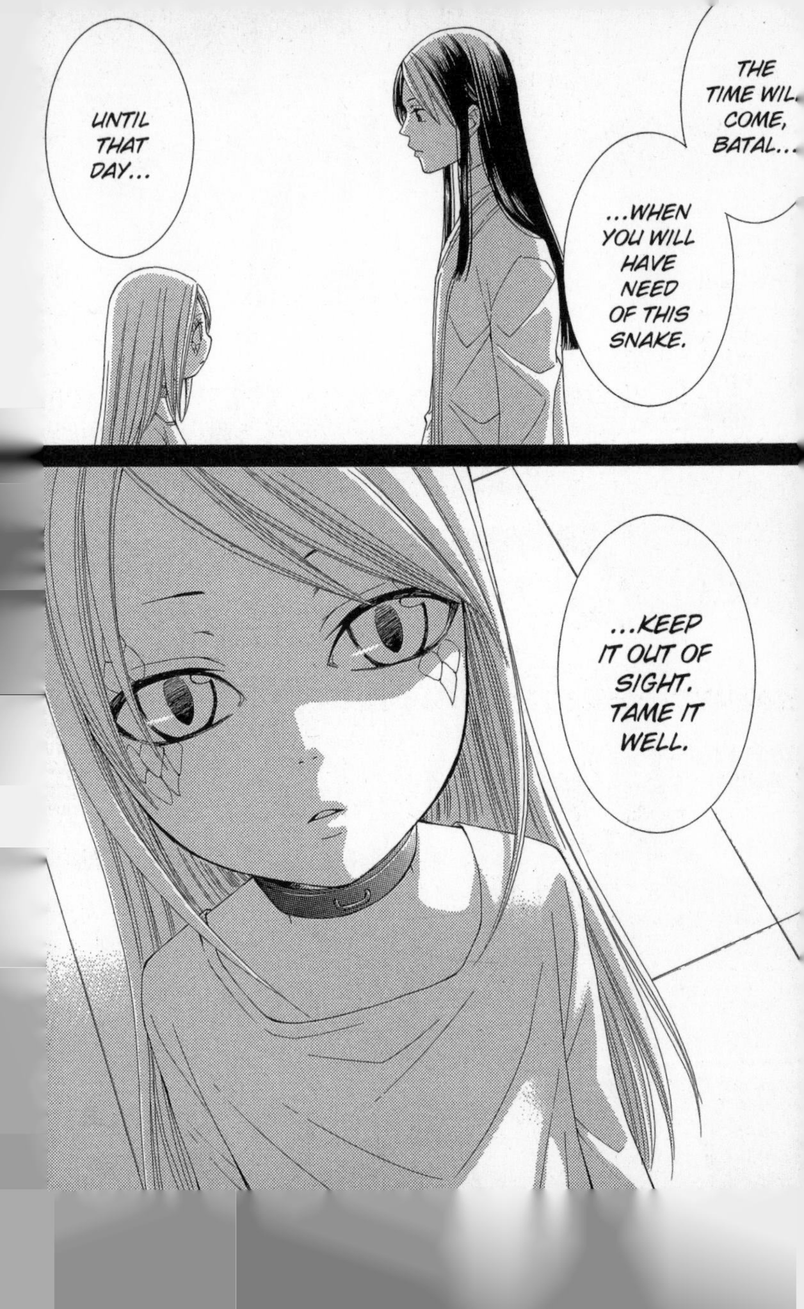
THE TIME WIL COME, BATAL...
...WHEN YOU WILL HAVE NEED OF THIS SNAKE.
UNTIL THAT DAY...
...KEEP IT OUT OF SIGHT. TAME IT WELL.

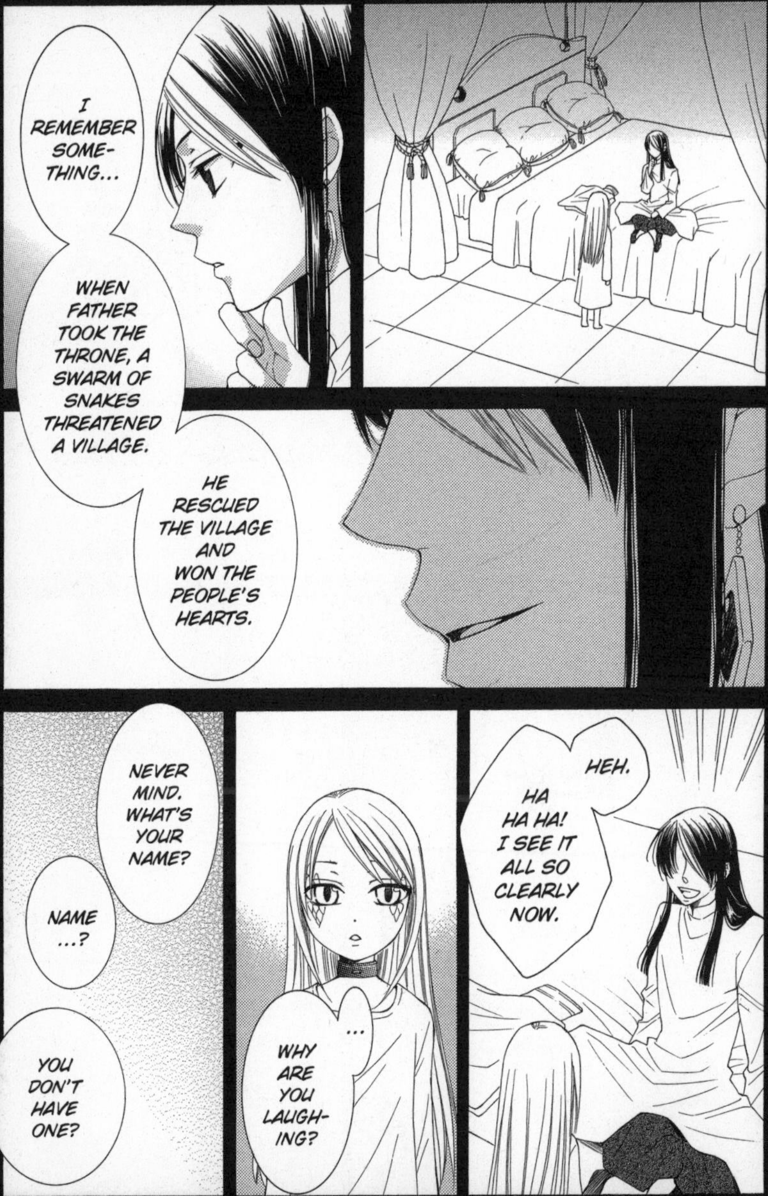
I REMEMBER SOME-THING...
WHEN FATHER TOOK THE THRONE, A SWARM OF SNAKES THREATENED A VILLAGE.
HE RESCUED THE VILLAGE AND WON THE PEOPLE'S HEARTS.
HEH.
HA HA HA! I SEE IT ALL SO CLEARLY NOW.
...
WHY ARE YOU LAUGH-ING?
NEVER MIND. WHAT'S YOUR NAME?
NAME ...?
YOU DON'T HAVE ONE?

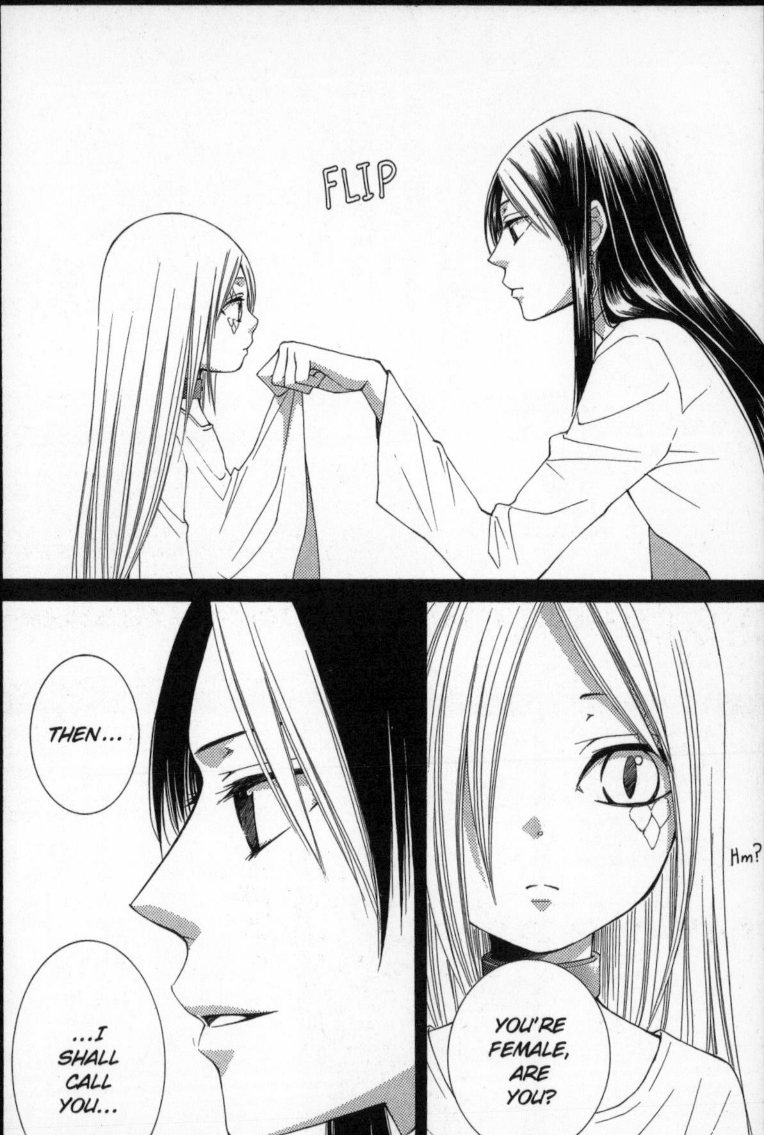
FLIP
Hm?
YOU'RE FEMALE, ARE YOU?
THEN...
...I SHALL CALL YOU...

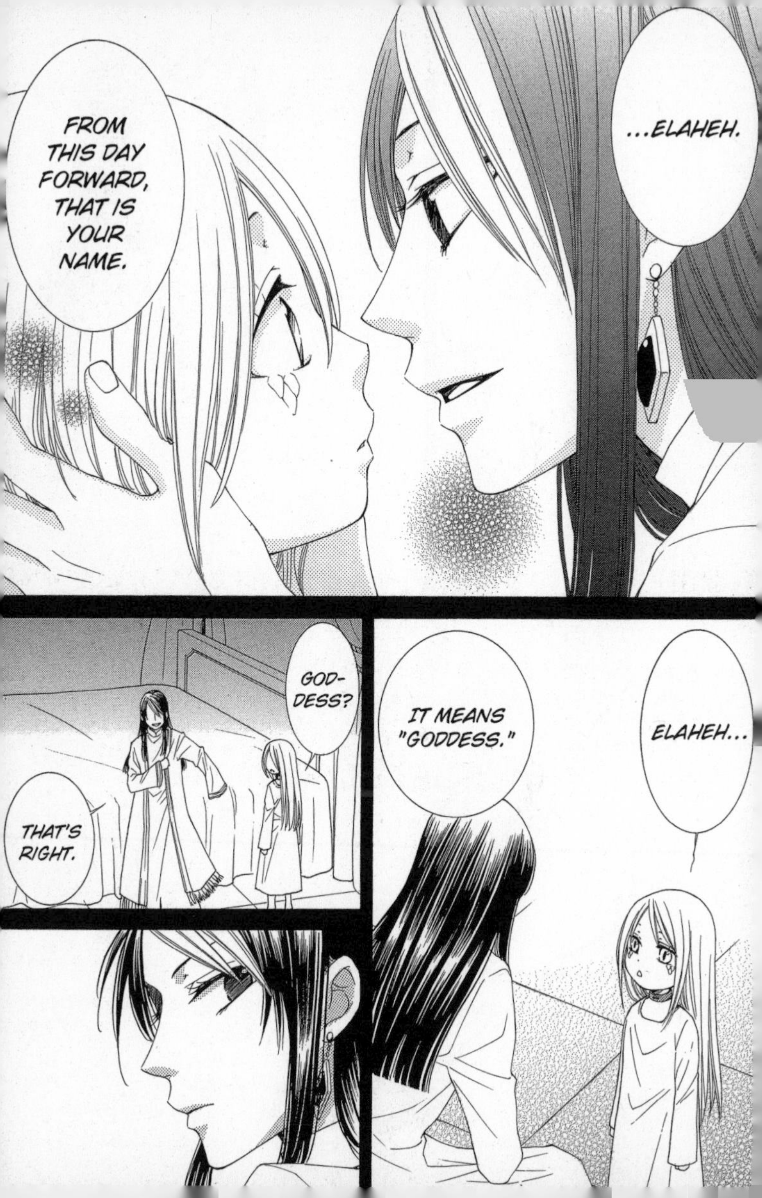
...ELAHEH.
FROM THIS DAY FORWARD, THAT IS YOUR NAME.
ELAHEH...
IT MEANS "GODDESS."
GOD-DESS?
THAT'S RIGHT.

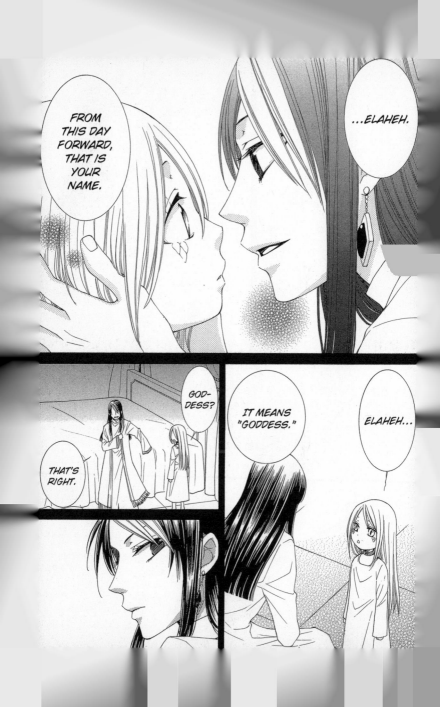

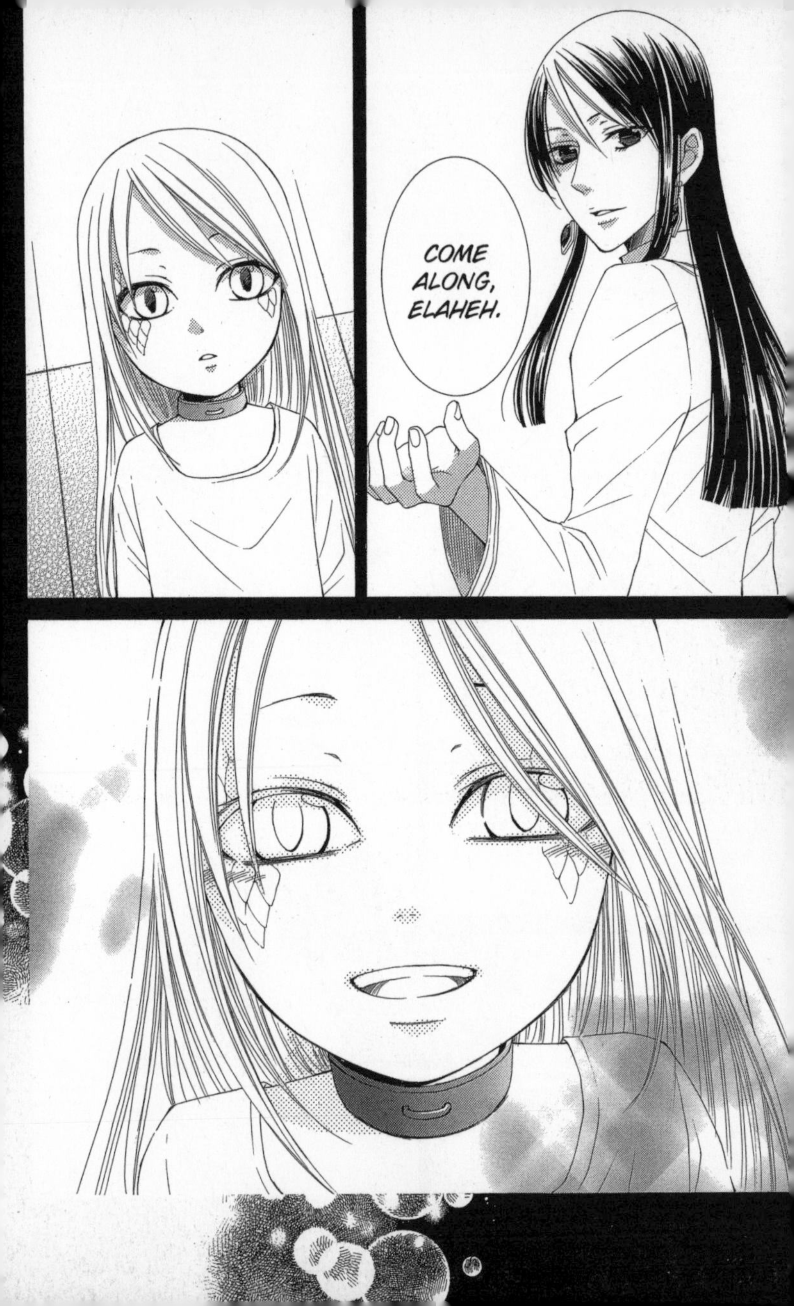
COME ALONG, ELAHEH.

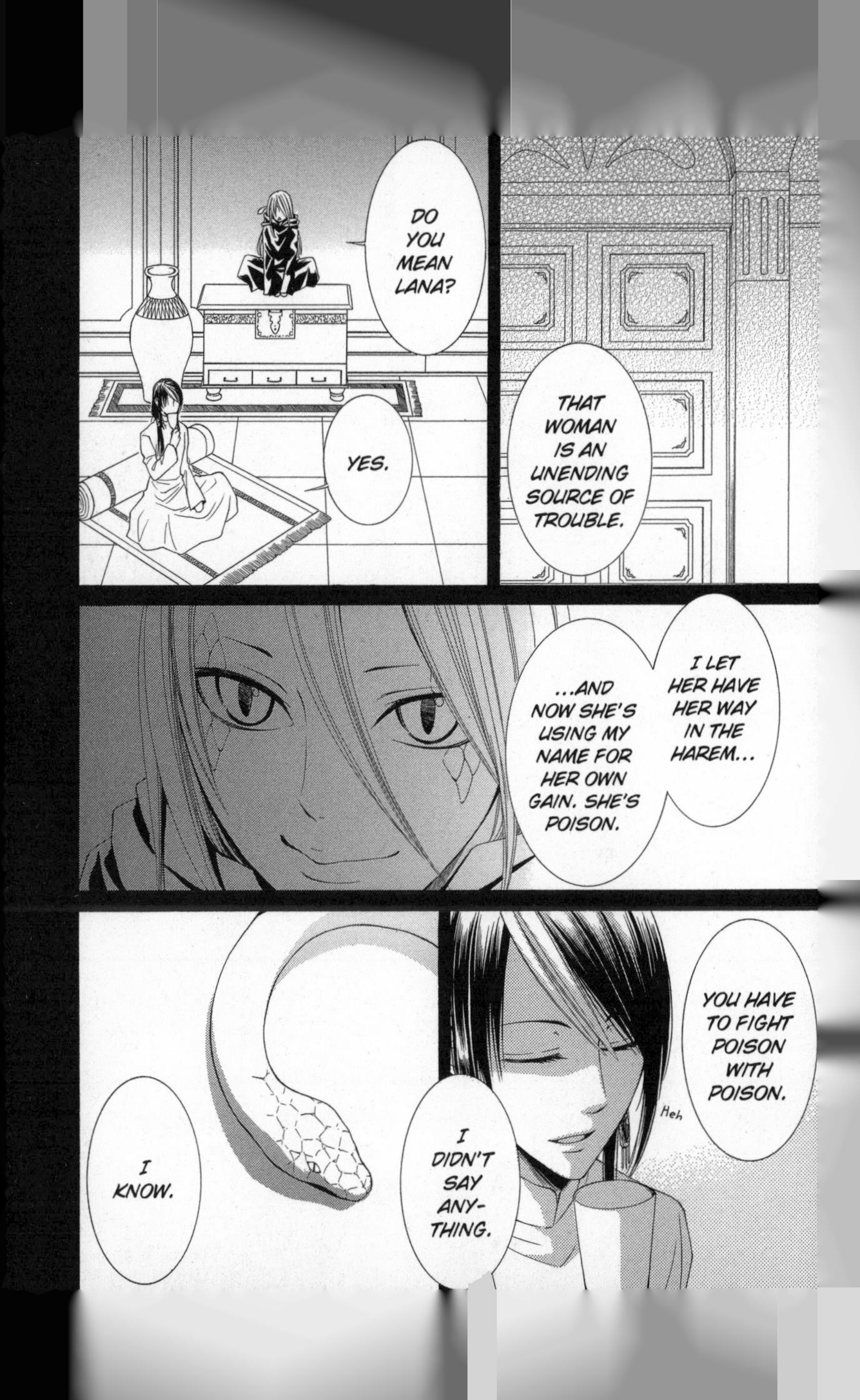
THAT WOMAN IS AN UNENDING SOURCE OF TROUBLE.
DO YOU MEAN LANA?
YES.
I LET HER HAVE HER WAY IN THE HAREM...
...AND NOW SHE'S USING MY NAME FOR HER OWN GAIN. SHE'S POISON.
YOU HAVE TO FIGHT POISON WITH POISON.
Heh
I DIDN'T SAY ANY-THING.
I KNOW.

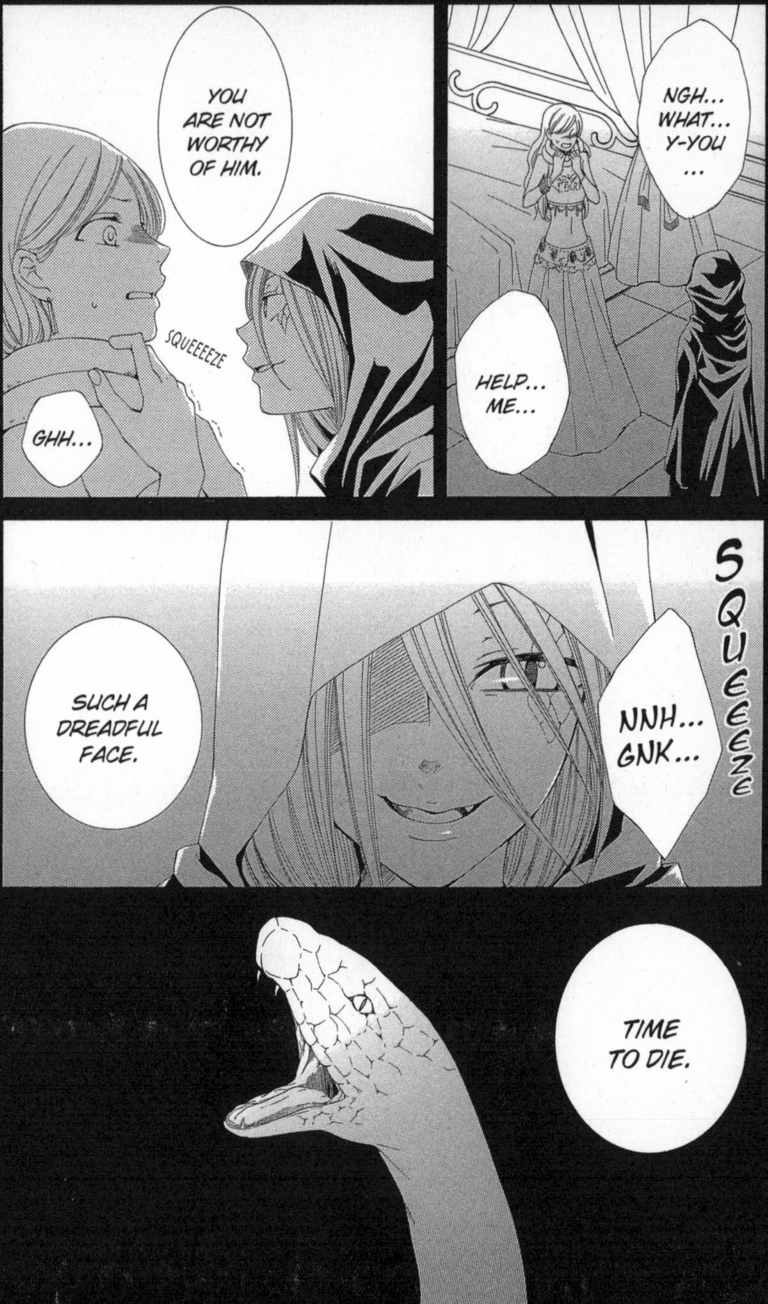
NGH... WHAT... Y-YOU ...
HELP... ME...
YOU ARE NOT WORTHY OF HIM.
SQUEEEEZE
GHH...
SQUEEEEZE
NNH... GNK...
SUCH A DREADFUL FACE.
TIME TO DIE.

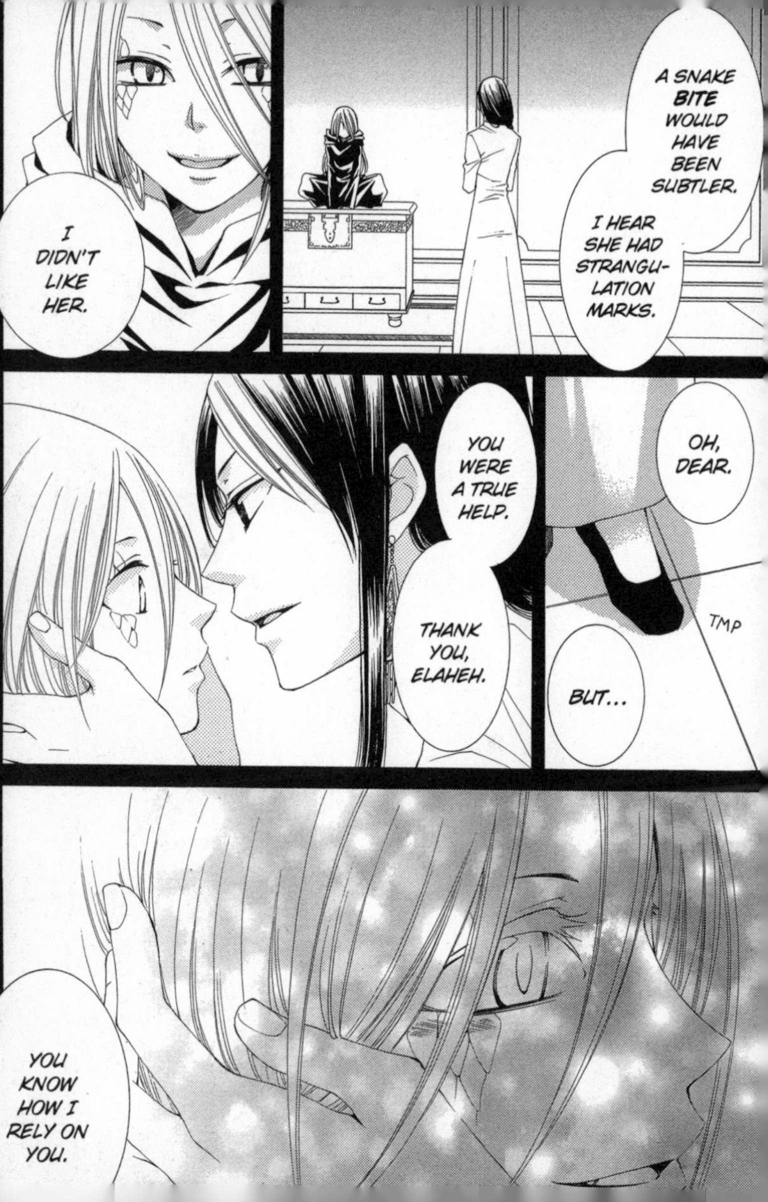
A SNAKE BITE WOULD HAVE BEEN SUBTLER.
I HEAR SHE HAD STRANGU-LATION MARKS.
I DIDN'T LIKE HER.
OH, DEAR.
TMP
BUT...
YOU WERE A TRUE HELP.
THANK YOU, ELAHEH.
YOU KNOW HOW I RELY ON YOU.

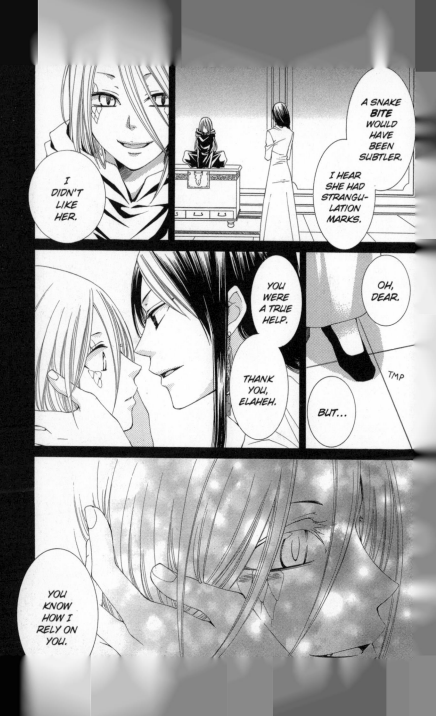

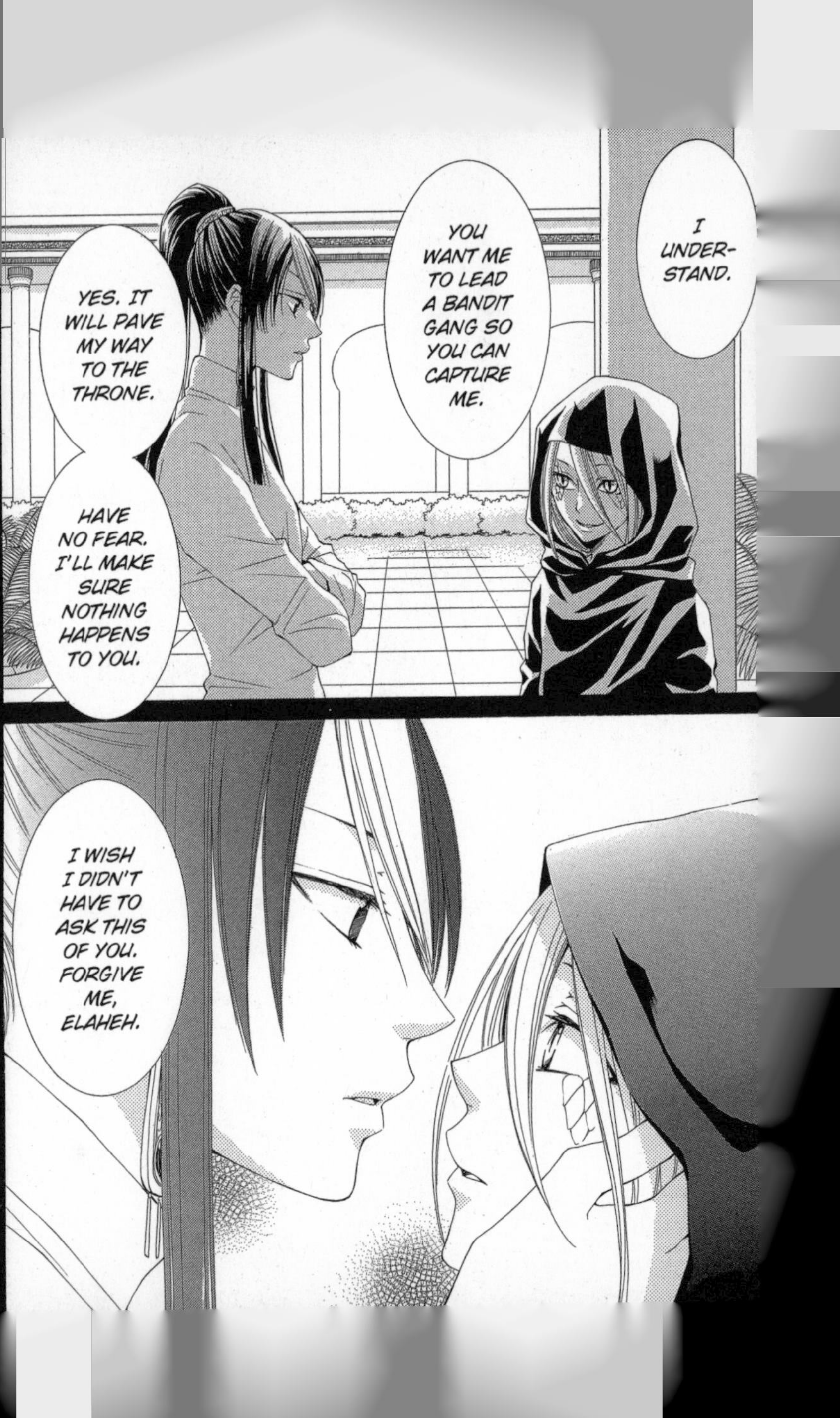
I UNDER-STAND.
YOU WANT ME TO LEAD A BANDIT GANG SO YOU CAN CAPTURE ME.
YES. IT WILL PAVE MY WAY TO THE THRONE.
HAVE NO FEAR. I'LL MAKE SURE NOTHING HAPPENS TO YOU.
I WISH I DIDN'T HAVE TO ASK THIS OF YOU. FORGIVE ME, ELAHEH.

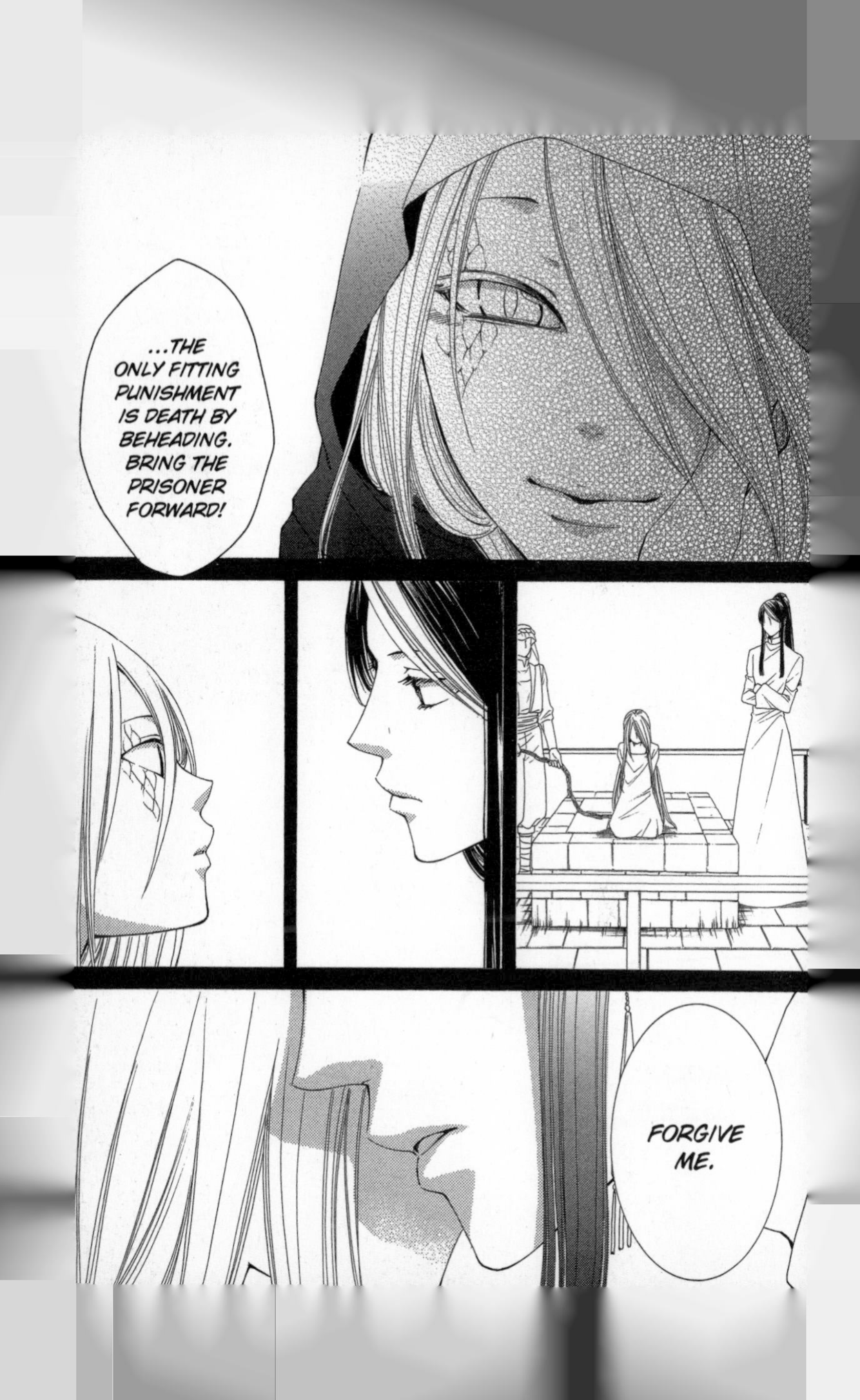
...THE ONLY FITTING PUNISHMENT IS DEATH BY BEHEADING. BRING THE PRISONER FORWARD!
FORGIVE ME.

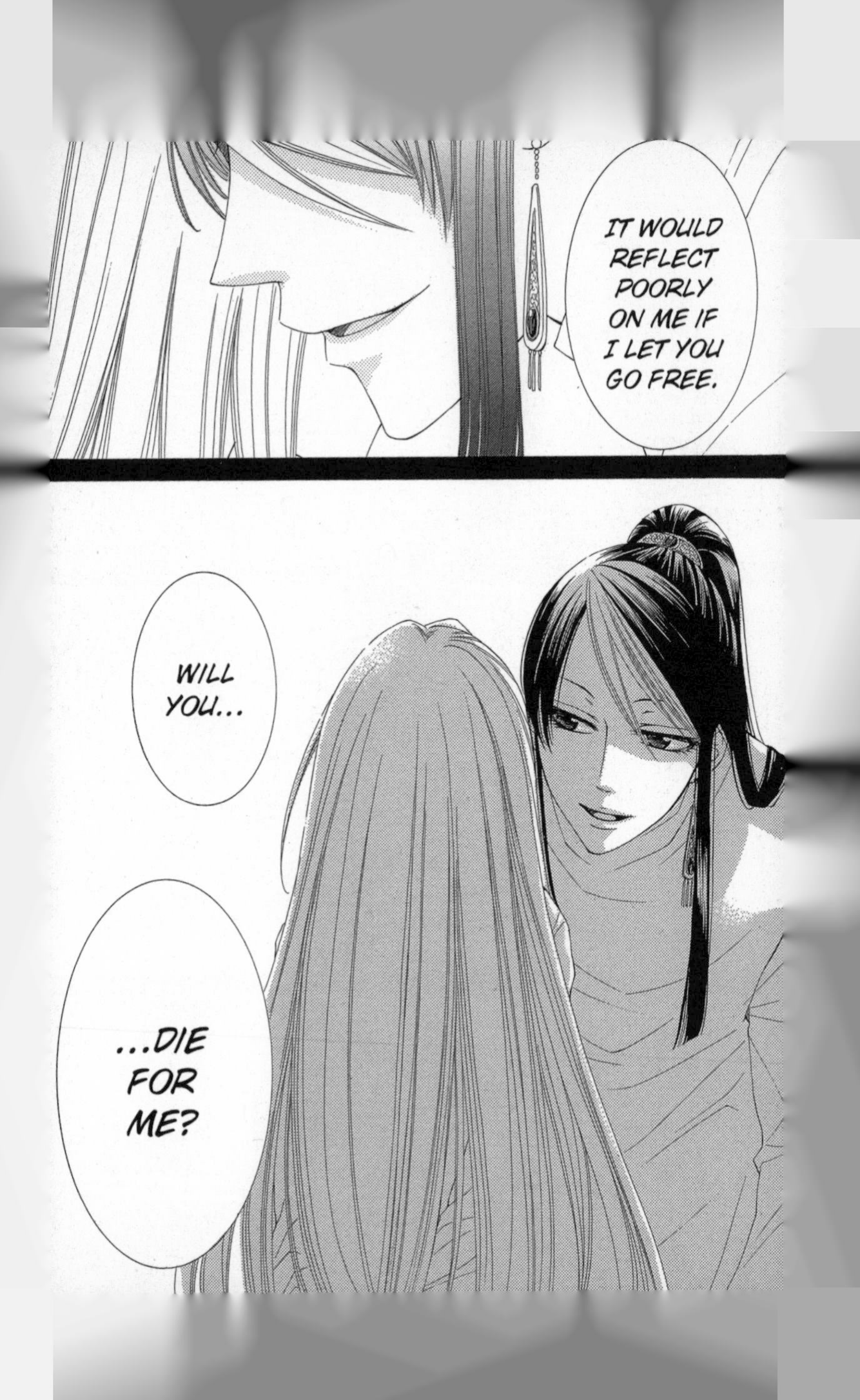
IT WOULD REFLECT POORLY ON ME IF I LET YOU GO FREE.
WILL YOU...
...DIE FOR ME?

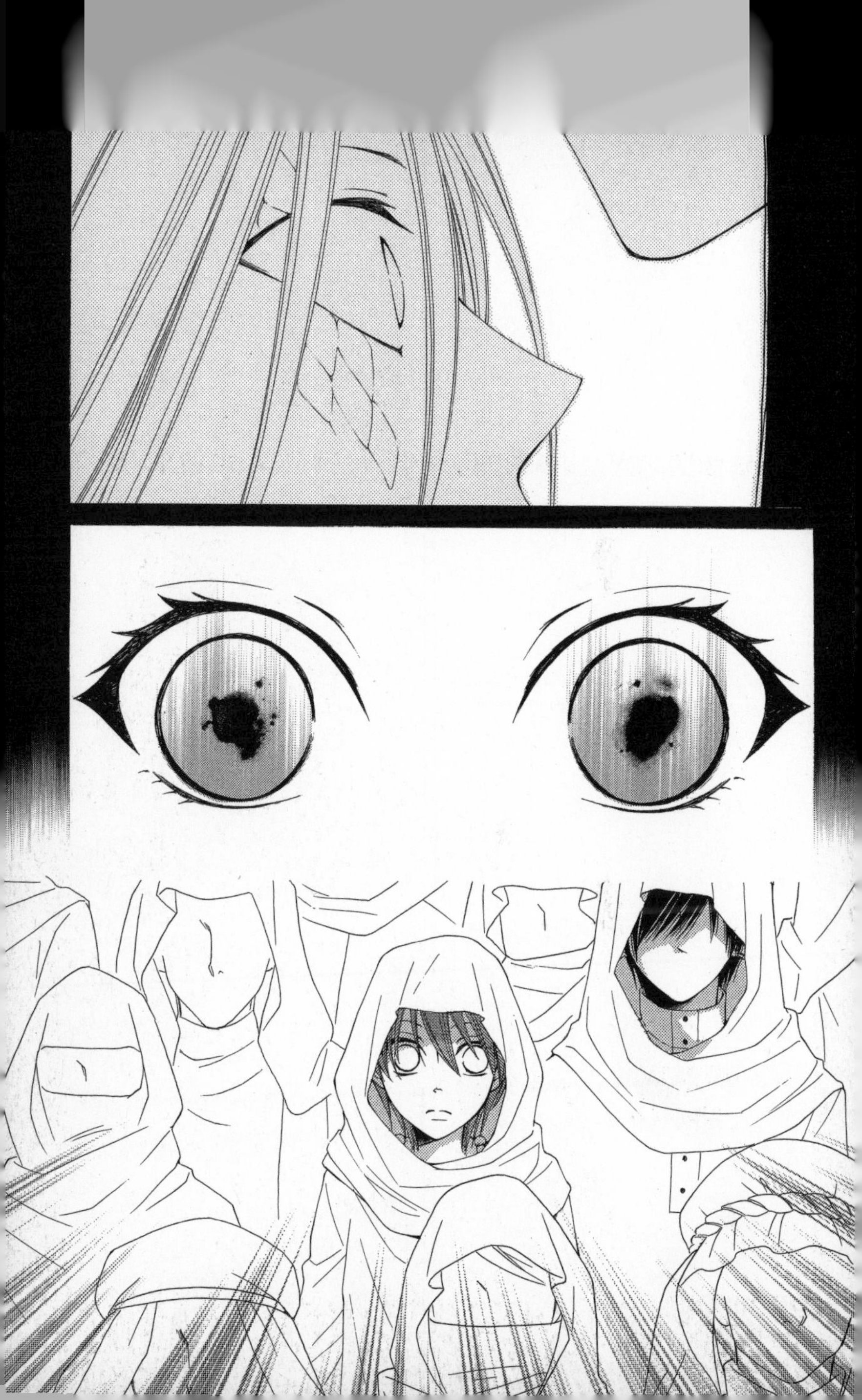

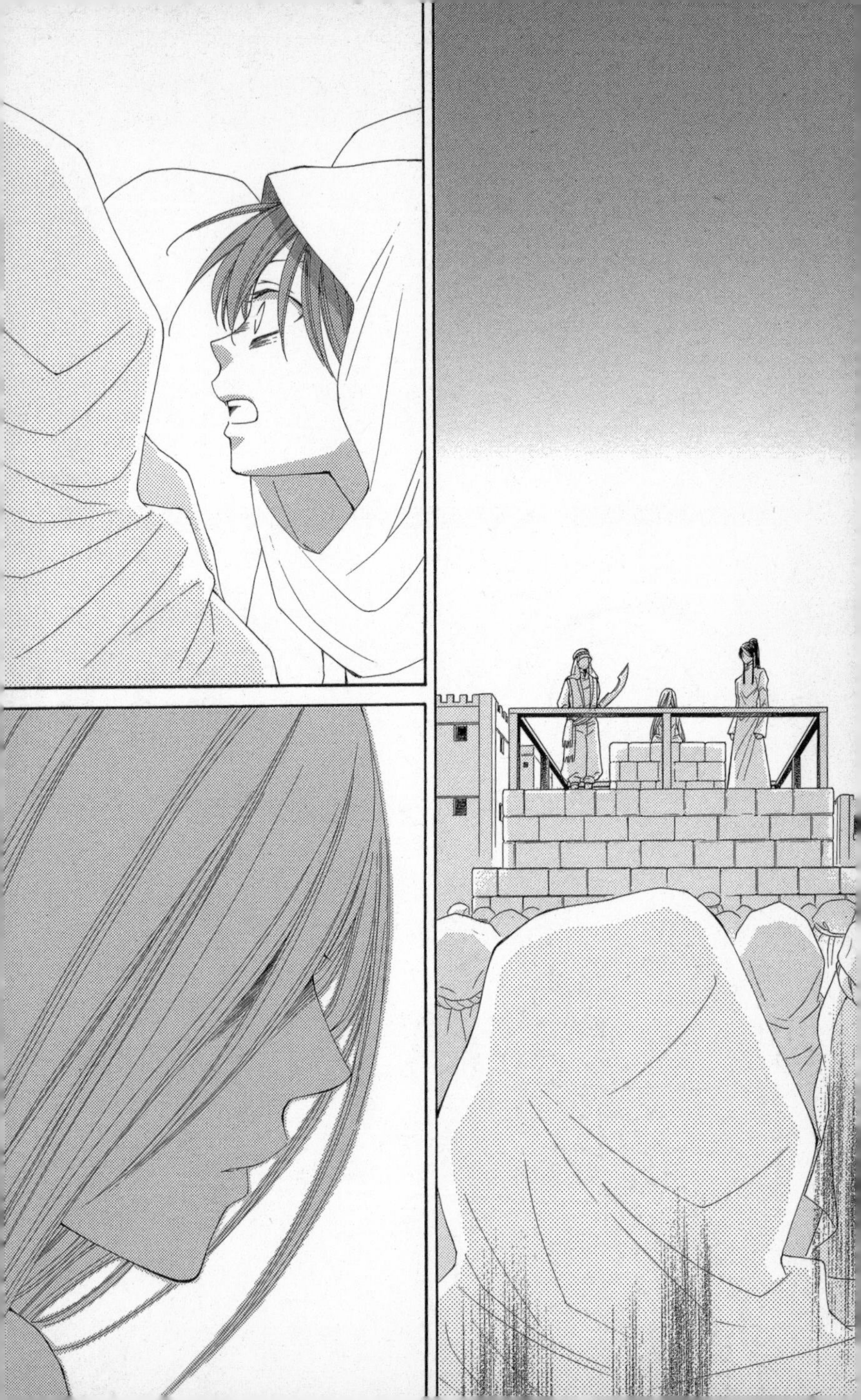

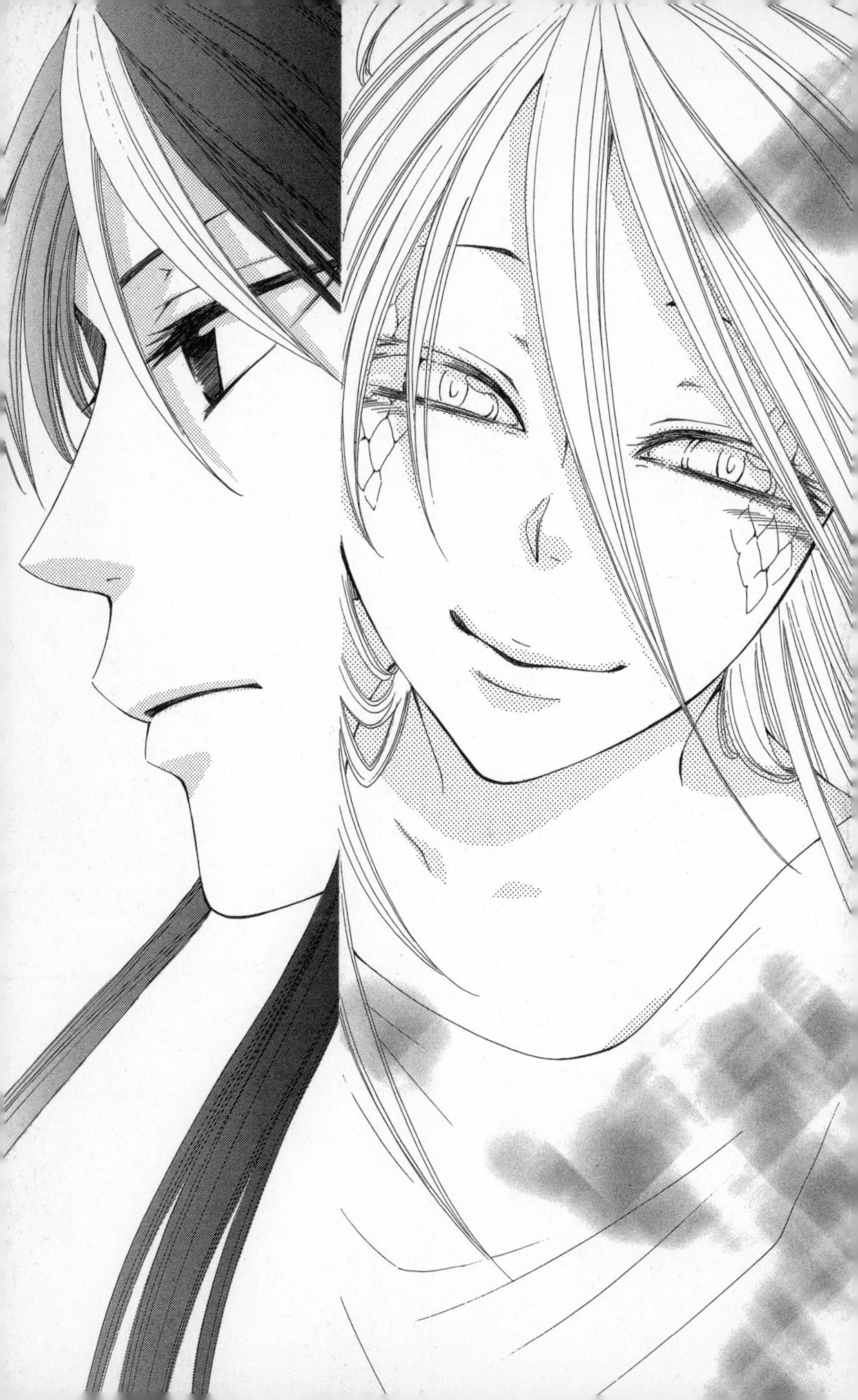

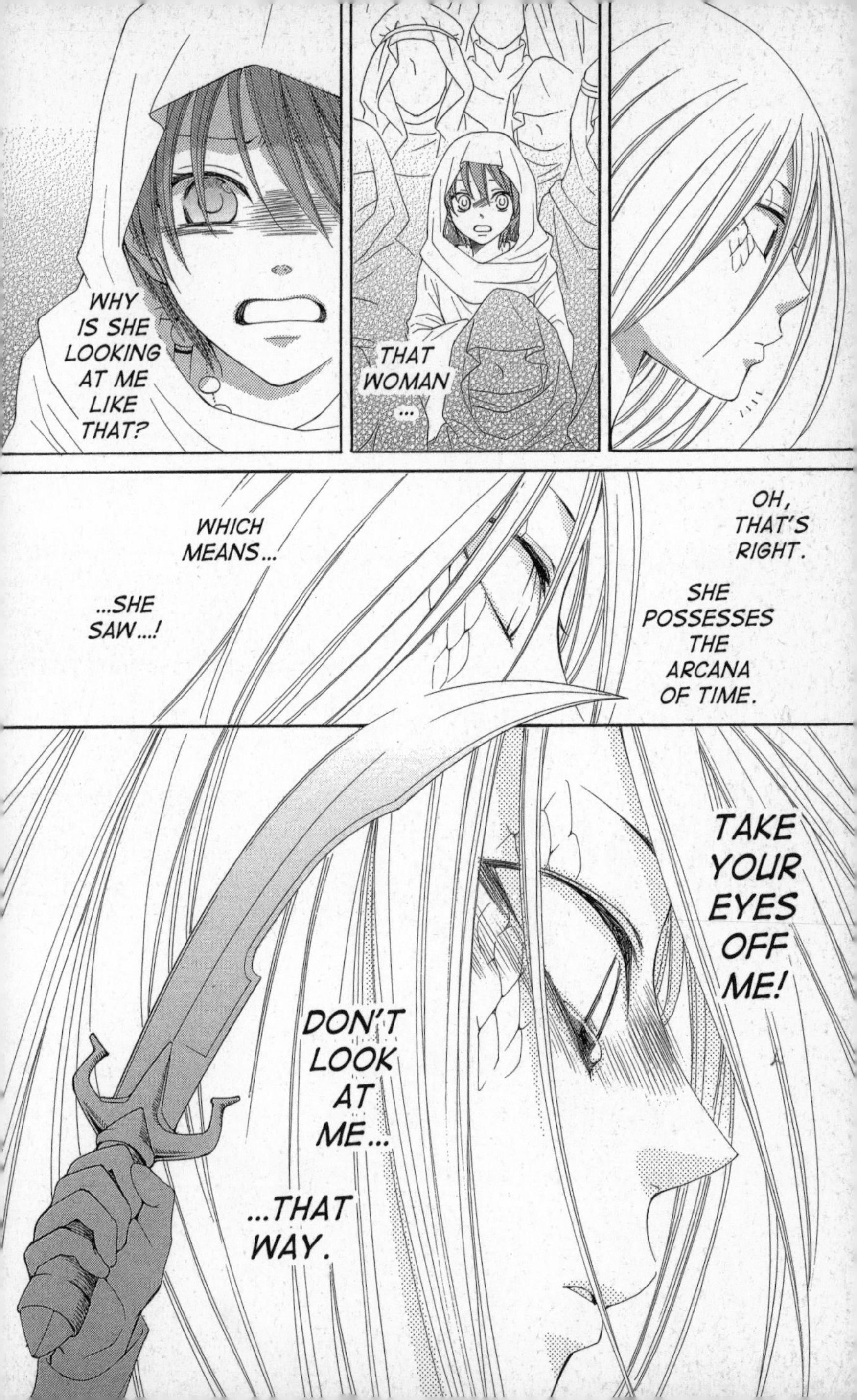
THAT WOMAN...
WHY IS SHE LOOKING AT ME LIKE THAT?
OH, THAT'S RIGHT.
SHE POSSESSES THE ARCANA OF TIME.
WHICH MEANS...
...SHE SAW...!
TAKE YOUR EYES OFF ME!
DON'T LOOK AT ME...
...THAT WAY.

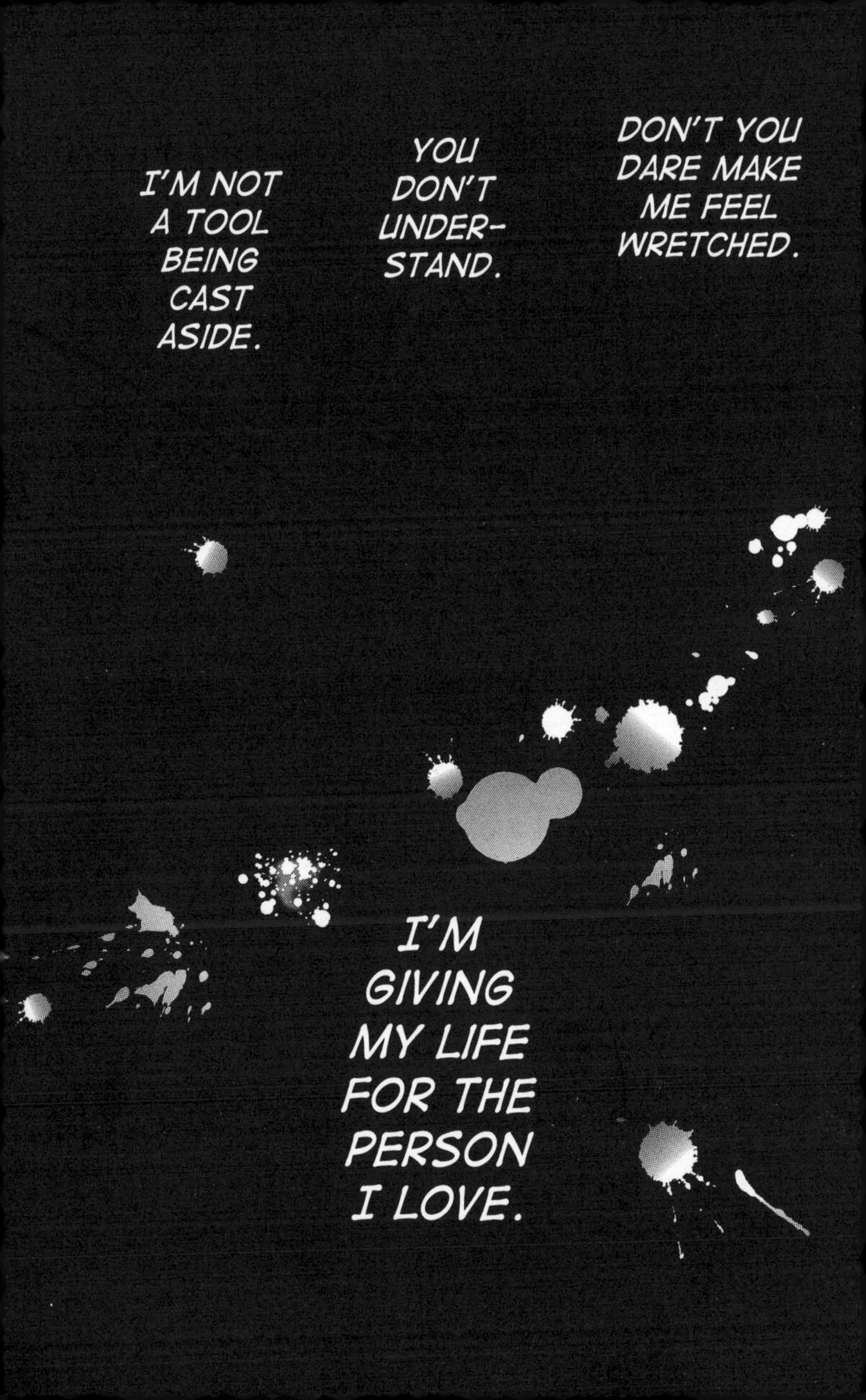
DON'T YOU DARE MAKE ME FEEL WRETCHED.
YOU DON'T UNDER-STAND.
I'M NOT A TOOL BEING CAST ASIDE.
I'M GIVING MY LIFE FOR THE PERSON I LOVE.

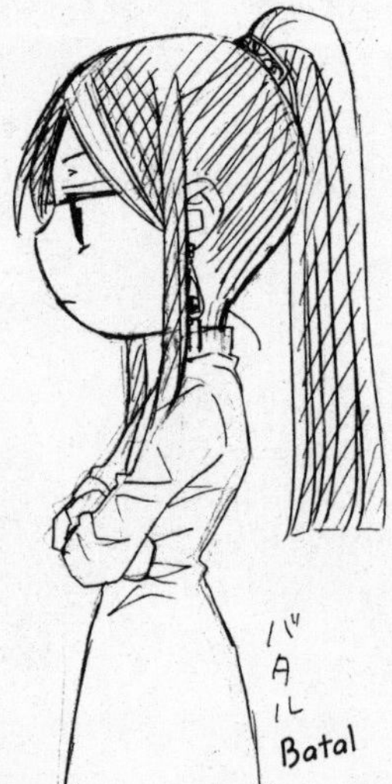
Batal

I like him quite a bit too.

Chapter 36

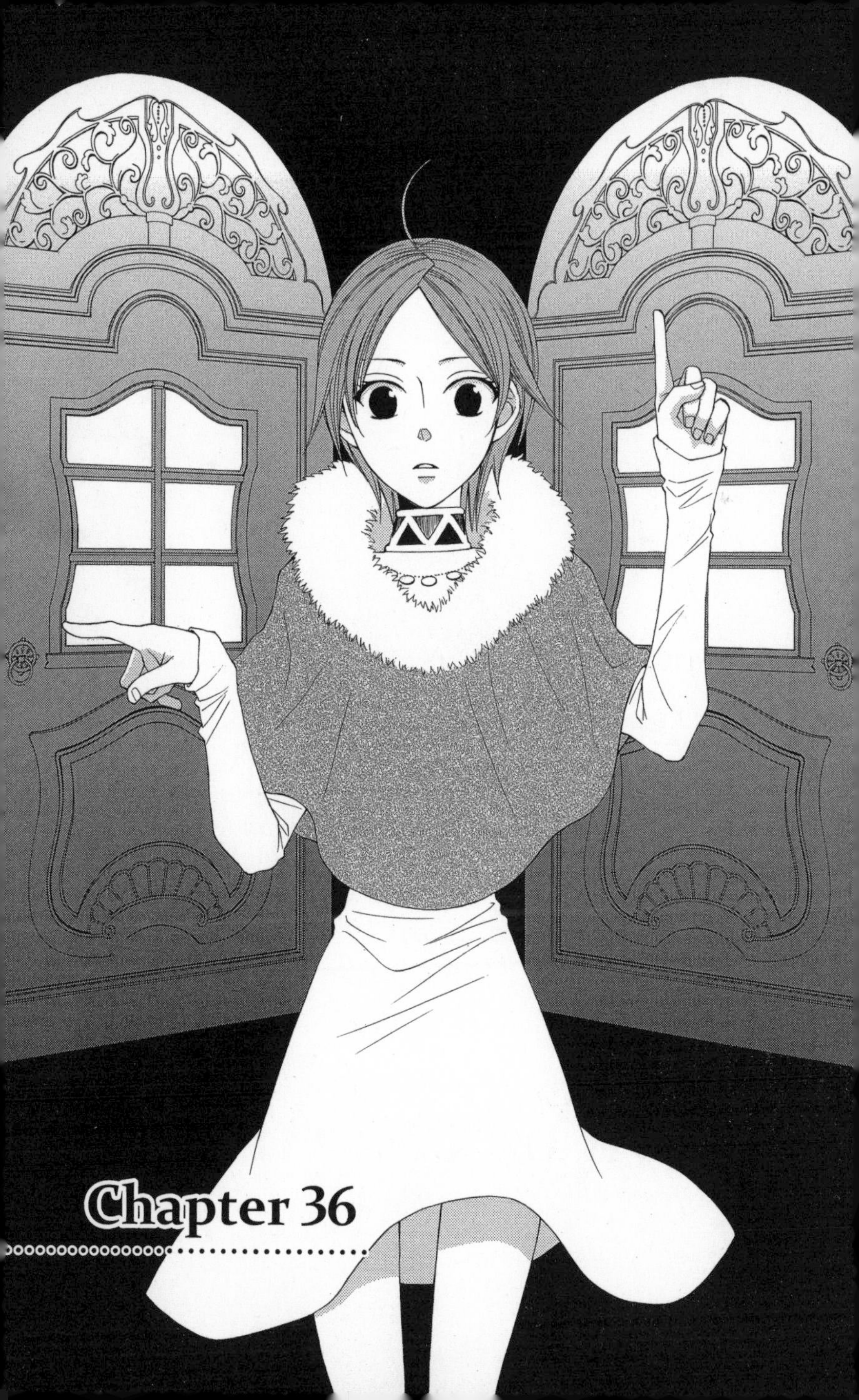

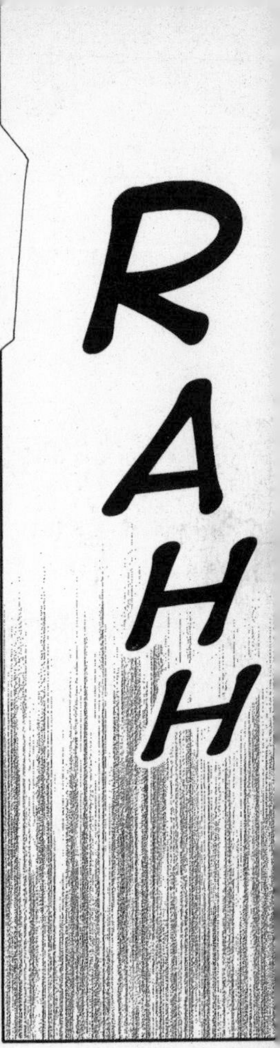
RAHH

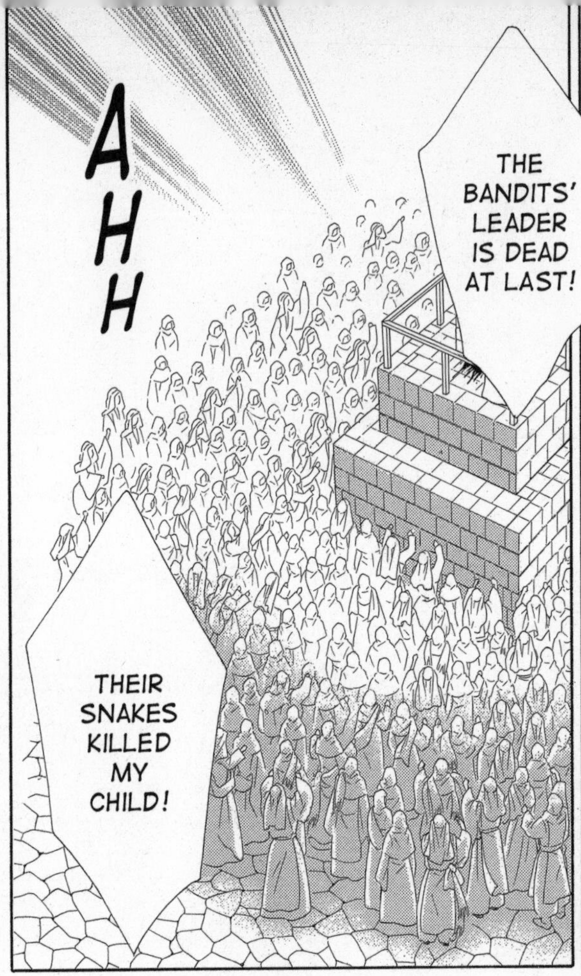
THE BANDITS' LEADER IS DEAD AT LAST!
AHH
THEIR SNAKES KILLED MY CHILD!

Dawn of the Arcana

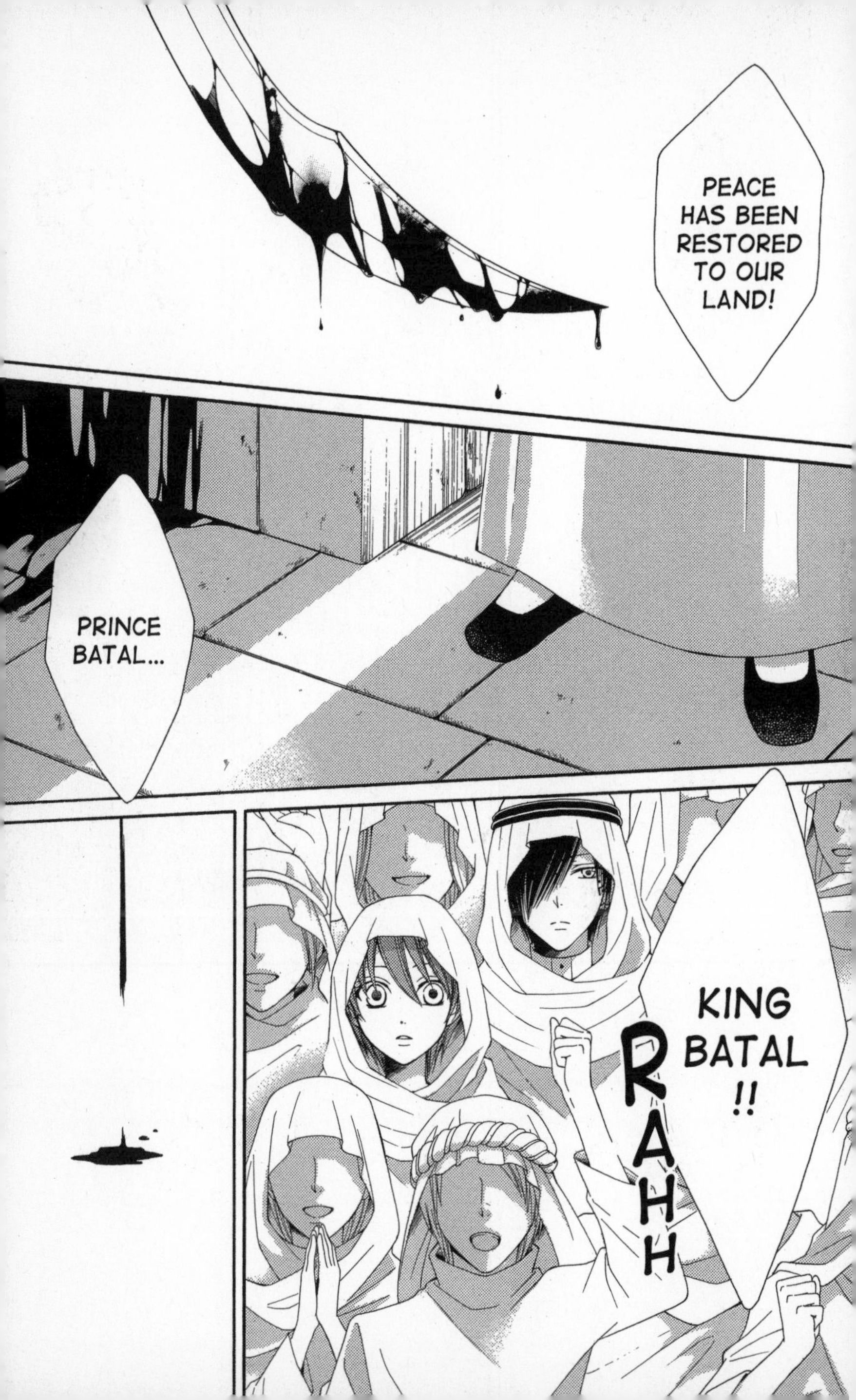
PEACE HAS BEEN RESTORED TO OUR LAND!
PRINCE BATAL...
KING BATAL !!
RAHH

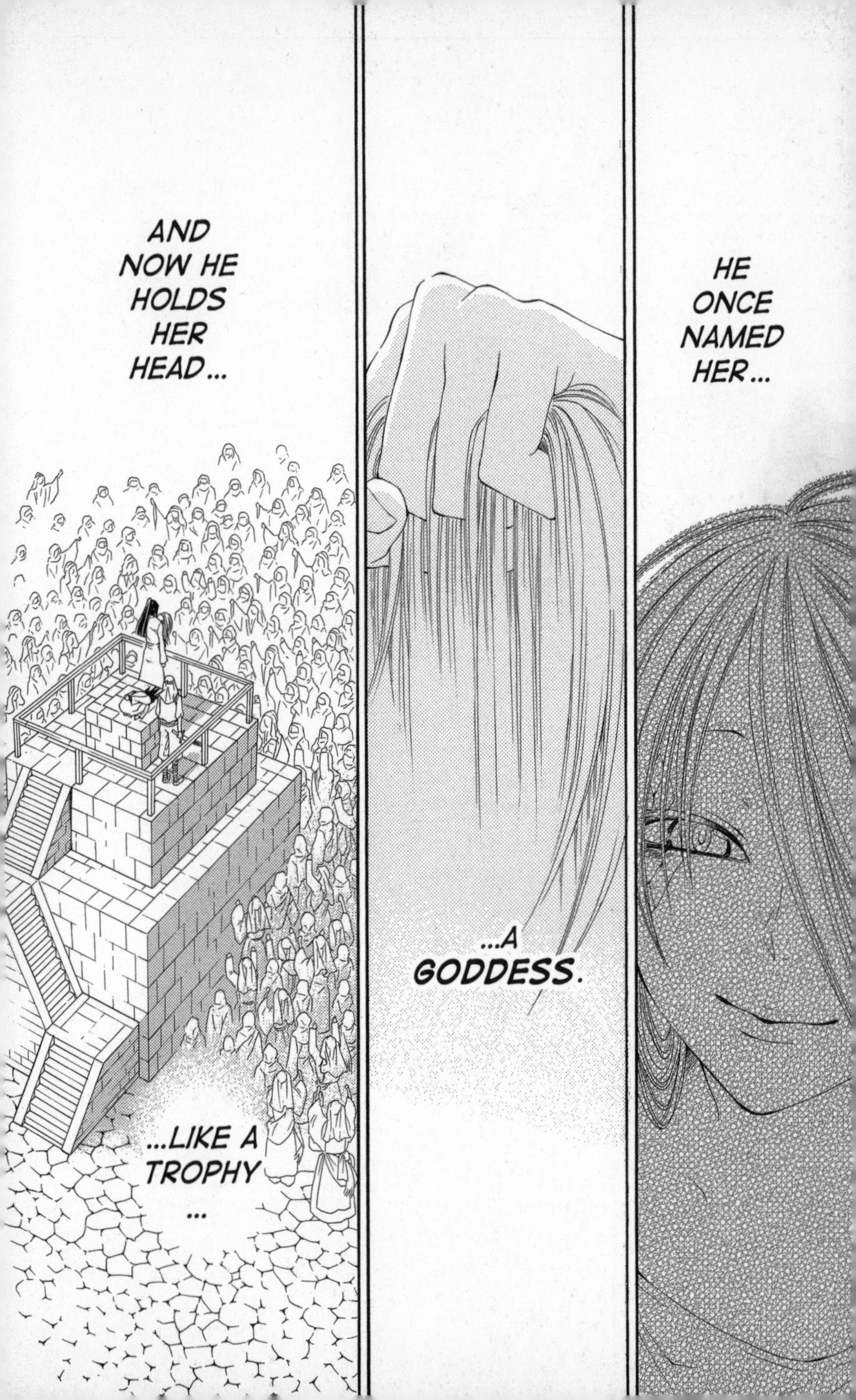
HE ONCE NAMED HER...
...A GODDESS.
AND NOW HE HOLDS HER HEAD...
...LIKE A TROPHY ...

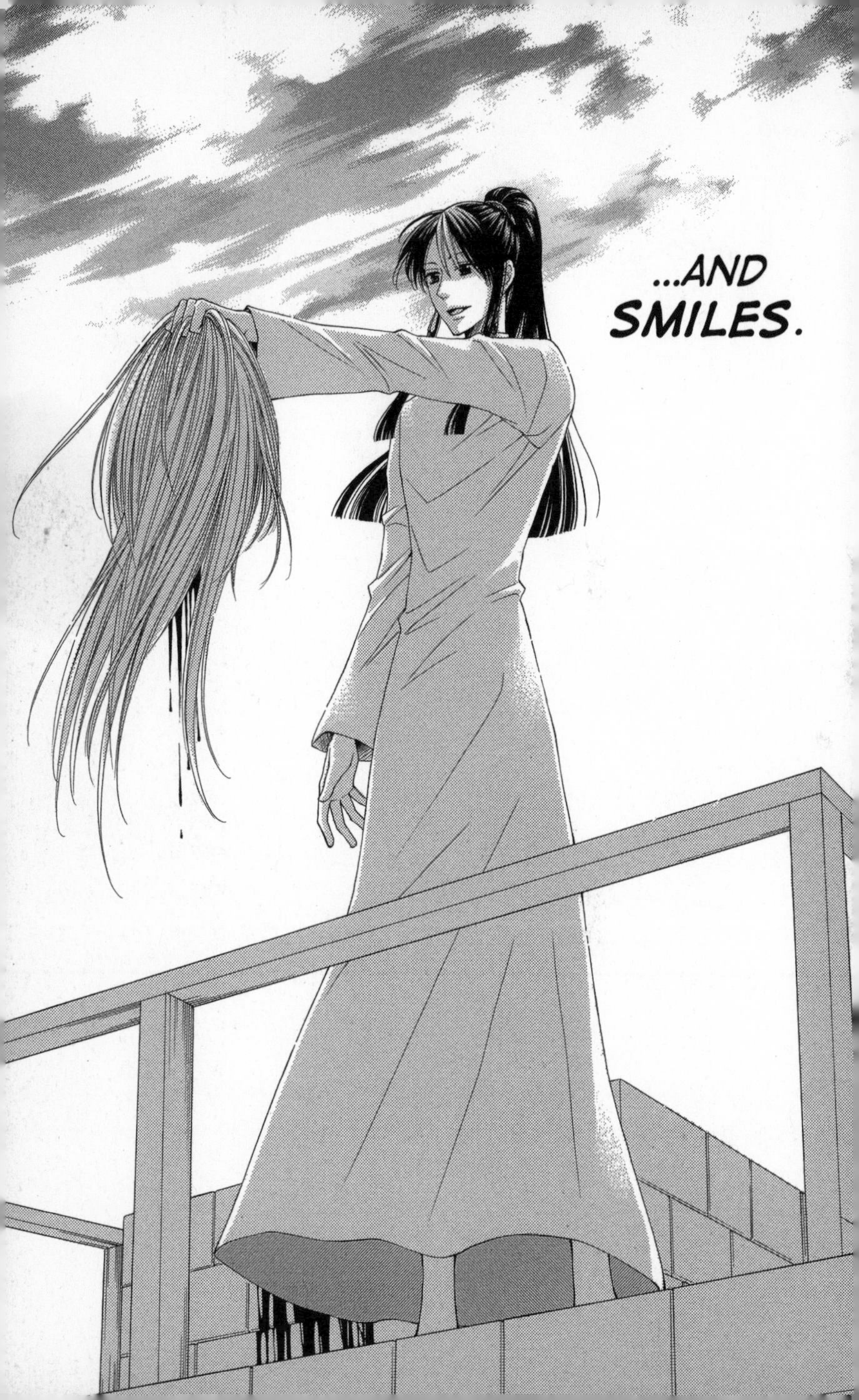
...AND SMILES.

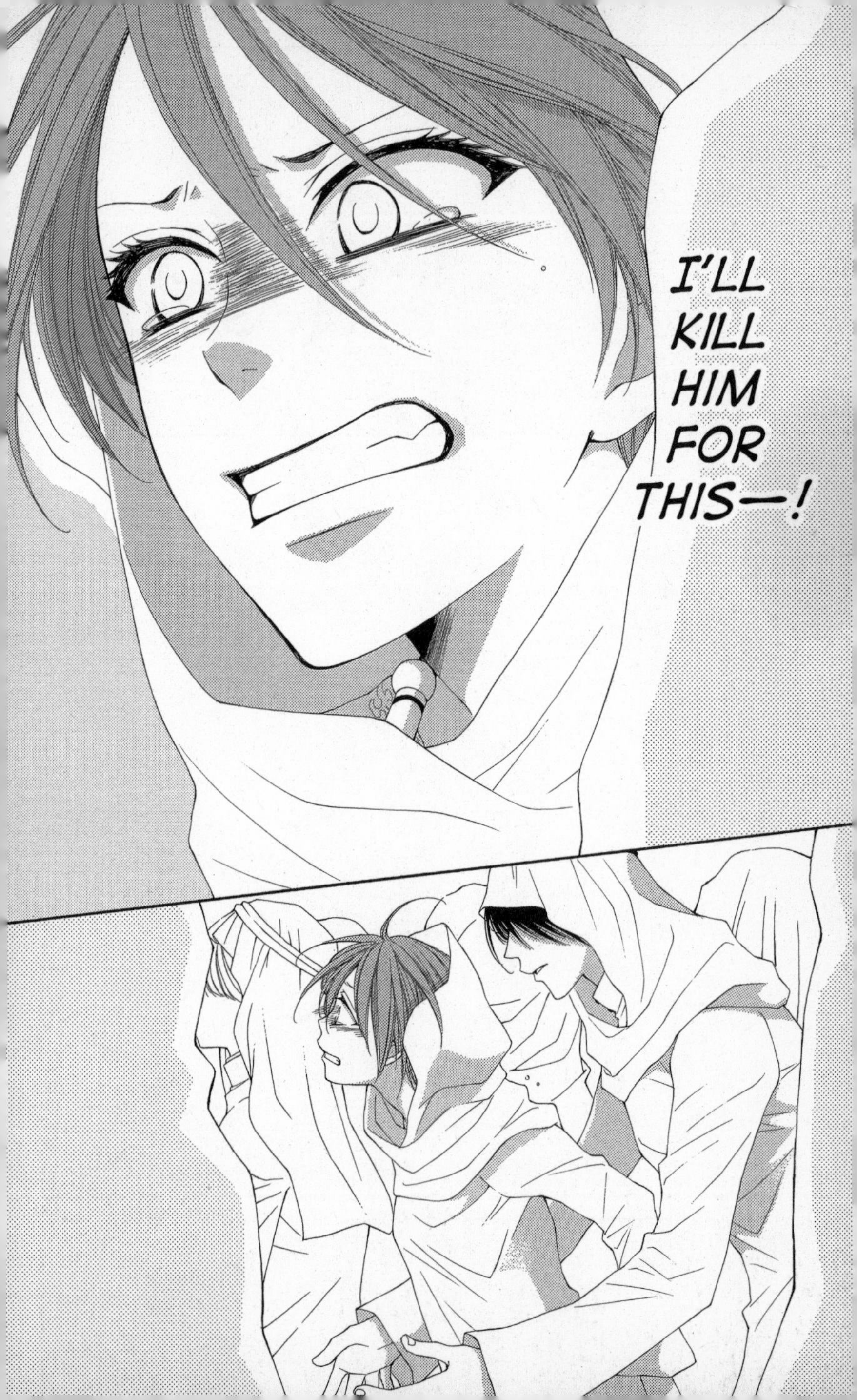
I'LL KILL HIM FOR THIS—!

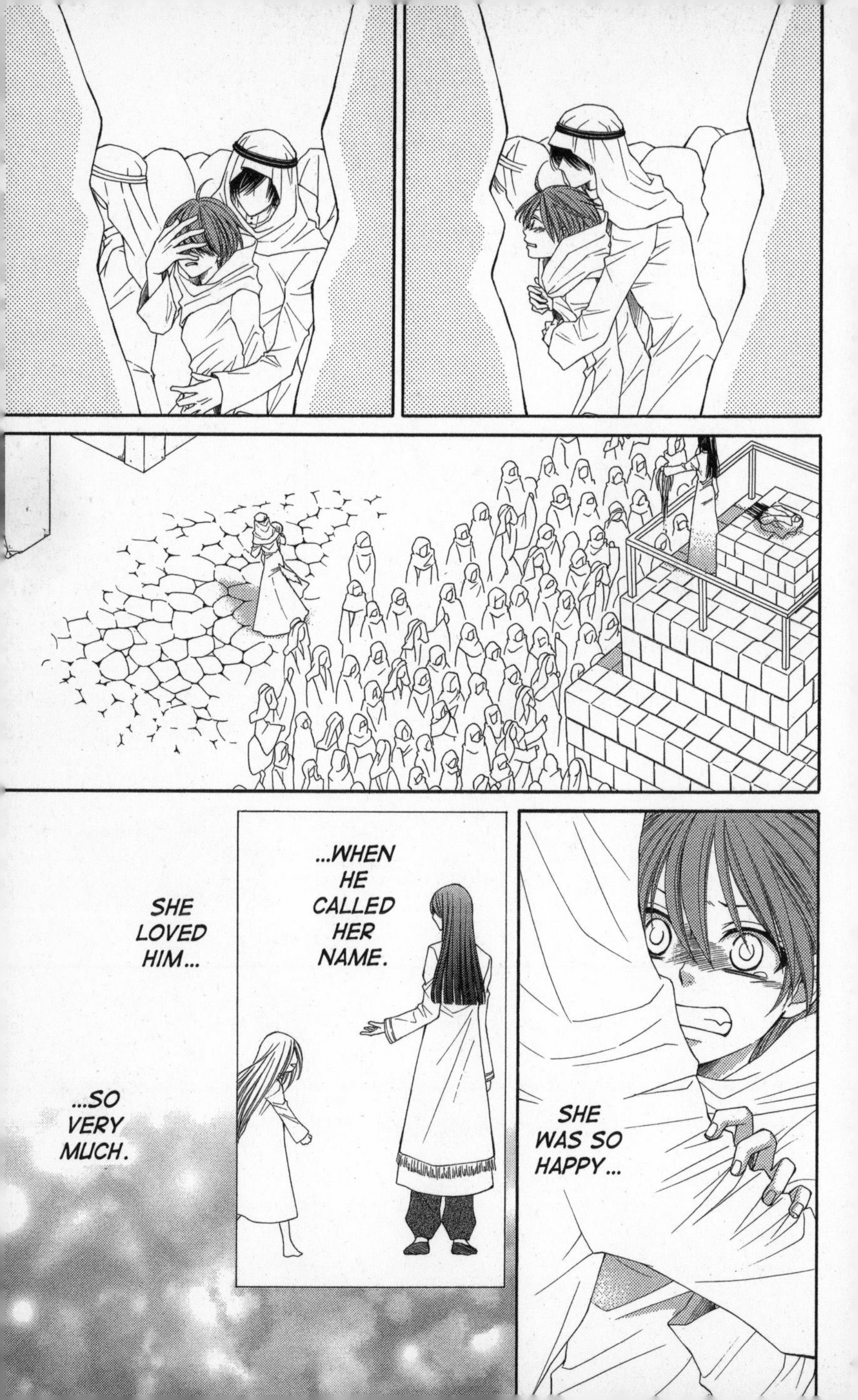
SHE WAS SO HAPPY...
...WHEN HE CALLED HER NAME.
SHE LOVED HIM...
...SO VERY MUCH.

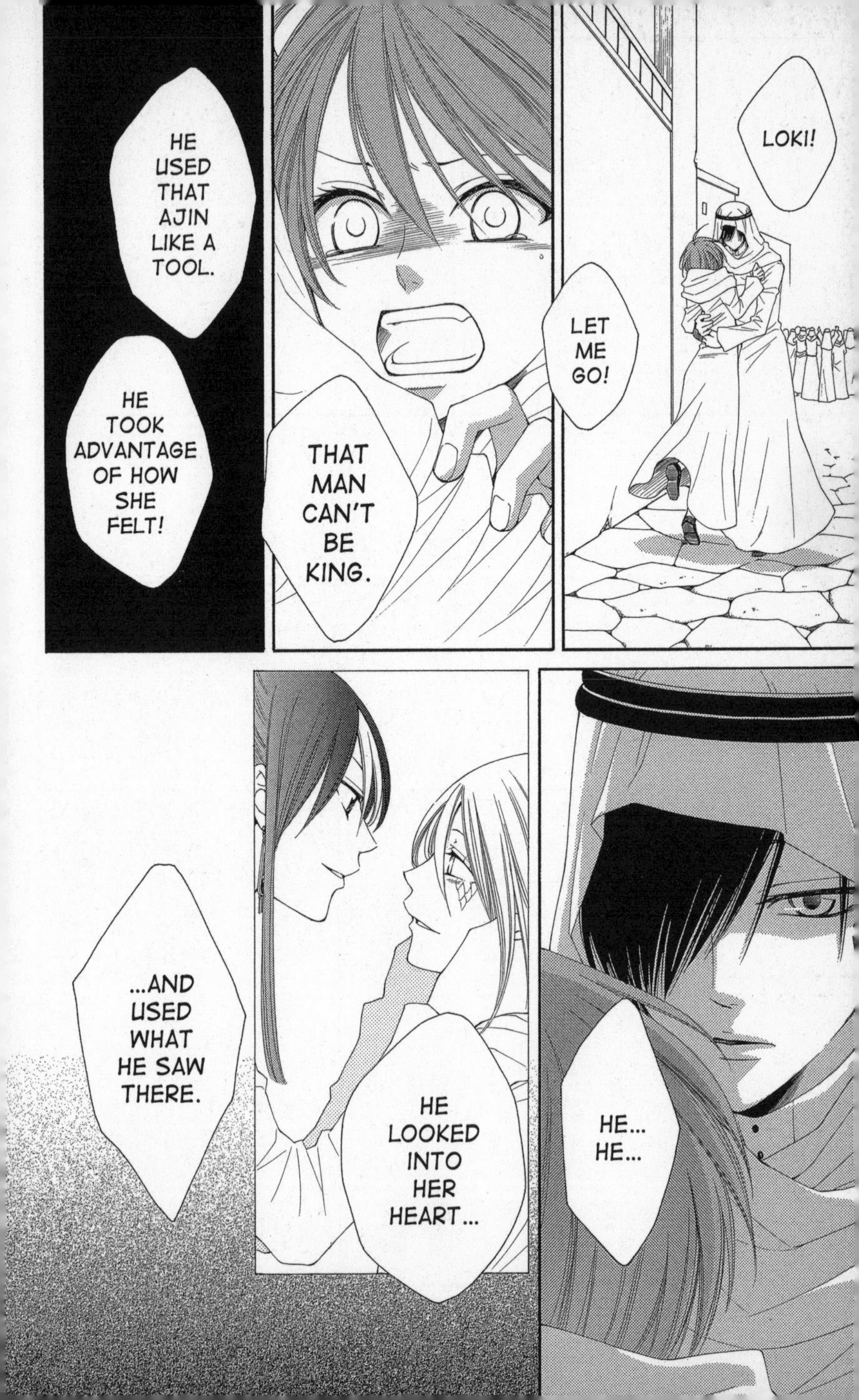
LOKI!
LET ME GO!
THAT MAN CAN'T BE KING.
HE USED THAT AJIN LIKE A TOOL.
HE TOOK ADVANTAGE OF HOW SHE FELT!
HE... HE...
HE LOOKED INTO HER HEART...
...AND USED WHAT HE SAW THERE.

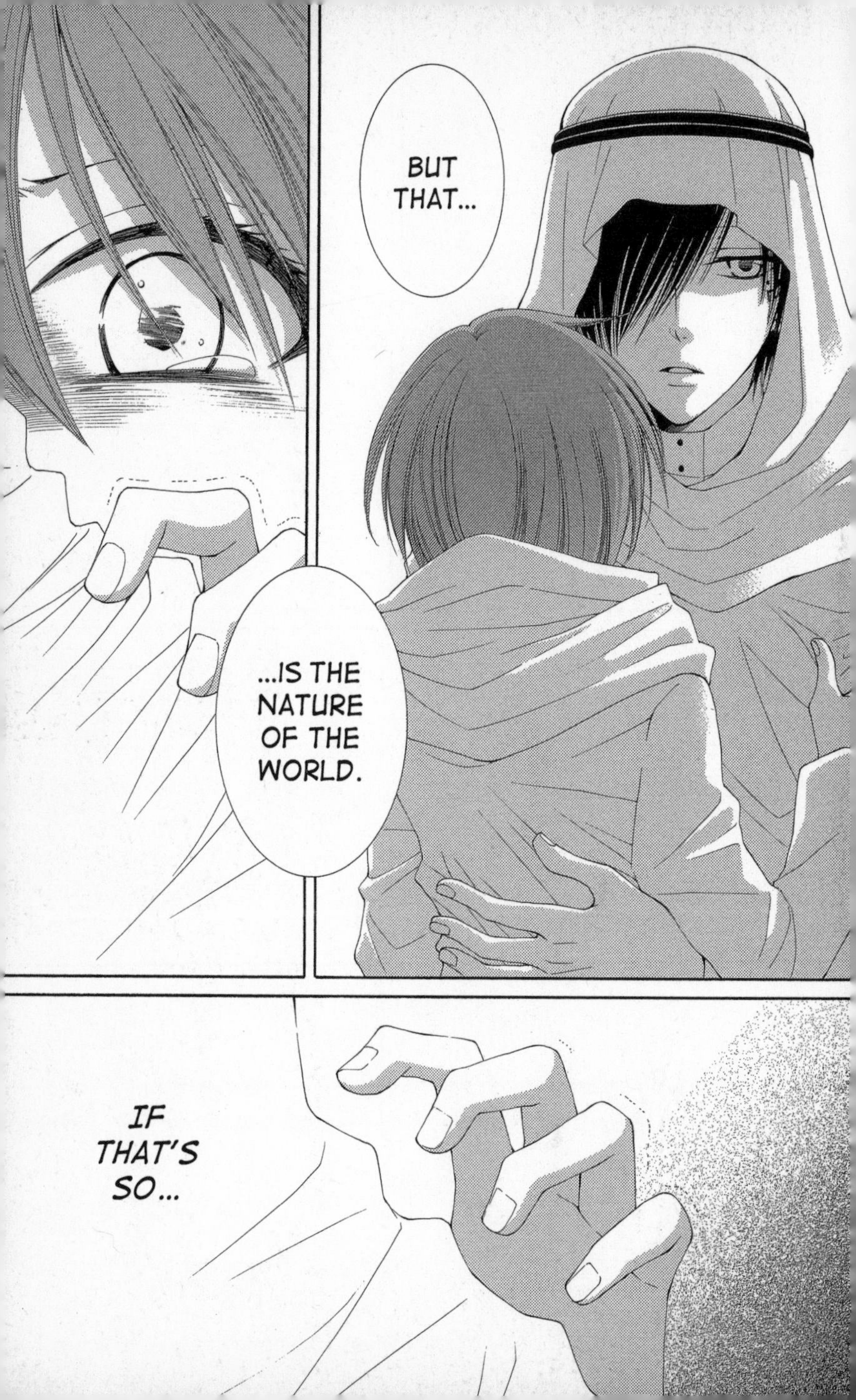
BUT THAT...
...IS THE NATURE OF THE WORLD.
IF THAT'S SO...

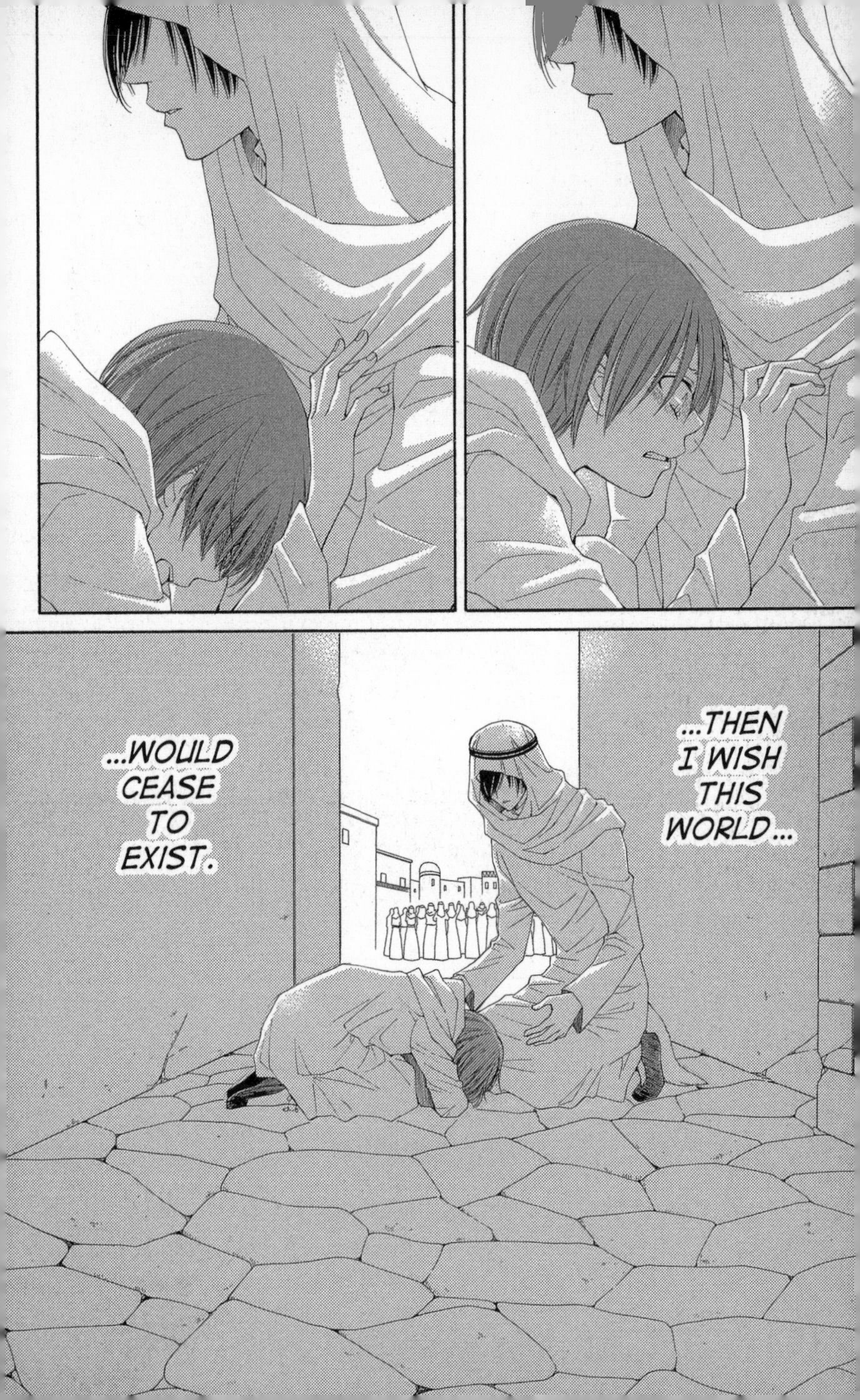
...THEN I WISH THIS WORLD...
...WOULD CEASE TO EXIST.

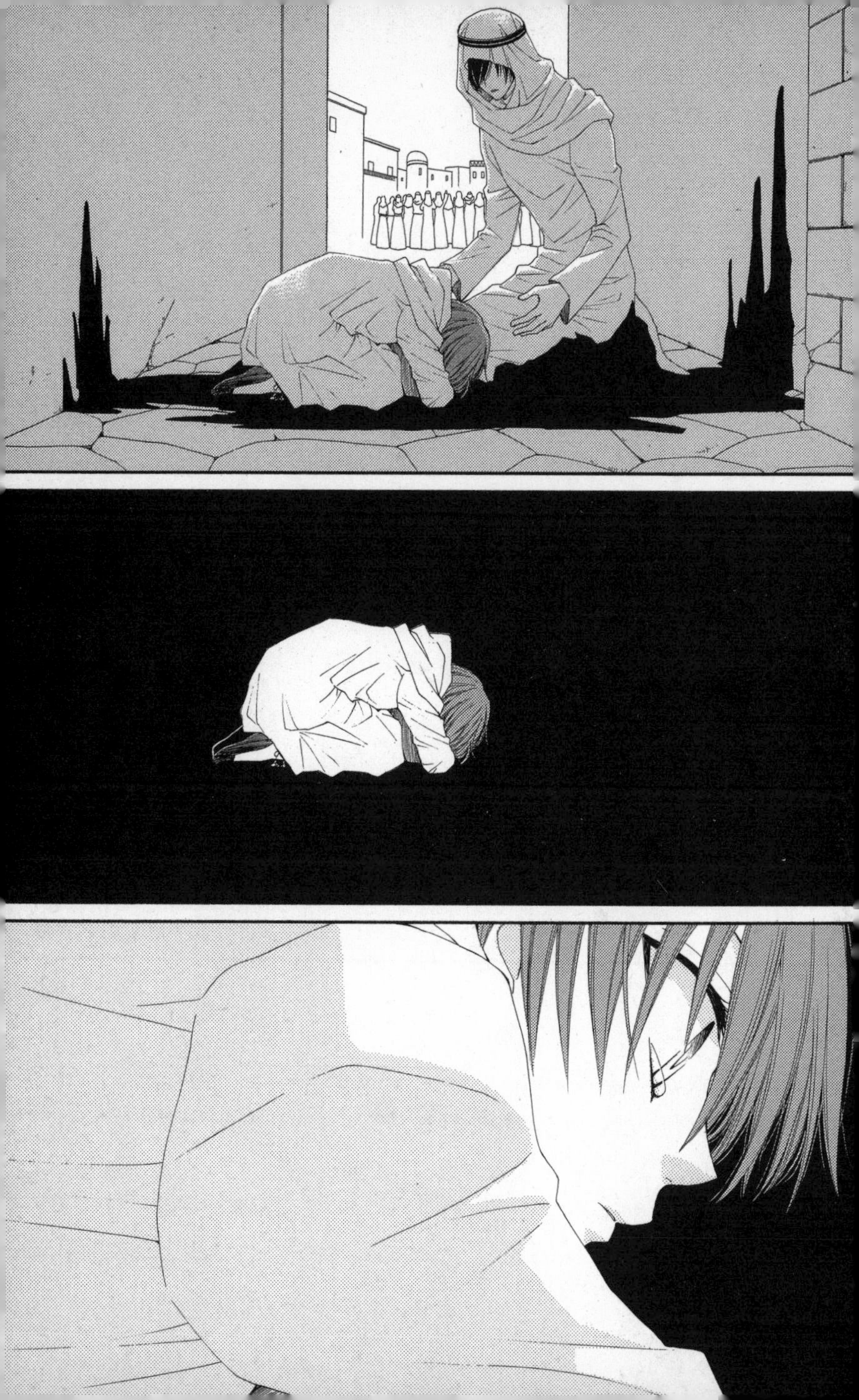

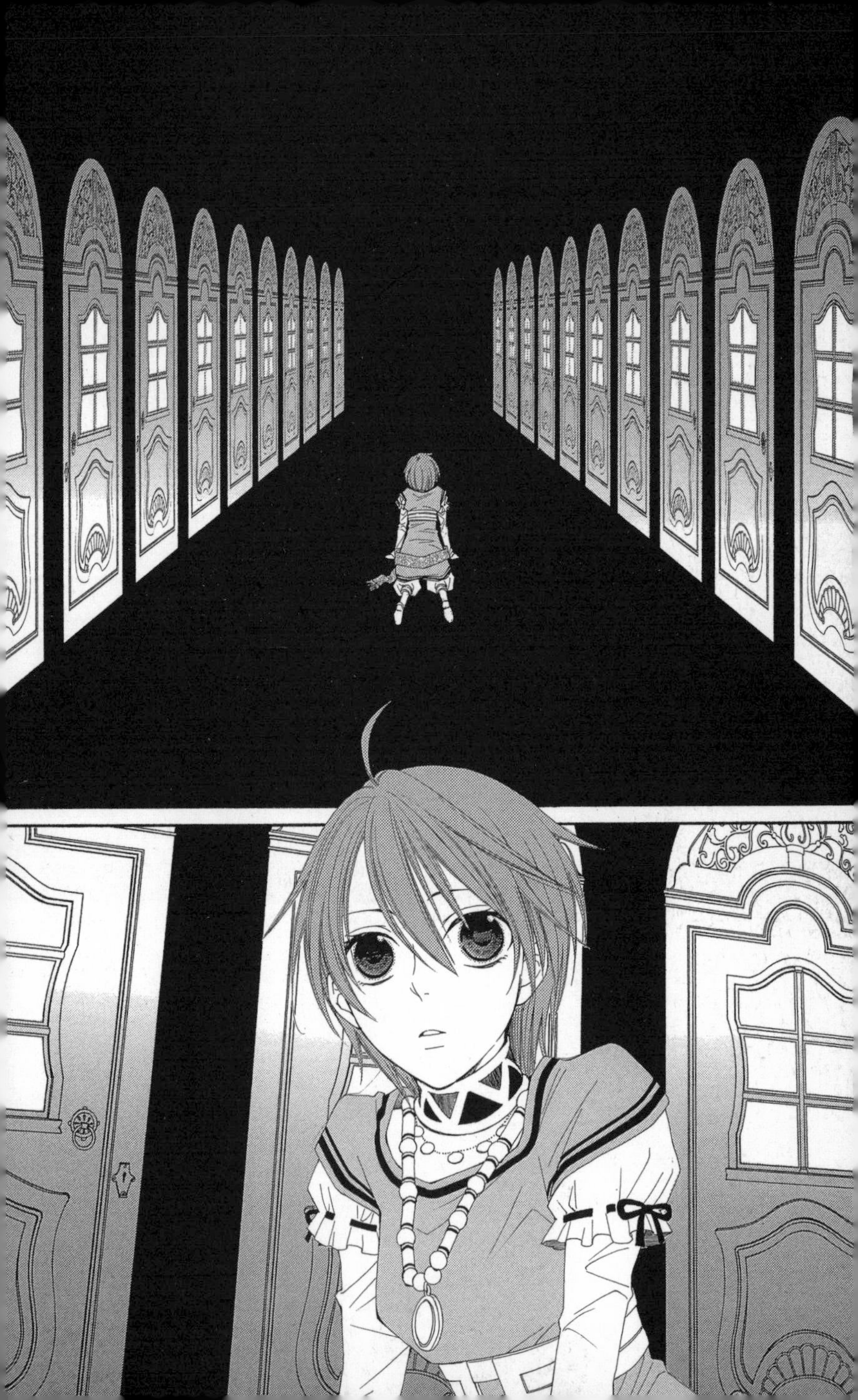

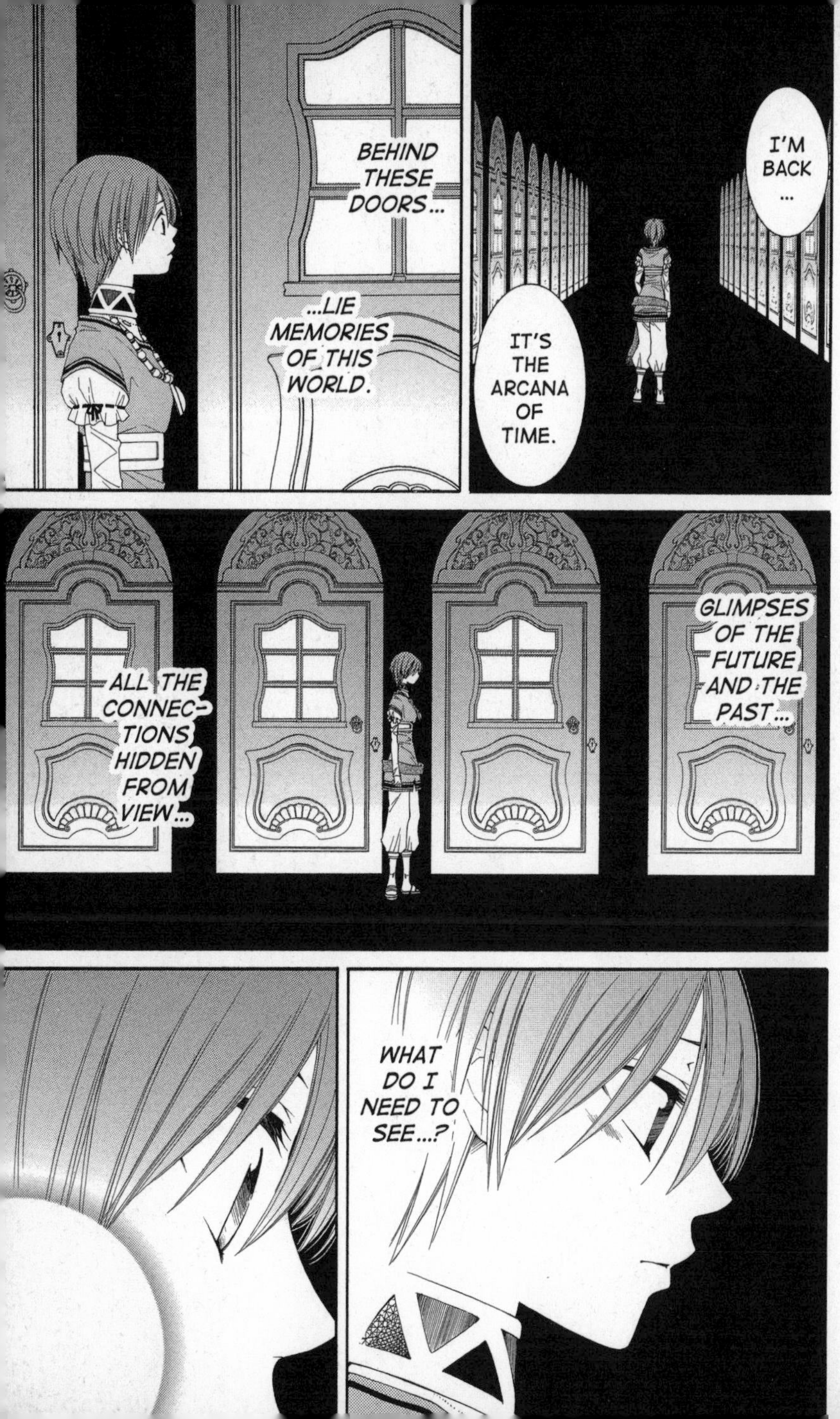
I'M BACK ...
IT'S THE ARCANA OF TIME.
BEHIND THESE DOORS...
...LIE MEMORIES OF THIS WORLD.
GLIMPSES OF THE FUTURE AND THE PAST...
ALL THE CONNECTIONS HIDDEN FROM VIEW...
WHAT DO I NEED TO SEE...?

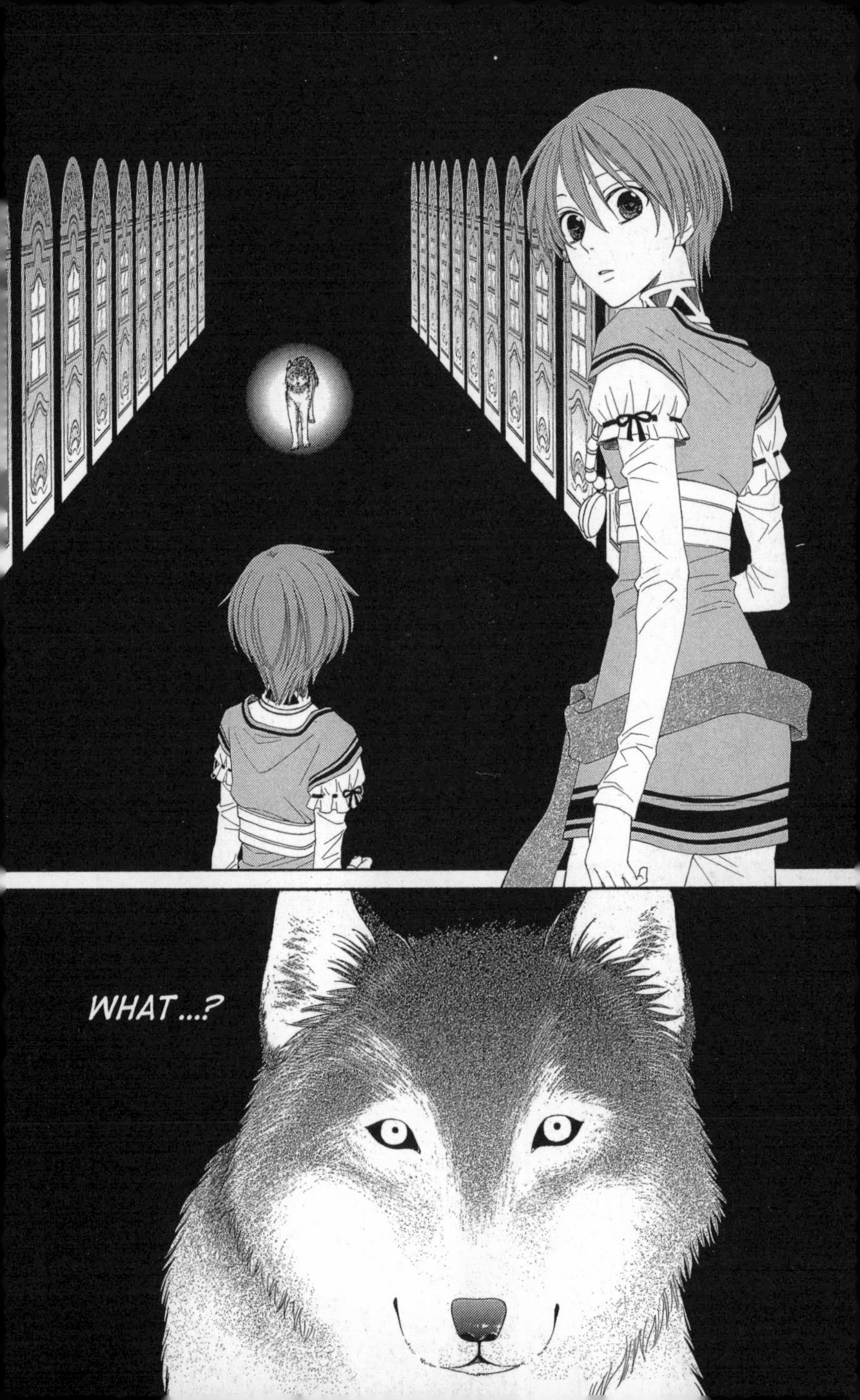
WHAT...?

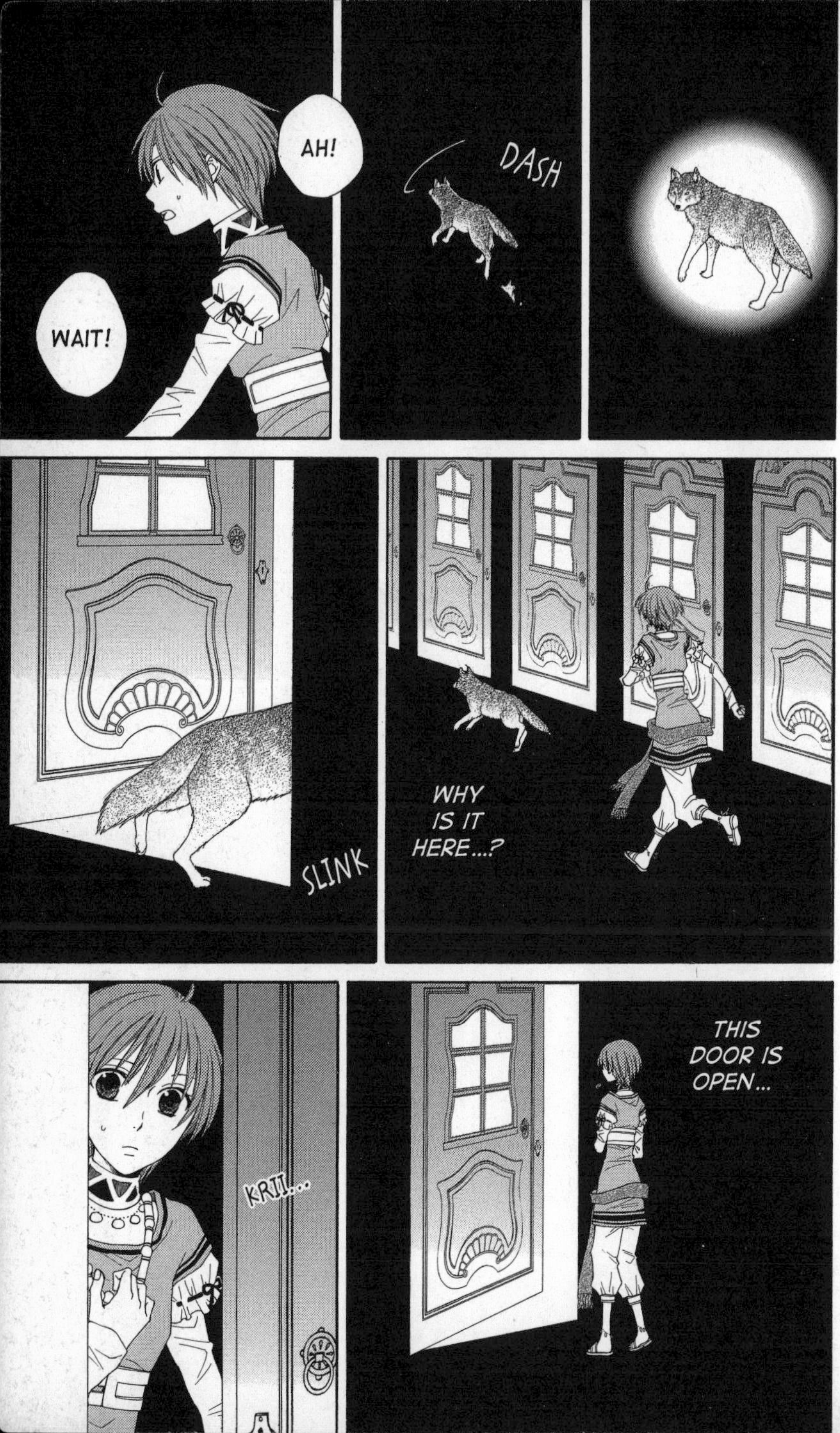
DASH
AH!
WAIT!
WHY IS IT HERE...?
SLINK
THIS DOOR IS OPEN...
KRII...

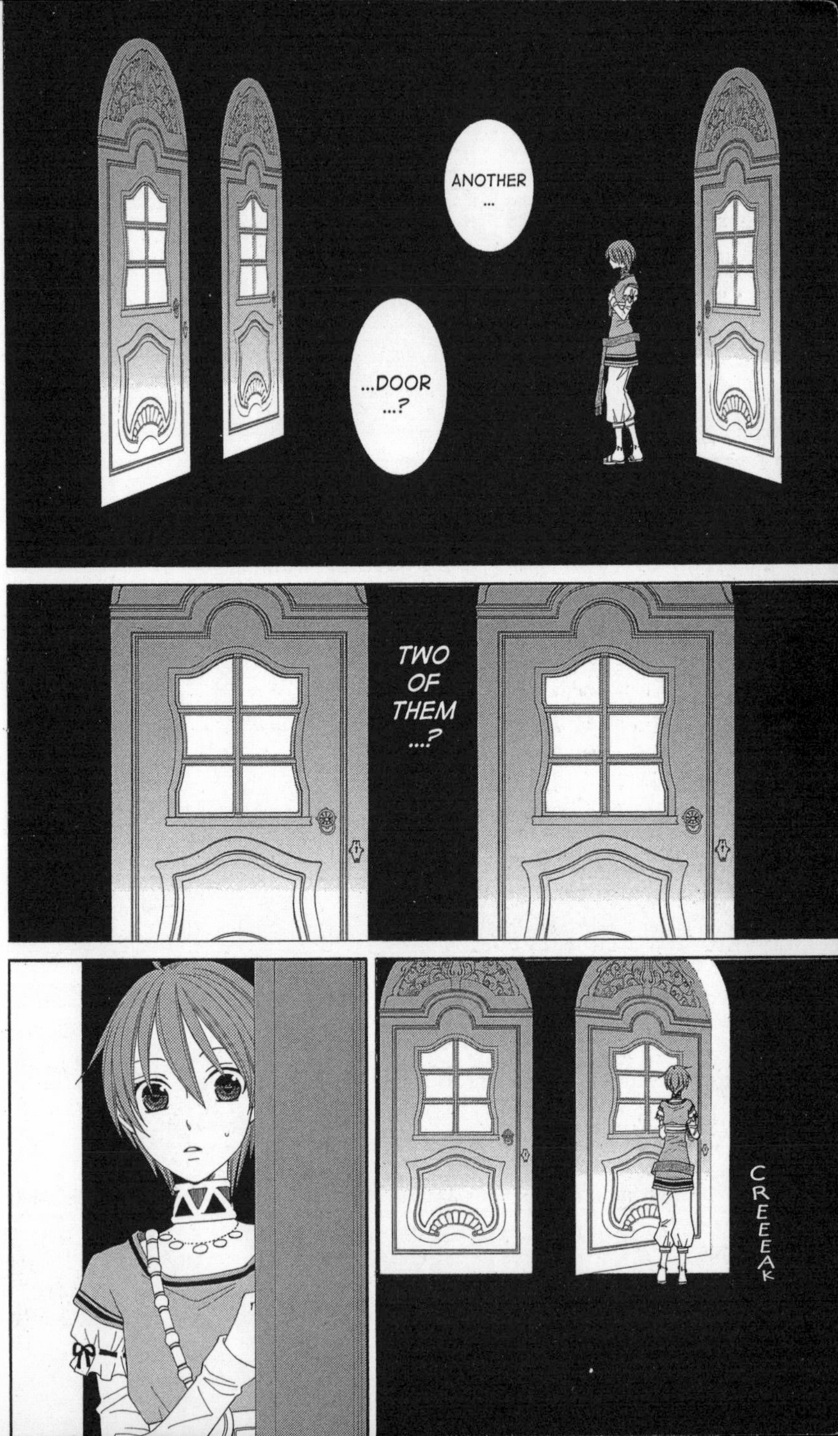
ANOTHER ...
...DOOR ...?
TWO OF THEM ...?
CREEEAK

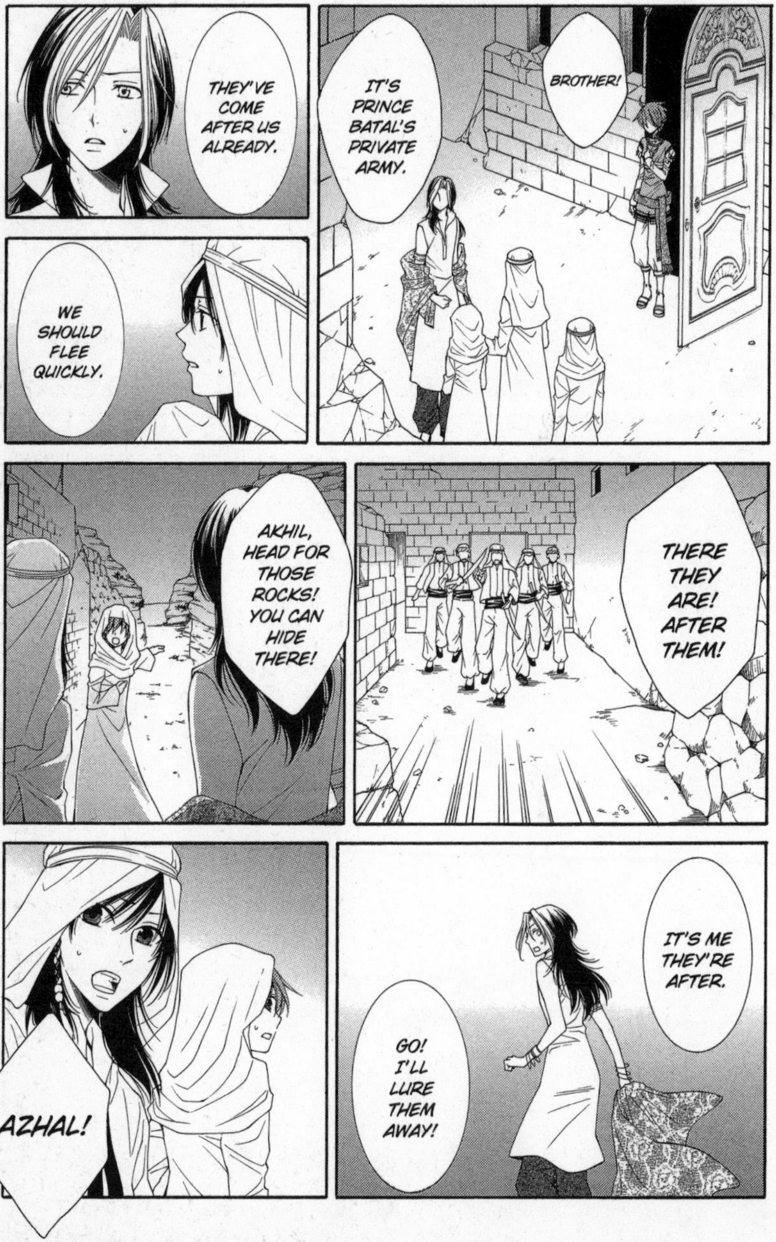
BROTHER!
IT'S PRINCE BATAL'S PRIVATE ARMY.
THEY'VE COME AFTER US ALREADY.
WE SHOULD FLEE QUICKLY.
THERE THEY ARE! AFTER THEM!
AKHIL, HEAD FOR THOSE ROCKS! YOU CAN HIDE THERE!
IT'S ME THEY'RE AFTER.
GO! I'LL LURE THEM AWAY!
AZHAL!

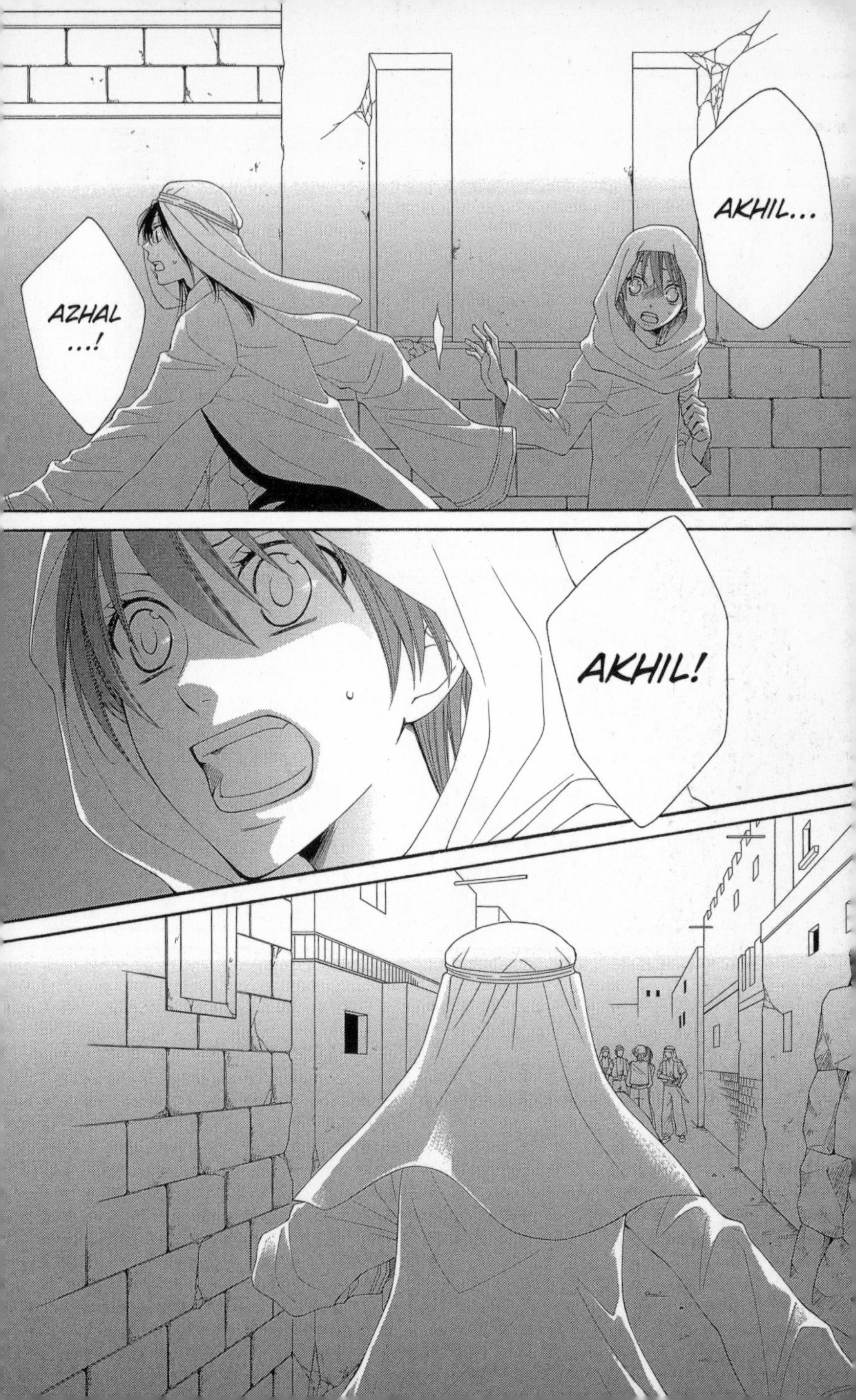
AKHIL...
AZHAL ...!
AKHIL!

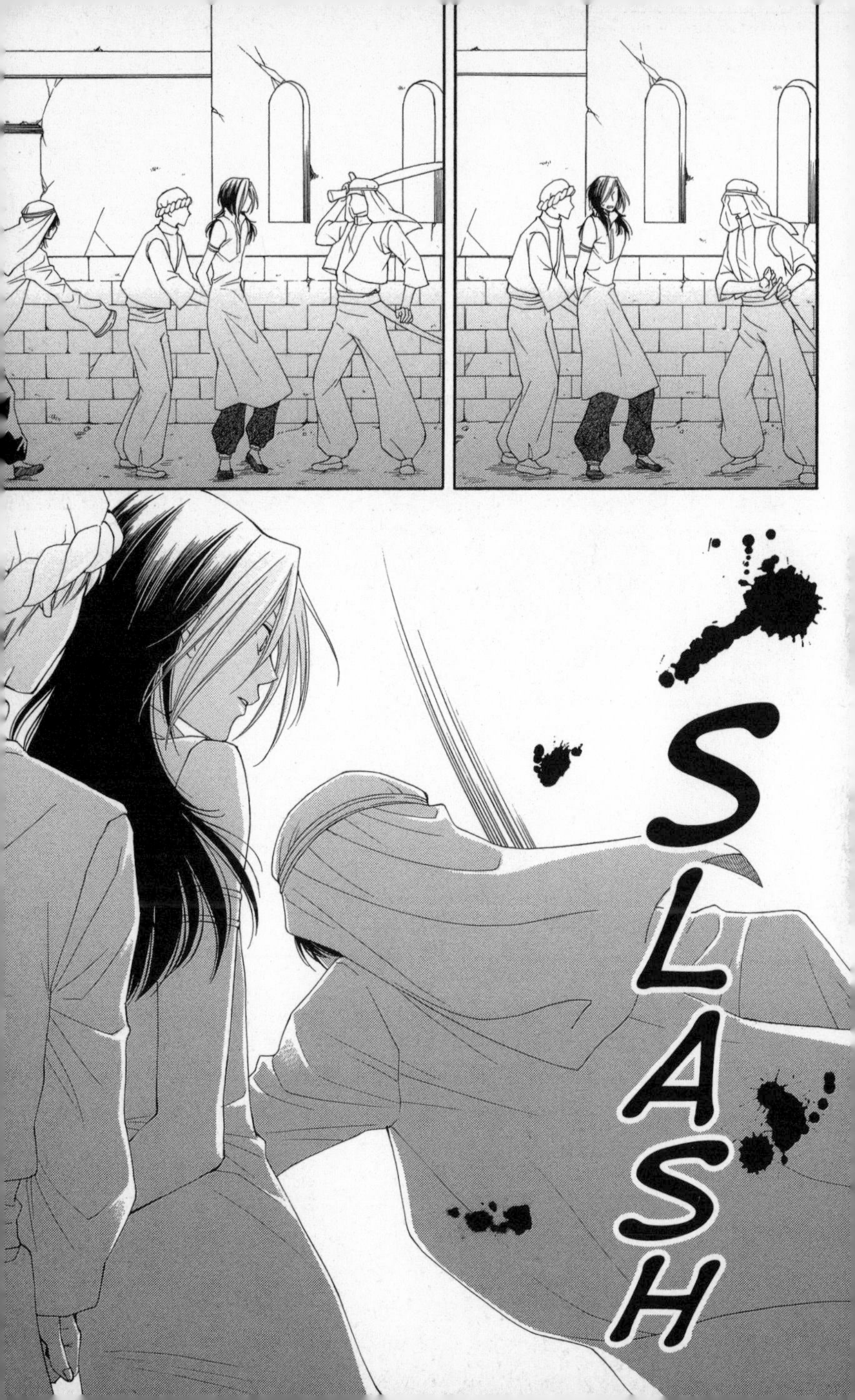
SLASH

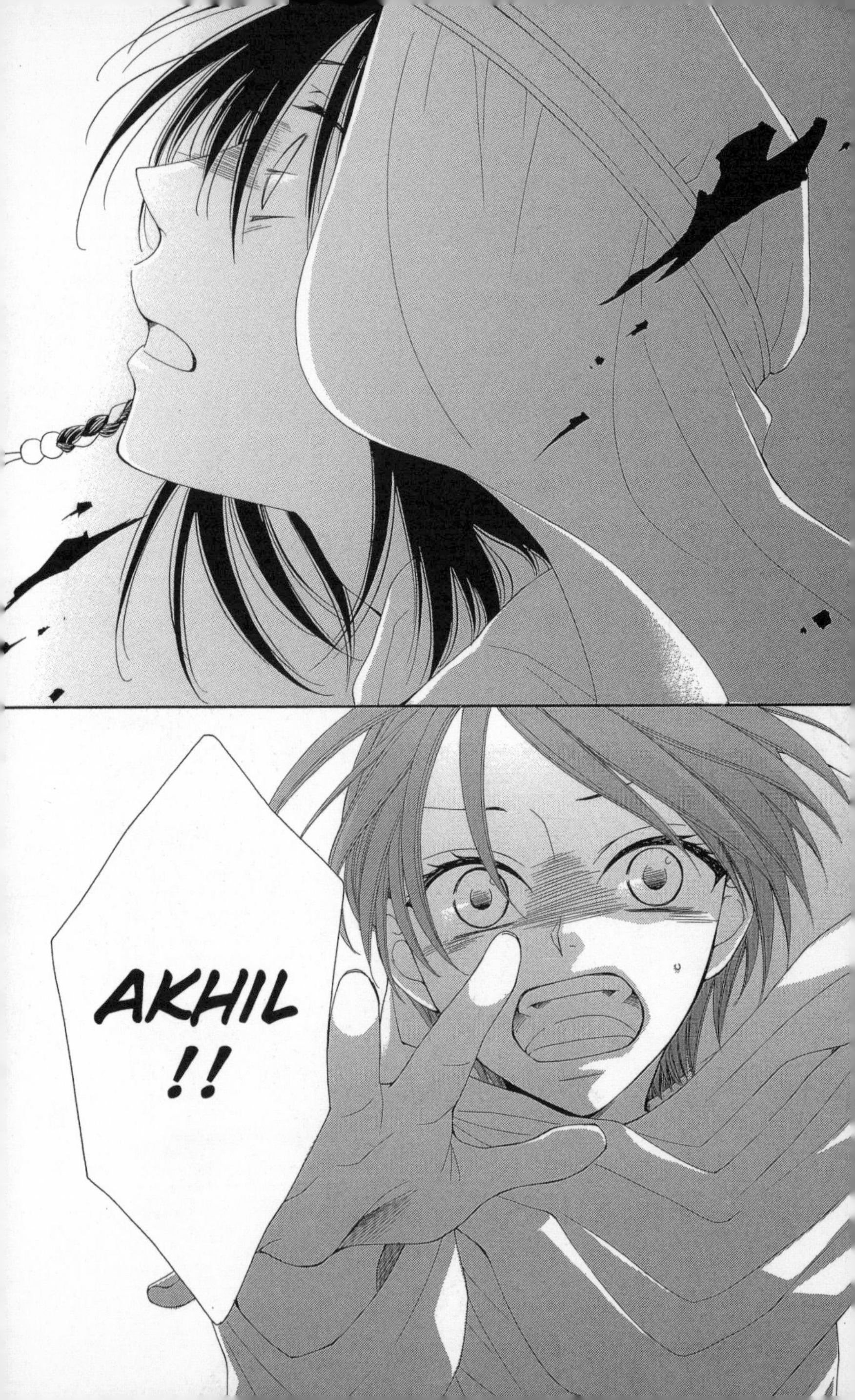
AKHIL !!

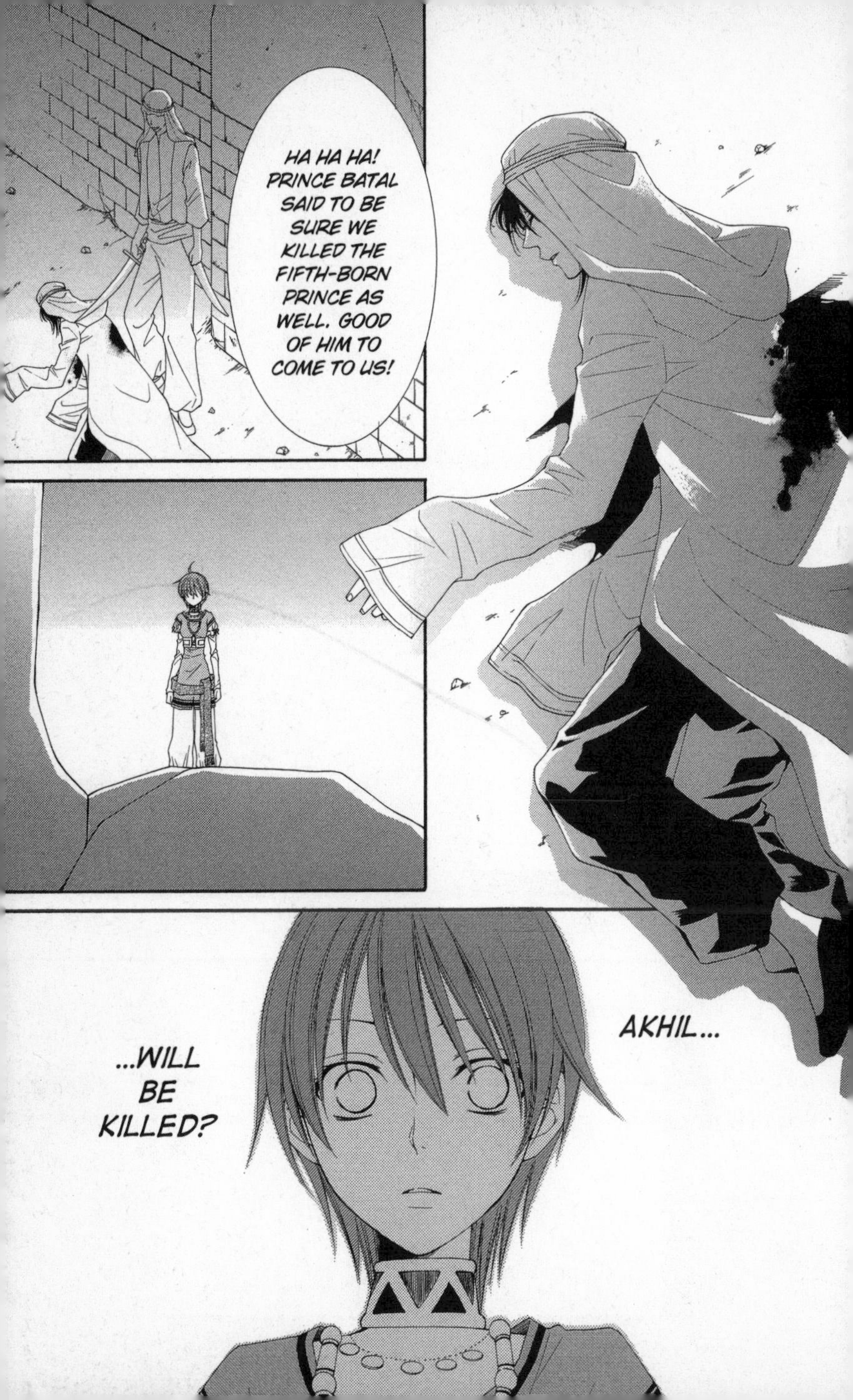
HA HA HA! PRINCE BATAL SAID TO BE SURE WE KILLED THE FIFTH-BORN PRINCE AS WELL. GOOD OF HIM TO COME TO US!
AKHIL...
...WILL BE KILLED?

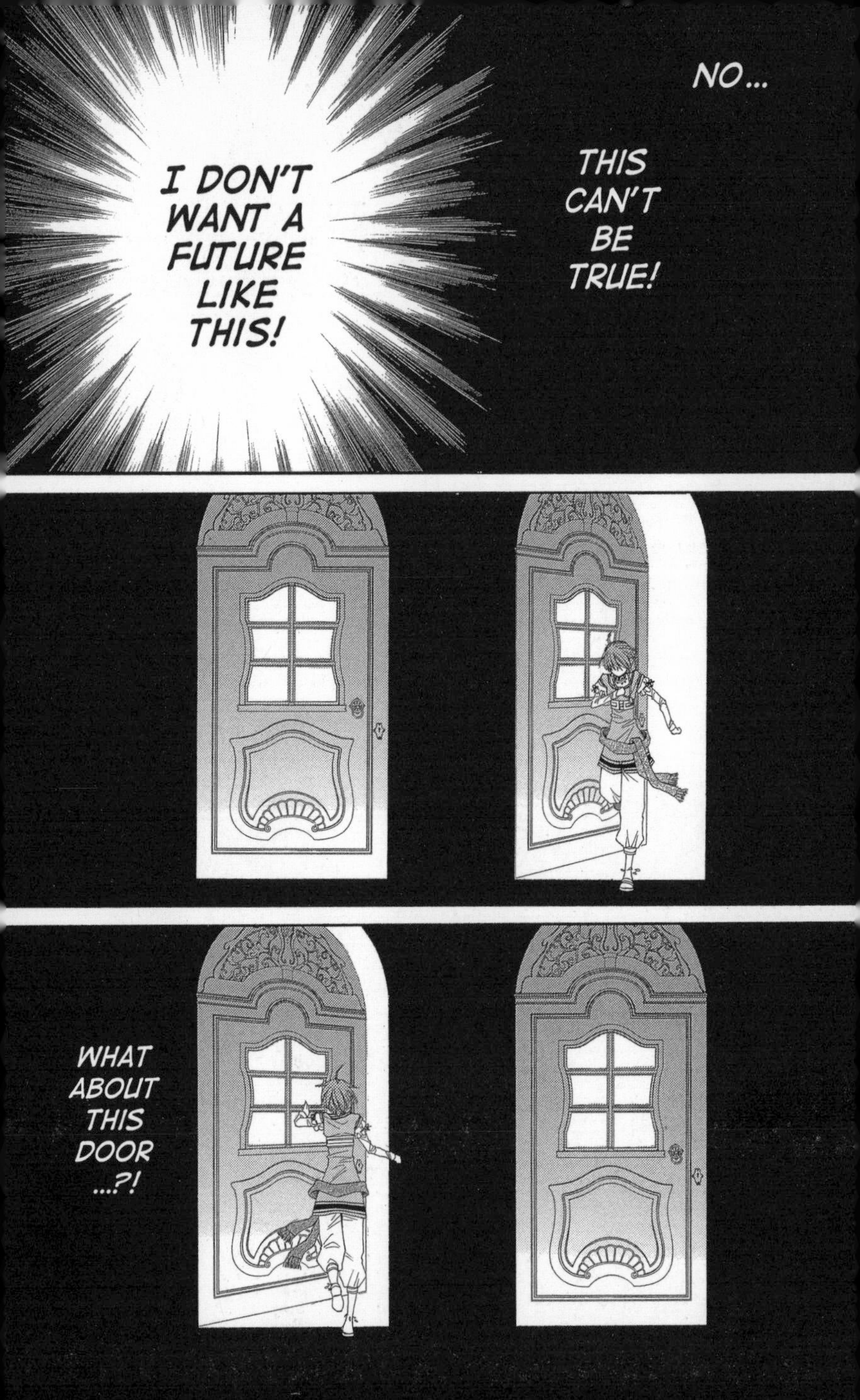
NO...
THIS CAN'T BE TRUE!
I DON'T WANT A FUTURE LIKE THIS!
WHAT ABOUT THIS DOOR ...?!

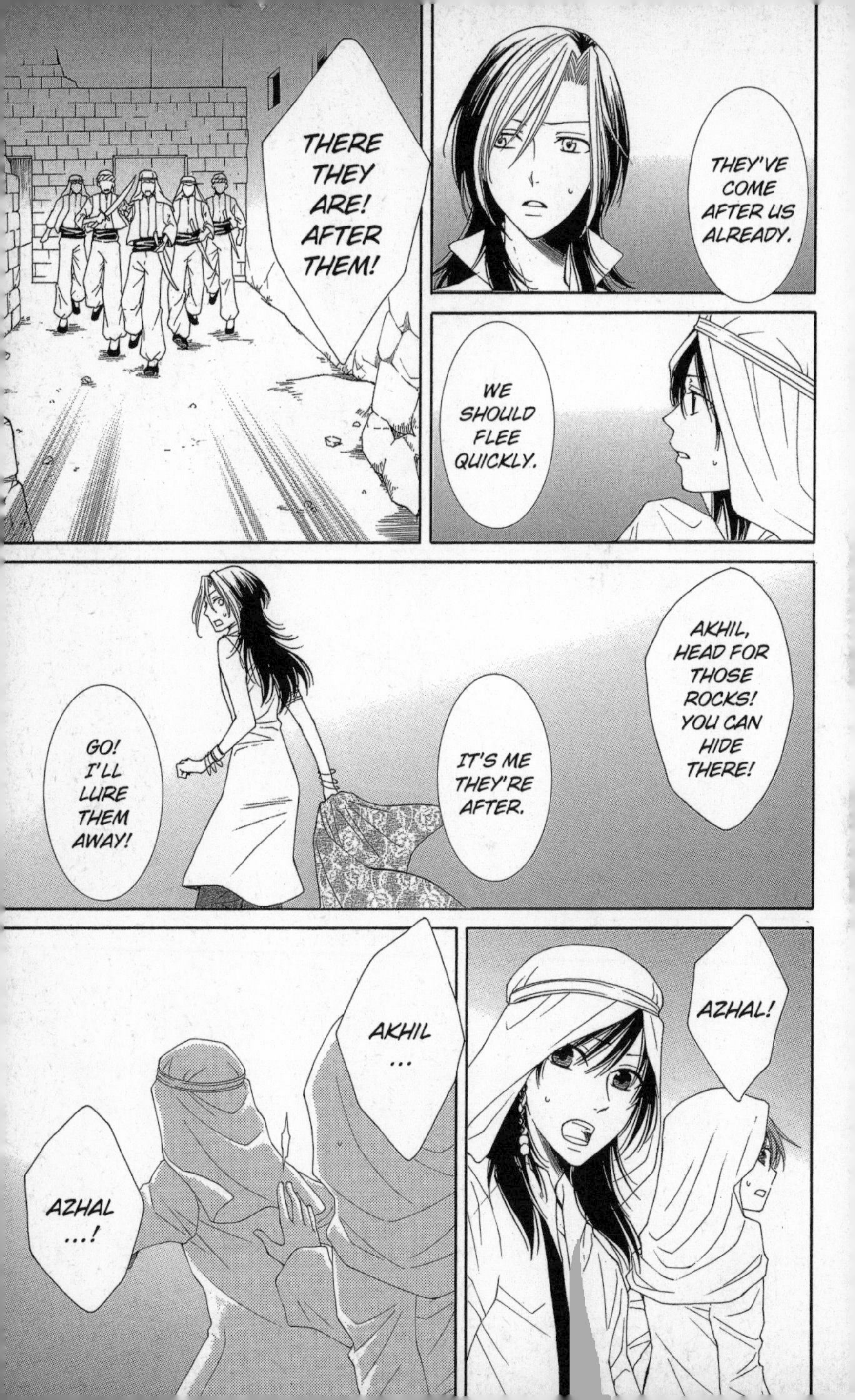
THEY'VE COME AFTER US ALREADY.
WE SHOULD FLEE QUICKLY.
THERE THEY ARE! AFTER THEM!
AKHIL, HEAD FOR THOSE ROCKS! YOU CAN HIDE THERE!
IT'S ME THEY'RE AFTER.
GO! I'LL LURE THEM AWAY!
AZHAL!
AKHIL ...
AZHAL ...!

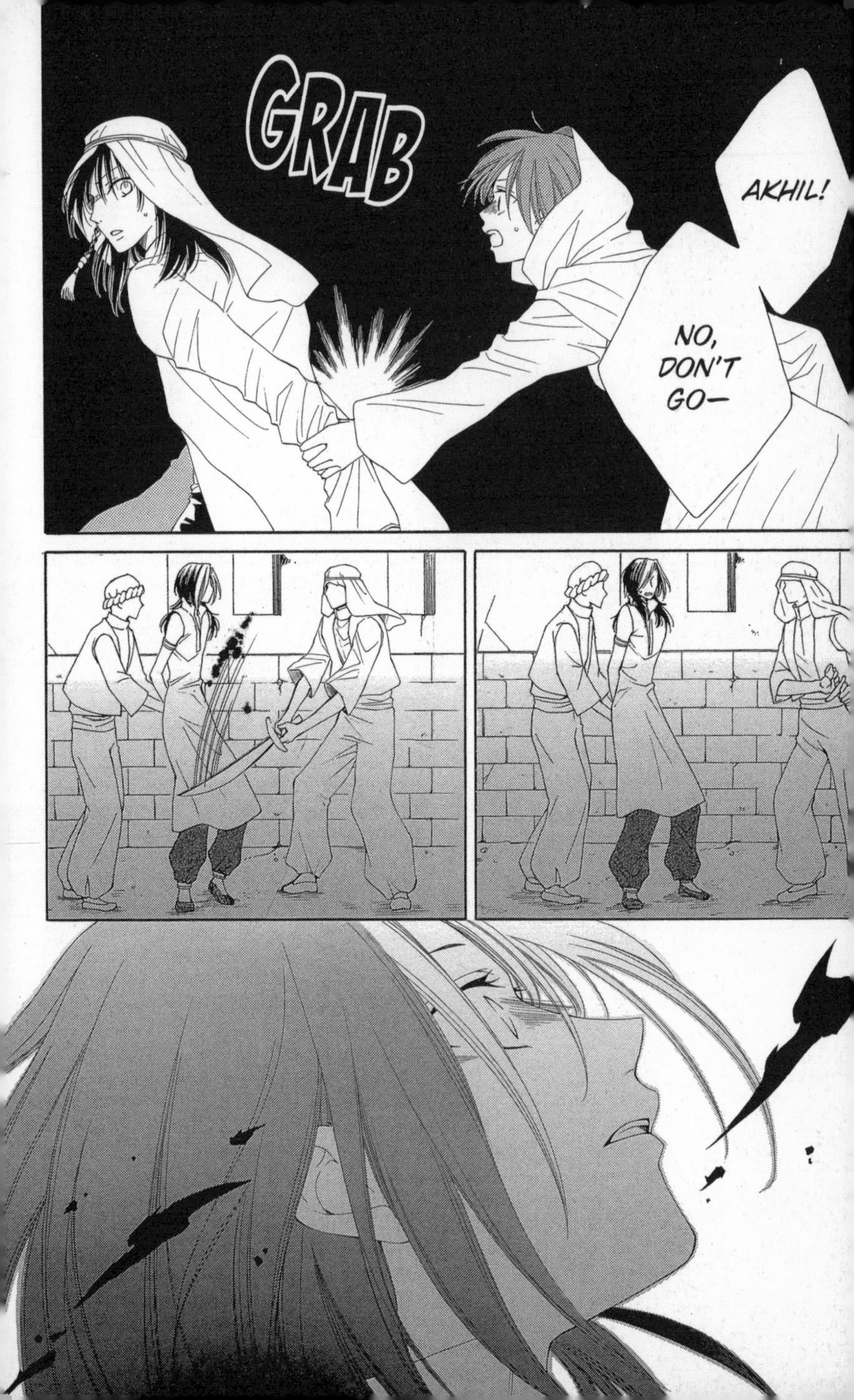
GRAB
AKHIL!
NO, DON'T GO—

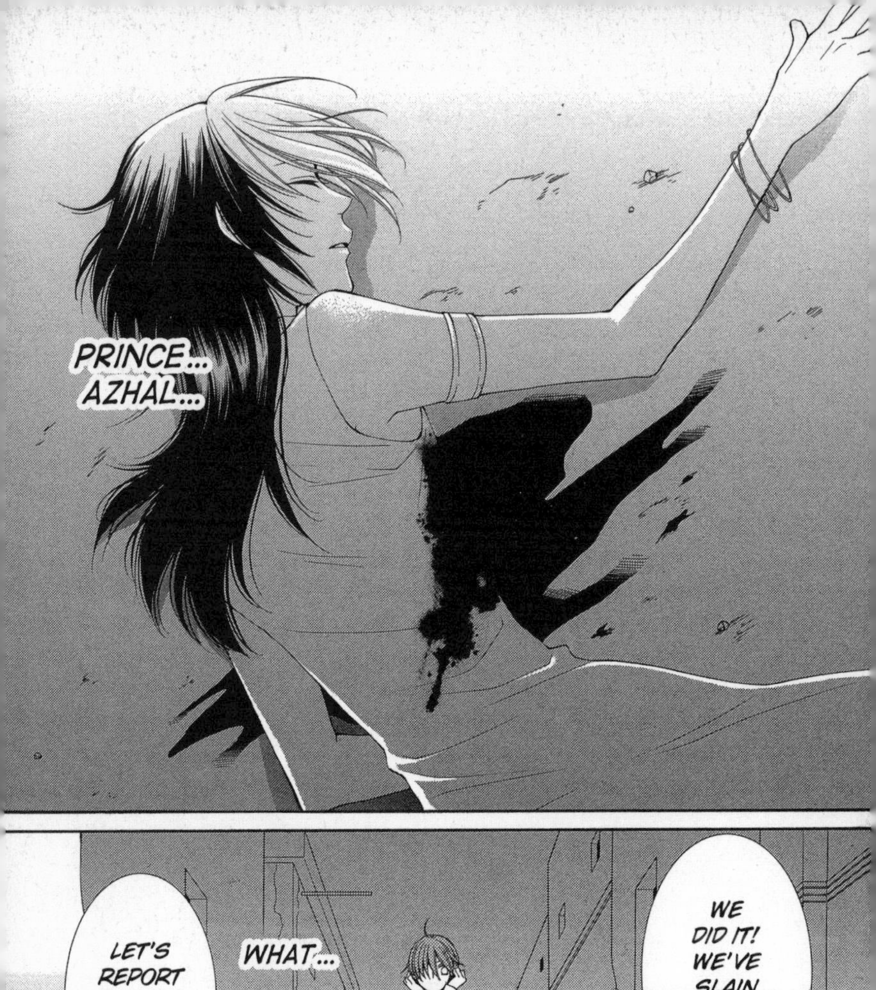
PRINCE... AZHAL...
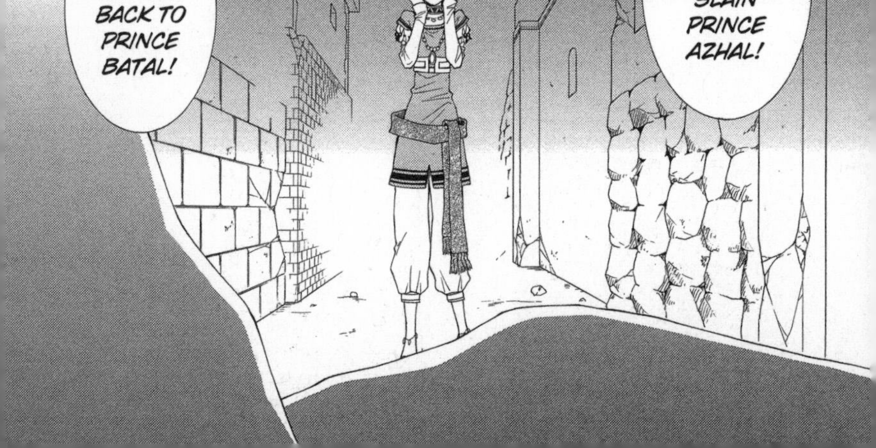
WE DID IT! WE'VE SLAIN PRINCE AZHAL!
WHAT...
LET'S REPORT BACK TO PRINCE BATAL!

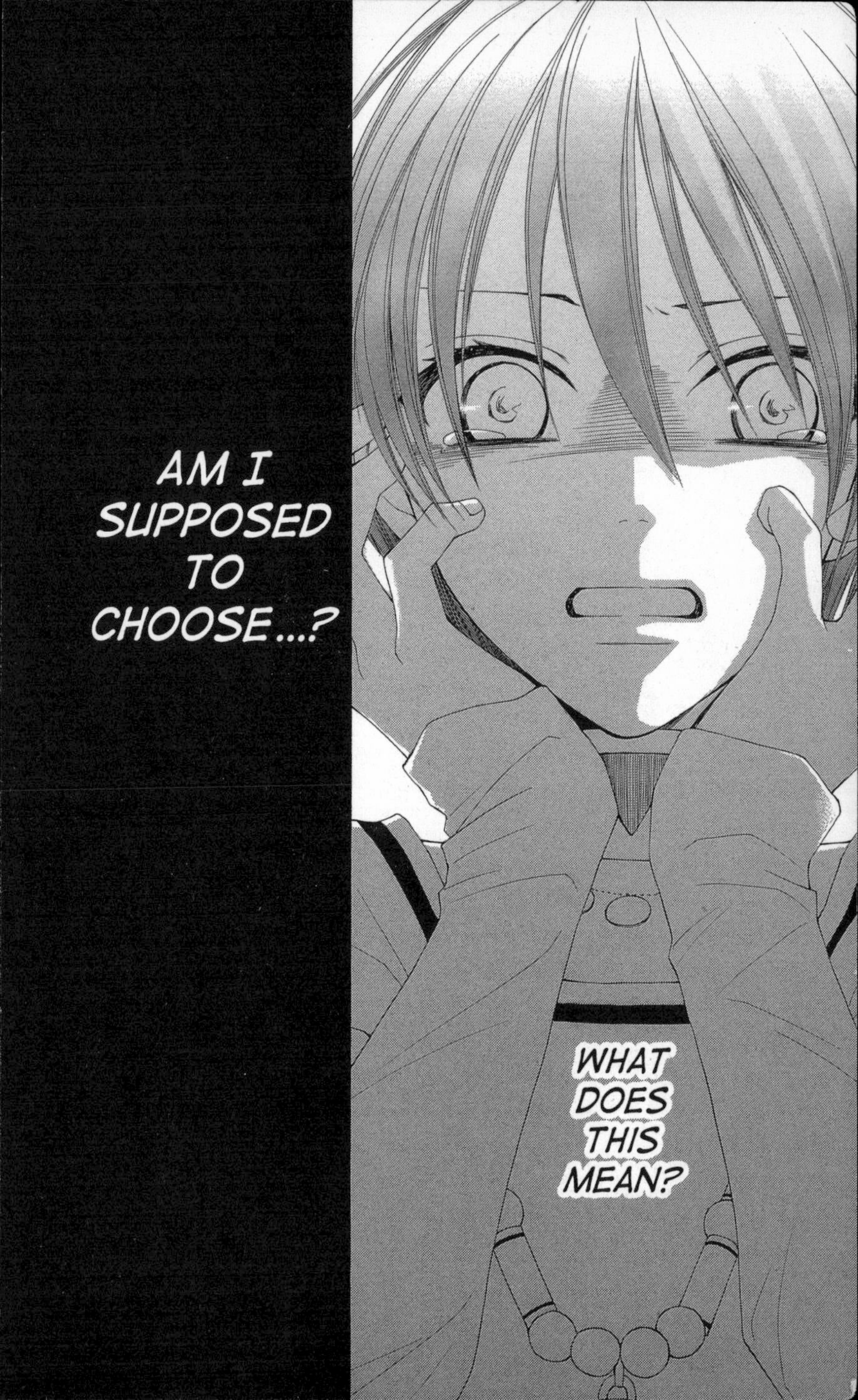
WHAT DOES THIS MEAN?
AM I SUPPOSED TO CHOOSE....?

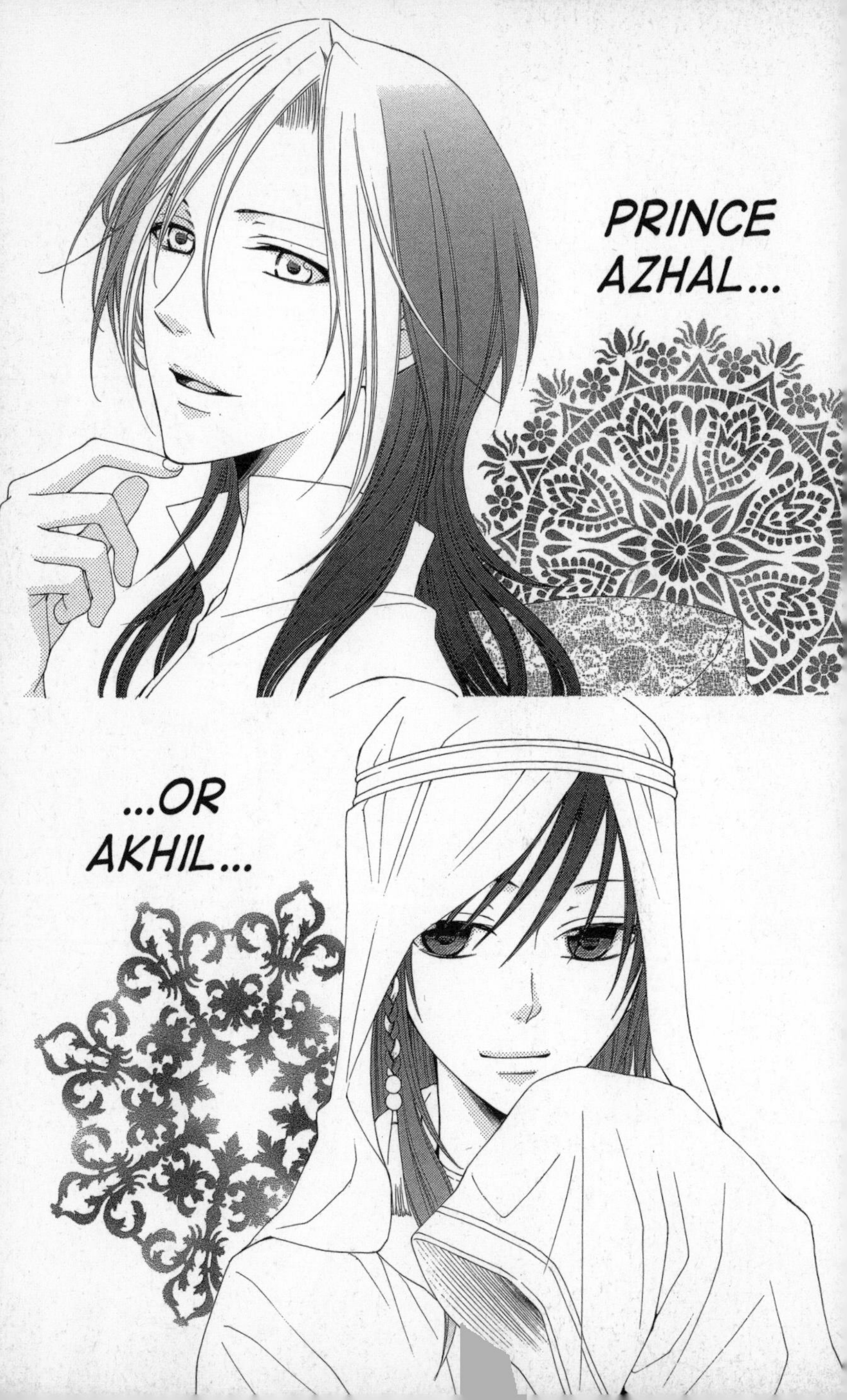

PRINCE AZHAL...
...OR AKHIL...

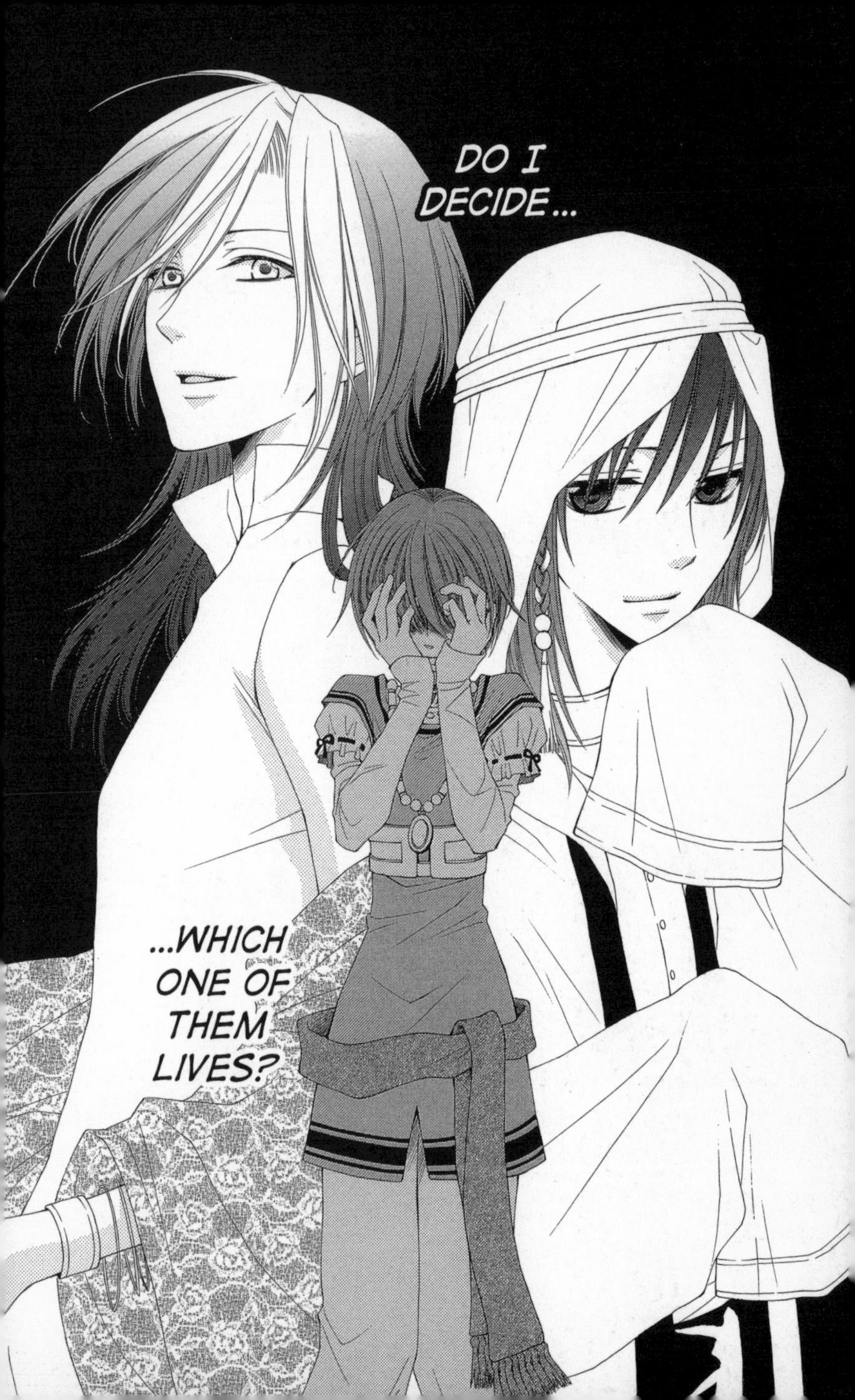
DO I DECIDE...
...WHICH ONE OF THEM LIVES?

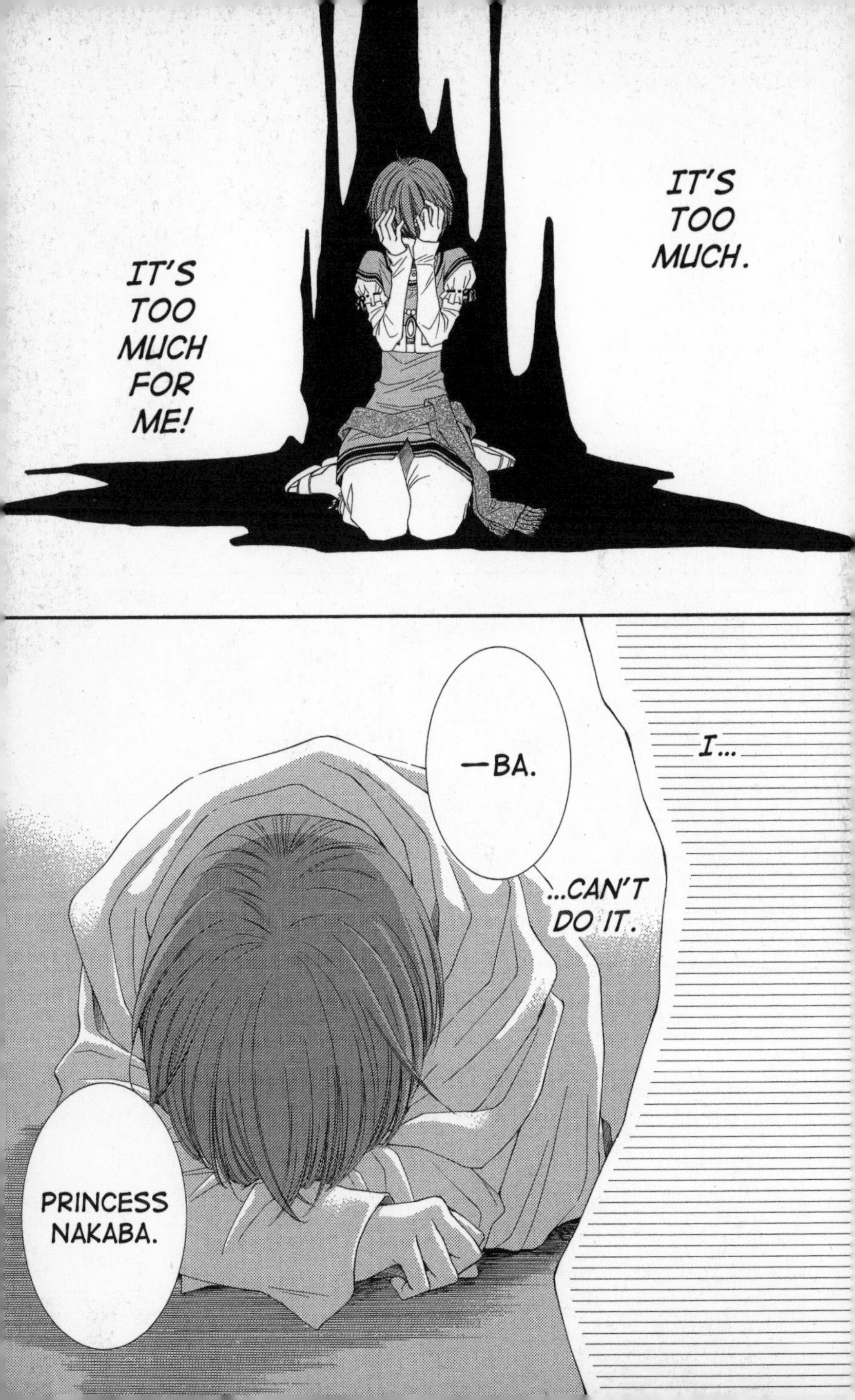
IT'S TOO MUCH.
IT'S TOO MUCH FOR ME!
I...
...CAN'T DO IT.
—BA.
PRINCESS NAKABA.

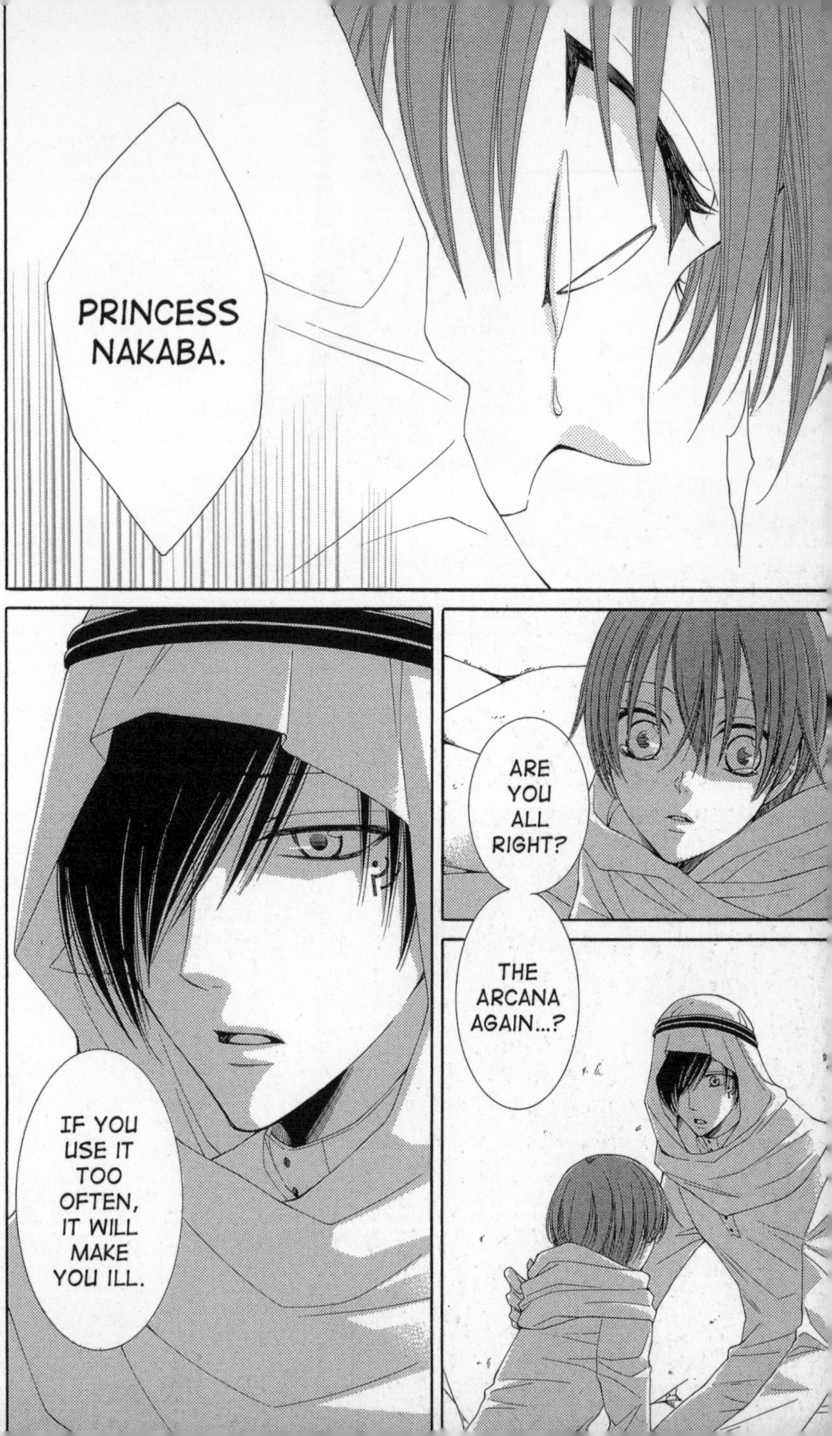
PRINCESS NAKABA.
ARE YOU ALL RIGHT?
THE ARCANA AGAIN...?
IF YOU USE IT TOO OFTEN, IT WILL MAKE YOU ILL.

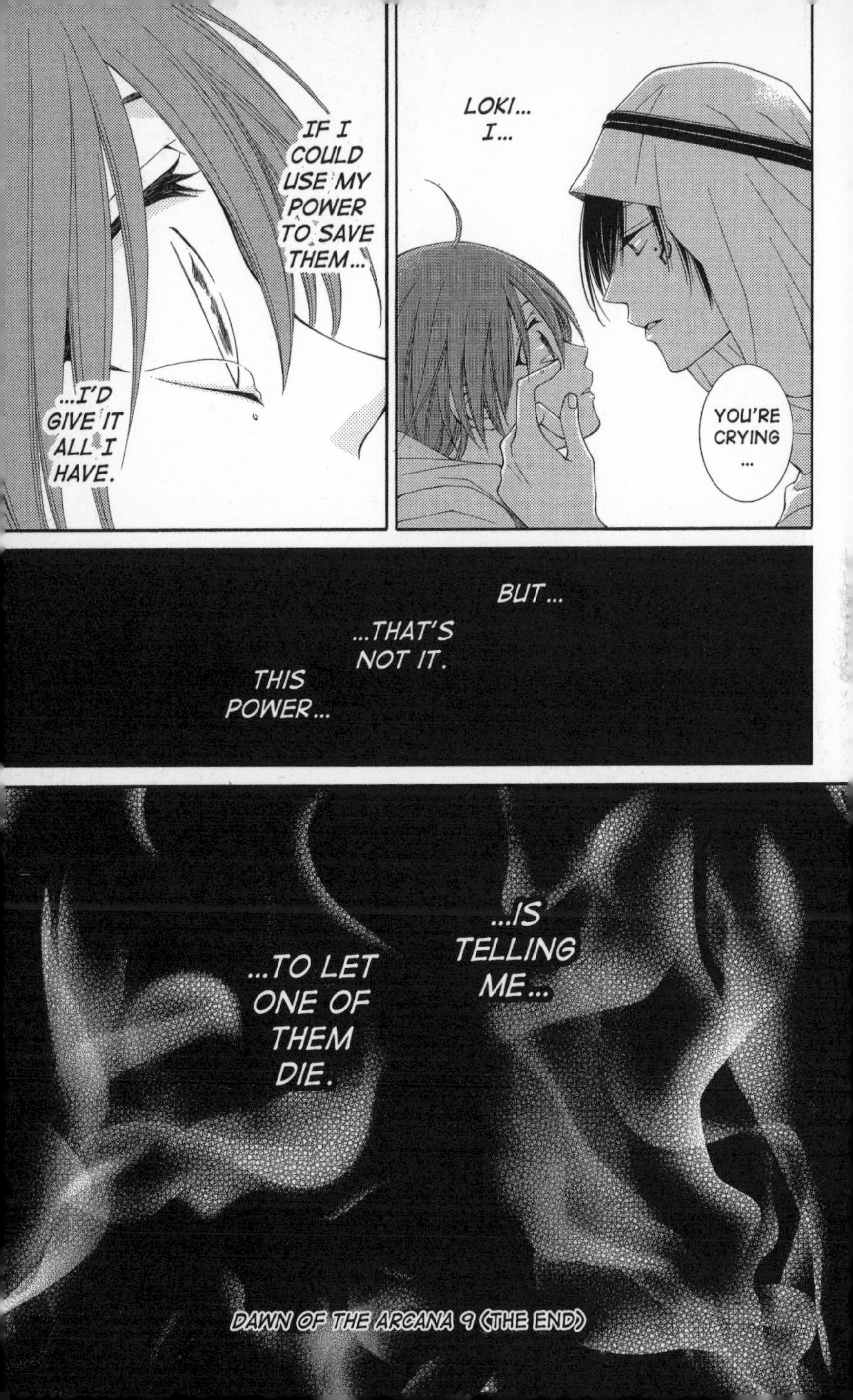
LOKI... I...
YOU'RE CRYING...
IF I COULD USE MY POWER TO SAVE THEM...
...I'D GIVE IT ALL I HAVE.
BUT...
...THAT'S NOT IT.
THIS POWER...
...IS TELLING ME...
...TO LET ONE OF THEM DIE.
DAWN OF THE ARCANA 9 (THE END)

Mr. Ser-cea.
Nope, I just can't
make him look cool.
I'm so sorry.

...

Bonus Chapter

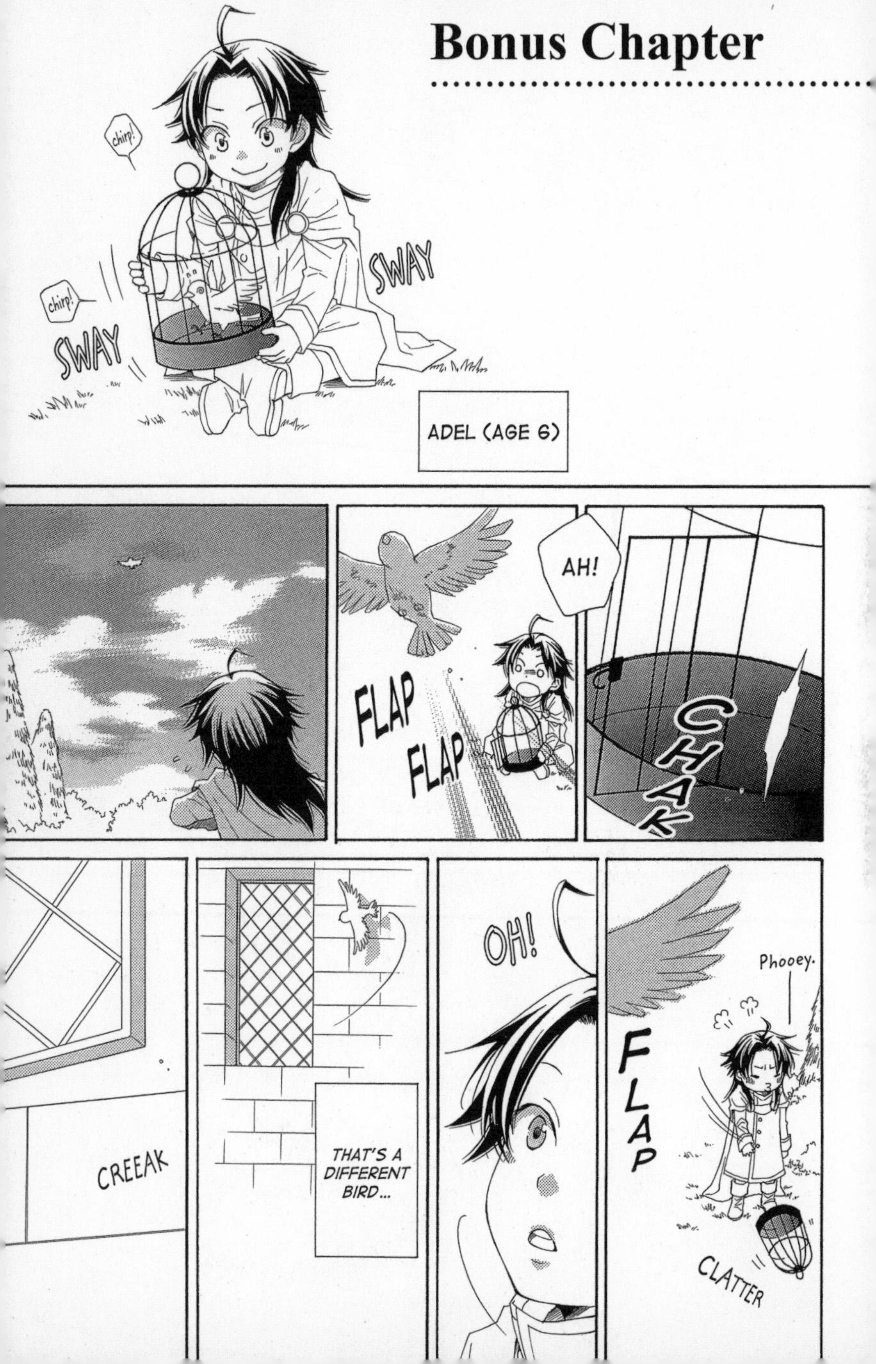
ADEL (AGE 6)
chirp!
SWAY
chirp!
SWAY
CHAK
AH!
FLAP
FLAP
Phooey.
FLAP
CLATTER
OH!
THAT'S A DIFFERENT BIRD...
CREEAK

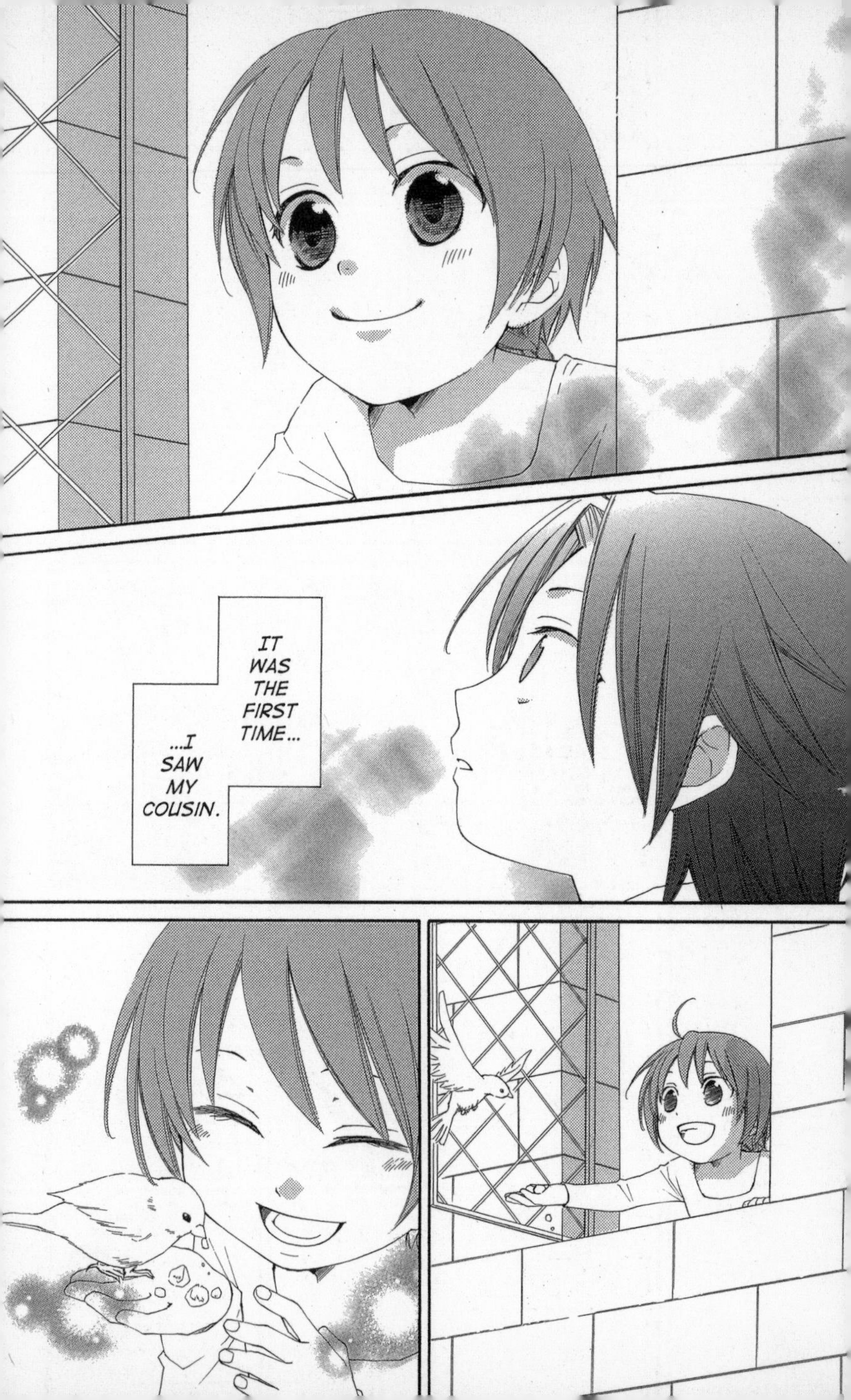
IT WAS THE FIRST TIME...
...I SAW MY COUSIN.

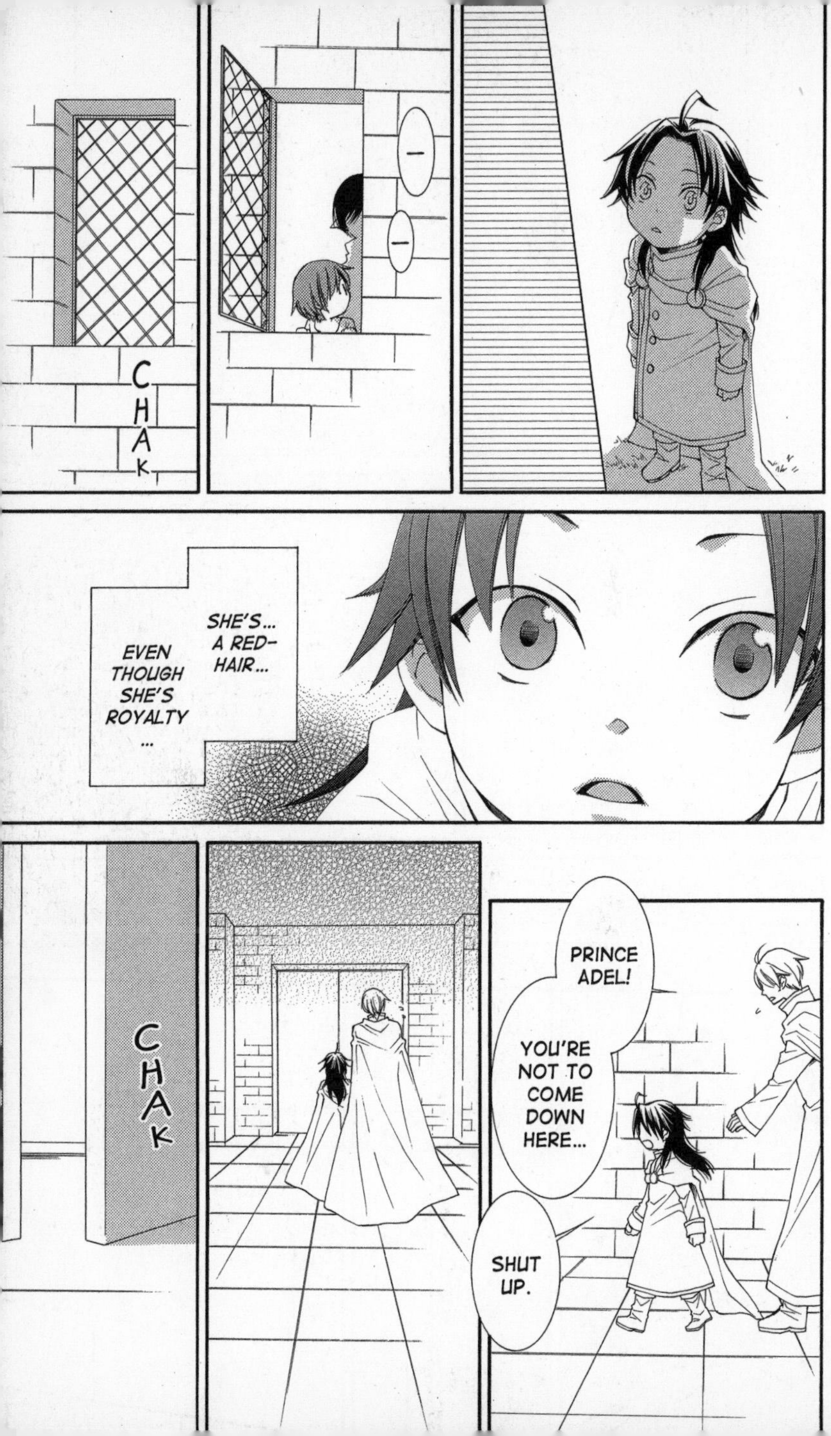
—
—
CHAK
SHE'S... A RED-HAIR...
EVEN THOUGH SHE'S ROYALTY ...
PRINCE ADEL!
YOU'RE NOT TO COME DOWN HERE...
SHUT UP.
CHAK

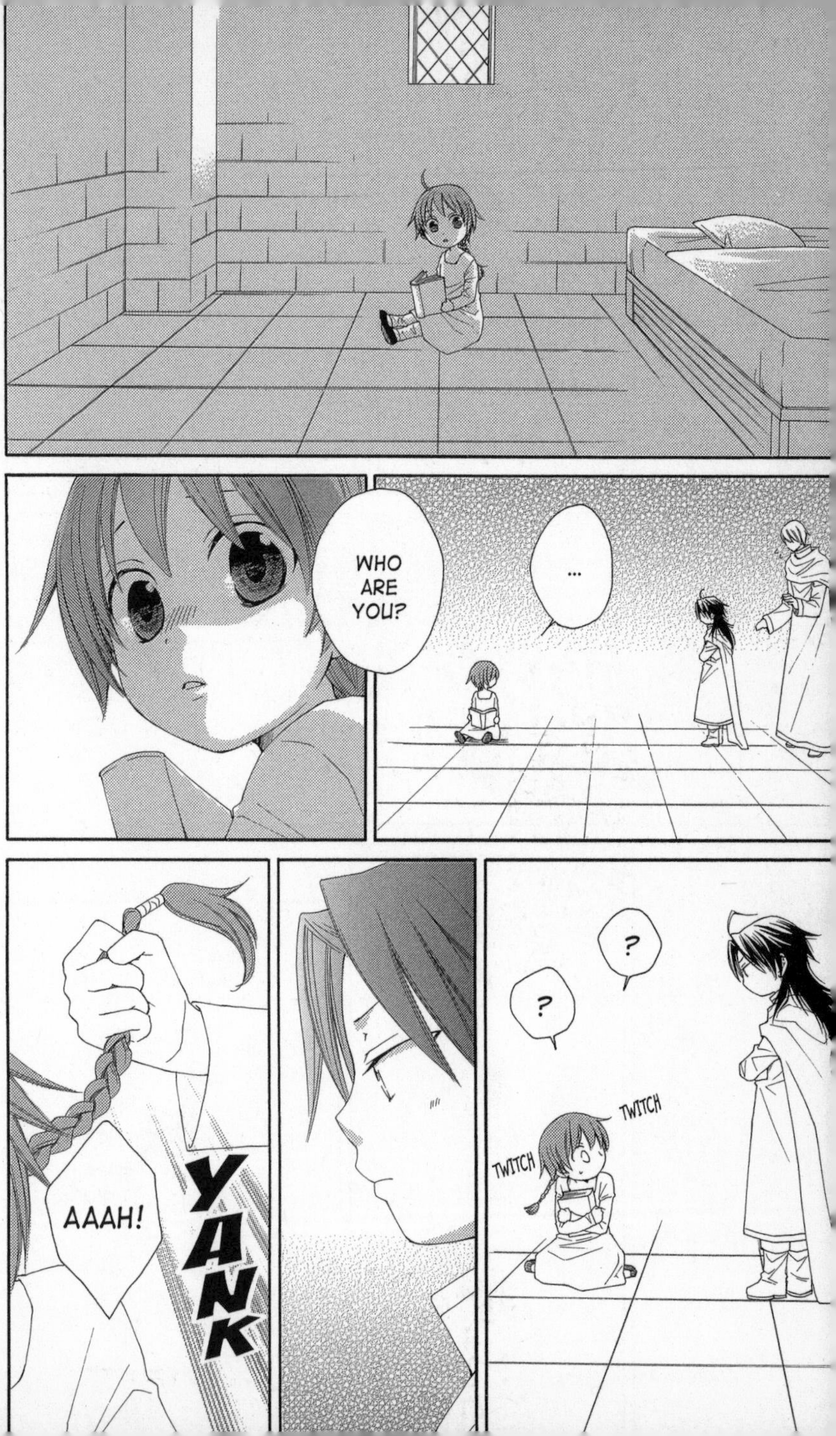
...
WHO ARE YOU?
?
?
TWITCH
TWITCH
YANK
AAAH!

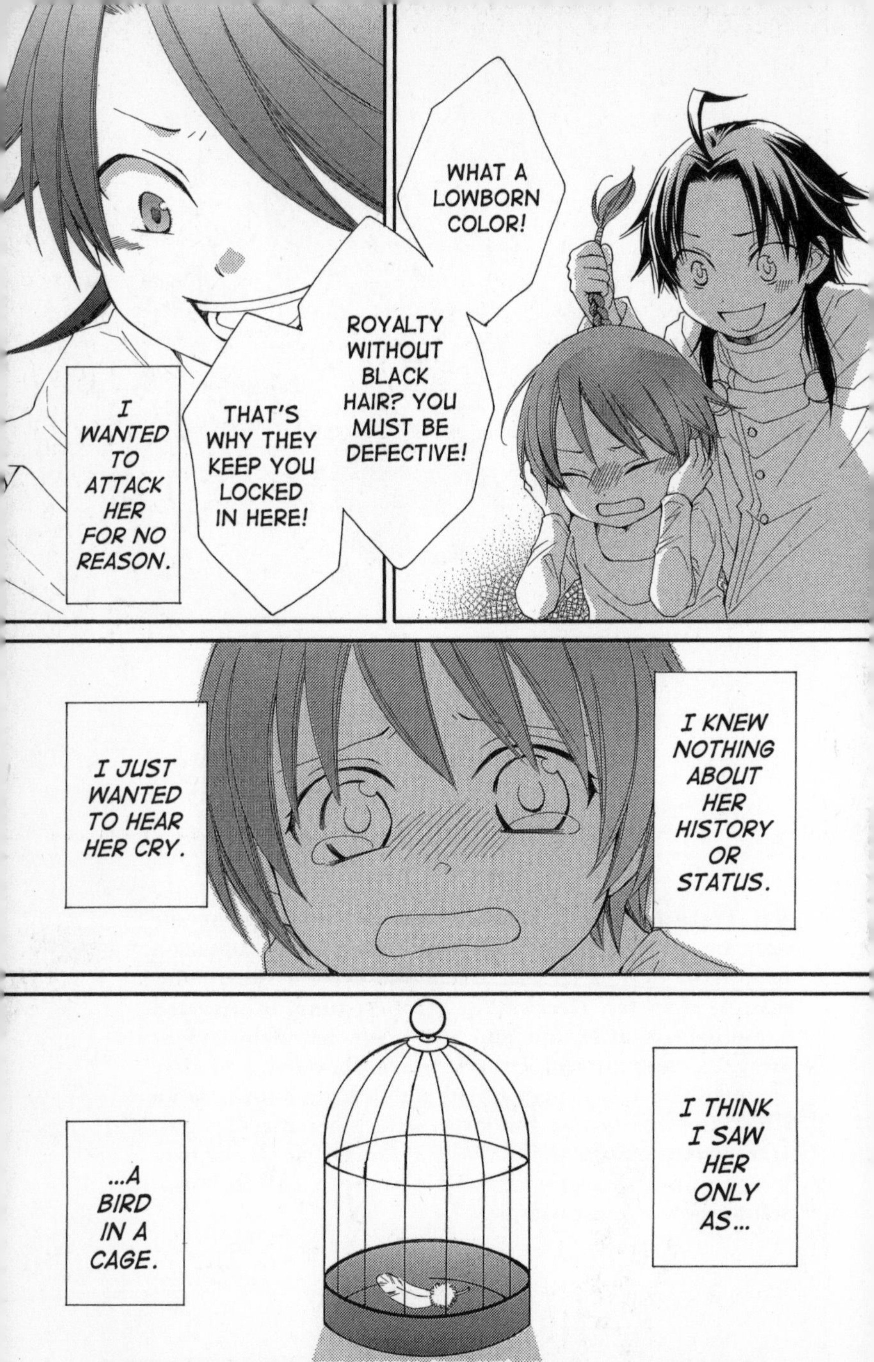
WHAT A LOWBORN COLOR!
ROYALTY WITHOUT BLACK HAIR? YOU MUST BE DEFECTIVE!
THAT'S WHY THEY KEEP YOU LOCKED IN HERE!
I WANTED TO ATTACK HER FOR NO REASON.
I KNEW NOTHING ABOUT HER HISTORY OR STATUS.
I JUST WANTED TO HEAR HER CRY.
I THINK I SAW HER ONLY AS...
...A BIRD IN A CAGE.

DAWN OF THE ARCANA BONUS CHAPTER (THE END) • *CHEESE!*, JULY 2011 EDITION

I honestly have a hard time drawing Caesar!

–Rei Toma

Rei Toma has been drawing since childhood, but she only began drawing manga because of her graduation project in design school. When she drew a short-story manga, *Help Me, Dentist,* for the first time, it attracted a publisher's attention and she made her debut right away. Her magnificent art style became popular, and after she debuted as a manga artist, she became known as an illustrator for novels and video game character designs. Her current manga series, *Dawn of the Arcana,* is her first long-running manga series, and it has been a hit in Japan, selling over a million copies.

DAWN OF THE ARCANA
VOLUME 9
Shojo Beat Edition

STORY AND ART BY
REI TOMA

Original Japanese edition "REIMEI NO ARCANA"
published by SHOGAKUKAN Inc.

English Adaptation/Ysabet MacFarlane
Translation/JN Productions
Touch-up Art & Lettering/Freeman Wong
Cover Design/Yukiko Whitley
Interior Design/Shawn Carrico
Editor/Amy Yu

Printed in the U.S.A.

Published by VIZ Media, LLC
P.O. Box 77010
San Francisco, CA 94107

10 9 8 7 6 5 4 3 2 1
First printing, April 2013

www.viz.com www.shojobeat.com

RATED T FOR TEEN

PARENTAL ADVISORY
DAWN OF THE ARCANA is rated T for Teen and is recommended for ages 13 and up. This volume contains suggestive themes and fantasy violence.

ratings.viz.com

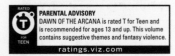

This is the last page.

In keeping with the original Japanese comic format, this book reads from right to left—so action, sound effects, and word balloons are completely reversed. This preserves the orientation of the original artwork—plus, it's fun! Check out the diagram shown here to get the hang of things, and then turn to the other side of the book to get started!

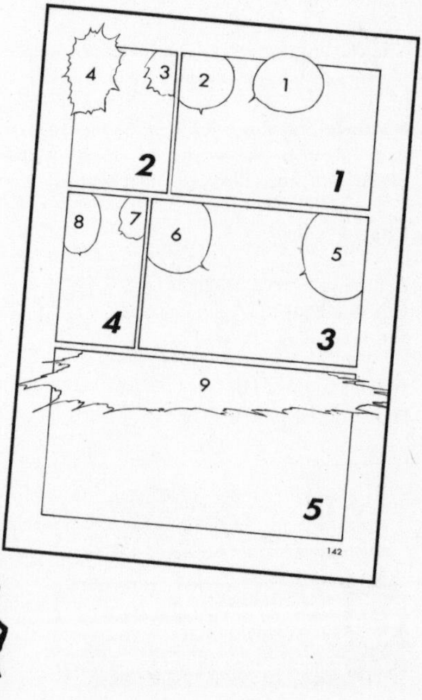
1
2
1
3
4
2
5
6
3
7
8
4
9
5
142

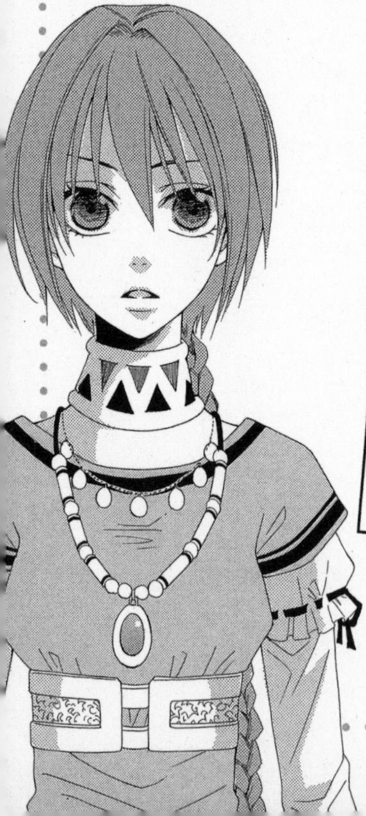